Advance

"Even as we attain greater and greater insights into the tangled web of 'nature' and 'nurture,' society stubbornly refuses to concede humankind's conformity as an animal species to the ongoing process of evolution. It instead imposes a mythological worldview almost entirely divorced from science: indeed, we see no contradiction in celebrating cultural diversity while simultaneously suppressing even a mention of genetic variance.

"Undaunted, Richard Lynn has with *The Chosen People* accomplished a yeoman's task in summing up work done thus far on Jewish intelligence. Given the disparate nature of the many studies that he cites, the relationship of intelligence to IQ is often problematic, and intelligence itself is but one piece in a complex mosaic, but this courageous and dispassionate book provides a platform for the study of a topic that is of considerable importance on the scientific plane, and–for the sophisticated reader–of even greater importance in the world of politics."
John Glad, author of *Jewish Eugenics*

"In *The Chosen People*, Professor Lynn has shown once again his talent for combining exhaustive research with daring scholarship. He is also an engaging writer, which is a quality in short supply among those who do detailed statistical work. Like his earlier books, this monograph should be read by anyone who is interested in the relation between innate intelligence and professional and social achievements. We ignore this historically significant subject at our peril and at the cost of future generations."
Paul E. Gottfried, Elizabethtown College

"Professor Richard Lynn's work addresses dispassionately and objectively the question of why Jews have been so remarkably successful as intellectuals and in professional and managerial life. Using a wealth of statistics and commentary from many different countries and societies, he demonstrates their success over and over again. Because of the odious uses to which the Nazis and their ilk put eugenically-based arguments, Jews and others have often been reluctant to engage in debating this question. Professor Lynn shows that this question ought to be addressed, and that it can be addressed objectively by philo-semites favourable to the Jews as well as by anti-semites who are hostile to them."
William D. Rubinstein, University of Aberystwyth

The Chosen People

A Study of Jewish Intelligence
and Achievement

Richard Lynn

WSP

Washington Summit Publishers
A National Policy Institute Book
2011

© 2011 by Richard Lynn. All rights reserved.

No part of this publication may be reproduced, distributed, or transmitted in any form or by any means, including photocopying, recording, or other electronic or mechanical methods, or by any information storage and retrieval system, without prior written permission from the publisher, except for brief quotations embodied in critical reviews and certain other non-commercial uses permitted by copyright law. For permission requests, write to the publisher at the address below.

Washington Summit Publishers
P. O. Box 1676
Whitefish, MT 59937

email: info@WashSummit.com
web: www.WashSummit.com

Library of Congress Cataloging-in-Publication Data:

Lynn, Richard, 1930–
The chosen people: a study of Jewish intelligence and achievement/ Richard Lynn.–1st ed.
    p.cm
Includes bibliographical references and index.
ISBN 978-1-59368-036-7
I. 1. Jewish history 2. Human genetics 3. Human evolution I. Title.
                                                                2011932717

Printed in the United States of America

10 9 8 7 6 5 4 3 2 1

To Joyce ,

> Ho tante cose che ti voglio dire
>
> O una sola,
>
> Ma grande come il mare,
>
> Come il mare profonda ed infinita...
>
> Sei il mio amore e tutta la mia vita.

Mimì, La Bohème

Acknowledgements

Many thanks to Louis Andrews and Richard Spencer (and his colleagues) for their expert editing; to all my Jewish friends for their comments and input; and to my wife, Joyce, for allowing me to disappear to my study to work on the book.

Richard Lynn
Bodrum, Turkey, 2011

Contents

1. Introduction — 1
2. The Four Jewish Peoples — 21
3. Australia — 33
4. Austria and Hungary — 41
5. Benelux — 57
6. Britain — 71
7. Canada — 97
8. Denmark — 111
9. France — 117
10. Germany — 131
11. Israel — 149
12. Italy — 181
13. Latin America — 191
14. Poland, Lithuania, and Latvia — 203
15. Russia — 213
16. South Africa — 237
17. Switzerland — 245
18. The Balkans — 253
19. United States — 271
20. Theories of Jewish Intelligence — 315
21. Conclusions — 341
References — 361
Index — 389
Biographical information — 407

CHAPTER 1

Introduction

1. Jewish Intelligence
2. Jewish Achievement in Historical Times
3. Jewish Achievements in Different Domains
4. Theories of Jewish Success
5. Definition of Intelligence

From the early 19th century, the Jews have been a remarkably successful people. Up to this time, Jews were discriminated against throughout virtually the whole of Europe, and their opportunities for achievement were severely limited. Except in the Balkans, they were not permitted to attend universities; they thus could not acquire the qualifications to practice as physicians and lawyers nor the education and skills required for success in science and mathematics. Most Jews in Eastern, Central, and Northern Europe spoke Yiddish, so they could not achieve much in philosophy and literature in a language that Gentile Europeans could understand.

In the first decade of the 19th century, the Jews were emancipated in France, and then throughout much of Europe, by Napoleon; during the course of the century, Jews were further emancipated in Britain, Russia, and Poland. Freed from the former restrictions, from the middle decades of the century on, Jews began to do conspicuously well in banking, commerce, industry, the professions, science, and the arts throughout Europe.

In the late 19th century, the great majority of Jews lived in the Russian Empire that included the Baltic States and the eastern half of present day Poland. They suffered severe pogroms from 1881 onward, and most of them immigrated to the countries of Central and Western Europe, the United States, and elsewhere in the Western world. They arrived as penniless refugees unable to speak the languages of their new countries; they were the "huddled masses" from the most backward region of Europe. Yet by the middle decades of the 20th century, the children and grandchildren of these immigrants were doing far better than their Gentile hosts on all indices of socioeconomic status and earnings and outperforming them by several orders of magnitude in obtaining elite academic distinctions for intellectual achievement.

In numerous countries throughout the world, Jews have become massively overrepresented in the professions, the universities, among business leaders, and the very rich. At the highest levels of intellectual achievement, Jews have won 27 percent of the A. M. Turing Awards that have been given annually from 1966 to 2009 for contributions of lasting and major technical importance to computer science. Jews have been about half of the world's chess grandmasters and champions: between 1851 and 1986 there were 15 world chess champions, and seven of these were Jewish—Steinitz, Botvinnik, Smyslov, Tal, Spassky, Fischer, and Kasparov (Cranberg & Albert, 1988; Rubinstein, 2004). Another cognitively demanding game is bridge. It has been estimated that more than half of the outstanding American bridge players and theoreticians have been Jewish (Storfer, 1990). The pinnacle of intellectual achievement in science and literature is the Nobel Prize. Jews have been hugely overrepresented among Nobel Prize winners. In the period from 1901–1962, 16 percent of Nobel Prize winners for science were Jewish (Weyl & Possony, 1963, p. 143). Estimating the world population of Jews in 1938 at 18 million and the world population of European Gentiles at 718 million, Jews were overrepresented by a factor of approximately 6.6.[*]

The purpose of this book is to document and explain such achievements. We shall be concerned with the theme that the remarkable Jewish successes can be largely explained by their high intelligence. This will take us into the further questions of why Jews have high intelligence, whether this is true of all Jews, and whether other qualities, such as a strong work ethic, also contribute to Jewish achievement. It is a strange fact that in the numerous books and articles that have been concerned with Jewish success in recent years, virtually none of them mention the high Jewish intelligence.

1. *Jewish Intelligence*

In the middle decades of the 19th century, people began to observe that Jews are outstandingly successful and speculate that this is attributable to their intellect. In 1847, Lord Ashley, speaking in the British House of Commons, observed:

> The Jews are a people of very powerful intellect.... [They] presented...in proportion to their numbers, a far larger list of men of genius and learning than could be exhibited by any Gentile country. Music, poetry, medicine, astronomy, occupied their attention, and in every field they were more than a match for their competitors. (Vital, 1999, p. 179)

A few years later in France, the Count de Gobineau (1853) discussed the cultural and intellectual achievements of different peoples and concluded that the Aryans (Northern Europeans) and the Jews were the two most intelligent peoples. Francis Galton (1869, p. 47) also believed the Jews were a highly intelligent people, writing in *Hereditary Genius* that they "appear to be rich in families of high intellectual breeds." In the United States, the physician Madison Marsh (1974, p. 343) discussed the Jews' "high average intelligence," and in 1898, Mark Twain (1985, p. 12) wrote that the Jew's "contribution to the world's list of great names in literature, science, art, music, finance, medicine, and abstruse learning is way out of proportion to the weakness of his numbers."

In the 20th century, a number of people reiterated the conclusion that the Jews have done well because they are highly intelligent. During World War I, the British writer John Fraser (1915, pp. 30–31), in his book *The Conquering Jew*, advanced the thesis that the principal reason for Jewish achievement is that Jews are more intelligent than Gentiles: "in alertness and knowledge... the Jew is the superior of the Christian." Fraser approvingly quotes a contemporary who avered, the struggle between the sons of the North, with their blond hair and sluggish intellects, and the sons of the Orient, with their black eyes, is an unequal one.

Fraser concludes,

> if the Russian dispassionately spoke his mind, I think he would admit that his dislike of the Jew is not so much racial or religious—though these play great parts—as a recognition that the Jew is his superior, and in a conflict of wits will get the better of him.

Writing four years later, Joseph Jacobs (1919, pp. 55–57) gave an account that attributed the Jews' success in Germany to their intelligence:

> [A] determinate number of Jews at the present time will produce a larger number of 'geniuses' (whether inventive or not, I will not say) than any equal number of men of other races. It seems highly probable, for example, that German Jews at the present moment are quantitatively (not necessarily qualitatively) at the head of European intellect.

In the same year, Thorstein Veblen (1919) also asserted that the secret of Jewish success lies in their high intelligence. He wrote of the "intellectual preeminence of Jews in modern Europe" (p. 35). His theory to account for this was that Jews are detached from the host societies in which they live. This frees them from the constraint of conventional ideas and allows them to think creatively. He argued (plausibly enough) that creative scientific achievement requires "a degree of exemption from hard and fast preconceptions, a sceptical animus, and release from the dead hand of conventional finality." Jews have this exemption:

> It is by the loss of allegiance…that he finds himself in the vanguard of American inquiry.... [H]e becomes the disturber of the intellectual peace, but only at the cost of becoming an intellectual wayfaring man, a wanderer in the intellectual no-man's land, seeking another place to rest.

He concluded with the logical inference that Jews would cease to be creative if and when they acquired their own homeland in Israel and were no longer rootless wanderers. Perhaps he would have changed his mind about this theory if he had lived to see the award of Nobel Prizes to six Israelis (see Chapter 11).

With the development of intelligence tests in the first decade of the 20th century, evidence on the intelligence of the Jews began to accumulate that substantiated the theory that Jews have high IQs. Studies showing this began to be published in the 1920s in Britain and the United States, and more studies confirming this in the United States were published from time to time throughout the 20th century. In the 1960s a landmark book was published by Nathaniel Weyl and Stefan Possony (1963). A further book by Weyl (1966) brought together the evidence of the high Jewish IQ and achievement and discussed the reasons for this.

By the 1990s, it began to be confidently asserted that Jews have a high IQ. For example, Richard Herrnstein and Charles Murray (1994, p. 275) have written, "Whenever the subject of group differences comes up one of the questions sure to be asked is 'Are Jews really smarter than everyone else?'" Their answer was that Ashkenazi Jews obtained an average IQ of 112.6 on the AFQT in relation to 100 for Whites. Others who have reviewed the evidence on Jewish intelligence and concluded that Jews have a high IQ include Kevin MacDonald (1994, pp. 188–190); Hans Eysenck (1995, p. 159): "as far as Jews are concerned, there is no question that they score very highly on IQ tests"; and Michael Levin, a philosophy professor at the City University of New York, who has written: "in every society in which they have participated, Jews have eventually been recognised (and disliked for) their exceptional talent" (1997, p. 132).

Numerous studies have shown that intelligence is a major determinant of economic and intellectual achievement. In a classical study, Christopher Jencks (1972) estimated that there is a correlation of 0.310 between IQ and income for men in the United States. This result has been confirmed and extended by a study in Britain showing that for a national sample of people whose intelligence was obtained at the age of eight years and whose income was obtained at the age 43, there were correlations between IQ and income of 0.368 for men (n=1280) and 0.317 for women (n=1085) (Irwing & Lynn, 2006). Many further studies showing that IQ is a substantial determinant of educational and intellectual attainment are summarized in *IQ and Global Inequality* (Lynn and Vanhanen, 2006). As all this is quite well known, and despite the accumulation of studies showing that Jews have a high IQ, it is curious that the high Jewish IQ has almost invariably been ignored by historians, sociologists, and economists who have written on the high achievements of the Jews, and even by psychologists who have written on intelligence. Numerous historians, sociologists, and economists have documented the high achievements of the Jews in various countries and suggested reasons for this, but virtually none of them have suggested that the explanation may be that Jews have a high IQ. There is no entry for intelligence in the 17 volume *Encyclopedia Judaica*, and only one paper on the intelligence of the Jews has been published in the *Jewish Journal of Sociology* and the Jewish journal *Commentary*.

2. Jewish Achievement in Historical Times

The Jews of Palestine before the Christian era do not appear to have been exceptionally gifted. They did not produce the great cultural and intellectual achievements of the Greeks. It is a disputed question whether the Jews have been exceptionally successful and disproportionately represented among the intellectually gifted for most of the last 2000 years or whether the high Jewish achievement did not appear until Jews were emancipated in the 19th century. One of those who have asserted that the high Jewish achievement is a recent phenomenon was Bertrand Russell (1945, p. 323), who wrote,

> Throughout the Middle Ages, Jews had no part in the culture of Christian countries, and were too severely persecuted to be able to make contributions to civilization, beyond supplying capital for the building of cathedrals and such enterprises.

In an attempt to answer this question, studies that have quantified Jewish achievement in different historical periods are summarized in Table 1.1. Jewish achievements are expressed as Jewish Achievement Quotients (AQs). These AQs have been calculated as the percentages of outstandingly gifted Jews in relation to their population numbers, as compared with the percentages of European Gentiles in relation to their population numbers, and the percentages of Jews expressed as a ratio of the percentage of European Gentiles. For instance, if two percent of Jews were found to be outstandingly gifted as compared with one percent of European Gentiles, Jews would have an Achievement Quotient of 2. We use this measure of Jewish achievement on numerous occasions throughout this book.

Row 1 in Table 1.1 gives the first historical evidence for Jewish achievement and comes from medieval times. The data are taken from Sarton (1948) who identified 626 gifted scientists living between 1150 and 1300 AD. Of these 95, approximately 16 percent were Jewish. Raphael Patai (1977) has estimated the numbers of Jews and Gentiles in Europe at this time and calculated that Jews were 32-fold overrepresented in relation to the non-Jewish population in the countries in which scientific work was carried out at that period, giving the Jews an Achievement Quotient of 32.

Table 1.1. Achievement Quotients of European Jews from 1150 to 1985

	Years	AQ	Reference
1	1150–1300	32.0	Patai, 1971
2	1000–1492	18.0	Patai, 1971
3	1830–1879	8.7	Berry, 1999
4	1880–1929	16.6	Berry, 1999
5	1830–1910	6.9	Murray, 2003
6	1900–1950	6.0	Murray, 2003
7	1950–2000	12.0	Murray, 2003
8	1901–1962	6.5	Weyl & Possony, 1963
9	1901–1985	8.0	Patai and Patai, 1989

Row 2 also comes from the medieval period, but is confined to scientific achievement in Spain. Patai (1977) has estimated that Jews were overrepresented among gifted scientists by a factor of 18 to 1, giving them an Achievement Quotient of 18. In this study the time period ends in 1492 with the expulsion of the Jews from Spain in that year. How seriously can these figures be taken? Not very, according to Murray (2003, p. 275), who observes, "few of those 626 are important enough in the broader sweep of scientific history to warrant a mention." I am inclined to agree. During this period, Jewish men were nearly all literate while most Gentile men were not. Because of this situation, proportionately more Jews wrote books on scientific subjects. But these were largely translations and commentaries on Arabic and Greek texts. Can anyone think of a single Jewish scientist or mathematician of any distinction during these years from 1150 and 1492, let alone one to compare with the Greek giants such as Aristotle, Pythagoras, Euclid, and Ptolemy? I would therefore follow Murray and place a large question mark over Patai's conclusions on high Jewish achievement in medieval Europe.

It has not proved possible to find any studies of Jewish achievement during the three and a half centuries from 1492 to 1830.

The next study, carried out by Colin Berry (1999), is for those born between 1830 and 1929; it is summarized in rows 3 and 4 of Table 1.1. Berry began by assembling a list of 1,352 outstandingly talented men of European ethnicity, born between 1830 and 1929, in the fields of engineering, astronomy, physics, chemistry, medicine, mathematics, literature, painting, and music. These were selected on a variety of criteria including the award of Nobel Prizes for Science and Literature and listing in reference works of those who had achieved eminence. Of the total number (1,352), 220 were Jewish. He then calculated the proportion of Jews and Gentile Europeans in relation to their numbers in the world for those born between 1830 and 1879 and between 1880 and 1930. The results showed that Jews were overrepresented in both periods in all nine fields and especially strongly in literature and in music. The Jewish Achievement Quotients were 8.7 for the first period and 16.6 for the second. Notice that the Jewish Achievement Quotient approximately doubled between the two periods.

Berry's paper attracted little or no attention and was not noticed by Murray (2003) in his monumental study of outstanding individuals in world achievement from the year 800 to 2000 AD. Murray analyses these by country, race, religion, and sex. He provides estimates of Jewish achievements, in relation to Gentile Europeans, for three periods. Rows 5 through 7 give his results for the period from 1870–2000 (Murray, 2003, pp. 279, 283). Row 5 gives an Achievement Quotient of 6.9 for Jewish achievements in music, science, art, philosophy and literature for those born between 1830 and 1910. (Murray presents the data for those aged 40 during the years 1870–1950, and hence to make his data comparable with those of Berry the period of their births is shown.) It will be seen that the Jewish Achievement Quotients found by Berry and Murray are in fairly close agreement (8.7 and 6.9) considering that some difference should be expected as a result of different samples and time periods. Murray was apparently unaware of Berry's work, so the two calculations were evidently made independently. Row 6 gives a Jewish Achievement Quotient of 6.0 based on the award of Nobel Prizes in Science and Literature during the period 1901 (the first year in which the prizes were awarded) to 1950 (these people would have been born roughly between 1850–1900). Row 7 gives a Jewish Achievement Quotient of 12.0 based on the award of Nobel Prizes in Science and Literature during the second half of the 20th century (1951–2000) and who would have been born roughly between 1900–1950.

Rows 8 and 9 give further estimates of Jewish Achievement Quotients also based on the award of Nobel prizes. Row 8 gives a Jewish Achievement Quotient of 6.5 for science derived from an analysis of Nobel Prize winners for Physics, Chemistry and Medice during the years 1901 to 1962, calculated by Nathaniel Weyl and Stefan Possony (1963). They found that 225 prizes were awarded and estimate that the world population of European peoples, including those in North America and Australasia as well as in Europe, was approximately 718 million. This can be expressed as a rate of 31.3 per 100 million. They estimate the world Jewish population in 1938 at 18 million and that 36 percent of Nobel Prize winners were Jewish, representing a rate of 203 per 100 million. Thus, Jews were approximately 6.5 to one overrepresented. The Jewish Achievement Quotient of 6.5 is closely similar to the 6.0 calculated by Murray for most of the same period (1901–1950), although Murray's figure includes the Literature Prize. Row 9 gives a Jewish Achievement Quotient of 8.1 based on all Nobel prizes (including those for Economics, Literature, and Peace, as well as for Science) awarded over the years 1901–1985 as calculated by Raphael and Jennifer Patai (Patai & Patai, 1989). They calculated that of the 541 prizes awarded, 91 were won by Jews. They do not attempt to estimate the ratio of Jewish to non-Jewish European Prize winners. This can be done using the same methodology as Weyl and Possony. If we adopt Weyl and Possony's estimate that the world population of European peoples was 718 million, the rate of Prize winners was 75 per 100 million. A reasonable estimate for the numbers of Jews for this period would be 15 million, since the numbers of Jews declined from approximately 18 million in 1938 to approximately 12 million for the period 1945–1985. Using this estimate, the rate of Jewish Nobel Prize winners was 667 per 100 million. Jews are thus overrepresented by a ratio of 8:1.

There are four comments to be made on the Jewish Achievement Quotients set out in Table 1.1. First, they all show that in all the studies Jews have been considerably overrepresented among outstandingly gifted individuals. Second, the Jewish Achievement Quotients for the medieval periods given in rows 1 and 2 are higher at 30 and 18 than any of those of the last two centuries from 1800 to 2000. However, we have noted that the high Jewish Achievement Quotients for the medieval period must be regarded with skepticism. There were no outstanding Jews during this period, and Gentile learning and scholarship were at a low ebb. Europe was emerging from the Dark Ages while among the Jewish communities, learning and scholarship flourished in these years. It was only from around the year 1200 that universities began to be founded in Europe for Gentiles, and it was largely these that nurtured Gentile European achievements over the next eight centuries.

Third, the Jewish Achievement Quotients in the two centuries from 1800 to 2000 are reasonably consistent, lying between 6.0 and 16.6. Some of these differences are no doubt sampling and measurement errors. Sampling errors arise because Jewish Achievement Quotients are higher in some fields than in others (they are particularly high in philosophy), so they will vary according to which fields are included in the calculation. Measurement errors may also be present because of errors in identifying Jews.

Fourth, there seems to be a real trend for the Jewish Achievement Quotients to increase during the last two centuries. This is found in the studies by Berry and Murray. Berry's calculations show the Jewish Achievement Quotients approximately doubled from 8.7 among those born between 1830 and 1879 to 16.6 among those born between 1880 and 1939. Similarly, Murray's calculations also show that Jewish Achievement Quotients doubled from 6.0 among those who received Nobel prizes between 1901 and 1950 to 12.0 among those who received Nobel prizes between 1950 and 2000. We shall find these results replicated in many countries. They are explained by Jews taking two or three generations to establish themselves fully in Gentile societies.

In the first half of the 19th century, Jews were prohibited in most countries from entering universities, music academies, and art colleges, and this handicapped them for achievement in science, philosophy, music, and art, and possibly in literature, for which a university or college education provides the foundation for achievement. In France and the Netherlands, Jews were permitted to enter universities in the 1790s, but it was not until 1848 that this was allowed in the Austro-Hungarian Empire and some of the German and Italian states; and it was not until 1871 that Jews were allowed to attend universities in England. In the United States, Jews were not given full civil rights at the state level until 1868.

3. Jewish Achievements in Different Domains

Are Jews exceptionally talented in all intellectual domains or only in some? Both Berry and Murray present data on this question and their calculations are shown in Table 1.2. Berry's and Murray's calculations for 1870–1950 (born 1830–1910) are derived from their inventories of gifted individuals, while Murray's calculations for 1951–2000 are based on Nobel Prizes.

Table 1.2. Achievement Quotients of European Jews at various time periods

Domain	Berry 1830–1879	Berry 1880–1929	Murray 1870–1950	Murray 1951–2000
Astronomy	1.2	3.4	1.0	-
Biology	-	-	8.0	-
Chemistry	3.5	5.3	6.0	10.1
Earth Science	-	-	3.0	-
Economics	-	-	-	45.0
Engineering	1.2	1.8	3.0	-
Mathematics	10.5	9.6	12.0	-
Medicine	5.5	10.5	8.0	14.1
Music	37.1	20.8	5.0	-
Literature	6.9	8.1	4.0	7.1
Painting	7.1	6.3	5.0	-
Philosophy	-	-	14.0	-
Physics	4.2	10.1	9.0	14.1

Five conclusions can be drawn from these results. First, Jews are better than Gentiles at everything intellectual. Second, the Berry 1880–1929 and Murray 1870–1950 data are closely similar, except for music and literature. Third, Jews are much more overrepresented among gifted musicians in Berry's results, where they have Achievement Quotients of 37.1 and 20.8; this is not confirmed by Murray's data, in which the Jewish Achievement Quotient is only 5.0 and is slightly lower than in most other domains. Fourth, there is a suggestion that the Jewish Achievement Quotient in mathematics is rather higher than in other domains. Mathematics is the highest Jewish Achievement Quotient in Berry's 1830–1879 data, apart from music. Mathematics is the third highest Jewish Achievement Quotient in Berry's 1880–1929 data, below medicine and music, and is second highest in Murray's 1870–1950 data, in which the highest Jewish Achievement Quotient is in philosophy. Fifth, the Jewish Achievement Quotient of 45.0 for economics based on Nobel Prizes which have been awarded since 1969 is clearly very high and is considered to be valid.

These results suggest that Jews may have a special aptitude for the abstract thinking required for mathematics, philosophy, and physics, and possibly also for economics, much of which is quite mathematical. Jews do less well in astronomy, engineering, and painting, and possibly in literature, although even in these, they do better than Gentiles.

4. *Theories of Jewish Success*

By the first two decades of the 20th century, it had become increasingly obvious to many people that Jews have been exceptionally successful; theories began to be advanced to explain Jewish success. A few people proposed that Jews are more intelligent than Gentiles, as noted in section 1, but most people preferred other theories. Five principal theories have been advanced to explain Jewish success. These are (a) strong motivation theory; (b) family and ethnic networks; (c) marginal man theory; (d) special aptitudes theory; and (e) luck. Several writers have asserted that Jewish success is attributable to more than one of these characteristics.

(a) Strong Work Motivation Theory. This states that Jews are strongly motivated to work hard and achieve success. Some have asserted that Jews have a strong form of the Protestant or Puritan work ethic, a commitment to work as a moral and religious obligation, which was proposed by Weber as the source of the economic advance of the Protestant nations from the 17th to the 19th centuries. Houston Stewart Chamberlain (1912, pp. 492–493) asserted that the principal reason why Jews had become "a disproportionately important and in many spheres actually dominant constituent of our life" is that Jews have an innate "abnormally developed will," by which he probably meant what today we would call strong motivation.

The German historian Werner Sombart (1919) attributed the Jewish success to their religion fostering a strong work ethic that gave them exceptional will power. He described this as *des Eigennutzes* (self-interest) and *Abstraktheit ihrer Geistesbeschaffenheit* (it is difficult to extract any meaning from this concept); literally it can be translated "the abstractness of their *nature* and *spirit*"; Mosse's (1987) translator renders it "abstract mentality." (My German friends assure me that it does not mean "a talent for abstract thought" or "thinking in abstractions," or anything associated with intelligence). Sombart also proposed that because Jews have been nomads for many centuries and generally had no land or property, they valued money and this ultimately led to their pre-eminence in banking.

In Russia in the 1920s, it was so obvious that Jews were prominent among the elite that people began to discuss why this should be. In 1929, Russian Larin published a book on this question and advanced the explanation that the hard life of Jews in previous centuries had produced "exceptional energy" (Slezkine, 2004, p. 252).

A variant of this theory is that Jews have a strong work ethic. This has received some confirmation from a study carried out in the United States by Gerhard Lenski (1963). He concluded that Jews are like White Protestants in possessing "individualistic, competitive patterns of thought and action linked with the middle class and historically associated with the Protestant ethic or its secular counterpart, the spirit of capitalism." Catholics and Blacks, he argued, have "the collectivist, security oriented working class patterns of action, historically opposed to the Protestant ethic."

A further variant of the strong work motivation theory is that Jews attach a high valuation to success. This has become a cultural norm in Jewish families. Parents bring up their children to achieve and socialize them to value success. Thus,

> Success is so vitally important to the Jewish family ethos that we can hardly overemphasize it.... [W]e cannot hope to understand the Jewish family without understanding the place that success for men (and recently for women) plays in the system. (Herz & Rozen, 1982, p. 306)

Jews attach a lot of importance to study and education and this socializes the children for educational and academic success: "Jewish youth used to spend long years bent over their books in an attempt to break out of the narrow circle of restrictions" (Slezkine, 2004, p. 252). Suzanne Rutland (1988, p. 259), writing on the success of Jews in Australia, has proposed that one of the reasons for this is that they "were highly motivated to create a new and more secure life for themselves," which gave them "the willingness to work hard."

The Harvard historian Stephan Thernstrom and his wife assert that the achievements of the Jews are "the product of cultural values that they have brought with them and transmitted from generation to generation over a very long time" (Thernstrom & Thernstrom, 2003, p. 98), although they fail to give any evidence that Jews have the requisite cultural values for educational and socioeconomic success. Gary Becker, the Nobel Prize winner for economics, is another who has pondered the problem of why Jews have done so well and concluded,

> The high achievement and low fertility of Jewish families are explained by high marginal rates of return to investments in the health, education, and other human capital of their children that lower the price of quality relative to quantity. (Becker, 1981, p. 110)

Translated from economists' jargon, this means that Jews have fewer children and devote more effort to their health care and to giving them a good education. He does not offer any explanations for why Jews do this but we are left to infer that this is part of their values.

(b) **Strong Family and Ethnic Networks.** Houston Stewart Chamberlain (1912, pp. 492–493) asserted that the Jewish religion (Judaism) inculcated "the idea of physical race-unity and race purity" that leads Jews to support each other through strong family and ethnic networks theory. In 1929, Larin proposed that because Jews have been discriminated against for many centuries, they have developed "an unusually strong sense of solidarity and a predisposition towards mutual help and support." Yuri Slezkine (2004), who quoted this opinion, agreed and has confidently asserted, "there is no doubt that their entrepreneurial success has been due to a combination of internal solidarity and external strangeness" (Slezkine, 2004, pp. 43, 252). It is not clear whether this trait was envisioned as genetic or cultural.

(c) Marginal Man Theory. This theory was advanced by Thorstein Veblen. David Hollinger (2002, p. 145–146), who has described Veblen as "the most creative American social theorist of the early 20th century," summarizes his theory as follows:

> The partial liberation of Jews from traditional Judaism yields a sceptical temper. The combination of withdrawal from Jewish tradition and only partial assimilation into Gentile society endows the intellectual Jew with the virtue of detachment. Skeptical, estranged, alienated, the liberated Jew was ideally suited for a career in science and scholarship. This Marginal Man, this 'wanderer in the intellectual no-man's land' could see 'unmediated facts' that were less readily observed by minds still clouded by Judaism, Christianity, local customs, tribal idols, or other pre-modern forms of reference.

There are several reasons for regarding Veblen's theory as implausible. First, as we shall see repeatedly throughout this book, Jews are good at everything, not only at science, for which a "skeptical temper" and "detachment" may be required. Second, as Jews ceased to be marginal in the second half of the 20th century, their success in all walks of life increased in the United States and Britain, as shown in the chapters on these two countries.

(d) Special Aptitudes. Several writers have proposed that Jews possess a number of special aptitudes that have been ingredients of success. High creativity has sometimes been advanced. For instance, the historian Lewis Bernstein Napier (1934, p. xx) attributed German anti-Semitism to the Jewish superiority and the inability of Germans to compete:

> [T]he German is methodical, crude, constructive mainly in the mechanical sense, extremely submissive to authority, a rebel or a fighter only by order from above... [whereas] the Jew, of the Oriental or Mediterranean race, is creative, pliable, individualistic, restless and undisciplined.

Napier seems to be groping towards the idea that Jews are more creative than Gentiles, but it is difficult to say whether he had any notion that they may be more intelligent. Rutland suggests that Jews have strong imagination, a concept akin to creativity:

> [I]magination is another essential ingredient in business success as new products must be conceived, new ways of doing things conjured up, and ways round problems solved. As a result of persecution and discrimination, Jews have always tended to be innovators and have come up with new ideas in science, commerce and industry, as well as in the arts. (1988, p. 261)

Daniel Moynihan (the former United States Senator) and Nathan Glazer (the Harvard sociologist) (1970, p. 153) have discussed why Jews have done so well in real estate in New York. They advanced the thesis that Jews have "exceptional skill in financial and business management, derived from a long history in business, that has unquestionably served many Jews well in a field that is incredibly complex and laden with pitfalls" (Moynihan and Glazer 1970, p. 153). It did not apparently occur to them that this "exceptional skill in financial and business management" could be an expression of high intelligence. They seemed to believe that it is a particular kind of aptitude independent of intelligence and, presumably, transmitted down the generations according to Lamarckian principles of the inheritance of acquired characteristics.

The British historian Paul Johnson has written,

> The great Jewish strength lay in the ability to take quick advantage of new opportunities, to recognise an unprecedented situation when it arose and devise methods of handling it. Christians had long learned how to deal with conventional financial problems, but they were slow to react to novelty. (2004, p. 253)

There is of course no special ability "to take quick advantage of new opportunities." The ability he describes is intelligence.

The American historian Stephen Steinberg (1981) suggests that Jewish craft and trading skills and high literacy level were the main factors accounting for Jewish success, but these, too, are expressions of intelligence.

Why have Jews been so good at chess? William D. Rubinstein (2004) has discussed this and begins by suggesting, great ability at chess appears to be an innate gift of some kind. There is universal agreement among experts that by constant practice, study, and lessons with outstanding players someone can improve... but that it is impossible to improve dramatically if the inherent ability is lacking—just as it is impossible for a tennis player to improve enough by practice to compete in the finals at Wimbledon unless he or she possesses the innate tennis ability of a great player (2004, p. 36).... It may be therefore that Jews are genetically good at chess" (p. 39).

This is very likely true in so far as Jews have a high level of general intelligence and some of them devote this to chess. Good chess players have high intelligence that they have directed into acquiring expertise at the game. An investigation I carried out in collaboration with Marcel Frydman of the University of Mons in Belgium (Frydman & Lynn, 1992) of 33 tournament level young chess players aged 8–13 found that they had an average IQ of 121, proving that a high IQ is required to do well in chess. Aljosha Neubauer (2006) of the University of Graz in Austria has also found that tournament standard chess players have high IQs.

(e) Luck. A. Godley (2007) asserts that the socioeconomic success of Jews who migrated to Britain and the United States between 1881 and 1914 has been largely due to luck. According to this account, Jews were just lucky that they went into the garment industry and that this happened to expand in the middle and later decades of the 20th century. This is surely the least plausible explanation for Jewish successes. It can hardly be luck that has made Jews in many countries the highest earning ethnic group, greatly overrepresented in the professions, among top chess and bridge champions, and among Nobel Prize winners.

(f). Multifactor theories. Many of those who have written on Jewish success have proposed multifactor theories incorporating several attributes. The American sociologist Paul Burnstein (2007) proposes five explanations of why Jews have done so well. These are

> getting more education and working long hours, faith that emphasizes pursuits in this world as opposed to the afterlife, mutual assistance through the self-help organizations they long maintained in the Diaspora, marginality that made them

skeptical of conventional ideas and stimulated creativity that led to intellectual eminence and, often, economic success, and social capital, the ability to secure benefits through membership in networks and other social structures.

The Irish economist Cormac O'Grada attibutes Jewish success to "bourgeois virtues such as sobriety, a desire to succeed, a dislike of violence, an emphasis on education and learning, and high self-esteem" (O'Grada, 2006, p. 162).

Neither of these eclectics mentions intelligence as a factor in Jewish success.

5. Definition of Intelligence

The nature of intelligence is poorly understood by those who have proposed that Jews have special aptitudes such as "problem solving" (Rutland, 1988, p. 261), the ability "to take quick advantage of new opportunities" (Johnson, 2004, p. 253), and "exceptional skill in financial and business management" (Moynihan & Glazer, 1970, p. 153). All these aptitudes are expressions of intelligence directed into particular fields. There is a virtually universal consensus among psychologists that intelligence is best conceptualized as a single broad construct that determines the efficiency of problem solving, learning and remembering in all areas. A useful definition of intelligence was provided by a committee set up by the American Psychological Association in 1995 under the chairmanship of Ulrich Neisser and consisting of 11 American psychologists whose mandate was to produce a report on what is generally known and accepted about intelligence. The definition of intelligence proposed by the Task Force was that intelligence is the ability "to understand complex ideas, to adapt effectively to the environment, to learn from experience, to engage in various forms of reasoning, to overcome obstacles by taking thought" (Neisser, 1996, p. 1). Intelligence is a determinant of success in a huge range of activites: "a century of research has shown that General Mental Ability is predictive of socioeconomic achievement, academic achievement, health-related behaviors, social outcomes, occupational status and even death" (Ones, Viswesvaran, & Dilchert, 2005, p. 431). This is precisely the ability that Jews have displayed since their emancipation in the early 19th century and which it is the objective of this book to suggest has been largely responsible for Jewish success.

However, achievement is not only determined by general intelligence. There are also different kinds of intelligence, notably in particular verbal and spatial abilities, that contribute to achievement in different fields; it is a peculiarity of Jews that they tend to be much stronger on verbal than on spatial ability. The consequence of this is that they tend to do particularly well in fields requiring strong verbal abilities such as law. Achievement is also determined by other attributes than intelligence, such as strong work motivation and family and ethnic networks. The question of whether these have also contributed to Jewish success will be discussed in the last chapter.

Note

* Since 1969, the Sveriges Riksbank (Swedish Central Bank) has recognized excellence in economics by awarding the Prize in Economic Sciences in Memory of Alfred Nobel. Though technically not equivalent to the Nobel Prize, it is often referred to as such. For the purposes of this book, no distinction is made between the separate but related awards. All Nobel Prize winners have been compiled from the Prize website and cross-referenced for Jews with the Israel Science and Technology Database, http://www.science.co.il/Nobel.asp

CHAPTER 2

The Four Jewish Peoples

1. The Mizrahim
2. The Sephardim
3. The Ashkenazim
4. The Ethiopian Jews
5. Genetic Differentiation after the Diaspora
6. Differences in Intelligence among the Four Jewish Peoples

In Chapter 1, we considered the intelligence and achievements of the Jews as if these were a single and homogeneous people. In reality, however, there are four Jewish peoples. These are the Mizrahim, the Sephardim, the Ashkenazim, and the Ethiopian Jews. There are also a few small Jewish sects in India.

1. *The Mizrahim*

The Mizrahim are the Jews of the Near East, the Middle East, and North Africa. They are sometimes known as the Oriental Jews, but this term is misleading since many of them come from North Africa. They are also sometimes aggregated with the Jews of Spain and Portugal and collectively called the Sephardim, but this is misleading because of their different histories. Many of the Mizrahim are descendants of the Jews of the first diaspora that occurred in the sixth century BC, when a number of them migrated to Babylon, broadly coterminous with contemporary Iraq. In the subsequent diasporas, others settled in Yemen, Syria, Iran, and elsewhere in the Near East and the Middle East where over the centuries, they became "Arabized in their language and habits" (Ma'oz, 2000, p. 108). Others settled in Egypt. During the Roman occupation of North Africa some groups of Jews migrated westward into Tunisia, Algeria, and Morocco.

In the seventh and eighth centuries AD, the Arabs conquered the Near East, Middle East and North Africa. Under Arab rule "Jewish life and culture flourished, despite periodic oppression" (Kosmin, Goldberg, Shain, & Bruk, 1999, p. 5). In Iraq, the Jews occupied a wealthy quarter of the new city of Baghdad, which the Abbasid dynasty founded in 762 as their capital. Here "the Jews provided court doctors and officials.... In 1170 it was estimated that there were about 40,000 Jews living there in the city." The scholars had the most prestige: "the phrase 'not of scholarly families being of merchants' was dismissive... the head of each academy came from one of six families" (Johnson, 2004, pp. 176, 181).

In North Africa, "a centre of Jewish prosperity was Kairouan in Tunisia; in the eighth century an academy was founded there and for the next 250 years it was one of the great centres of Jewish scholarship. Jews supplied the court with doctors, astronomers, and officials" (Johnson, 2004, p. 177).

In 1516, the Ottomans, from their base in Turkey and capital Istanbul, gained control of most of the Near and Middle East, including present day Syria, Lebanon, and Palestine. In the 17th century, the Ottomans extended their empire to include Georgia, Armenia, Iraq, Syria, the whole of North Africa, and the southern part of the Balkans. Many towns and cities in the Ottoman Empire had Jewish populations. Those with the greatest numbers of Jews were Baghdad and Jerusalem.

The Ottomans ruled these territories until the early 20th century. In the early 19th century, there were about 80,000 Jews in the Ottoman Empire in the Near East and North Africa. By 1900, there were about 400,000 Jews in the Near East and North Africa. The greatest number of Jews was in Baghdad, where there were about

52,000 (Montgomery, 1902). Egypt's 1907 census recorded 38,635 Jews living in the country. A much higher percentage of Jews than of Muslims were literate (44 percent as compared with four percent) (Landau, 2000).

The Ottomans provided a generally benign environment for Jews and other non-Muslims in their African and Asian territories, as well as in their European dominions in the Balkans: "the Ottoman Levant did not see much anti-Semitism" (Benbassa and Rodrigue, 1995, p. 159); and "Jews fared better under Muslims than under Christian and pagan rule" (Entine, 2007, p. 174). In the 19th century,

> a noticeable number of Jews held senior positions in commerce and finance as merchants, bankers, and treasury officials; Jews periodically served as physicians, interpreters, and advisers in the courts of sultans and provincial governors.... In addition to good economic conditions (and personal achievements), for centuries Jews enjoyed a considerable degree of communal autonomy (during the nineteenth century this was formalized as part of the reforms in the *millet* system) in matters of religious worship, jurisdiction in issues relating to personal status, the levying of certain taxes, and managing educational and welfare institutions. (Ma'oz, 2000, pp. 108–9)

For the most part, Jews did not challenge Muslim supremacy, and relations between the two groups were not hostile. Jews were, however, "occasionally subject to oppression, extortion and violence by both local authorities and segments of the Muslim population" (Ma'oz, 2000, p. 114).

2. The Sephardim

The Sephardim are the descendants of the Jews who lived for many centuries in Spain and Portugal. Jews settled in Spain in the first three centuries AD, when it was part of the Roman Empire. After the fall of Rome, Spain was occupied by the Visigoths, under whose rule "systematic anti-Semitism was pursued.... Throughout the seventh century, Jews were flogged, executed, had their property confiscated, were subject to ruinous taxes, forbidden to trade, and, at times, dragged to the baptismal font" (Johnson, 2004, p. 177). The

Arabs invaded Spain in 711 and rapidly conquered the whole country. Arab rule lasted for 783 years until 1492. For the first 300 or so years, the Arabs "treated the Jews with extraordinary favour and tolerance.... Jews were not only craftsmen and traders but doctors." The capital city of Cordoba became the "leading centre of Jewish culture in the world" (Johnson, 2004, p. 177). "The Jewish elite in Spain were tax farmers over the centuries" (Benbassa & Rodrigue, 1995, p. 37). However, in 1013 "the primitive Berber Moslems took Cordoba.... Prominent Jews were assassinated. At Grenada there was a massacre of Jews" (Johnson, 2004, p. 177). During the next four centuries, the Jews were persecuted and a number of them fled to France or to North Africa.

The most famous of the Jewish scholars in Spain in the early medieval period was Moses Maimonides (1135–1204). He was born and grew up in Cordoba, but to escape persecution, moved to Fostat (Cairo) in Egypt, where he was a physician to Saladin, the sultan of Egypt and Syria. Maimonides's chief philosophical work, *Guide to the Perplexed,* was addressed to those who had lost their faith and attempted to reconcile the work of Aristotle with Jewish theology.

In the 15th century, there were about 250,000 Jews in Spain out of a total population of about four million. At the end of the century, in 1492, the Spanish drove the Arabs out of Spain and expelled the Jews, unless they converted to Christianity; about 165,000 chose to leave. The Jews were also expelled from Portugal in 1496. Most of those who left went to the Balkans; others went to a variety of places in the Levant (the lands of the eastern Mediterranean, including present-day Turkey, Syria, Lebanon, Israel, and Egypt), notably in Izmir (in present-day Turkey), Jerusalem, Damascus, Alexandria, Cairo, and Tangier. Others went to the Netherlands and Italy. Their descendants in the mid-20th century numbered about two million and were widely dispersed throughout the world. Most of those in the Balkans were killed by the Germans during World War II. The majority of those who escaped moved to Israel.

3. *The Ashkenazim*

The Ashkenazim are the descendants of the Jews who migrated from Palestine into Central and Northern Europe. The word Ashkenazi means "German" in Yiddish, the language they spoke. The theory advocated by Arthur Koestler (1977) that the Ashkenazim are mainly the descendants of Caucasian Khazars in present day Ukraine who converted to Judaism in the eighth and ninth centuries has now been rejected by most scholars (Brook, 2006; Entine, 2007), although David B. Goldstein (2008) believes it is possible some Khazars may have converted, migrated west, and assimilated into Jewish communities. Between 300 and 600 AD, Jews are known to have lived in Cologne and in several towns in what is now France, from which they were expelled by King Dagobert of the Franks (c.603–639) in 629 AD. When these first Ashkenazi communities came under the rule of Charlemagne about the year 800, he gave freedoms to the Jews in his lands that stretched from western Germany through France to northeast Spain. These favorable conditions stimulated more Jewish migration from southern Europe. This period also saw Jewish merchants taking up the occupation of money-lending when Church legislation banned Christians from the practice of "usury," defined as lending money in exchange for interest, making the Jewish presence a necessary part of the economy.

By the early 900s, Jewish populations were well-established in Northern Europe. Some of them settled in England following the Norman Conquest of 1066. In the period between 1290 and 1500, Jews were extensively persecuted and expelled from Western and Central Europe. They were expelled from England (1290), France (1394), and parts of Germany (1400s). Most of them migrated eastward into present day Poland, Lithuania, Latvia, and Russia. They mainly remained there until 1881–1914, when there were pogroms against them in the Russian empire. There was an exodus from Central and Eastern Europe between 1918 and 1939 when the Jews experienced further persecution. They migrated principally to the United States and also to Britain, Canada, Continental Europe, Australia, South Africa, South America, and Israel. In the second half of the 20th century, around 95 percent of Jews in the world outside Israel were Ashkenazi (Rubinstein, 1985).

4. *The Ethiopian Jews*

The fourth group of Jews are the *Falashas,* who are also known as the Black or Ethiopian Jews. They believe they are descended from Ham, one of Noah's sons. As they are black, this is improbable and in fact they are Ethiopians who converted to Judaism at some uncertain time many centuries ago. Genetic studies have shown that they are closer genetically to sub-Saharan Africans, including South African Bantu, San Bushmen, and Senegalese, than to Ashkenazi and Asian Jews (Kobyliansky, Micle, Goldschmidt, Arensburg & Nathan, 1982; Zoossmann-Diskin, Ticher, Hakim, Goldwitch, Rubinstein, & Bonnie-Tamir, 1991). The most definitive study found no Jewish genetic markers in the Ethiopian Jews and concluded that they are descended from Ethiopians who converted to Judaism (Lucotte & Smets, 1999).

In the 1970s, there was discussion among the rabbis in Israel as to whether they should be recognized as Jews. In 1973, the Chief Rabbi decided that the Falashas were, indeed, Jews. The Israeli government accepted this decision, and as a result, allowed Ethiopian Jews to migrate to Israel. From 1977 onward, many thousands of them took advantage of this concession, and by 1998, virtually all of them had left Ethiopia and taken up residence in Israel. They numbered about 80,000, according to the Central Bureau of Statistics, and were approximately 1.4 percent of the population of Israel.

In addition to these four Jewish groups, there is a small population of Jews in India. There were about 26,000 of these Indian Jews in the late 1940s, mainly living in and around Mumbai (Bombay). Some of these were "genetic Jews" who had migrated to India at various times and for various reasons, while others were converts. About 10,000 of these migrated to Israel after the state was established in 1948. There was also a small community of about 1,000 Tibeto-Burmese Jews in northern India, who appeared not to be genetically Jewish (Halkin, 2008) and who migrated to Israel.

5. Genetic Differentiation after the Diaspora

The Ashkenazim, the Sephardim, and the Mizrahim have some genetic affinity, as a result of their common origin in Palestine. The Ethiopian Jews are not related genetically to these three populations of "genetic Jews." These three populations of Jews have affinity derived from their common origin. The first evidence for the genetic relatedness of the Ashkenazim, the Sephardim, and the Mizrahim was published by L. Sachs and M. Bat-Miriam (1957). They examined fingerprints and devised a method for quantifying the number of whorls, the distinctive ring patterns on the fingertips. They then measured the number of whorls in eight samples of Jews in Israel who had come from different countries (Bulgaria, Turkey, Germany, Morocco, Egypt, Yemen, Poland, and Iraq) and compared these with four samples of non-Jewish Arabs and with six samples of European Gentiles. The study showed that the whorl count of the Jews from the eight geographically disparate locations was similar and different from those of the Arabs and European Gentiles. Jews in the United States also have the same numbers of whorls. The authors concluded that "even Jews living in Europe and North America show clear evidence of their original Eastern Mediterranean gene pool" (p. 125).

These results have been confirmed and extended by Michael Hammer et al. (2000) in a study in which they examined the genetic profiles of 1,371 men from seven Jewish populations (Ashkenazi, Roman, North African, Kurdish, Near Eastern, Yemenite, and Ethiopian) and 16 non-Jewish populations (Russians, Poles, Greeks, Turks, Italians, Germans, Austrians, Egyptians, Tunisians, Palestinian Arabs, Syrians, Lebanese, Moroccans, Kurds, and the Lemba (a tribe of Blacks in South Africa)). They found that all the Jewish samples (except for the Ethiopian Jews) shared a degree of genetic similarity that differentiated them from non-Jews; all the Jewish samples (again, except for the Ethiopian Jews) also displayed a genetic similarity to Palestinian Arabs, Syrians, and Lebanese. This proved that the Jews are a Semitic people who have evolved a genetic identity that differentiates them from other Semitic peoples.

While the three populations of Jews have some genetic affinity derived from their common origin, they have also become genetically differentiated. It was inevitable that this would happen because it is a law of evolutionary biology that when populations become isolated from one another, they grow apart genetically. There are two principal reasons for this. First, populations adapt to their local environments. For instance, the incidence of G6PD deficiency is 58.2 percent among Jews in Iraq but only 0.4 percent among Ashkenazi Jews in Northern Europe and the United States (Szeinberg, 1963). The deficiency provides some protection against malaria, which is why it has become so common among Jews in Iraq, where malaria is prevalent, but has not spread among Ashkenazi Jews because malaria is absent in Northern and Central Europe. Second, genetic mutations occur in some populations but not in others; for instance, the recessive gene for Tay-Sachs disease is present in approximately 1.8 percent of Ashkenazi Jews but in only about 0.2 percent of Mizrahim Jews (Bodmer & Cavalli-Sforza, 1976, p. 629). This gene appeared as a mutation in Ashkenazi Jews and has spread among them, but it has not appeared to anything like the same extent in other Jews. Two further factors have led to genetic differentiation among the three Jewish peoples. The first of these consists of some interbreeding over the centuries between Jews and their Gentile host communities. Some of the offspring of these Jewish-Gentile unions have been absorbed into Jewish communities. The second is that some Gentiles have converted to Judaism, sometimes as individuals and occasionally as groups. The result of these two processes has been that each of the three Jewish peoples has developed some genetic similarities with the Gentile populations among whom they have lived. Thus, while virtually all the Sephardim and the Mizrahim have dark eyes and dark, straight hair, significant numbers of Ashkenazim have blue eyes as well as fair and wavy hair. M. Fisberg (1904) summarized a dozen studies of a total of 75,377 Ashkenazi Jews in Germany carried out at the end of the 19th century and found that approximately 47 percent had the dark hair and dark eyes of the original Southwest Asian stock; 42 percent had mixed hair and eye color (fair hair with dark eyes or dark hair with blue eyes), while 11 percent had fair hair and blue eyes. Thus, 53 percent of German Jews had some North European ancestry.

The genetic differentiation of the three Jewish peoples has been further demonstrated by Hammer et al. (2000) in their study of the genetic profiles of 1,371 men from seven Jewish populations (Ashkenazi, Roman, North African, Kurdish, Near Eastern, Yemenite, and Ethiopian) and 16 non-Jewish populations. They found that (1) Ashkenazi Jews had some genetic affinity with European peoples including Germans, Austrians, Russians, Greeks, and Spaniards; this shows that there was some interbreeding and genetic admixture of Ashkenazi Jews with various non-Jewish European populations; (2) Mizrahim had some genetic affinity with non-Jewish Tunisians and Egyptians, again showing that there was interbreeding and some genetic admixture of the Mizrahim with non-Jewish North African populations among whom they lived; (3) the South African Lemba also had some genetic affinity with the Jews, presumably because many centuries ago some Jewish merchants traded with them and interbred with some Lemba women.

DNA research has shown that the Y-chromosome of both Ashkenazi and Sephardic Jews are of Middle Eastern origin, similar to Lebanese and Syrian DNA types. The Y-chromosome is only passed from father to son and can be used to trace Jewish male origins. Another study of Ashkenazi mitochondrial DNA, which can only be passed from mother to child, allows the tracking of maternal origins and showed that the mtDNA generally matched that of local European populations and not Middle Eastern populations (Hammer et al., 2000). The Y-chromosome study showed that gene flow into the Jewish community from female European Gentiles was low at about 0.5 percent per generation. However, over some 40 generations, this small amount of gene flow would have an appreciable effect. This and further studies indicate that a number of male Jewish traders moved from the Middle East into Europe and married local women. The children of these marriages assimilated into Jewish communities (Behar, Garrigan, Kaplan, Mobasher, et al., 2004; Entine, 2007; Goldstein, 2008; Halkin, 2008).

The four Jewish peoples, each with their distinctive genetic profiles, differ considerably in their intelligence and achievements. In subsequent chapters this is documented for all the countries in which there are significant Jewish populations. We shall see that it is only the Ashkenazim that have the exceptional intelligence, which is estimated at 110 (all these IQs are calculated in relation to 100 for Britain and other countries of Northwest Europe, which has become known as the "Greenwich standard," analagous to longitude which is measured in degrees distant from Greenwich). The IQ of the Sephardim is considered in Chapter 17 on the Balkans and is estimated at 99, about the same as the average of Europeans. The IQ of the Mizrahim is considered in Chapter 11 on Israel and is estimated at 91, about 7 IQ points higher than that of other peoples of the Near and Middle East. The IQ of the Ethiopian Jews is also considered in Chapter 11 and is estimated at 66, about the same as that of other peoples of sub-Saharan Africa (Lynn, 2006). Chapter 20 considers theories to explain the differences in intelligence among the four Jewish peoples and between these and Gentiles. Chapter 21 considers the general implications of the study of Jewish intelligence and achievements and the future of the Jewish peoples. The IQs of these peoples have been obtained from a literature search using PsychINFO, PsychNet, ISI Web of Science, and Web of Knowledge.

Chapter 3

Australia

1. Numbers of Jews
2. Educational Achievement
3. Socioeconomic Status
4. Earnings
5. Intermarriage
6. Conclusions

Small numbers of Jews were transported to Australia as convicts from Britain between 1788 and 1852. Others migrated voluntarily in the early 19th century. Even at this early date, "Australian Jews played a more dominant role in commercial life than their numbers would suggest" (Rutland, 1988, p. 121). In New South Wales, the most prominent Jewish business was run by the Cohen family. The business was started by Samuel Cohen (1815?–1890?), who set up a shop in 1836 in West Maitland. His son George (1842–1937) moved the business to Sydney, where he became one of the leading businessmen. George's son, Samuel (1869–1948), was a director of numerous companies and was knighted in 1937 in recognition of his public work. Sir Samuel Cohen's son, Paul (1909–2007), changed his surname to Cullen, entered the army, and rose to the rank of Major General. Other prominent Jews in Sydney were Sir Adolph Basser, who established a leading jewelery business and founded Basser College at the University of New South Wales, and Abram Coppleson, who founded the Coppleson Institute for medical research at the University of Sydney.

Jews immigrated in the 1850s to participate in the development of the goldfields at Ballarat and Bendigo, and also in the mining of coal, as well as copper, silver, and lead. Few Jews worked as miners. They worked more as provisioners for the miners, setting up hotels and shops and supplying the mines with food, clothing, sieves, and pickaxes. A population survey of the state of Victoria in 1881 found that fewer than 10 percent of Jews were unskilled laborers, while nearly all the rest were skilled workers, salesmen, storekeepers, hotel owners, bakers, and caterers. Jews had a higher socioeconomic profile than Gentiles (Rutland, 1988, pp. 53–4).

In Melbourne, the Michaelis family ran one of the most prominent Jewish businesses. Moritz Michaelis (1820–1902) arrived in Australia in 1853 and set up an import business. When he died in 1902, he was one of the hundred richest men in Victoria. Another was the Myers family. Sidney Baevski Myer (1878–1934) arrived in Australia in 1897, established the Myer Emporium "which has been ranked with the famous international stores such as Macy's in New York and Selfridges in London" (Rutland, 1988, p. 124). Other prominent Jews included Sir Isaac Isaacs (1855–1948), whose father arrived from Poland in 1854 and who was Chief Justice of Australia and Governor-General (1931–1936); and Sir Zelman Cowen (b. 1 919), whose grandparents had fled Russia in the 1880s to escape the pogroms. Zelman's paternal grandfather went to Britain, from which his father immigrated to Australia, while his maternal grandfather went to the Australian gold-mining town of Ballarat. Cowen studied law at the University of Melbourne, where he became professor; he later became vice-chancellor of the University of Queensland (1970–1977) and then Governor-General of Australia. Yet another eminent Jew was Lieutenant General Sir John Monash (1865–1931), whose father arrived from Poland in 1853. John was Commander-in-Chief of the Australian Army Corps on the Western Front during World War I. In 1923, he was appointed vice-chancellor of the University of Melbourne. In 1958, Monash University in Melbourne was named after him. The most internationally famous of the Melbourne Jewish community was Helena Rubinstein (1879-1965), who migrated to Australia from Kracòw in 1891. She observed that women's complexions suffered in the Australian climate and opened a shop to sell face cream to afford some protection against the strong Australian sun. From this modest beginning she built her worldwide cosmetics business that survives to this day.

1. Numbers of Jews

The approximate numbers of Jews in Australia and their percentages of the population for various dates from 1851 to 2001 are given in Table 3.1. The increase of about 36,000 in the numbers from 1933 to 1961 was partly due to the immigration of about 8,000 Jews from Austria, Germany, Hungary, Lithuania, and Poland seeking to escape anti-Semitism and persecution. The numbers were quite small because Australia had a quota of 1,800 Jews a year, which was raised to 5,000 a year in 1938. About another 23,000 or so Jews entered after World War II up to 1960 as survivors of the Holocaust, including a few thousand from Egypt and other countries in the Near East from which they were expelled following the Arab-Israel conflict. A further 36,000 came between 1961 and 2001, a number of them from South Africa and Israel. Most of the Austrian, German, and Hungarian Jews settled in Sydney, while most of the Polish Jews settled in Melbourne (Rutland, 1988). In the 1980s, about 10,000 Jews migrated to Australia from South Africa. Despite the increase in the numbers of Jews, the Gentile population increased at about the same rate, with the result that the percentage of Jews in the population has remained fairly stable from 1851 to 2001 at between 0.36 and 0.56 percent.

Table 3.1. Numbers and Percentages of Jews in Australia

Year	Jewish Population	% of Total
1851	1,778	0.53
1933	23,553	0.36
1961	59,343	0.56
2001	98,000	0.50

2. Educational Achievement

Jews in Australia have had higher levels of education than Gentiles. Some statistics for the educational achievement of Jews in Australia are given in Table 3.2. Row 1 shows that already by 1921, Jews were more than five times overrepresented as students in Australian universities, as compared with Gentiles. Row 2 shows that by 1933, this had increased to an overrepresentation of 5.8 times. Rows 3 through 5 show the percentages of Jews and Gentiles that passed the high school matriculation examinations and who were university graduates in New South Wales, recorded in the 1966 and 1976 censuses in New South Wales and in Victoria. Jews were greatly overrepresented and obtained Achievement Quotients of 5.3 in New South Wales in 1966 and of 3.9 in Victoria in 1976.

Table 3.2. Educational Achievement of Jews and Gentiles (percentages)

Year	Education	State	Jews	Gentiles	AQ
1921	College students	Australia	3.74	0.71	5.2
1933	College students	Australia	4.26	0.73	5.8
1966	Matriculation	N. S.Wales	33.0	9.4	3.5
1966	Graduates	N. S.Wales	5.8	1.1	5.3
1976	Graduates	Victoria	10.2	2.6	3.9

Sources: rows 1–2: Elazar & Redding, 1983, p. 280; rows 3–5: Rubinstein, 1986, p. 122)

3. Socioeconomic Status

Jews had achieved higher socioeconomic status than Gentiles by 1947, when a survey found that 53 percent of Jews were in white-collar occupations compared with 25 percent of Gentiles (Elazar & Redding, 1983, p. 280). In 1986, the Australian magazine *Business Review Weekly* published a "Rich List" of the 200 Australians who possessed more than $100 million and found that 50 of these were Jewish business people, mostly immigrants from Central and Eastern Europe (Rutland, 1988, p. 200). Jews were about 0.5 percent of the population, giving them an Achievement Quotient of 50.

Australia   37

The percentages of Jews and Gentiles in professional and administrative occupation and in sales in New South Wales recorded in the 1966 census are shown in Table 3.3. It will be seen that for both men and women, Jews were greatly overrepresented and obtained Achievement Quotients of 3.2 and 6.4, respectively. Jews were also overrepresented as salesmen and saleswomen. Jews were correspondingly underrepresented in blue-collar occupations. William Rubinstein (1987) gives figures from the 1971 census for the whole of Australia, showing that for all workingmen, 46.1 percent were in professional and managerial occupations, quite similar to the 49.8 percent in New South Wales in 1966; in the 1971 census, 21.2 percent of working Jewish men were in small business and clerical occupations, and 6.7 percent were in semiskilled and unskilled occupations. (Rubinstein does not give the corresponding figures for Gentiles.)

Table 3.3. Occupational Distribution of Jews and Gentiles in New South Wales in 1966 (percentages)

Occupation	Sex	Jews	Gentiles	AQ
Prof/Admin	Men	49.8	15.4	3.2
Prof/Admin	Women	15.9	2.5	6.4
Sales	M & W	14.8	5.8	3.9

An analysis of the numbers and percentage of Jews among the elite defined as the 370 leading Australians was carried out by Higley, Deacon, and Smart (1979). Their results are summarized in Table 3.4.

Table 3.4. Percentages of Jews in the Elite

Field	% Jews	AQ
Politics & media	3.5	6.2
Business	6.0	10.7
Civil servants	12.0	21.4
Academics	15.0	26.8

We see that Jews were considerably overrepresented in politics and the media, and among business leaders, and massively overrepresented among senior civil servants and leading academics with Achievement Quotients of 21.4 and 26.8, respectively.

4. Earnings

Jews in Australia have higher average earnings than Gentiles. Statistics for the earnings of Jews and Gentiles in Victoria in 1976 and 1981 taken from the Federal census have been given by Rubinstein (1987, p. 122) and are given in Table 3.5. For 1976, he gives the percentages of men with annual earnings of $18,000 and above as 30.5 for Jews and 9.5 for Gentiles. Among low earners, there were fewer Jews than Gentiles. Only 17.8 percent of Jewish men had annual earnings of under $7,000, as compared with 28.5 percent of Gentiles. In 1981, the percentages of men with annual earnings of $26,000 and above were 25 percent for Jews and 11 percent for Gentiles.

Table 3.5. Annual Earnings of Jews and Gentiles in Victoria (percentages)

Year	Annual Earnings	Jews	Gentiles
1976	$18,000+	30.5	9.5
1976	Under $7,000	17.8	28.5
1981	$26,000+	25.0	11.0

5. Intermarriage

Many Jews in Australia have assimilated with Gentiles. The rates of intermarriage between Jews and Gentiles recorded in the censuses of 1921, 1961, and 1971 are shown in Table 3.6. In 1921, the rates of exogamy were quite high at 28 percent for Jewish men and 15 percent for Jewish women. The exogamy rates declined in 1961 and 1971. This was due to the greater numbers of Jews in Australia in the second half of the 20th century and hence the greater availability of Jewish marriage partners. The greater percentages of Jewish men marrying Gentiles than of Jewish women have been found in a number of other countries and implies that a higher proportion of Jewish women remain unmarried.

Table 3.6. Percentages of Jews Marrying Gentiles

Year	Men	Women
1921	28	15
1961	10	4
1971	10	6

6. Conclusions

The Jews have been remarkably successful in Australia. They have been overrepresented in the universities, the professions, and business. They have also made their mark in chess: the Hungarian-born Lajos Steiner (1903–1975) won the New South Wales chess championship for five consecutive years (1941–1945) and later became the all-Australia chess champion.

How can the Jewish successes be explained? Suzanne Rutland (1988, p. 259–261), who has written the standard text on Jews in Australia, believes there are five reasons for Jewish success. First, many of them had "entrepreneurial flair and business acumen." Second, they "were highly motivated to create a new and more secure life for themselves." Third, they had "the willingness to work hard, 'often seven days a week and sixteen hours a day', usually with the assistance of their wives." Fourth, they had "imagination":

> Imagination is another essential ingredient in business success, 'as new products must be conceived, new ways of doing things conjured up, and ways round problems solved'. As a result of persecution and discrimination, Jews have always tended to be innovators.

Fifth, "self-help was also an important factor in Jewish business success," as Jews excelled at exploiting the ethnic-religious networks they brought over from Europe. (p. 264). Rutland does not mention intelligence as a possible factor in the success of the Jews. There is no direct evidence on the intelligence of the Jews in Australia, but studies in Britain, Canada, and the United States have shown that it is higher than that of Gentiles at an IQ of approximately 110. The Jews of Australia are the same Ashkenazi stock, most likely have about the same IQ, and this has almost certainly been a significant factor in their success.

CHAPTER 4

Austria and Hungary

1. Austria
2. Austrian Nobel Prize winners and Chess Grandmasters
3. Czechoslovakia
4. Hungary
5. Hungarian Nobel Laureates, Wolf Prize winners, and Chess Grandmasters
6. Infant Mortality

In this chapter, we consider the position of Jews in Central Europe, a region that comprised the Austro-Hungarian Empire from 1815 to 1918 and now includes not only present-day Austria and Hungary but the Czech Republic and Slovakia. In 1867, Hungary (which included Slovakia) became an autonomous region of the Austro-Hungarian Empire. In 1918, as a result of the First World War, the Austro-Hungarian Empire was split up: Austria and Hungary became independent states, and the northern provinces of both were hived off to form the independent state of Czechoslovakia.

Jews settled in this region of Central Europe from at least 800 AD. From time to time, they were persecuted and expelled. In 1298, it is estimated that approximately 100,000 Jews were killed in Austria. The Jews were expelled from Hungary in 1360 and from Austria in

1420 (Barnaav, 1998). Despite these tribulations, Jews flourished in this region. The 1918 *American Jewish Yearbook* calculated that at the turn of the century, there were 2,258,000 Jews in the Austro-Hungarian Empire, 4.4 percent of a total population of 51,100,000.

Charles Murray (2003, p. 280) has calculated the numbers of Jewish and Gentile "significant figures" (important names in science and the arts) in Central Europe whose careers peaked in the years 1870-1950. He finds 21 Jews and 50 Gentiles. Calculating the ratio of Jewish to Gentile "significant figures," he concludes that Jews were overrepresented by a factor of 7.1.

1. Austria

The number of Jews in Austria during the 19th century and up to 1940 was approximately 233,000 and comprised approximately 3.5 percent of the population. About 90 percent of these (approximately 209,000) were estimated to have been killed in the Holocaust. Of the 32,000 or so that survived, many immigrated to Israel, leaving approximately 9,000 (0.1 percent of the population) in 2002.

Jews were emancipated and given full civil rights in Austria in 1867. From this time up to the end of World War I, Jews in Austria became prominent in the professions, in intellectual life, banks, commerce, and industry. Several of the most famous Austrians of this period were Jews, including the philosophers Karl Popper (1902–90) and Ludwig Wittgenstein (1889–1951), whose family had a large engineering business; the founder of psychoanalysis, Sigmund Freud (1856–1939), his daughter Anna Freud (1895–1982), and Alfred Adler (1870–1937), Freud's sometime colleague and later apostate; the novelist Stefan Zweig (1881–1942); and the Rothschilds whose Creditanstalt was one of the largest banks in the country.

Within a couple of decades following emancipation, Jews became greatly overrepresented among university students, in the professions, and in business in Austria. Statistics showing this for the years 1873–1918 are given in Table 4.1. The first row shows that in the 1880s, Jews (who were approximately 3.5 percent of the population) were 17 percent of all university students in the country, giving them an overrepresentation Achievement Quotient of 4.9. Row 2 of Table 4.1 shows that in the 1880s, Jews were 50 percent of the students at the University of Vienna, where they comprised approximately 10 percent of the population, giving them an Achievement Quotient of 5.0. The next eight rows show that in the period 1873–1910, Jews were 40 percent of graduates of the Gymnasium (elite high schools), 40 percent of directors of the public banks, 70 percent of the members of the Vienna stock exchange council (the Borsenrath), and were overrepresented in the professions of law, medicine, and journalism, and among the Faculty at the University of Vienna. The last row shows that in 1917 Jews comprised 50 percent of the directors of industrial companies who held more than seven simultaneous directorships.

Table 4.1. Jews in Austria 1870–1918

Years	Occupation	% Jews	AQ
1880s	University Students	17	4.9
1880s	Vienna Students	50	5.0
1873–1910	Gymnasium Students	40	11.4
1873–1910	Bank Directors	40	11.4
1873–1910	Stock Exchange	70	20.0
1873–1910	Lawyers	62	17.7
1873–1910	Doctors	50	14.3
1873–1910	University Faculty	25	7.1
1873–1910	Journalists	57	16.3
1917	Company Directors	50	14.3
Source: Slezkine (2004)			

Austrian Jews continued to do well in the interwar period. Statistics showing the overrepresentation of Jews in the professions and business in Austria for the years 1918–1939 are given in Table 4.2. Jews (who were still approximately 3.5 percent of the population) had high achievement quotients among university professors, jewellers, chemists, booksellers, shoe manufacturers, and hat manufacturers.

Table 4.2. Jews in Austria 1918–1929

Occupation	% Jews	AQ
Professors	23.7	6.8
Jewellers	55.6	15.9
Chemists	26.0	7.4
Booksellers	71.5	20.4
Shoe Manufacturers	35.0	10.0
Hat Manufacturers	45.0	12.9
Source: Fraenkel (1967)		

2. Austrian Nobel Prize winners and Chess Grandmasters

Austrian Nobel Prize winners, representing the peak of intellectual achievement in the country, are listed in Table 4.3. Of the total of 16 Nobel Laureates, seven have been Jews. (Friedrich von Hayek is not identified as Jewish, but this is uncertain; he is not listed as Jewish on many websites of Jewish Nobel Prize winners, but he was a cousin of Ludwig Wittgenstein, who was Jewish, so he likely had some Jewish ancestry).

Table 4.3. Nobel Prize winners (Jews are asterisked)

Year	Name	Subject	Year	Name	Subject
1914	Robert Bárány *	Medicine	1945	Wolfgang Pauli*	Physics
1923	Fritz Pregl	Chemistry	1962	Max Perutz*	Chemistry
1927	Julius Wagner-Jauregg	Medicine	1973	Konrad Lorenz	Medicine
1930	Karl Landsteiner*	Medicine	1973	Karl von Frisch	Medicine
1933	Erwin Schrödinger	Physics	1974	Friedrich von Hayek	Economics
1936	Otto Loewi*	Medicine	1998	Walter Kohn*	Chemistry
1936	Victor F. Hess	Physics	2000	Eric R. Kandel*	Medicine
1938	Richard Kuhn	Chemistry	2004	Elfriede Jelinek	Literature

Thus, Jews, comprising about 1.8 percent of the population over the 20th century, have won 43 percent of the Nobel Prizes, giving them an Achievement Quotient of 24.

Austrian chess grandmasters are listed in Table 4.4. These are taken from the list of the 141 top-rated chess grandmasters for the years 1851 to 2000–the title of grandmaster was first introduced in 1851–compiled by William Rubinstein (2004). In this period, there were four Jews and four Gentiles among the top-rated grandmasters. From 1940–2000, there was only one top-rated grandmaster (Portisch) who was a Gentile.

Table 4.4. Jewish and Gentile Top-rated Chess Grandmasters

Year	Jews	Gentiles
1851–1939	Englisch	Hamppe
	Spielmann	Maroczy
	Kostic	Schlecter
	Chajes	Duras
1940–2000	-	Portisch

3. Czechoslovakia

The most famous Jews from Czechoslovakia are Sigmund Freud, who was born in the present-day Czech Republic but studied medicine at the University of Vienna and conducted his medical practice in the city; Franz Kafka (1883–1924), who was born in Prague and is best remembered for his novels *The Trial* and *The Castle*; and the British publishing tycoon Robert Maxwell (born Ludvík Hoch) (1923–1991).

From the emancipation of the Jews in 1867 up to 1940, Jews were approximately 2.4 percent of the population of Czechoslovakia. In the census of 1930, there were 354,342 Jews recorded in Czechoslovakia, representing 2.42 percent of the population. Most of these were in the eastern provinces of Slovakia and Subcarpathian Rus, where they were 8.4 percent of the population. In the western provinces of Bohemia and Moravia, they were only 1.1 percent of the population. According to Ezra Mendelsohn (1983, p. 152), "the Jews did not, on the whole, suffer discrimination in the state bureaucracy or the universities, unlike the case almost anywhere else in East Central Europe." Jews assimilated well in Bohemia, where 32 percent of Jewish men married Gentile women in 1931, and only slightly fewer Jewish women married Gentile men.

Jews did well in Czechoslovakia after the emancipation. In the 1880s, Jews were 15 percent of university students in Czechoslovakia and were overrepresented by a factor of 5.6 in relation to their proportion in the population (Slezkine, 2004). In 1935–1936, 11.9 percent of the university students were Jewish, giving them an Achievement Quotient of 4.9. While in Slovakia, "Jewish professionals, especially doctors and lawyers, constituted an inordinately high proportion; in the late 1930s, 40 percent of doctors in Slovakia were Jews" (Mendelsohn, 1983, p. 145). This gives them an Achievement Quotient of 4.8.

There have been three Czech Nobel Prize winners: Carl Cori (1896–1984) and Gerty Cori (1896–1957), who were jointly awarded the Prize for Medicine in 1947, and Jaroslav Seifert (1901–1986), who was awarded the Prize for Literature in 1984. Carl Cori was Jewish, so Jews, who composed about 2.4 percent of the population in the first half of the 20th century, won two thirds of the Nobel Prizes. The Czechs have produced three of the top-rated chess grandmasters: Wilhelm Steinitz (1836–1900), Solomon Flohr (1908–1983), and Oldrich Duras (1882–1957). All three were Jewish.

In World War II, it is estimated that about 90 percent of Jews in Czechoslovakia perished in the concentration camps. In 2002, there were an estimated 2,800 Jews in the Czech Republic and 3,300 Jews in Slovakia, comprising 0.02 and 0.06 percent of the populations, respectively.

4. Hungary

Jews were approximately five percent of the population of Hungary during the 19th century and up to 1910. In 1920, the percentages of Jews in the population was a little higher at 5.9. In the 1920s, the numbers of Jews and their percentages of the population declined because Jews had lower fertility than Gentiles, and there were also some conversions and emigration. The fall from 444,567 in 1930 to 170,000 in 1949 was a result of the Nazi exterminations in World War

II. The further falls to 75,000 in 1985 and 52,000 in 2000 were largely due to emigration, principally to Israel, and to low fertility (Johnson, 2004, p. 563). These figures are given in Table 4.5.

Table 4.5. Numbers and Percentages of Jews in Hungary

Year	Jewish Population	% of Total
1800–1910	-	5.0
1920	473,355	5.9
1930	444,567	5.1
1949	170,000	1.9
1985	75,000	0.75
2000	52,000	0.5

The Jews prospered in Hungary after their emancipation in 1867. According to a leading historian of the Austro-Hungarian Empire: "the capitalist development of modern Hungary...has been almost entirely of the Jews' making" (Macartney, 1969, p. 710). Another historian of the Austro-Hungarian Empire has written, Hungary was "a paradise for the Jews":

> By the late 19th century a small but potent Jewish oligarchy, mostly ennobled and partly converted to Christianity, held overriding economic power.... Budapest was sometimes called *Judapest*.... The Jewish impact on Hungary was not limited to economic activity. The children of Jewish bankers, industrialists, and businessmen, here as elsewhere in Europe, flocked to the universities and became doctors, lawyers, editors, journalists, scholars, musicians, and, perhaps most notably, scientists.... In the immediate prewar period, Jews constituted some fifty percent of the students in the University of Budapest medical faculty." (Mendelsohn, 1983, pp. 89, 92, 94)

"How are we to explain the unprecedented Jewish penetration of Hungarian economic and cultural life in the prewar period?" asks this same historian. To this question he gives the cogent answer that "the fact is that the general environment was unusually favourable to Jews" (p. 93).

Among the most internationally famous of the Jews in Hungary

48   THE CHOSEN PEOPLE

in this period were the composer Franz Lehar (1870–1948), best known for his operetta *The Merry Widow,* first performed in 1905; the escapologist Harry Houdini (1874–1926), who was born Ehrich Weisz; the writer and novelist Arthur Koestler (1905–1983); and David Gestetner (1854–1939) who invented the stencil duplicating process and whose copiers—*Gestetners*—were an essential item of equipment of offices throughout the world until they were replaced by photocopiers in the 1970s.

Some statistics showing how well Jews were doing in the second half of the 19th century up to World War I are given in Table 4.6. Row 1 shows that in 1857, 12.5 percent of wealthy landowners (defined as those in the class of the highest taxpayers) were Jewish (305 out of 2,450). Row 2 shows that in 1887, 62.3 percent of wealthy businessmen defined as those in the class of the highest taxpayers were Jewish (362 out of 588). Row 3 shows that between 1880 and 1900, Jews were 25 percent of all university students in the country which, considering that they were approximately 5 percent of the population, gives them an Achievement Quotient of 5.0.

Table 4.6. Jews in Hungary, 1857–1900 (percentages)

	Year	Occupation	% Jews	AQ
1	1857	Landowners	12.5	2.4
2	1887	Businesses	62.3	12.2
3	1880–1900	University Students	25.0	5.0
4	1880–1900	Budapest Students	43.0	8.6
5	1900	Doctors	49.0	9.8
6	1900	Lawyers	45.0	9.0
7	1900	Journalists	42.0	8.4
8	1900	Writers and artists	26.0	5.2

Sources: rows 1–4: Slezkine (2004); rows 5–8: Encyclopedia Judaica.

Row 4 shows that in the same period Jews were 43 percent of students at the elite Budapest Technological University, giving them an Achievement Quotient of 8.6.

Rows 5 through 8 shows that in 1900 Jews were massively overrepresented among doctors, lawyers, and journalists, and among writers and artists.

In 1918, Hungary became an independent country. After a tumultuous period, a Communist government gained power in 1919, headed by Béla Kun (1886–1938?), who was Jewish. Twenty of the 26 ministers in the government were also Jewish. This gave Jews a bad name among much of the population who disliked life under Communist rule. The fires of anti-Semitism were fuelled and there were a number of pogroms against Jews in which Jews were murdered in some 50 cities throughout the country. In August of 1919, Hungary was invaded by Romania, and Kun's reign of terror was put to an end. The Romanians installed a Social Democratic government, but in the next year, this was replaced by the conservative regime of Admiral Miklós Horthy (1868–1957).

Jews continued to do well in Hungary in the new order between the wars:

> Hungarian Jewry was basically distributed among the middle class, ranging from the haute to the lower bourgeoisie. At its apex were the giants of finance and industry. At the bottom were the artisans and small merchants of the little towns. There was no Jewish factory proletariat. (Mendelsohn, 1983, p. 100)

Only 4.2 percent of Jews worked in agriculture as compared with 59.7 percent of Gentiles, who were largely peasants (Slezkine, 2004). During this period, five percent of Jews were university graduates, compared with 1.7 percent of Protestants, 1.3 percent of Catholics, and 0.8 percent of Greek Orthodox (von Hentig, 1948, p. 339).

Statistics showing the prominence of Jews among the business elite and in the professions are given for 1920 in Table 4.7. Row 1 shows that in 1920, 54.0 percent of the owners of prominent commercial businesses were Jewish and row 2, that Jews owned 85.0 percent of banks and other financial institutions. Row 3 shows that in 1920, 12.5 percent of the owners of industrial businesses were Jewish. Row 4 shows that 60 percent of the doctors were Jews. Rows 5, 6, 7, and 8 show that 51 percent of lawyers, 39 percent of the privately employed engineers and chemists, 34 percent of the journalists, and 29 percent of the musicians were Jews. These figures are for those who identified themselves as Jews by religion. If Jewish converts and nonbelievers had been added, the percentages of Jews in these professions would have been higher.

Table 4.7. Occupational Profile of Jews in Hungary in 1920

	Occupation	% Jews	AQ
1	Commerce	54.0	10.6
2	Banks	85.0	16.7
3	Industrialists	12.5	2.4
4	Doctors	60.0	12.0
5	Lawyers	51.0	10.1
6	Engineers/Chemists	39.0	7.8
7	Journalists	34.0	6.8
8	Musicians	29.0	5.8
9	University students	13.4	2.3
Source: Slezkine (2004)			

Row 9 shows that 13.4 percent of the university students were Jewish. This figure is for the years 1921–1922 and is lower than might be expected due to a law passed in 1920 limiting the numbers of Jews admitted to the universities.

The prominence of Jews among the business elite was still present in 1930, as shown in Table 4.8.

Table 4.8. Economic position of Jews in Hungary in 1930

	Ownership	% Jews	AQ
1	Large commercial firms	61.7	12.1
2	Large industrial firms	47.4	9.3
3	Wealth	71.0	14.2
Source: Mendelsohn, 1983, p. 101			

Row 1 shows that in this year, 61.7 percent of the commercial firms (defined as those employing 20 or more people) were Jewish and row 2, that Jews owned 47.4 percent of the large industrial firms (similarly defined). Row 3 shows that Jews were 71 percent of the most wealthy taxpayers, defined as those whose income exceeded 200,000 pengo (the Hungarian currency) a year.

A significant number of Jews married Gentiles during this period. Between 1931 and 1935, 19.3 percent of Jewish men married Gentile women, while 16.5 percent of Jewish women married Gentile men (Mendelsohn, 1983, p. 102). Jews were well acculturated. Nevertheless, anti-Semitism increased in the 1920s when a quota for Jews was instituted for university admissions and Jews were effectively kept out of the civil service and army officer corps. Anti-Semitism became more virulent toward the end of the 1930s. In 1938, a law was passed restricting the proportion of Jews to 20 percent of the workforce, and Jews were limited to five percent of those admitted to the legal, medical, and engineering professions. In 1939, a further law prohibited Jews from all managerial positions in newspapers, theatres, cinemas, and film production; limited Jews to six percent of students at universities; and required all Jewish public prosecutors and professors and teachers in universities and high schools to retire by 1943. In industrial corporations, banks, mines, and insurance companies, Jews were to be limited to 12 percent of the workforce.

Hungary entered World War II as an ally of Germany. This was, up to a point, good for Jews because the Hungarians retained control of the country and Admiral Horthy (the regent) and other political leaders were sympathetic to the Jews, or at least not as virulently anti-Semitic as the Nazis. The Germans exerted pressure on the Hungarian government for the extermination of the Jews, but the Hungarian political leaders did their best to avoid complying with this demand. To accommodate the Germans, they passed more anti-Semitic legislation in 1941 prohibiting marriage between Jews (defined as having at least one Jewish grandparent) and Gentiles, and in 1942, Jewish estates were confiscated. Jews were conscripted into labor battalions and sent unarmed to the Russian front, where many of them died. In March 1944, the Germans occupied and took control of Hungary and organized the transportation of approximately 300,000 Jews to the concentration camps. These came largely from rural areas. Horthy managed to protect most of the Jews in Budapest from deportation, and more than half of them survived the war. By the year 2000, there were still 52,000 Jews in Hungary.

5. Hungarian Nobel Laureates, Wolf Prize winners, and Chess Grandmasters

In the 1920s and 1930s, Hungary produced a number of brilliant Jewish physicists. They included Leo Szilard (1898–1964), born in Budapest the son of a civil engineer, who won the Hungarian national prize in mathematics at the age of 18. He studied physics and engineering at the University of Berlin, where he developed a friendship with Einstein. When Hitler came to power he fled to Britain and in 1938 moved to the United States, where he was a prominent member of the Manhattan Project for the development of the atom bomb. Other renowned Hungarian Jewish physicists of this period were Eugene Wigner (1902–1995), John von Neumann (1903–1957), Edward Teller (1908–2003), Theodor von Kármán (1881–1963), Georg von Hevesy (1885–1966), and Michael Polanyi (1891–1976). In the 1930s, all of these men moved to the United States, where the first three (Wigner, von Newman, and Teller) joined Szilard as key members of the Manhattan Project.

Hungary has produced 12 Nobel Prize winners and four recipients of the Wolf Prize, awarded for outstanding work in mathematics. They are listed in Table 4.9.

Table 4.9. Hungarian Nobel and Wolf Prize winners (Jews are Asterisked)

Year	Nobel Prize	Subject	Year	Wolf Prize
1937	Albert Szent-Györgyi	Medicine	1983	Paul Erdos*
1943	George de Hevesy*	Chemistry	1987	Peter Lax*
1943	Jaroslav Heyrovsky*	Chemistry	1999	László Lovász
1944	Isidor Isaac Rabi *	Physics	2000	Raoul Bott*
1945	Wolfgang Pauli*	Physics		
1961	Georg von Békésy	Medicine		
1963	Eugene Wigner*	Physics		
1971	Dennis Gabor*	Physics		
1994	John C. Harsanyi*	Economics		
1994	George A. Olah*	Chemistry		
2002	Imre Kertész*	Literature		
2004	Avram Hershko*	Chemistry		

Of the total of 12 Nobel Prize winners, 10 have been Jews, while three of the four Wolf Prize winners have been Jews. Thus, Jews, comprising about 3.2 percent of the population during the 20th century, have produced 81 percent of the Nobel and Wolf Prize winners, giving them an Achievement Quotient of 25.

Hungarian Jews have excelled in chess. Table 4.10 gives the names of the top-rated Jewish and Gentile chess grandmasters in Hungary for the years 1851 to 2000. Between 1851 and 1939, there were four Jews and three Gentiles among top-rated grandmasters (Rubinstein, 2004).

Table 4.10 Jewish and Gentile Top-rated Chess Grandmasters

Year	Jews	Gentiles
1851–1939	Lowenthal	Szen
	Kolisch	Maroczy
	Gunsberg	Charousek
	Reti	
1940–2000		Leko

From 1940 to 2000, there was only one, a Gentile. Over the whole period, there were four Jews and four Gentiles. Jews were approximately 3.7 percent of the population during the period, giving them an Achievement Quotient of 13.5. Hungarian Jewry is also notable for producing Judit Polgár (b. 1976), from a Jewish family in Budapest (a number of her family were killed in the Holocaust, and her grandmother survived Auschwitz). She was among the best 20 players in the world in the 1990s and is widely considered the best female chess player of all time. Her two older sisters, Zsuzsa and Zsófia, are also good players, though not in the same class as Judit.

6. Infant Mortality

There is an association between high intelligence and low infant mortality that has been found among individuals and between groups. For instance, S.W. Savage (1946) found that in Britain the mothers of infants who died in their first year of life (this is the definition of infant mortality) had below average intelligence; this correlation was confirmed in the United States by Richard Herrnstein and Charles Murray (1994), who reported in their analysis of the *American Longitudinal Study of Youth* that mothers of infants who died in their first year of life had an average IQ of 92, eight points below the national average. One of the principal reasons for this is that more intelligent mothers look after their babies more effectively, for example, by feeding them properly, taking care of them when they are ill, and insuring that they do not have accidents.

Infant mortality was lower among Jews in the late 19th and early 20th centuries. Studies showing this have been summarized by Gretchen Condran and Ellen Kramarow (1991) and are shown in Table 4.11; infant mortality of Gentiles was between four and 67 percent higher than that of Jews.

Table 4.11. Infant Mortality per 1,000 Live Births

Years	Location	Jews	Gentiles	% Difference
1851	Hungary	153	251	64
1851	Bohemia	162	271	67
1851	Moravia	163	226	39
1880–1899	Budapest	129	210	63
1900–1912	Budapest	95	152	60
1894–1913	Vienna	78	81	4

Chapter 5

Benelux

1. Numbers of Jews in the Netherlands and Belgium
2. Socioeconomic Status of Jews in the Netherlands, 1860–1909
3. Crime Rates among Jews in the Netherlands, 1910–1920
4. Position of Jews in the Netherlands, 1930
5. Educational and Occupational Status, 1999
6. Nobel and Mathematics Prize winners
7. Fertility, Mortality, and Exogamy

Benelux is the convenient, if unlovely, name for the area of Northwest Europe that includes Belgium, the Netherlands, and Luxembourg. Jews were first recorded in these parts around the year 1200. By 1261, Henry III of Brabant (c. 1230–1261), the ruler of much of what is now this region, became concerned about the Jews' profession of money-lending, regarded as the sin of usury, and ordered them to leave unless they desisted from this occupation. However, he died before his order was carried out, and his widow decided not to proceed with the order because the Jews paid substantial taxes that she did not wish to forego.

A number of Jews came to Belgium and the Netherlands in 1290 following their expulsion from England. The first major persecution of

Jews in Belgium and the Netherlands occurred in 1348–1350 when the bubonic plague, known as the Black Death, swept though Europe and was responsible for the deaths of about a third of the population. Many people blamed the Jews for this terrible and inexplicable epidemic, since Jews were widely believed to be the enemies of Christians and wished to harm them. Throughout Europe, Jews were attacked and killed in revenge; Belgium and the Netherlands were no exceptions. A contemporary monk, Henry of Hereford, wrote:

> In that year of 1349 the Jews were exterminated most cruelly. This was done either on account of their wealth, which many people were able to seize illegally, or because they, as the general rumour hath it, maliciously poisoned the wells all over the world. (Blom, Fuks-Mansfeld, & Schoffer, 1996, pp. 19–20)

In the 15th century, Jews were discriminated against in a number of ways. They were prohibited from being money-lenders and from living in several towns. The only city to provide a benign environment for Jews was Nijmegen, and this was where the majority of Jews in the region lived. Many Jews left as a result of this hostile environment in the rest of the Low Countries and settled in Germany, mainly in Cologne and Frankfurt am Main.

From 1540 onward, a number of Sephardic Jews from Portugal settled in Antwerp. The Jews were officially given notice to leave Portugal in 1496, but were given some years grace to wind down their affairs. In 1511, some of them left for Antwerp, where they founded a colony of 20 families and traded in imports of salt, figs, oranges, and lemons from Portugal; sugar and tobacco from the Portuguese colony in Brazil; and spices and silks from the East, largely shipped via Lisbon. They also exported grain and textiles back to Portugal. In the next few years, more Jewish families moved to Antwerp as the Inquisition made life increasingly uncomfortable for them in Portugal. In 1549, Charles V (1500–1558), the ruler of the Benelux region at the time, became concerned at the growing numbers of Jews in Antwerp and expelled those who had arrived since 1543. Those who remained continued to increase in numbers, and by 1598, there were 93 Jewish family households in the city.

In 1587–88, the States of Zeeland and the States General permitted Portuguese Jews to come to the northern provinces. These included

Amsterdam, where a number of Sephardic Jews settled. In the early 1600s, they were joined by a number of Ashkenazim refugees from Germany and Poland. The Ashkenazim and the Sephardim coexisted as separate communities with their own synagogues and burial sites. Many of the Sephardim were rich, and the wealthiest were among the social elite:

> The Sephardi elite retained its aristocratic ways in every area: some of the splendid houses they purchased in Amsterdam became tourist attractions... Those who lived in The Hague bought homes on the prestigious boulevard, the Lange Voorhout.... They kept carriages and servants some of whom were Negroes and mulattos, who were slaves brought in from the Caribbean" (Blom, Fuks-Mansfeld, & Schoffer, 1996, p. 147).

The Ashkenazim were the Sephardim's poor relations, and the latter took measures to prevent intermarriage. In 1671, the Sephardim decreed that any of their men who married an Ashkenazi should be expelled from the Sephardic community. About this time, an Ashkenazi middle class began to emerge, and by the middle of the 18th century, mixed marriages became common and the two communities came together.

From the early 1600s, Amsterdam became the major Jewish city in the Netherlands. By the 1650s, Jews held 10 percent of the accounts in the Amsterdam Exchange Bank and were 10 percent of the registered brokers for commerce and shipping. Jews were prominent in share dealing in the Dutch East India Company and the West India Company:

> All reports agree that by the end of the seventeenth century these activities were dominated by Jews, who before 1700 were almost always Sephardim. They acted as specialist buyers and vendors on behalf of Dutch regents, Christian merchants and shopkeepers, and sometimes on behalf of foriegn noblemen (Blom, Fuks-Mansfeld, & Schoffer, 1996, p. 110).

In the mid-17th century, Jewish communities were established in several other Dutch cities, including the major ports of Rotterdam, Middleburg, and Antwerp, and also in the inland towns of Amersfoort and The Hague. At this time the Netherlands became the most important European center of international trade with the Americas and the East and the Jews were prominent among the Dutch merchants.

By the year 1700, there were 6,200 Jews in Amsterdam, comprising three percent of the population of the city, with approximately equal numbers of Ashkenazim and Sephardim (Blom, Fuks-Mansfeld, & Schoffer, 1996, pp. 91, 100). The city became the center for the import of wool from Spain and rough diamonds from the Portuguese colony of Goa in India. The Jews in Amsterdam established the two major centers for cutting and polishing rough diamonds, and then selling them on. In the late 17th century, the wealthiest Sephardim were Jacob Delmonte, Jeronimo Nunes da Costa, Antonio and Francisco Lopes Suasso, Manuuel de Belamonte, and the De Pintos and Pereiras. The wealthiest Ashkenazim were the Gompertz family in Amsterdam and the Boas family in The Hague. The Amsterdam Jew who acquired the greatest permanent reputation was Baruch Spinoza (1632–1677), who was born into a Sephardic family from Spain. He was critical of Judaism, denying the divine origin of the Bible and the authority of the rabbis. The Sephardi community convicted him of heresy and excommunicated him in 1656.

In the 17th century, Jews had greater civil rights in the Netherlands than in the rest of Europe. They were permitted to attend the Dutch universities, where a number of them qualified in medicine. At the end of the century, there were 30 Jewish physicians in the Collegium Medicum, the professional medical association of Amsterdam.

In the 1650s, there was a community of Dutch Jews in the British colony of Barbados, who exported sugar and tobacco to Amsterdam and Hamburg. Toward the end of the 17th century, Jews played a significant part in the development of the Dutch colony of Surinam in South America. In 1730, Jews owned 115 of the 400 sugar plantations in the colony. Jews were also prominent as traders in the Dutch island of Curacao in the Caribbean.

1. Numbers of Jews in the Netherlands and Belgium

During the 18th century, "stockbroking and share dealing remained key sectors of Jewish economic activity in Amsterdam. Furthermore, a growing number of Ashkenazim gradually found a place in what had hitherto, to all intents and purposes, been a Sephardic preserve" (Blom, Fuks-Mansfeld, & Schoffer,1996, p. 110). The first half of the 18th century saw a huge increase in the numbers of Ashkenazim, largely due to immigration from Eastern and Central Europe after 1726, while the numbers of Sephardim declined slightly as a result of emigration to London, Surinam, and the Caribbean, where many of the sugar plantations were in Sephardi ownership. In the middle of the century, the Benelux region had by far the largest concentration of Jews in Western and Central Europe. Among the social elite, Jews and Gentiles mixed together comfortably in social life. Many Jews, however, were poor and were supported by charities established and administered by wealthy Jews. At the time of the first census carried out in 1795, there were approximately 25,000 Jews recorded in the city, comprising about 12 percent of the population, of whom 22,000 were Ashkenazi and only 3,000, Sephardic.

In 1796, Napoleon emancipated the Jews from restrictions on where they were permitted to live and gave them full civil rights. In the 19th century, Amsterdam continued to be the major Jewish city in the Netherlands. In 1869, there were 29,952 Jews in the Amsterdam, comprising 11.3 percent of the population of the city and 44 percent of Jews in the Netherlands.

Over the course of the 19th century, efforts to integrate the Jews into Dutch society increased. In 1808, Jewish schools were required to teach Dutch, and in 1814, Yiddish was proscribed in official Jewish affairs. Within a generation, the Ashkenazim abandoned Yiddish and began to speak Dutch as their first language. Amsterdam remained the major Jewish city. In the middle decades of the century, the German Rothschild and the French Pereire banking houses established branches in Amsterdam and recruited Jews to work in them; young, well-educated Jews began to enter the civil service, the professions, education, and the army and navy. In Amsterdam and Antwerp, Jews dominated the diamond trade that consisted of importing rough diamonds and cutting and polishing them. In Amsterdam, in the middle decades of the 19th century, Jews were 43 out of the 50 diamond dealers and retailers in the city. In the last two decades of the 19th century, about 12,000 refugees from Russia and Poland came to the Netherlands, increasing the Jewish population by around 15 percent.

The numbers and percentages of Jews in the Netherlands and Belgium in the 19th and 20th centuries are given in Table 5.1. In the Netherlands, about five percent of these were Sephardic Jews of Portuguese origin. The increase in the number of Jews from 1899 to

1929 was largely caused by an influx of refugees from Eastern Europe. In 1930, there were an additional 20,900 who were half or a quarter Jewish. Following the accession of Hitler to power in Germany in 1933 and the rise of virulent anti-Semitism, about 35,000 German Jews fled to the Netherlands, and about 20,000 of these moved on to other countries during the course of the 1930s.

Table 5.1. Numbers and Percentages of Jews in the Netherlands and Belgium 1869–2001

	The Netherlands		Belgium	
Year	N. Jews	% Population	N. Jews	% Population
1869	68,000	1.9	-	-
1879	81,000	2.1	-	-
1899	103,000	2.0	-	-
1920	115,000	1.7	-	-
1930	112,000	1.4	-	-
1941	140,522	1.6	65,000	1.4
1947	28,000	0.16	25,000	0.3
2001	26,500	0.16	31,500	0.3

Nazi Germany invaded the Netherlands in May 1940. In the following year, the Germans carried out a census of the whole population in which everyone was required to register and receive identity cards. The Jews were required to identify themselves as such and had a J stamped on their cards. The census produced a figure of 140,522 full Jews, 14,549 half-Jews, and 5,719 quarter-Jews. Between 1941 and 1942, Jews were prohibited from sending their children to Gentile schools and from entering the universities; were dismissed from their jobs; and stripped of their civil rights, goods, and property. In July 1942, the Germans began to send the Jews to the concentration camps for extermination. Over the next two years, about 107,000 were deported, of whom an estimated 5,500 survived. Some 5,000 Jews were exempted from deportation, mainly because they assisted the Germans in various ways such as by working in industries that served the war effort. A further 10,500 were partners of mixed marriages and were also exempted. About 25,000 Jews were able to avoid deportation by going into hiding: some 9,000 were detected and killed, while 16,000 survived. About 1,000 wealthy Jews were permitted to leave the country on payment of large sums. And somewhere between 1,800 and 2,700 were able to escape by boat to England or overland to Switzerland and Spain. After the liberation in 1945, it is estimated that there were about 28,000 Jews left in the Netherlands.

There was some increase in numbers and percentages of Jews in the Netherlands from 1930 to 1941 as a result of the immigration of about 15,000 German Jews. The huge fall from 1941 to 1947 reflects the deaths in the concentration camps. In the post World War II period, an increasing number of Jews abandoned their Jewish identity and about one half married Gentiles. It thus becomes difficult to define and identify their numbers. In the 1947 census, 14,346 people declared themselves to be Jews. This was about half the number with Jewish ethnicity, the remainder of whom did not consider themselves Jews or did not care to reveal this to the census. There was therefore an estimated total of 28,000 Jews (Brasz, 1996, p. 345). In the 1960s, around 10,000 Israelis came to the Netherlands, and in the early 1990s, they were joined by about 2,000 Jews from Eastern Europe. In the 1980s, the number of Jews affiliated to Jewish congregations had declined to around 9,000. And by 2001, this had fallen further to 5,139. The total number of Jews in the Netherlands at the turn of the century has been estimated in the *American Jewish Yearbook* at about 30,000, not including the 10,000 or so Israelis.

In Belgium there were approximately 65,000 Jews in 1940. Approximately 40,000 of these were killed in the German occupation. By 2001, the numbers had increased to 31,500, largely as a result of immigration from the Soviet Union and Eastern Europe.

2. Socioeconomic Status of Jews in the Netherlands, 1860–1909

The socioeconomic status of Jews in the Netherlands in the second half of the 19th century has been analysed by Jona Schellekens and Franz van Poppel (2006). They took The Hague as a typical city and examined the socioeconomic status of Jews, Protestants, and Catholics from population registers and census returns for the period

1860–1909. The percentages of the three religious denominations in various socioeconomic categories are shown in Table 5.2. We see that Jews were overrepresented in the first three higher socioeconomic status categories, and underrepresented in the second three lower socioeconomic status categories.

Table 5.2. Socioeconomic Status of Jews in the Netherlands, 1860–1909

Group	Jews	Protestants	Catholics
Numbers	727	1,114	621
Upper class	7.4%	6.8%	3.2%
Petty bourgeoisie	57.8%	17.0%	24.5%
Lower white collar	8.1%	6.6%	6.1%
Farming & fishing	0.1%	7.5%	2.4%
Skilled laborers	13.1%	36.3%	35.3%
Unskilled laborers	3.7%	9.3%	9.7%
Unknown	9.8%	16.4%	18.8%

3. Crime Rates among Jews in the Netherlands

Some useful information about the crime rates of Jews in the Netherlands during the years 1910–1920 has been given by Willem Bonger (1943). He has provided statistics for those sentenced, subdivided by Jews, Protestants, Catholics, and No Church. His results are shown in Table 5.3. The first row gives the percentages of the four groups (aged 20 and over) in the population. The next rows give the percentages of those sentenced for various crimes. The general pattern of results is that Jews were underrepresented among those sentenced for what may be regarded as the less intelligent crimes of violence (rape, murder, assault, etc.), but were overrepresented among those sentenced for the more intelligent financial crimes of embezzlement, swindling, and receiving stolen goods.

Table 5.3. Crime Rates of Jews in the Netherlands, 1910–1920

	Jews	Protestants	Catholics	No Church
Percent in population	**1.8**	**54.4**	**35.5**	**7.3**
Rape	0.0	59.7	39.0	0.0
Murder/manslaughter	0.4	58.3	38.3	2.0
Sexual offences by teachers	0.5	59.8	38.1	1.6
Serious assault	0.6	48.2	49.3	1.5
Domestic violence	0.8	58.2	38.1	2.6
Assault	1.3	56.3	40.1	2.0
Theft	1.3	52.4	43.9	1.8
Minor sexual offences	1.4	72.7	24.1	1.7
Embezzlement	2.5	56.3	37.8	2.6
Swindling	4.6	53.8	38.1	2.6
Receiving stolen goods	4.9	51.5	41.1	1.9

4. Position of Jews in the Netherlands, 1930

The 1930 Dutch census provides some of best information about the position of the Jews in the Netherlands in the first half of the 20th century. Amsterdam continued to be the major Jewish center. The 1930 census recorded that the number of Jews in the city had risen to 65,523; Jews comprised 8.65 percent of the population of the city and 58 percent of Jews in the Netherlands. They became increasingly integrated with Dutch society. In Amsterdam, the percentage of mixed marriages increased from six percent in 1901 to 17 percent in 1934 (Blom, Fuks-Mansfeld, & Schoffer, 1996, p. 234). Holland's 1930 census, which showed that Jews comprised 1.4 percent of the population, provided information about the numbers and percentages of Jews with university educations and in the major professions. It was found that 2.6 percent of Jews were university graduates. The percentages of Jews who were lawyers, doctors, and dentists are summarized in Table 5.4. Jews were overrepresented in all three professions by factors of between 2.3 and 5.7. J. C. H. Blom, R. G. Fuks-Mansfeld, and Ivo Schoffer (1996, p. 248), who present these data and are the authors of the standard text on the Jews in the Netherlands, explain that the large proportion of Jewish university graduates and professionals "was related to Jewish traditions, in which learning is highly esteemed."

Table 5.4. Occupations of Jews in the Netherlands in 1930 (percentages)

Occupation	% Jews	AQ
Lawyers	3.2	2.3
Doctors	3.8	2.7
Dentists	7.4	5.3

As in the United States, Jews in the Netherlands were prominent in the music business: "A remarkably large number of musicians had Jewish origins, among them Lez van Delden, Sem Dresden, Jo Juda, Bertus van Lier, Max Tak, and the musical educator Oskar Back" (Blom, Fuks-Mansfeld, & Schoffer, 1996, pp. 248, 267). Two Dutchman are listed among the 141 top-rated chess players from 1851 to 2000 (Rubinstein, 2004, p. 37). One of these was the Jew Max Euwe (1901–1981), the only Dutch world champion. He defeated the legendary Russian champion Alexander Alekhine in 1935 and held the world title for two years until he was defeated by Alekhine in 1937. The other was Jan Timman (b. 1951), a Gentile who appeared among the top-rated chess players in the 1980s.

5. Educational and Occupational Status in the Netherlands, 1999

A survey carried out in 1999 compared the educational and occupational status of Jews (18–64 years of age) in the Netherlands with the general population. The results are summarized in Table 5.5. The samples consisted of 776 Jews and 10,617 non-Jewish Netherlanders. Among men, nine percent of the general population had university degrees, whereas the percentage of Jews was almost four times greater at 34 percent. Among women, Jews were four times overrepresented among university graduates. Occupational status was scored on a scale that ran from 13 for garbage collectors to 89 for surgeons. For both men and women, Jews had higher average scores than the general population.

Table 5.5. Educational and Occupational Status of Jews in the Netherlands, 1999

Status	Jews	Population
University degree: % Men	34	9
% Women	21	5
Occupational status: % Men	55	45
% Women	47	39

6. Nobel and Mathematics Prize winners

The Dutch have won 13 Nobel Prizes for science, literature, and economics. One of these was Jewish—Tjalling Koopmans (1910–1985), who received the prize for economics in 1975. (In addition Tobias Asser (1838–1913), a member of the Dutch Jewish Asser banking family, won the Nobel Peace Prize in 1911.) Five Belgians have won Nobel Prizes; none of whom were Jewish. Belgium has produced three prize-winning mathematicians: the Fields Medalist Jean Bourgain (1994), who is a Gentile, the Wolf Prize winners Elias Stein (1999), who is Jewish, and Pierre Deligne (2007), who is a Gentile. The two countries together have produced 18 Nobel Prize winners, of whom one has been Jewish. Jews, who have been about 0.23 percent of the population of the two countries during the second half of the 20th century, have produced approximately five percent of the Prize winners, giving them an Achievement Quotient of 22.

7. Fertility, Mortality, and Exogamy

In the 19th century, Jews in the Netherlands had higher fertility than Gentiles. The average Jewish family has 11 children, as compared with eight children for Gentiles. In the early 20th century, this fertility differential was reversed, as Jews developed the low fertility characteristic of middle-class and more intelligent subpopulations that I have reviewed in *Dysgenics*. Among those married between 1906 and 1910, Jews had an average of 3.4 children compared with 5.2 children for Gentiles (Blom, Fuks-Mansfeld, & Schoffer, 1996, p. 235).

Infant mortality, child mortality, and general mortality were lower among Jews in the 19th and early 20th centuries: in the period between 1905 and 1910, for instance, the mortality rate of Jews was about 20 percent lower than that of Protestants, whose rate in turn was about 20 percent lower than that of Catholics. The figures for infant and child mortality show similar differences. Studies showing this for Amsterdam have been summarized by Gretchen Condran and Ellen Kramarow (1991) and U. O. Schmelz (1971) and are shown in Table 5.6.

Table 5.6. Infant and Child Mortality per 1,000 Live Births

Mortality	Years	Jews	Gentiles
Infant	1901–1913	77	101
Infant	1914–1918	52	58
Infant	1919–1920	41	48
Child	1900–1910	112	182

Blom, Fuks-Mansfeld, and Schoffer (1996, p. 235) suggest the explanations of the comparatively low infant mortality of Jews include better parental care, closer family ties in general, a healthier lifestyle (due to Jewish dietary and other ritual laws), a different occupational structure (a marked preference for commerce and the liberal professions), and a greater number living in large cities; in addition, Jews were less subject to tuberculosis, syphilis, other infections, and respiratory and intestinal diseases. They do not mention that low mortality is associated with higher intelligence and that this might be a factor in the lower rate of infant mortality of Jews.

In the post-World War II period, Jews in the Netherlands increasingly married Gentiles. In 1934, 17 percent of Jews married Gentiles; while between 1946–1999, 61 percent of Jewish men and 48 percent of Jewish women married Gentiles (Kalmijn, Liefbroer, van Poppel, & van Solinge, 2006).

Chapter 6

Britain and Ireland

1. Numbers of Jews
2. Intelligence
3. Educational Attainment
4. Earnings and Wealth
5. Socioeconomic status
6. The Professions
7. The Royal Society and the British Academy
8. Significant Figures
9. Eminence
10. Chess Champions
11. Bridge
12. Nobel Prize winners
13. Infant Mortality
14. Ireland
15. Conclusion

Jews first came into England shortly after the Norman Conquest in 1066. In the 12th century, the largest community was in Norwich, where it numbered around 200. There were also Jewish communities in London, York, Oxford, Winchester, and some other cities. In the year 1290, their total number in England has been estimated at around 2,500.

Jews made a living as money-lenders, as elsewhere in Europe, and as traders, particularly in eastern goods such as spices and silk, for which they had a virtual monopoly.

There were large-scale attacks on Jews during the Third Crusade of 1189–1190, during which a number of Jews were massacred in London, York, and Norwich (Russell, 1945, p. 434). In 1290, Edward I confiscated the Jews' money and property and expelled them *en masse*. There were virtually no Jews in England until the end of the 15th century, when a few of those expelled from Spain in 1492 and Portugal in 1497 arrived in England. There were, however, no significant numbers until they were officially permitted to settle by Oliver Cromwell (1599–1658) in 1656. From this time on, many Ashkenazi Jews from East and Central Europe settled in England; a number of Sephardim came from the Netherlands, which was in decline economically in the 18th century. Nearly all these immigrants settled in London.

In the 19th century, Jews were not subjected to violence in Britain. However, they suffered certain disabilities. For most of the century, they were not permitted to become members of parliament, hold public office, or enter the universities of Oxford and Cambridge, which only began admitting Jews in 1871. Despite this, a number of Jews excelled intellectually in the 19th century. David Ricardo (1772–1823), the economist and author of *Principles of Political Economy and Taxation*, came from a wealthy Jewish family, converted to Christianity, and became a Member of Parliament. Nathan Mayer Rothschild (1777–1836) was sent by his father from Frankfurt to set up a bank in Britain, made a fortune in the Napoleonic War, and established the bank as the greatest in the world. His grandson, also Nathan Mayer (1840–1915) was made Baron Rothschild in 1885, and the family joined the ranks of the British aristocracy. Benjamin Disraeli (1804–1881) entered parliament in 1837, which he was able to do after his conversion to Christianity, and became Prime Minister from 1874 to 1880. Sir Moses Montefiore (1784–1885) was the first Jew to become Sheriff of London and was created a baronet in 1846. Sir William Herschel (1792–1871), who was half-Jewish, was a distinguished astronomer who discovered the planet Uranus, and was appointed president of the Royal Astronomical Society in 1848. In 1858, Lionel de Rothschild (1808–1879) became the first professing

Jew to enter parliament and in taking the oath was allowed to omit the words "on the true faith of a Christian."

1. Numbers of Jews

By 1730, there were about 6,000 Jews in Britain. By 1800 this had grown to about 20,000 and by 1860, to approximately 60,000, partly through immigration and partly through natural increase. In the first half of the 19th century, the Jewish community in London was dominated by a dozen or so very rich families, among whom the leading were the Rothschilds, Montefiores, Goldsmids, Cohens, Mocattas, and Samuels.

Between 1881 and 1900, the number of Jews increased nearly fourfold. This was due to the immigration of about 100,000 Jews from Russia and Poland, where they were persecuted following the assassination of Tsar Alexander II in 1881, for which the Jews were widely blamed. This was largely responsible for the increase in the number of Jews to around 300,000 by 1920. Most of these settled in London, which has been home to around 65 to 70 percent of Jews in Britain in the 20th century. The next largest communities have been in Manchester, followed by Leeds and Glasgow. The majority of Jews in Britain at the end of the 20th century were the descendants of those who had fled from Russia between 1881 and 1905 (Waterman & Kosmin, 1986).

Estimates of the size of the Jewish population in Britain and of their percentage of the population from the Middle Ages to the end of the 20th century have been given by Stephen Brook (1990) and by Stanley Waterman and Barry Alexander Kosmin (1986) and are shown in Table 2.1. It appears from these figures that the size of the Jewish population peaked around 1950 and declined substantially over the next 50 years. The reason for the increase in the number of Jews, from 330,000 in 1930 to 380,000 in 1940, was the immigration of about 50,000 Jewish refugees from Germany and Austria in the 1930s. From 1940 to 2001, the numbers of Jews declined. The main reason for this is that many Jews assimilated into the Gentile community and lost their Jewish identity. The figure for 2001 is the number who identified themselves as Jewish in the census of that year. It should be noted that these figures are difficult to estimate with any precision because many Jews have taken British sounding surnames and the numbers of these cannot be ascertained from electoral rolls or from records of births, deaths, and marriages; also, substantial numbers who are ethnically Jewish do not subscribe to Judaism, so they do not appear in statistics of religious affiliation.

Table 6.1. Numbers of Jews in Britain

Year	Jewish Population	% of total
1290	2,500	0.005
1730	6,000	0.01
1800	20,000	0.01
1850	30,000	0.01
1880	60,000	0.20
1900	225,000	0.59
1910	280,000	0.67
1920	310,000	0.70
1930	330,000	0.71
1940	380,000	0.79
1970	360,000	0.65
1980	340,000	0.60
1990	304,000	0.54
2001	267,000	0.46

Jews in Britain range between the strictly Orthodox and those with no Jewish affiliation designated secular and nonpractising. In the 1990 "National Jewish Population Survey" (Schmool & Cohen, 1998), 47 percent of the sample considered themselves as having been raised in traditional Jewish homes. The percentages of these who identified with different degrees of Judaism are given in Table 2.2. The last three groups who identified themselves as "Just Jewish," "Progressive," and "Secular/Nonpractising," together totalling 44 percent, had moved toward a more liberal identification than the traditional homes in which they had been reared. This trend away from traditional and Orthodox Judaism was confirmed by asking the total sample how similar their Jewish identity was to that of their parents: 49 percent said they were the same as their parents; 38 percent considered themselves less Orthodox; and only 13 percent considered themselves more Orthodox.

Table 6.2. Identities of Jews in Britain in 1990 (percentages)

Identity	Percent
Strictly Orthodox	5
Traditional	51
Just Jewish	16
Progressive	13
Secular	15

Despite some degree of social and legal discrimination, Jews did well in Britain. In 1857, a survey in London found Jews overrepresented in the middle class: 76 percent of Jews had incomes of more than £100 a year, compared to 69 percent of Gentiles (Feldman, 1994). Jews had lower infant mortality than Gentiles in the early 20th century. In 1903, the infant mortality per 1,000 live births was 128 for Jews; the rate for Gentiles was 161, a full 25 percent higher. (Condran & Kramarow, 1991).

2. Intelligence

By the end of the 19th century, it was noted that Jewish children in London took a disproportionate number of prizes and awards in schools (Russell & Lewis, 1900). In the 1920s, studies began to be published reporting that Jews had high IQs. Subsequent testing only confirmed these findings. There have been five studies of the intelligence of Jews in Britain. These are summarized in Table 6.3.

Rows 1 through 3 give the results of a study carried out in the mid-1920s in London. Children aged 8–14 were tested in three schools in which Jewish and Gentile children were present in approximately equal numbers. The children were tested for general intelligence with the Northumberland Test. The Jewish children obtained a mean IQ of 110.5. The children were also tested on arithmetic and reading and obtained an arithmetic quotient of 110.6 and a reading quotient of 113.0. These EQs (educational quotients) are both very close to their IQ and show, as in many other studies, that differences in educational attainment are closely similar to differences in intelligence and are likely largely due to differences in intelligence.

Table 6.3. IQs and Educational Attainment of Jews in Britain

	Age	N. Jews	N. Gentiles	Test	IQ/EQ
1	8–14	1081	813	IQ	110.5
2	8–14	1081	813	Arithmetic	110.6
3	8–14	1081	813	English	113.0
4	6–14	303	221	IQ	113.0
5	10	907	-	IQ	111.5
6	8	22	3,350	IQ	108.5
7	7–16	39	11,101	IQ	108.2

Sources. Rows 1–3: Davies & Hughes, 1927. Row 4: Winch, 1930. Row 5: Vincent, 1966. Rows 6–7: Lynn and Longley, 2006

Row 4 gives an IQ of 113 obtained on a reasoning test for Jewish children attending two schools together with Gentile children in the East End of London. The East End was a lower socioeconomic community, so the Gentile children were probably a little below average. Typically, the IQ gap between lower- and middle-class children is about 10 IQ points, suggesting that the IQ of the Jewish sample in relation to a socially representative sample of Gentile children would have been approximately 108–110. Row 5 gives an IQ of 111.5 for a sample of 907 10-year-old Jewish children in the city of Glasgow. These children were found to have a mean IQ of 117.8 on the Moray House Test, a verbal comprehension and verbal reasoning test, compared with an IQ of 100 for Gentile children (number not given) tested at the same time in the same city. The unusually high IQ of the Jewish children in this study is explained by the intelligence of non-Jewish children in Scotland being somewhat depressed as compared with that in Great Britain as a whole (see Lynn, 1979). The extensive data presented by Vernon (1951) on mean IQs in different regions of Great Britain put the mean IQ in Glasgow at 93.7 in relation to 100 for the country as a whole. To compare the mean IQ of Jewish children in Glasgow with that of Gentile children, we must therefore subtract 6.3 IQ points from their score, giving them a mean IQ of 111.5. This brings the mean IQ of the Jewish children in

Glasgow obtained in this study closely into line with results of the London studies given in rows 1 through 4. Although the samples whose IQs are given in rows 6 and 7 are small, they are well drawn and representative of the British population.

Row 6 gives a mean Jewish IQ of 108.5 derived from the British 1946 national cohort study (NCS-46) of all babies born in the first week of March of that year. The sample was intelligence tested at eight years, but their religious affiliation was not recorded until the age of 26, when 22 described themselves as having been brought up Jewish out of a total of 3,374. There were four intelligence tests given at age 8 (a 60-item nonverbal picture test, a 35-item reading comprehension test, a 50-item word-reading test, and a 50-item vocabulary test). The scores on the four tests were summed to give an IQ. The higher Jewish IQ is statistically significant (t=2.31, p<0.031).

Row 7 gives an IQ of 108.2 for a sample of 39 Jewish children in the British National Cohort Study (NCS-58) of all babies born in the week 3–9 March, 1958. The children were tested on reading and arithmetic at the age of 7, on reading comprehension, mathematics, verbal and nonverbal IQ at the age of 11, and on reading comprehension and mathematics at 16 years. The total sample size at age 7 was 11,140, among whom 39 were Jewish. The sample size fell to 29 among the 16-year-olds because of attrition inevitable in longitudinal studies. The number of Jews is quite small and comprises 0.3 percent of the sample. This is roughly what would be expected, as the numbers of Jews in Britain in 1970 was estimated at 360,000 (Waterman & Kosmin, 1986), approximately 0.65 percent of the population. The percentage of Jews among the children in the sample may appear too small, but Jews in Britain were an aging population (Waterman & Kosmin, 1986), so the percentage of Jewish children would be expected to be lower than their percentage in the population. The average IQ of the five studies is 110.3 and is regarded as the best reading for the IQ of Jews in Britain in relation to White Gentiles.

The results of the NCS-58 study are given in detail in Table 6.4. The right-hand column gives the IQs and EQs (Educational Quotients) of the Jewish children in relation to 100 for the Gentiles. At all three ages and on all the tests, the Jewish children score higher than the Gentiles.

Table 6.4. IQs and Educational Attainment of Jews in the NCS–58 Sample

Test	Age	Jews			Gentiles			Jewish IQ
-	-	N	Mean	Sd	N	Mean	Sd	-
Arithmetic	7	36	6.50	2.61	11,104	5.19	2.47	108
Reading	7	37	26.57	5.39	11,104	23.67	9.95	104
Verbal IQ	11	39	27.95	8.38	11,104	22.63	9.25	104
Nonverbal IQ	11	39	25.13	7.70	10,790	21.27	7.52	108
Reading	11	39	20.49	6.33	10,789	16.31	6.20	110
Math	11	39	25.67	10.25	10,785	17.19	10.30	112
Reading	16	29	29.21	6.75	9,508	25.72	6.84	108
Math	16	29	18.56	6.94	9,467	13.09	6.98	112

Despite the small numbers of Jews, all the differences are highly statistically significant ($p<.001$). The IQs have been averaged to 108.25, giving an overall IQ for the sample. This is the figure entered in row 7 of table 6.3.

3. Educational Attainment

The educational attainment of all 11-year-old children in England attending state schools was collected in 2004 under the direction of the Government Department for Education and Skills (DfES). The children were tested in English, mathematics and science using a program known as Key Stage 2. On the basis of their performance in the tests, the children were graded into levels 2, 3, 4, and 5. The DfES released the results as percentages of those attending Jewish schools and White Gentiles from all schools passing at levels 4 and 5. These are shown in Table 6.5. We see that a higher percentage of Jewish children passed in all three subjects. As the sample consisted of all the children attending state schools, it did not include children at independent schools, who are approximately six percent of the cohort. Children attending these independent schools come largely from affluent families and perform well in educational tests, so the exclusion of these is likely to have reduced slightly the attainment scores of both the Jews and the Gentiles. Affluent Jews as well as Gentiles typically send their children to independent schools, so it is doubtful whether the omission of small numbers of these has any significant effect on the differences shown in Table 6.5.

Table 6.5. Educational Attainment of Jews and Gentiles in 2004 (percentages passing)

Group	N	English	Math	Science
Jews	905	92	91	95
Gentiles	489,887	78	74	87

In recent decades, greater proportions of Jews than of Gentiles have attended universities and attained advanced degrees. This trend was first discovered in the 1960s by E. Krause (1969), who estimated that about three percent of university students were Jews, even though Jews at this time were approximately 0.5 percent of the population. This was confirmed in the "National Jewish Population Survey" of 1990, which related that 48 percent of Jewish men aged 18–64 held university degrees, as compared to 10 percent of Gentile men (Schmool & Cohen, 1998). Among women, 45 percent of Jews held university degrees, as compared with eight percent of Gentiles. The 2001 census contained a question on religious identity from which information about educational qualifications has been analysed by David Graham and Stanley Waterman (2005). Their results for educational qualifications of Jews and the total population in England and Wales are shown in Table 6.6. We see that Jews attained university degrees at almost double the rate of the general public. On the other hand, the percentage of Jews with no educational qualifications was approaching half that of the total population.

Table 6.6. Educational Qualifications of Jews and the Total Population in 2001 (percentages)

Group	Education	25–34	35–49	50–59	60–64	65–74
Jews	U. Degree	56	44	32	25	22
Population	U. Degree	29	23	18	14	12
Jews	None	7	9	23	33	45
Population	None	13	21	39	55	64

80   The Chosen People

The greater percentage of Jews with high educational qualifications has remained remarkably constant over the 40-year period covered by the age range. Thus, among the 65–74 year olds born between 1927 and 1936, almost twice as many Jews than Gentiles had university degrees. Jews had just about the same advantage among the 25–34 year olds born between 1967 and 1976.

4. Earnings and Wealth

Using probate returns on death, William Rubinstein (2000) calculated the numbers of Jews and Gentiles possessing great wealth in the 19th and first half of the 20th centuries . He found 7,574 persons leaving estates worth £100,000 or more during the period 1809–1899; 179 of these were Jews, representing 2.4 percent. Rubinstein's detailed figures are shown in Table 6.7. These include the numbers of Jews leaving these large estates, the percentage of Jews among all estates of this size, the percentage of Jews in the population, and finally the Jewish Wealth Quotient calculated by dividing the percentage of Jews among the wealthy by their percentage in the population given in Table 2.1 (0.01 percent in 1809-1849 and 0.30 percent in 1850-1899). Thus, in the first period, the Jewish Wealth Quotient of 10.5 indicates that Jews were 10.5 times overrepresented among the very wealthy, relative to their numbers in the population. In the second half of the century, the Jewish Wealth Quotient fell slightly because of the large number of impoverished Jewish immigrants from 1881 on. Row 3 gives the number of Jews who died leaving in excess of £1 million during the period 1809-1939. Rubinstein found 199 such individuals, of whom 28 were Jews (14.1 percent). Taking the average number of Jews in the population during this period as 0.4 percent, Jews obtain a Wealth Quotient of 28.4. Row 4 gives the number of Jews who died leaving in excess of £2.5 million during the period 1870-1919. Rubinstein found 24 such individuals, of whom four were Jews (16.7 percent). Adopting the average number of Jews in the population during this period as approximately 0.59 percent (the percentage in 1900), Jews obtain a Wealth Quotient of 28.3. All these figures show that Jews were greatly overrepresented among the very wealthy.

Table 6.7. Percentages of Jews among the very wealthy

	Years	Wealth	N Jews	% Jews	WQ
1	1809–1849	£100,000	13	1.05	10.5
2	1850–1899	£100,000	166	2.58	8.6
3	1809–1939	£1 million	28	14.10	28.4
4	1870–1919	£2.5 million	4	16.70	28.3

5. Socioeconomic Status.

Jews have higher socioeconomic status than Gentiles. An early study showing this was published by E. Krause in 1969. He examined the occupational structure of the London district of Edgware and found that 57 percent of Jewish men worked in professional or managerial occupations, compared with 39.4 percent of Gentiles. Figures giving national statistics for the overrepresentation of Jews in the professional class and their underrepresentation in the manual class and among the unemployed are given in Table 6.8. The table gives these as percentages of Jews and Gentiles in the socioeconomic classes and the right-hand column gives the odds ratios, representing the proportion of Jews in relation to a Gentile proportion set at 1.0. Row 1 gives results from a study of the percentages of Jews and Gentiles in 1961 by S. J. Prais and M. Schmool (1975), showing that 10 percent of Jews and 4 percent of Gentiles were in the higher professions and hence a Jewish Achievement Quotient of 2.5, signifying that Jews were 2.5 times overrepresented.

To obtain a comparison of the occupational distribution of Jews and Gentiles in 1990, the proportions of Jews in the professions and in manual work are taken from the "National Jewish Population Survey" of 1990 (Schmool & Cohen, 1998). The proportions of White Gentiles are taken as the averages obtained in the 1982 and 1994 surveys carried out by the Policy Studies Institute (Modood & Berthoud, 1997). The results are given in rows 2 through 5 of Table 6.8 and show that Jews were substantially overrepresented in the professions and underrepresented among manual workers. Row 6 gives the percentage of Jews and Gentiles who were unemployed for men and women combined aged 16-64 (men) and aged 16-59 (women) from the same two sources and show that the percentage of Jews who were unemployed was 40 percent of the rate of Gentiles.

82   THE CHOSEN PEOPLE

Table 6.8. Jewish and Gentile socioeconomic status, 1961–1990 (percentages)

	SES	Year	Sex	Jews	Gentiles	AQ
1	Professional	1961	M & W	10	4	2.5
2	Professional	1990	Men	54	25	2.2
3	Professional	1990	Women	50	14	3.6
4	Manual	1990	Men	6	17	0.4
5	Manual	1990	Women	2	25	0.1
6	Unemployed	1990	M&W	6	14	0.4

6. The Professions

An analysis of the numbers and proportions of Jews in most of the major professions around 1985 has been made by Asher Tropp (1991). He began by noting that it is impossible to find the numbers of Jews in professions by searching through the directories for Jewish names because many Jews have anglicized their names and cannot be identified. This is a common problem that is not confined to identifying Jews in Britain. His method of overcoming it was to select 40 indisputably Jewish names (Cohen, Goldberg, Stein, etc.). He found that these comprise seven percent of Jews in the Jewish Board of Deputies list of Jewish names. He inferred that in directories of members of professions, the number of those with these Jewish names would represent seven percent of the number of Jews. To obtain an estimate of the number of Jews in each of a number of professions, he multiplied this number by 14.26 (7 x 14.26 = 100). He then counted the total number in the profession and calculated the percentage of these who are Jews. His figures are shown in Table 6.9.

Tropp did not take the final step of comparing the percentages of Jews in the professions in relation to their percentages in the population. I have made good this omission by calculating the percentage of Jews in the professions as a proportion of their percentages in the population in 1985. To make this calculation, the number of Jews in the population in 1985 is taken as 322,000 (given in Table 6.1), and the total population in the United Kingdom is taken as 56,379,000, the figure in the 1981 census. Thus, in 1985, Jews were approximately 0.6 percent of the population. I have constructed an index of the comparative representation of Jews by calculating the ratio of their percentage in the professions to their percentage in the population to give Jewish Achievement Quotients.

Table 6.9. Percentages and Achievement Quotients of Jews in the Major Professions

Profession	% Jews	AQ
Ophthalmic Opticians	7.8	13.0
Barristers	7.5	12.5
Dentists	4.9	8.2
Pharmacists	4.6	7.7
University Faculty	4.3	7.2
Doctors	4.0	6.6
Solicitors	4.0	6.6
Dispensing Opticians	4.0	6.6
Accountants	3.6	6.0
Architects	2.3	3.8
Chartered Surveyors	1.3	2.2

It will be seen that in all of the 11 professions, Jews have Achievement Quotients much greater that 1.0; hence Jews are substantially overrepresented in relation to their proportion in the population. The magnitude of their overrepresentation varies considerably among the professions. It is greatest among ophthalmic opticians and barristers, with Achievement Quotients of 13.0 and 12.5, respectively, and lowest among architects and chartered surveyors, with Achievement Quotients of 3.8 and 2.2, respectively. Tropp does not suggest any reasons for these differences. A possible explanation for the relatively low ratios of architects and chartered surveyors may lie in American studies that have found that Jews are less strong on visualization abilities than on verbal and reasoning abilities; it is likely that visualization abilities are required to succeed in the professions of architecture and chartered surveying. (Tropp omits some professions from his study, including veterinary surgeons, chiropodists, members of parliament, clergymen, senior civil servants, and senior members of the armed forces on the grounds that these are too few for analysis.)

I have examined two further high status professions for the percentages of Jews. The first is Members of Parliament and the second vice-chancellors of universities. The results are summarized in Table 6.10. There were 29 Jewish Members of Parliament (MPs) elected to the House of Commons in 1950, 4.5 percent of the total. In 2000, 21 Jews were elected, representing 3.2 percent of the total (these figures come from the *Jewish Yearbooks* for each year). In 1950, Jews were approximately 0.70 percent of the population, giving Jews an Achievement Quotient of 6.4. In 2000, Jews were 0.46 percent of the population, giving Jews an Achievement Quotient of 7.0. These are just about the average of their overrepresentation in the 11 professions shown in Table 6.8. As regards university vice-chancellors, in 2006, there were 161 of these, of whom seven were Jews (4.3 percent of the total). University vice-chancellors were all middle aged or elderly, so we should compare this 4.3 percent with the percentage of Jews in the population around 1970 (0.65 percent) to give an Achievement Quotient of 6.6.

Table 6.10. Numbers and Percentages of Jewish MPs and University Heads

Year	Profession	N. Jews	% Jews	AQ
1950	MPs	29	4.5	5.4
2000	MPs	21	3.2	7.1
2006	University heads	7	4.3	6.6

7. The Royal Society and the British Academy

We look now at two indices of Jewish intellectual distinction of a more elevated order than membership of a profession. These are Fellowship of the Royal Society and the British Academy. The Royal Society was founded in 1660 for leading British scientists. Its web site asserts that election to its fellowship is an intellectual distinction second only to the Nobel Prize. The Jewish fellows are given in the British *Jewish Yearbooks*. The numbers and percentages of Jewish Fellows of the Royal Society are shown for selected years from 1901 through 2005 in Table 6.11. The percentages (but not the numbers) for the years 1901 through 1940 are given by Tropp (1991). The Achievement Quotients of Jews have been calculated in the same way as described above for the professions.

We can see that Jews have been overrepresented in all years except 1910. The reason for this lies in the large immigration of impoverished Jews from Russia between 1881 and 1914 that increased their percentage in the population. The newcomers had not acquired the education to achieve the degree of eminence required for fellowship of the Royal Society. As they established themselves in Britain, they took advantage of the educational opportunities and their overrepresentation (shown by their Achievement Quotients) increased steadily. Notice that from 1901 to 1920, the average Achievement Quotient was 1.8; from 1930 to 1950, it increased to 4.7; and from 1965 to 2005, it improved to 9.6. This reflects the rise and rise of Jewish attainment over the course of the century.

Table 6.11. Jewish Fellows of the Royal Society

Year	N. Jews	% Jews	Jewish AQ
1901	-	1.0	1.7
1910	-	0.6	0.9
1920	-	2.0	2.8
1930	-	3.0	4.3
1940	-	3.7	4.7
1950	19	3.7	5.1
1965	36	5.2	8.0
1985	53	7.6	13.3
1995	47	4.6	9.2
2005	48	3.7	8.0

We look next at the numbers of Jewish Fellows of the British Academy. This was founded in 1902 as a society for eminent scholars in History, Philosophy, and Philology, and was later extended to those who have achieved distinction in the social sciences. Fellowship of the British Academy was intended to confer the same distinction for eminent scholars in these subjects as fellowship of the Royal Society conferred on scientists. Whether it has quite succeeded in this aspiration, I will not venture to say, but it is a satisfactory criterion for those who have achieved distinction in the humanities and social sciences. The numbers of Jewish fellows are given in the *Jewish Yearbooks* and are shown for selected years from 1950 through 2005 in Table 6.12 (the *Yearbooks* do not give this information for the first half of the century). The Achievement Quotients of Jews have been calculated in the same way as described above for the professions and the Royal Society, namely, by calculating the ratio of the percentage of Jewish Fellows to their percentage in the population. We can see that Jews have been overrepresented with Achievement Quotients of between 8.0 and 10.7 throughout the period, just about the same as their overrepresentation among fellows of the Royal Society

Table 6.12. Jewish and Gentiles Fellows of the British Academy

Year	N. Jews	N. Gentiles	% Jews	AQ
1950	10	140	6.7	9.6
1965	19	235	7.5	10.7
1985	25	444	5.3	9.3
1995	26	622	4.0	8.0
2005	28	725	3.7	8.0

8. Significant Figures

Charles Murray (2003, p. 280) has calculated the numbers of Jewish and Gentile "significant figures" (great names in science and the arts) in Britain who had most of their careers between 1870 and 1950. He finds eight Jews and 185 Gentiles. Calculating the ratio of Jewish to Gentile "significant figures," he arrives at an Achievement Quotient (that is, the measure of Jewish overrepresentation) of 8.1. This is close to the Jewish Achievement Quotients for Fellowship of the Royal Society and the British Academy.

9. Eminence

There are four further apogees of eminence in Britain. The first is a life peerage that confers on the holder the title of baron or baroness; the second the Order of Merit, which is confined to a maximum of 24 members; the third is the Companion of Honour; and the fourth is the title of Dame, reserved for eminent women. These honors are conferred on those who have achieved distinction in a variety of fields. For instance, life peerages have been conferred on Maurice Saatchi (b.1946), the advertising tycoon, and George Weidenfeld (b.1919), the publisher, who are both Jewish, and on John Birt (b.1944), a former director of the BBC, and William Rees-Mogg (b.1928), a former editor of the *Times*, who are Gentiles. The Order of Merit has been conferred on Lucian Freud (b.1922), the painter, Lord Rothschild, the banker, and Tom Stoppard (b.1937), the playwright, who are Jewish, and on Norman Foster (b.1935), the architect, and Joan Sutherland (1926–2010), the soprano, who are Gentiles. The Companion of Honour has been conferred on Harold Pinter (1930–2008), the playwright), and Eric Hobsbawm (b.1917), the historian, who are both Jewish, and on Paul Scofield (1922–2008), the actor, and Peter Brook (b.1925), the theatre producer, who are Gentiles.

The numbers of Jews and Gentiles who held these honors in 2002 are given in Table 6.13. Those holding the Order of Merit and the Companion of Honour have been combined because they are so few, amounting to only 64.

Table 6.13. Jewish and Gentile Life Peers, Holders of the Order of Merit, and the Companion of Honour, and Dames.

Honor	Year	N. Jews	N. Gentiles	% Jews	AQ
LifePeers	2002	43	439	8.7	14.5
OM/CH	2002	9	55	14.0	27.3
Dames	2002	7	251	2.3	3.8

Column 5 gives the percentages that are Jewish. Column 6 gives the Jewish Achievement Quotients calculated on the basis of 0.6 for the percentage of Jews in the population in 1980, adopted because these honors are normally awarded to those in late middle age and the old, so it is appropriate to use an earlier figure when Jews formed a larger percentage of the population. We can see that Jews are hugely overrepresented with AQs of 14.5 for Life Peers and 27.3 for the Order of Merit and the Companion of Honour. Jewesses are less overrepresented among Dames, with an AQ of only 3.8.

10. Chess Champions

The British Chess Federation was formed in 1904 and has held tournaments every year except during World Wars I and II. The winners of these tournaments are given in Table 6.14. Some people won in more than one year, but their names are only given once. Jewish winners are asterisked. Of the 47 chess champions, seven have been Jewish (15 percent). Adopting a figure of 0.65 percent for the percentage of Jews in the population during the 20th century, Jews have an Achievement Quotient of 23.

Table 6.14. British Chess Champions (Jews are asterisked)

Napier	Barden	Short
Atkins	Philips	Adams
Griffiths	Fazekas*	Plaskett
Yates	Penrose	Hodgson
Scott	Haygarth	Hennigan
Thomas	Lee	Watson
Khan	Keene	Sadler
Winter	Eley	Ward
Fairhurst	Hartston*	Adams
Alexander	Botterill	Short
Coombe	Mestel*	Gallagher
Golombek*	Speelman*	Ramesh
Broadbent	Bellin	Kunte
Klein*	Nunn	Rowson
Wade	Littlewood	
Yanofsky*	Miles	

11. Bridge

Britain does not produce many top-level bridge players. There are only seven British players among the 157 top rated names among the Open World Champions recognised by World Bridge Federation in 2004. Their names ranked by their position are given in Table 6.15. Two of them are Jews, denoted by asterisks. Hence, Jews who were

0.46 percent of the population produced 29 percent of the top bridge players, giving them an Achievement Quotient of 63.

Table 6.15. British Bridge Champions in 2004; (Jews are denoted by asterisks.)

Boris Schapiro*	Kenneth Konstram	Terence Reese
Leslie Dodds	Adam Meredith	
Nico Gardener*	Jordanis Pavlides	

12. Nobel Prize winners

British Nobel Prize winners are listed in Table 6.16. (These were born in Britain; the list does not include those who were born elsewhere but assumed British nationality.) Britain has produced 79 Nobel Prize winners, three of whom have been Jews: Brian Josephson (b.1940), physics (1973), Herbert Brown (1912–2004), chemistry (1979), and Harold Pinter (1930–2008), literature (2005). Thus, Jews have been 3.8 percent of British Nobel Prize winners. In 1970 the Jewish population in Britain was around 360,000 or 0.65 percent of the population. Adopting this figure, Jews are overrepresented by a factor (Achievement Quotient) of 5.8. All the Jewish Prize winners were in the second half of the 20th century, confirming the same trend that was found for Fellows of the Royal Society.

Table 6.16. British Nobel Prize winners (Jews are asterisked)

Year	Name	Subject	Year	Name	Subject
1902	Ronald Ross	Medicine	1960	Maurice Wilkins	Medicine
1904	William Ramsay	Chemistry	1963	Alan Hodgkin	Medicine
1904	Lord Rayleigh	Physics	1963	Andrew Huxley	Medicine
1906	J. J. Thomson	Physics	1964	Dorothy Hodgkin	Chemistry
1907	Rudyard Kipling	Literature	1967	Ronald Norrish	Chemistry
1915	William Bragg	Physics	1969	George Porter	Chemistry
1915	Lawrence Bragg	Physics	1969	Derek Barton	Chemistry
1917	Charles Barkla	Physics	1972	John Hicks	Economics

90 THE CHOSEN PEOPLE

Year	Name	Subject	Year	Name	Subject
1908	Frederick Soddy	Chemistry	1972	Rodney Porter	Medicine
1922	Francis Ashton	Chemistry	1973	Geoffrey Wilkinson	Chemistry
1922	Archibald Hill	Medicine	1973	Patrick White	Literature
1927	C. T. R. Wilson	Physics	1973	Brian Josephson*	Physics
1928	Owen Richardson	Physics	1974	Paul Flory	Chemistry
1929	Arthur Harden	Chemistry	1974	Antony Hewish	Physics
1929	Frederick Hopkins	Medicine	1974	Martin Ryle	Physics
1932	John Galsworthy	Literature	1977	James Meade	Economics
1932	Edgar Adrian	Medicine	1977	Neville Mott	Physics
1932	Charles Sherrington	Chemistry	1978	Peter Mitchell	Chemistry
1933	Paul Dirac	Physics	1979	Herbert Brown*	Chemistry
1935	James Chadwick	Physics	1974	Godfrey Housefield	Medicine
1936	Henry Dale	Medicine	1980	Frederick Sanger	Chemistry
1937	Norman Haworth	Chemistry	1982	John Vane	Medicine
1937	George Thompson	Physics	1983	William Golding	Literature
1945	Alexander Fleming	Medicine	1984	Richard Stone	Economics
1947	Robert Robinson	Chemistry	1988	James Black	Medicine
1947	Edward Appleton	Physics	1993	Michael Smith	Chemistry
1948	Patrick Blackett	Physics	1993	Richard Roberts	Medicine
1950	Bertrand Russell	Literature	1996	Harold Kroto	Chemistry
1950	Cecil Powell	Physics	1996	James Merrlees	Economics
1951	John Cockcroft	Physics	1997	John Walker	Chemistry
1952	Archer Martin	Chemistry	1998	John Pople	Chemistry
1950	Richard Synge	Chemistry	2001	Tim Hunt	Medicine
1953	Winston Churchill	Literature	2001	Paul Nurse	Medicine
1956	Cyril Hinchelwood	Chemistry	2003	Peter Mansfield	Medicine
1956	William Shockley	Physics	2003	Anthony Leggett	Physics
1958	Lord Todd	Chemistry	2005	Harold Pinter*	Literature
1958	Frederick Sanger	Chemistry	2007	Martin Evans	Medicine
1960	Peter Medawar	Medicine	2007	Oliver Smithies	Medicine
1962	John Kendrew	Chemistry	2009	Jack Szostak	Medicine
1960	Francis Crick	Medicine			

Britain has also produced seven mathematicians who have received the Fields Medal or the Wolf Prize awarded for outstanding work in mathematics. These are Michael Atiyah (1966), Alan Baker (1970), David Mumford (1974), Simon Donaldson (1986), Andrew Wiles (1995), Richard Borcherds (1998), and Timothy Gowers (1998). None of these is Jewish.

13. Infant Mortality

Despite the poverty of Jews in Britain in the early 1900s, they had comparatively low rates of infant mortality. In London as a whole, the infant mortality at this time was 102.8 per 1,000 live births, while in the heavily Jewish districts of Spitalfields and Goodman's Fields, it was 85.4 and 95.0 per 1,000, respectively (O'Grada, 2006).

14. Ireland

There was a small number of Sephardic and Ashkenazi Jews in Ireland in the 17th and 18th centuries; these were "mainly commercial and middle class" (O'Grada, 2006, p. 33). The majority of Jewish immigration took place from the 1870s until 1914. Most of these came from Lithuania, then from parts of Russia, and were known as "Litvaks." Most of them settled in Dublin, while a few settled in Belfast and Cork. The numbers of Jews recorded in censuses from 1981 to 2001 are shown in Table 6.17. The fall in numbers from the peak in 1936 has been due to low fertility, assimilation with Gentiles, and emigration, principally to Israel, Britain, and the United States.

Table 6.17. Numbers and Percentages of Jews in Ireland

Year	N. Jews	% Population
1871	285	0.00
1911	5,148	0.01
1936	5,221	0.01
1971	3,592	0.01
2001	2,000	0.00

The first generation of Jewish immigrants to Ireland nearly all spoke Yiddish and made a living principally as itinerant peddlers of cloth, cotton, needles, scissors, cereals, seeds, and household furnishings, frequently supplied on credit to the Irish poor. Others worked as tailors, cabinetmakers, and as money-lenders. As elsewhere, the second generation prospered and "within a decade or two, many of them entered careers in dentistry, medicine, or the law, or became merchants or factory owners" (O'Grada, 2006, p. 3).

Among the Jews who achieved prominence in Ireland was Chaim Herzog (1918–1997), who grew up in Dublin in the 1920s and immigrated to Israel where he became president. In 1956 and again in 1961, Robert Briscow, whose father came from Lithuania, was elected mayor of Dublin; he also sat in the Irish Parliament for a number of years.

The socioeconomic profile of Jews in Ireland is given in the censuses of 1926 and 1946 and is shown for men in Table 6.18. We see that in 1926, 11.5 percent of Jews worked in the professions compared with only 2.7 percent of the total population. Thus, Jews were 4.2 times overrepresented–4.7 times by 1946. Jews were also considerably overrepresented in commerce, (including banking, insurance, and finance), in production and repairs, and among clerks. In contrast, Jews were underrepresented in public administration (includes the police and the military), transport, and in agriculture. The reason for the underrepresentation of Jews in public administration is attributable to "a lingering anti-Semitism in the public sector and in government" (O'Grada, 2006, p. 210).

Table 6.18. Socioeconomic Profile of Jewish Men in Ireland

Occupation	1926		1946	
	Total	Jews	Total	Jews
Professions	2.7	11.5	3.5	16.6
Commerce	5.9	52.7	5.8	40.3
Production, repairs	16.0	27.1	15.8	35.3
Clerks, typists	1.8	2.8	2.1	1.8
Public administration	3.5	0.5	3.8	0.6
Transport	6.6	1.1	6.0	0.5
Agriculture	57.1	0.3	53.2	0.2

The socioeconomic profile of Jewish women in Ireland is shown in Table 6.19. It is broadly similar to that of Jewish men. We see that in 1926, slightly fewer Jewish women worked in the professions compared with the total population. In 1946, however, the position was reversed, with Jews slightly overrepresented. Jewish women were also considerably overrepresented in commerce, including banking, insurance, and finance, in production and repairs, and among clerks, including typists. In contrast, Jews were underrepresented in public administration (includes the police and the military), transport, and agriculture. The socioeconomic profiles as a whole show that already by 1926, Jewish men and women had become upwardly mobile in Ireland and were numerous in middle-class occupations; by 1946 their position had further improved.Infant mortality in Dublin recorded in the 1911 census was 3.2 percent for Jews, 15.3 percent for Catholics, and 13.4 percent for others, who were mainly Protestants (O'Grada, 2006a). Child mortality from birth to 14 years was 9.6 percent for Jews in Dublin, and 20.8 percent for non-Jews in the city. But "even today, we do not fully understand why Jewish parents were so good at looking after their children" (O'Grada, 2006, p. 201).

Table 6.19. Socioeconomic Profile of Jewish Women in Ireland

Occupation	1926 Total	1926 Jews	1946 Total	1946 Jews
Professions	8.6	6.8	11.0	13.3
Commerce	8.3	42.3	8.9	31.0
Production, repairs	9.5	20.0	10.5	18.0
Clerks, typists	3.7	18.7	7.1	28.7
Public administration	1.2	0.3	0.9	0.6
Transport	3.7	0.0	0.4	0.3
Agriculture	35.5	1.6	24.3	0.3

15. Conclusion

Most of the Jews in Britain and Ireland came as impoverished immigrants between 1881 and 1914 seeking refuge from the pogroms in Russia and as economic migrants. In both countries, Jews have prospered. In Britain, already by the 1920s, Jewish children had a substantially higher average IQ at approximately 110 than that of Gentiles, and by the second half of the 20th century, Jews were massively overrepresented in the professions, among fellows of the Royal Society and the British Academy, among the top chess and bridge players, and among Nobel Prize winners.

In Ireland as well, Jews have been economically more successful than their non-Jewish neighbors. How to explain this? Cormac O'Grada offers five explanations. First, "men were prepared to work hard at jobs that most people in the host community found distasteful, particularly peddling and petty money-lending, or dealing in scrap and rags and second-hand furniture." Second, "the immigrants saved and invested in property, education, and business. They worked harder, they probably saved more." Third, "the Jews helped one-another; their community was rich in networks and institutions offering mutual support." Fourth, "Jewish demography was characterized by adaptability and flexibility; while the first generation stood out for low infant and child mortality, the second led the transition toward ever smaller families, trading child quantity for child quality." Fifth, "the career expectations of the second generation stretched beyond those of the first, and many of the younger generation received second-and even third-level education" (O'Grada, 2006, p. 210–11). No mention is made of the possibility that Jews might be more intelligent than Gentiles.

Chapter 7

Canada

1. Numbers and Percentages of Jews in Canada
2. Intelligence
3. Educational Attainment
4. Earnings
5. Socioeconomic Status
6. Nobel and Wolf Prize winners
7. Fertility and Mortality
8. Conclusions

A small number of Sephardic Jews, originally from Spain and Portugal, settled in Montreal in the middle decades of the 19th century. But the great majority of Canada's Jews are the Ashkenazim descendants of immigrants who sought refuge from Russia, Poland, and Lithuania from 1881 on, particularly between 1900 and 1918. In the 1930s, there was some further immigration from Germany, Austria, and Czechoslovakia.

1. Numbers and percentages of Jews in Canada

Numbers and percentages of Jews in Canada from 1901 through 2002 are shown in Table 7.1. There were very few Jews in Canada in 1901, but the country experienced a considerable increase by 1911, resulting from refugees from Russia. The numbers had increased again by 1931, as a consequence of natural increase and further immigration, and had risen again by 1981 and 2002. The percentage of Jews in the population, however, remained more or less constant, between 1.0 and 1.5 percent.

Table 7.1. Numbers and Percentages of Jews in Canada

Year	N. Jews	% population
1901	16,000	0.2
1911	75,681	1.0
1931	156,726	1.5
1981	264,020	1.0
2002	362,000	1.1

2. Intelligence of Jews in Canada

There have been two studies of the intelligence of Jews in Canada. The results are given in Table 7.2. Row 1 gives the results of the first study carried out by R. A. Wendt and Elinor Burwell (1964) in the early 1960s in three schools: two were Jewish; one was mixed. They were tested with the WISC and obtained a Full Scale IQ of 111.1, a verbal IQ of 113.1, and a "performance" IQ (a nonverbal test that to some degree, meaures spatial-visualization ability) of 107.8. These results need adjustment for the secular rise of IQs known as the "Flynn Effect," a secular trend in which Full Scale IQs have been increasing at 3 points a decade, verbal IQs, at two points a decade, and performance IQs, at four points a decade (Flynn, 1984). The WISC standardization sample was obtained in 1949, and the adjusted results are a Full Scale IQ of 107.1, a verbal IQ of 108.1, and a performance IQ (entered as "spatial") of 104.8.

The second study was carried out by Kevin Majoribanks (1972). He compared 100 Jewish boys aged 11 years with 200 White Gentile boys (100 Protestant Anglos and 100 French Canadians). His results are shown in row 2 of Table 7.2. In relation to the combined scores of the two Gentile groups set at 100, the Jewish boys obtained a nonverbal reasoning IQ of 105, a verbal IQ of 119, a spatial IQ of 103, and a numerical IQ of 115. To calculate a general IQ, these have been averaged to give a figure of 110.5. The two studies can be averaged to give an IQ of 108.8 for Jews in Canada, or 109 to the nearest whole number. This is close to the mean IQs of Jews in the United States and in Britain of about 110. Both the Canadian studies show the strong verbal/weaker spatial-ability profile that has also been found among Jews in the United States.

Table 7.2. IQs of Jews in Canada

Test	IQ	Reas	Verb	Spatial	Num
WISC	107.1	-	108.1	104.8	-
PMA	110.5	105	119.0	103.0	115

3. Educational Attainment

Canadian Jews' educational attainment compared with that of ethnic British, French, and other Europeans are shown in Table 7.3. Row 1 gives the percentages that were illiterate found in the 1921 census. The British had the fewest (one percent) illiterates, reflecting their higher educational and socioeconomic status in Canada at this time. Next come the Jews (seven percent), showing that even at this early date, the Jews were relatively well educated. They were followed closely by the French (eight percent), who performed consistently at a lower level than the British until the end of the 20th century. Then come the Other Europeans (14 percent), reflecting the immigration of large numbers of illiterate Italians (19 percent), Poles (20 percent), and Ukrainians (30 percent) in the last decades of the 19th century and early decades of the 20th.

Row 2 gives the percentages that were found to be illiterate in the 1931 census. As in 1921, the British had the fewest (1 percent) illiterates, reflecting their continued high status in Canada. Once again, Jews (four percent) came next, followed closely by the French (six percent). The Other Europeans had eight percent illiteracy, a significantly lower percentage than their 14 percent in 1921.

Table 7.3. Literacy and Educational Attainment of Jews and Gentiles

	Measure	Year	Jews	British	French	European
1	Illiterate %	1921	7	1	8	14
2	Illiterate %	1931	4	1	6	8
3	10th grade %	1951	53	55	30	35
4	10th grade %	1961	64	63	38	31
5	10th grade %	1971	80	77	59	58
6	10th grade %	1981	85	84	77	72
7	Years-NB	1981	13.5	11.7	11.1	11.9
8	Years-FB	1981	12.7	12.7	12.4	10.7
9	Years-M	1991	15.0	12.3	11.7	12.4
10	Years-W	1991	14.6	12.6	12.2	12.5

Sources: rows 1–6: Herberg, 1990b; rows 7–8: Li, 1988; rows 9–10: Sweetman & Dicks, 2000

Rows 3 through 6 give percentages of the ethnic groups who had reached the 10th grade of secondary school found in the censuses of 1951, 1961, 1971, and 1981. Row 3 gives the data for 1951, showing that the British had the greatest percentage (55 percent), followed closely by the Jews (53 percent). There is a considerable drop to the Other Europeans (35 percent) and the French (30 percent).

Row 4 gives the data for 1961 and shows that the Jews had marginally overtaken the British to become the group with the highest percentage (64 percent) with 10th-grade education. The British came second with 63 percent, followed by the French at 38 percent. The Other Europeans came next at 31 percent, a little lower than the 35 percent of 1951, reflecting the post-World War Two immigration of substantial numbers of illiterate Poles (40 percent) and Ukrainians (38 percent). Once again, the Native American Indians had by far the fewest with 10th-grade education at only nine percent.

Row 5 gives the data for 1971 and shows that the Jews were again the group that boasted the highest percentage (80 percent) of people with at least 10th-grade education. The British came second with 77 percent. There is then quite a drop, with the French at 59 percent and the Other Europeans at 58 percent. Row 6 gives the data for 1981. Once again, the Jews were the group with the highest percentage (85 percent) with 10th-grade education, followed by the British with 84 percent. The French came next at 77 percent, followed by the Other Europeans at 72 percent.

Rows 7 and 8 give the average years of education given in the 1981 census, broken down by the native born (NB) and the foreign born (FB). Among the native born, the Jews had the most years of education (13.5 years), followed by the Other Europeans (11.9), the British (11.7), and the French (11.1). The figures for the foreign born are a little different. The foreign-born Jews and Other Europeans had fewer years of education than the native born, while the foreign-born British and French had more years of education than the native born. These differences reflect different patterns of immigration. The Jews and Other Europeans who entered Canada were less educated than their native-born co-ethnics; the reverse was true for British and French.

Rows 9 and 10 give the average years of education measured in the 1991 census, separately for men (row 9) and women (row 10). Among the men, the Jews once again had the most years of education (15.0 years), followed by the Other Europeans (12.4 years), the British (12.3), and the French (11.7).

Table 7.4 gives Jewish and European figures for the percentages with any kind of tertiary (college or university) education found in the censuses of 1951 through 1991. Row 1 gives the data for 1951 and shows that Jews had the greatest percentage (13 percent) with some tertiary education, followed by the British (11 percent). The French (4 percent) and Other Europeans (5 percent) had much lower percentages. Row 2 gives the data for 1961 and shows that again the Jews had the highest percentage (15 percent), followed by the British (8 percent), the French (5 percent), and Other Europeans (5 percent). Row 3 gives the data for 1971 and shows that once more, the Jews had the greatest percentage (40 percent) with some tertiary education, followed by the British (29 percent), the Other Europeans (26 percent), and the French (23 percent).

Table 7.4. Jews and Gentiles with Tertiary Education (percentages)

	Year	Jews	British	French	European
1	1951	13	11	4	5
2	1961	15	8	5	5
3	1971	40	29	23	26
4	1981	53	38	29	34
5	1981	32	10	8	9
6	1991	55	12	13	15

Sources: 1951–1981: Herberg, 1990a & b; 1981: Li, 1988; 1991: McMullin, 2004.

In 1981, shown in row 4, the Jews still had the greatest percentage with tertiary education at 53 percent, again followed by the British (38 percent), the Other Europeans (34 percent), and the French (29 percent).

Row 5 gives the percentages with university degrees in 1981. The figures are lower than those in row 4 because they exclude those with other forms of tertiary education. The rank order of the ethnic groups, however, remains the same, with a much greater percentage of Jews than the three categories of Gentiles. Row 6 gives the percentages of those aged 25–34 with university degrees in 1991. Once again, the Jews had by far the highest percentage with university degrees (55 percent) followed by the British, Other Europeans, and the French with between 12–15 percent.

Further evidence for the better educational attainment of Jews comes from grade-eight high school students (approximately 14 year olds) in Ontario in 1994. At this stage, the students are streamed by ability into three groups: (1) basic–where students are two years behind the average for grade eight; (2) general–for students of average abilities; and (3) advanced–for high ability students who achieve more than 70 percent in both English and in mathematics. The percentage of Jews and Whites are shown in Table 7.5. It will be seen that a much higher percentage of Jewish children were placed in the high ability advanced streams, and a much lower percentage, in the basic streams.

Table 7.5. Jews and Gentiles in Advanced Streams and Basic School Streams (percentages)

Group	Advanced	Basic
Jews	42	13
Whites	26	25
Source: The Toronto Star, February 11, 1995		

4. Earnings

The earnings of Jews compared with those of ethnic British, French, and Other Europeans are shown in Table 7.6. The figures are for the employed labor force obtained from census returns for 1941 through 2001.

Table 7.6. Jewish and Gentile Earnings, 1941–2001

	Year	Jews	British	French	European
1	1941	1,327	1,515	1,007	1,115
2	1951	2,619	2,481	2,150	2,232
3	1961	7,426	4,852	3,872	3,319
4	1971	12,368	8,500	7,307	7,846
5	1981	21,349	15,100	13,831	13,367
6	1991	50,100	34,660	31,615	33,100
7	2001	73,928	51,985	-	-
Sources: Meng & Sentence, 1984; Herberg, 1990b, 1981; Li, 1988, 1991; Sweetman & Dicks, 2000, 2001.					

Row 1 gives the average earnings for 1941 and shows that the British had the highest average earnings ($1,515), reflecting their dominant position in Canada at this time. The Jews came next ($1,327), followed by a substantial drop to the Other Europeans (Germans, Italian, Dutch, Scandinavians, and Poles) ($1,115), and the French ($1,007). Row 2 gives the average earnings in 1951 and shows that the Jews had overtaken the British as the group with the highest average earnings ($2,619 as compared with $2,481). Other Europeans (Germans, Italian, Dutch, Scandinavians, Ukrainians, and Poles) came next at ($2,232), followed by the French ($2,150).

Row 3 gives the average earnings in 1961 and shows that the Jews had increased their lead as the highest earning group ($7,426) with a substantial advantage over the British ($4,852). These groups were followed by the French ($3,872) and the Other Europeans ($3,319). Row 4 gives the average earnings in 1971 and shows that the Jews retained their position as the highest earning group ($12,368), again with a substantial lead over the British ($8,500); Other Europeans come next ($7,846), followed by the French ($7,307).

Row 5 gives the average earnings in 1981 and shows that the Jews continued to retain their lead as the highest earning group ($21,349) with a substantial lead over the British ($15,100). The French ($13,831) still had significantly lower average earnings than the British; Other Europeans were fractionally lower ($13,167). Rows 6 and 7 give the average earnings in 1991 and 2001 and show that Jews continued to maintain their position as much higher earners than Gentiles.

Abdolmohammad Kazemipur and Shiva Halli (2001) give the percentages of native-born Canadians living in poverty found in the 1996 census as British: 19.3 percent; French: 19.6 percent; and Jews: 12.2 percent. Consistent with the Jews' high average earnings, there are fewer Jews in poverty.

5. Socioeconomic Status

The percentages of Jews and Gentiles in the professions in the censuses of 1921 through 1981 are shown in Table 7.7. Row 1 gives the percentages in the professions in 1921 and shows that the British, not surprisingly, had by far the highest percentage (12 percent). The French had five percent in the professions, well below the British, and reflecting the under-performance of the French in all indices of education and socioeconomic status in the early and middle decades of the 20th century. The Jews also had five percent in the professions; they were not doing particularly well in 1921. The reason for this is that nearly all of them were recent immigrants from Eastern Europe and had not been able to obtain the educational qualifications for entry into the professions.

Table 7.7. Jews and Gentiles: Percentages in the Professions, 1921–1981

Year	Jews	British	French	European
1921	5	12	5	4
1931	7	11	9	4
1941	7	10	8	4
1951	45	19	14	5
1961	48	23	17	14
1971	32	21	16	15
1981	45	26	24	18

Source: Herberg (1990a, 1990b)

In the years 1931 and 1941, we see that the British retained their leading position (11 percent and 10 percent), but the French had narrowed the gap (9 percent and 8 percent). The Jews had also improved their position to 7 percent, but were below the British and the French.

The 1951 census reveals a dramatic shift in the position of the Jews in Canada. They were by far the most overrepresented group with 45 percent in the professions. The British had lost their hitherto dominant position and dropped to 19 percent. The French were still behind at 14 percent. The censuses of 1961, 1971 and 1981 saw a continuation of these trends. The Jews remained by far the most overrepresented group in the professions. The British continued to be second; the French, third; and Other Europeans, fourth. The underrepresentation of Other Europeans reflects the immigration of numbers of Greeks, Portuguese, and Italians without professional qualifications.

The occupations of Jewish men and all Canadian men found in the 1991 census are given in Table 7.8. Row 1 shows Jews massively overrepresented among doctors and dentists, while row 2 shows Jews substantially overrepresented among lawyers and accountants. Row 3 shows Jews only slightly overrepresented among architects and engineers, as to be expected. Rows 4 through 6 show Jews moderately overrepresented among teachers, managers, and salesmen. Row 7 shows Jews highly underrepresented among manual workers.

Table 7.8. Occupations of Jews and All Canadians; Men, 1991 (percentages)

Occupation	Jews	All	AQ
Doctor, dentist	4.6	0.5	9.2
Lawyer, accountant	8.1	1.8	4.5
Architect, engineer	5.8	5.1	1.1
Teacher	12.5	6.4	1.9
Manager	19.2	10.6	1.8
Sales	16.3	8.0	2.0
Manual	16.3	47.3	0.3
Source: Torczyner & Brotman, 1995			

The occupations of Jewish females and all Canadian females found in the 1991 census are given in Table 7.9 The figures mirror those for men.

Table 7.9. Occupations of Jews and All Canadians; Women, 1991 (percentages)

	Occupation	Jews	All	AQ
1	Doctor, dentist	1.1	0.2	5.5
2	Lawyer, accountant	2.7	1.5	1.8
3	Architect, engineer	1.7	1.3	1.3
4	Teacher	22.0	14.4	1.5
5	Manager	11.0	6.2	1.8
6	Sales	11.0	7.3	1.5
7	Manual	7.2	18.8	0.4
Source: Torczyner & Brotman, 1995				

6. Nobel and Wolf Prize winners

There have been eight Canadian Nobel Prize winners and one Wolf Prize winner for mathematics. These are listed in Table 7.10. Four of the nine have been Jewish. Thus, Jews, who comprised about 1.25 percent of the population of Canada during the 20th century, have produced 44 percent of the Nobel and Wolf Prize winners, giving them an Achievement Quotient of 35.

Table 7.10. Canadian Nobel and Wolf Prize winners (Jews are asterisked)

Year	Name	Subject	Year	Name	Subject
1976	Saul Bellow*	Literature	1995	Robert Langlands	Mathematics
1983	Henry Taube	Chemistry	1996	William Vickrey	Economics
1989	Sidney Altman*	Chemistry	1997	Myron S. Scholes*	Economics
1990	Richard E. Taylor	Physics	1999	Robert A. Mundell	Economics
1992	Rudolph A. Marcus*	Chemistry			

7. Fertility and Mortality

Jews in Canada have resisted assimilation with Gentiles more than in the United States. In 1991, only 12.9 percent of Canadian Jews had married Gentiles (Torczyner & Brotman, 1995). This has contributed to the continued survival of Jews as an ethnic group. Acting against this trend, however, is the low fertility of Jewish women in Canada. Canadian Jewish women have had the lowest fertility of the four major religious groups. Table 7.11 gives statistics from the 1981 census showing this expressed as children ever born per 1,000 ever-married women aged 15–44 and aged 44 and up (Brym, Shaffir, & Weinfeld, 1993, p. 32). As these figures are for ever-married women, and therefore exclude unmarried women, the true fertility of Canadian women is actually lower, possibly below replacement level in the case of Jewish Canadian women.

Table 7.11. Children Ever Born per 1,000 Ever-married Women, 1981

Group	Age 15–44	Age 44+
Catholic	1.78	3.85
Protestant	1.80	2.80
Eastern Orthodox	1.80	2.80
Jewish	1.60	2.24
All	1.78	3.30

Child mortality has been lower among Jews than among Gentiles in Canada. In 1931 the rates were 13.6 percent for Jews and 36.7 percent for the general population (Schmelz, 1971).

8. Conclusions

The Jews have been the most successful ethnic group in Canada. In the second half of the 20th century, they had the most education, the highest percentage with university degrees, the greatest proportion in the professions, and the highest average earnings of all racial and ethnic groups.

The success of the Jews is difficult for social scientists to explain. The Canadian sociologist Peter Li has written that "the income advantage enjoyed by Jews and those of West European origin, except the French, is probably due to their historical position in which they already enjoyed an advantage over other groups" (Li, 1988, p. 138). This is not convincing. Most of the Jews arrived in Canada between 1881 and 1914 as impoverished refugees fleeing persecution in Russia and Poland. When they arrived in Canada, they could not speak English or French and were, for the most part, penniless and at the bottom of the earnings and socioeconomic status hierarchy. The British possessed the wealth and held the powerful positions in most of Canada; the French were the established dominant ethnic group in Quebec. The Europeans discriminated against Jews to some degree by excluding them from clubs and associations, as they did in the United States and Europe. Yet by 1951, the Canadian Jews had a far greater proportion in professional occupations than the British, at 45 percent as compared with 19 percent, and they maintained this advantage in the successive censuses of 1961, 1971 and 1981 (Table 7.7). They have also had higher average earnings from 1951 through 1991 (Table 7.6). The high IQ of Canadian Jews, measured at 109, must be a major factor in their overrepresentation in the professions and their high average earnings. It may or may not be surprising that this is not mentioned by sociologists such as Li (1988) and Edward Herberg (1990a, 1990b) in their analyses of the success of the Jews in Canada.

Chapter 8

Denmark

1. 1814–1939
2. Nobel Prize winners
3. The Royal Danish Academy

Jews first began to settle in Denmark in the 17th century. Virtually all of them went to Copenhagen, where many have remained. More Jews came to Denmark from Germany in the 18th century. Jews were discriminated against in Denmark until the early 19th century. They were not allowed to vote, hold public office, or marry non-Jews.

1. 1814–1939

The 19th century witnessed a transformation of the socioeconomic position of Jews in Denmark from poverty to predominantly bourgeois status. Thus, "at the beginning of the nineteenth century, the majority of Jews in Denmark were in poor circumstances, but by 1900 they mostly belonged to the middle and upper middle classes" (Encylopedia Judaica, 1968, 15, p. 1537). The socioeconomic ascent of the Jews in Denmark began with their partial emancipation in 1814 when Jews were given citizenship and were permitted to hold public office and marry Gentiles. In 1834, Jews were allowed to vote. In 1843, Jews could be appointed to medical professorships at the University of Copenhagen, but it was not until 1872 that all formal restrictions on the appointment of Jews to the University were lifted. During the course of the 19th century, Jews became well assimilated in Denmark. From 1880 to 1889, 35.9 percent of Jewish marriages were to Gentiles. From 1890 to 1899, this figure had increased to 40.7 percent, and between 1900 and 1905, it had increased further to 48.2 percent. Only about half of the children of these mixed marriages were raised as Jews, so there was some reduction in the number of those who were identified as Jews. Thus, in 1834, there were 4,064 Jews in Denmark, while in 1902, there were only 3,476. Immigrants seeking refuge from Eastern Europe in the early 20th century pushed the number of Jews in Denmark up to 5,875 in 1921 (Buckser, 2003, pp. 37–38, 41).

From 1881 onward, Jews came to Denmark as refugees from the pogroms in Russia, and there was some further immigration from the Middle East in the 1990s. Throughout the 19th and 20th centuries, Jews have been about 0.10 percent of the total population in Denmark. In 2002, there were 6,400 Jews in Denmark, representing 0.11 percent of the population of 5,360,000.

During the 19th century, Jews prospered socially and economically in Denmark. According to the leading historian of Danish Jewry, "over the course of the nineteenth century, Jews found their way into almost all of the nation's most prestigious positions."

> This process drastically transformed the economic position of the community.... [B]y the opening of the twentieth century, most Jews belonged to the upper end of the middle class, with incomes and living standards far above the Danish average (Buckser, 2003, p. 39).

One of the most successful Danish Jews in the 19th century was I. C. Jacobsen (1811-1887), the brewer of Carlsberg lager. In 1876, he founded the Carlsberg Foundation, which remains one of the leading Danish foundations for the support of research. The trust stipulates that 51 percent of the shares of the Brewery must be owned by the Foundation at all times. One of the best known of the Danish Jews is Victor Borge (1909-2000), the pianist and comedian.

In April 1940, the Germans occupied Denmark, but did not treat it as a conquered country but as a "protectorate." Danes kept their own civil government and administration. The Germans exerted pressure on the Danes to round up and transport the Jews, but the Danes did not cooperate and resisted these demands. In August 1943, the protectorate was abolished, and the Germans took control of the country. They tried to round up the Jews with a view to eliminating them, but word of the plan got out and the great majority of the Jews were able to go into hiding. Later, the Danes ferried many of them across the sea to Sweden. In the event, almost all of the approximately 7,000 Jews in 1943 were saved from the Holocaust.

2. Nobel Prize winners

The best-known Danish Nobel Prize winner is the physicist Niels Bohr (1885–1962). His mother, Ella Adler, was a member of a prominent Jewish banking family. (Jews count those who have Jewish mothers as Jews.) Niels Bohr's father was a Gentile and Professor of Physiology at the University of Copenhagen. Bohr was a brilliant student at the University. After graduating in Physics, he worked with J. J. Thomson in Cambridge and was appointed Professor of Physics at the University of Copenhagen at the early age of 21. His principal achievement was the formulation of a theory of the spectrum of hydrogen based on an atomic model and quantum theory structure, for which he was awarded the Nobel Prize for Physics in 1922. In the early years of World War II, he was visited by Werner Heisenberg, the German theoretical physicist, who tried to recruit him to work on the development of a nuclear bomb. Bohr declined and was among those who escaped to Sweden in 1943. He then went to the United States and joined the Manhattan Project that developed the atom bomb. His son, Aage Neils Bohr (1922–2009), was also a physicist and succeeded his father as Professor of Physics at the University of Copenhagen. In 1975, he too won the Nobel Prize for Physics. There has been one other Danish Nobel Prize winner who was Jewish. This is the Danish American Benjamin Mottelson (b.1936), who won the Prize for Physics in 1975.

In total, there have been 11 Danish Nobel Prize winners; they are listed in Table 7.1. Three of them have been Jews. Thus, Jews, who comprise 0.1 percent of the Danish population, have won 27 percent of the Nobel Prizes, giving them an Achievement Quotient of 270.

Table 7.1. Nobel Prize winners (Jews are asterisked)

Year	Name	Subject	Year	Name	Subject
1917	Karl Gjellerup	Literature	1944	Johannes V. Jensen	Literature
1917	Henrik Pontoppidan	Literature	1975	Ben Mottelson*	Physics
1920	August Krogh	Medicine	1975	Aage N. Bohr*	Physics
1922	Niels Bohr*	Physics	1984	Niels K. Jerne	Med.
1922	Johannes Fibiger	Medicine	1997	Jens C. Skou	Chem.
1922	Henrik Dam	Medicine			

3. The Royal Danish Academy

The Royal Danish Academy for Arts and Sciences was established in 1742 as an institution for the most eminent scholars in Denmark, akin to the National Academy of Sciences in the United States and the Royal Society in Britain. In 1999, it had 236 members, of whom 143 were in the sciences and 93 in the humanities and social sciences. Eleven of these were Jewish or partly Jewish, including three members of the Bohr family (Aage, Henrik, and Tomas). Thus, the Jews, who comprise 0.1 percent of the Danish population, are 4.7 percent of the Academicians, giving them an Achievement Quotient of 47. Because many of these were partly Jewish, this Achievement Quotient should be halved to 23.5.

Chapter 9

France

1. Numbers of Jews in France
2. 1789–1945
3. 1945–2010
4. Socioeconomic Status
5. Nobel Prize winners
6. Fields Medallists and Wolf Prize winners
7. Significant Figures
8. Bridge Champions

Jews are known to have lived in what is now France between 300 and 600 AD. They were expelled by King Dagobert (c.603–639) of the Franks in 629. Early in the ninth century, Charlemagne (768–814) ruled a large empire that covered France, western Germany, northeastern Spain, and northern and central Italy (including Rome). Charlemagne was keen to promote culture and learning in his empire, and he observed that the Jews in Italy were strong in this regard. Accordingly, he invited the Italian Jews to relocate to France and the Rhineland. He promised good conditions for them, including physical protection; liberty to travel; the freedom to practice their religion and build synagogues; property rights; and the rights to hold public office and adjudicate their own disputes. A number of Jews took up this invitation. They did, however, suffer some discrimination in so far as they were banned from the guilds, and they were heavily taxed.

In France, as throughout Europe, many Jews became money-lenders and traders. Money-lending was a good niche for them because of the Christian prohibition against charging interest on loans, promulgated by the Pope in 1179. This prohibition was based on Deuteronomy, which decrees "thou shalt not lend upon usury to thy brother." This was Church law and therefore applied only to Christians, not to Jews. Few Christians were willing to incur the risk of lending money without the incentive of receiving interest, so there was a demand for money-lenders that Jews took advantage of. They extended loans to a wide range of borrowers, including peasants, tradesmen, knights, courtiers, and occasionally even to monasteries. A record from Perpignan in southwest France states that in 1270, 80 percent of the 228 adult Jewish men made their living lending money to their Gentile neighbors (Arkin, 1975).

Jews were also traders and were

> practically alone in maintaining links between the primitive and agrarian Carolingian society and the most important trading centers in the Middle East, India, and even China. In exchange for slaves, furs, and arms, they brought back spices, perfumes, precious cloth, jewels, and many other goods. (Blom, Fuks-Mansfeld, & Schoffer, 1996, p. 13)

In the 10th century, the Carolingian Empire founded by Charlemagne collapsed, and it broke up into a number of independent states. In most of these, Jews had a number of their privileges withdrawn. They were no longer permitted to own land or hold public office, and they were banned from the trade and craft guilds that had monopolies. Money-lending remained one of the few activities open to them, together with street peddling, the repair of utensils and clothing, and the practice of medicine.

In 1096, at the time of the First Crusade, "Jews were murdered on a large scale for the first time, by the Crusaders themselves and by the rabble that followed in their wake" (Blom, Fuks-Mansfeld, & Schoffer, 1996, p. 15). The reason for this was that Jews were perceived to be ethnically related to the Saracens, who then occupied the Holy Land, and therefore sympathetic to the enemy.

The second major persecution of Jews occurred in 1348–1350, when the Black Death (the bubonic plague) swept though Europe and was responsible for the demise of about a third of the population. Many people blamed the Jews for this terrible and inexplicable epidemic, since Jews were widely believed to be the enemies of Christians. Throughout Europe, Gentiles attacked and killed the Jews in revenge, and France was no exception: in 1394, the Jews were expelled from the country.

In the late 16th century, King Henry II invited the Jews, who were being harassed by the Inquisition in Portugal, to settle in southwest France between Bordeaux and Spain, and a number of them did so. Most of them worked as traders importing goods from Lisbon and exporting grain back to Portugal. Some of the Jews in the Southwest did well, including the philosopher Michel deMontaigne (1533–1592), who was half-Jewish and mayor of Bordeaux.

In the 18th century, Jews were subject to restrictions in France similar to those in most of the rest of continental Europe. A poll tax levied on Jews was abolished in 1784, but in the same year, the rights of Jews to lend money and trade in grain and cattle were curtailed. Jews were required to obtain crown permission to marry and secure residence qualifications, without which they could be expelled. The Revolution of 1789 saw the emancipation of the Jews from these restrictions. The revolutionaries appreciated that their slogan "Liberty, Equality, Fraternity" was inconsistent with the limited rights of Jews, and in 1781, these restrictions were abolished. Jews became full citizens and were able to enter the universities and, at least in theory, any occupation.

1. Numbers of Jews in France

The numbers of Jews and their percentages of the population are shown in Table 9.1. The big jump in numbers from 1890 to 1914 was due to the immigration of approximately 120,000 refugees from Russia. The increase from 1914 to 1940 was largely due to refugees from Germany. The fall from 340,000 in 1940 to 250,000 in 1945 was a result of the killing of approximately 90,000 Jews in World War II.

Table 9.1. Numbers of Jews in France

Year	N. Jews	% population
1890	86,000	0.2
1914	296,000	0.5
1940	340,000	0.8
1945	250,000	0.6
1985	670,000	1.1
2002	520,000	0.86

2. 1789–1945

Following their emancipation in 1789, Jews in France had considerable freedom and generally prospered. Most Jews in the 19th century "were modest garment makers, small provincial salesmen, sellers of livestock, furniture, iron or canvas" (Birnbaum, 1992, p. 98).

The first field in which Jews began to achieve success was banking. In the middle decades of the 19th century, about a third of the major banks in France were run and owned by Jews, including Deutsch, Bamberger, Heine, Lippman, Periere, Ephtussi, Stern, Bischoffsheim, Hirsch, Reinach, and Rothschild. Pre-eminent among these were the Rothschilds who were "almost certainly the richest family in France during the 19th and 20th centuries" (Rubinstein, 2000, p. 32). In 1858, Emmanuel Lambert (1814–1860) became the first Jew to be appointed a *prefet* (a senior public official). In the second half of the 19th century, Jews who achieved prominence included Camille Pissarro (1830–1903), the early impressionist painter, Georges Bizet (1838-75), the composer (who was half-Jewish) and is best remembered for his opera *Carmen*, and Sarah Bernhardt (1844–1923), who became the most acclaimed actress of her day.

In the closing decades of the 19th century, Jews began to gain acceptance in French professional life. From this time up to 1940, a number of the most famous intellectuals and public figures were Jews, including Léon Blum (1872-1950), who was Prime Minister in 1936; the sociologist Emile Durkheim (1858-1917); the novelist Marcel Proust (1871-1922); the writer Emile Herzog (1885-1967), better known by his penname "Andre Maurois"; the anthropologist Claude Lévi-Strauss (1908-1988); and the psychoanalyst and literary critic Jacques Lacan (1901-1981). In the 20 years from 1895 to 1914, 148 Jews graduated from France's most prestigious college, the Ecole Polytechnique. Jews became quite prominent in public life during the Third Republic, which began in 1870. In the period 1870–1914, 21 Jews were elected deputies to the French Parliament, and between 1914 and 1940, a further 31 were elected. In the years 1870–1940, 25 generals in the French army were Jews (Birnbaum, 1992, pp. 186, 383-384—He does not give the total numbers of Ecole Polytechnique graduates, deputies or generals). In the 1930s, an estimated 15 percent of doctors in France were Jews (Brustein, 2003), drawn from a Jewish population of about 0.8 percent of the French population.

Despite the absence of legal restrictions, there was a strong undercurrent of anti-Semitism in the 19th century that persisted up to the deportation of many Jews to the concentration camps during World War II. Although Jews were admitted to the civil service, by an unwritten rule, none were appointed to the three most important ministries: the Quai d'Orsay (the ministry for foreign affairs), the Cour des Comptes (Court of Audit), and the Inspection des Finances (finance ministries). In 1853, Arthur de Gobineau (1816–1882) published his *Essai sur l'inegalite des races humaines* (*An Essay on the Inequality of the Human Races*), which maintained that Aryans (Northern Europeans) are a superior race, though Jews are highly gifted. The Jews are, in de Gobineau's mind,

> a people capable of all it undertook, an intelligent people.... [W]e marvel at the variety of Jewish aptitudes, at their singular ability to assimilate, at the speed with which they appropriate our knowledge and our methods. (Baker, 1974, p. 36)

Three years later Ernest Renan (1823–1892) published his *Vie de Jesus* (*Life of Jesus*), the best selling book in France in the whole of the 19th century, which maintained "the Semitic race, compared to the Indo-European, represents an inferior level of human nature"; he asserted that Jesus was an exception who "was immune to all the defects of his race" (Johnson, 1987, p. 282). Those who held such anti-Semitic sentiments encountered a problem: If Jews were inferior, why were they so successful? The answer was provided by Édouard Drumont (1844–1917) in his widely popular *La France Juive* (*Jewish France*, 1886), in which he argued that Jews succeeded by cheating and conspiring together to advance their own kind.

In 1893, a further discussion of the reasons for the remarkable success of the Jews was offered by Anatole Leroy-Beaulieu (1842–1912) in his book *Israel chez les Nations* (*Israel Among the Nations*). He wrote, "We marvel at the variety of Jewish aptitudes, at their singular ability to assimilate, at the speed with which they appropriate our knowledge and our methods." How to explain these Jewish aptitudes?

> They have been prepared by heredity, by two thousand years of mental gymnastics. By taking up our sciences, they do not enter an unknown territory, they return to a country already explored by their ancestors. The centuries have not only equipped them for stock-market wars and assaults on fortune, they have armed them for scientific battles and conquests. (p. 221)

Leroy-Beaulieu was perceptive in identifying high intelligence as the key to Jewish success and in noting that this could be channelled into a variety of fields, including commerce and science. He erred only in his Lamarckian theory of the inheritance of historically acquired characteristics in so far as he evidently believed that high intelligence of the Jews had been acquired by "two thousand years of mental gymnastics."

Anti-Semitism erupted in 1895 in the now-legendary "Dreyfus Affair." This case involved Captain Alfred Dreyfus (1859–1935), who was the only Jew serving in the French army general staff. He was accused of handing military secrets to the Germans. He was tried, found guilty, and sentenced to imprisonment on Devil's Island. The case aroused tremendous passions between the supporters of Dreyfus and his opponents. There were anti-Semitic riots in Paris and a number of provincial cities. After 11 years in prison, Dreyfus was released and pardoned.

At the time of the Dreyfus case, in the last decade of the 19th century, there was growing unease over the apparently large numbers of Jews in the public services. In 1895, two deputies raised this matter in the French parliament. One asked, "what measures the government intends to take to stop the predominance of Jews in various branches of the French administration," while the other called for an inquiry "into the dangers of the continual infiltration of the Jewish race into our midst" (Birnbaum, 1992, p. 301).

The German invasion of France took place in May 1940, and it took the German army only a few weeks to secure victory. The

Germans partitioned the country, occupying Paris and the north, while allowing the remainder to be governed from Vichy by Marshal Philippe Pétain (1856–1951), a German sympathizer. In October 1940, the Germans and the Vichy government issued statutes that banned Jews from all public offices, including school and university teaching and the armed services. Jewish generals and other officers were retired. Many prominent Jews were stripped of their French citizenship, including Maurice de Rothschild (1881–1957), the head of the banking family, and Pierre Mendes-France (1907–1982), who was later to become Prime Minister. A census of Jews was drawn up, and all Jews were required to wear a yellow badge. In June 1942, Adolf Eichmann issued instructions that Jews in France should be rounded up and taken to camps, where they would await deportation to Germany, often for the purpose of extermination. In August, this plan began to be implemented with the deportation of approximately 10,000 Jews. The writer and novelist Arthur Koestler was among those imprisoned in transit camps, though he managed to escape. It is estimated that the Germans and the Vichy government deported approximately 90,000 French Jews (about 26 percent of the total) who died in the concentration camps during World War II.

3. 1945–2010

The increase in the number of Jews in France from 250,000 in 1945 to 670,000 in 1985 was largely due to the immigration of North African Jews from Algeria (120,000), Tunisia (80,000), Morocco (65,000), and Egypt (25,000), and of Southwest Asian Jews from Syria, Lebanon, and Turkey (Johnson, 2004, p. 563). In addition, about 40,000 Jews were admitted from Poland.

In the post-World War Two period, Jews were prominent in public life, in the professions, in intellectual life, banks, commerce and industry. Distinguished Jews included the politicians Leon Blum, Prime Minister (1946–1947); René Mayer, Prime Minister (1953); Pierre Mendès-France, Prime Minister (1954–1955); Michel Debré, Prime Minister (1959–1962); Rabrice Reinach, Prime Minister (1960); Laurent Fabius, Prime Minister (1984–1986); Simone Veil, Health Minister (1974–1976), President of the European Parliament (1979–1982); and Dominique

Strauss–Kahn, Finance Minister, (1997–1999), Managing Director of the International Monetary Fund (2007–2011).

Prominent Jewish activists include: René Cassin (1887-1976), who drafted the Universal Declaration of Human Rights and won the Nobel Peace Prize 1968; Daniel Cohn-Bendit (b. 1945), student leader and Green MEP; Bernard Kouchner (b.1939), founder of Médecins Sans Frontières (Doctors Without Borders); and Alain Krivine (b.1941), student leader and Trotskyist MEP; the cleric Jean-Marie Lustiger (1926–2007), former Archbishop of Paris and Cardinal (born Jewish; converted to Roman Catholicism).

Eminent Jewish academics in the social sciences and humanities include: Raymond Aron (1905-1983), sociologist and journalist; Jacques Attali (b.1943), economist; Claude Lévi-Strauss, anthropologist; George Steiner (b.1929), historian and literary critic; Simone Weil (1909–1943), philosopher; and the impenetrable philosopher and deconstructionist Jacques Derrida (1930–2005).

In music, distinguished Jews include the composers Alain Boublil (b. 1941) and Claude-Michel Schonberg (b. 1944), who composed the musicals *Les Miserables* and *Miss Saigon*; the composer Adolphe Adam (1803-1856); Jacques Canetti (1909–1997), music producer and brother of writer Elias Canetti (1905–1994), the Nobel Prize winner; and Sacha Distel (1933–2004), the celebrated singer and guitarist.

In business distinguished Jews have included Marcel Bleustein (1906–1996) and Maurice Lévy (b.1942), founder and head of Publicis Groupe; Isaac (1874–1939) and his son Daniel Carasso (1905– 2009), leaders of multinational Gouppe Danone (Dannon); André Citroën (1878–1935), founder of Citroën automobiles; Marcel Dassault (1892–1986) (born Marcel Bloch), aerospace industrialist; Maurice Girodias (1919–1990), founder of Olympia Press; Philippe Kahn (b. 1962), founder of Borland; Alexandre, Simon, and Elie Lazard, founders of the Lazard bank; Armand, Georges, Maurice and Paul Marciano (b. 1952), founders of Guess; Gilbert Trigano (1920–2001), founder of "Club Med"; and Pierre Wertheimer (1888–1965), co-founder of Chanel, the perfume business

4. Socioeconomic Status

The socioeconomic status distribution of Jews and Gentiles in 1988 has been given by Della Pergola (1993) and is shown in Table 9.2. We see that Jews are highly overrepresented in the major professions and senior management, and also among traders, which includes the proprietors of medium-sized and small businesses. Jews are also highly overrepresented among skilled craftsmen. Jews and Gentiles are about equally represented in the minor professions. Jews are underrepresented among the clerical workers and in the "Other blue-collar" category.

Table 9.2. Socioeconomic status of Jews and Gentiles

Socioeconomic status	Jews	Gentiles
Professional & managerial	41.7	12.2
Traders	19.4	5.8
Minor professional	18.1	17.5
Clerical	11.1	25.0
Skilled craftsmen	8.3	2.1
Other blue-collar	1.4	37.4

5. Nobel Prize Winners

France has produced 41 Nobel Prize winners, who are listed in Table 9.3. Six of these have been Jews: Henri Moissan, Chemistry (1906); Gabriel Lippmann, Physics (1908); Henri Bergson, Literature (1927); François Jacob, Chemistry (1965); André Lwoff, Medicine (1965); Claude Cohen-Tannoudji, Physics (1997). Thus, Jews, who have made up about 0.8 percent of the population during the 20th century, have produced 15 percent of French Nobel Prize winners, giving them an Achievement Quotient of 19. In the first half of the 20th century, three of the 21 Nobel Prize winners were Jewish, representing a rate of 8.8 per million. In the second half, three of the 16 Nobel Prize winners were Jewish, but the number of Jews in France had almost doubled from 340,000 to 670,000, so Jewish Nobel Prize winners as a rate per million approximately

126 THE CHOSEN PEOPLE

halved. The explanation for this is that many of the new Jews in France came from North Africa and have lower IQs than the Ashkenazim of Europe (see Chapter 11).

Table 9.3. French Nobel Prize winners (Jews are asterisked)

Year	Name	Subject	Year	Name	Subject
1901	Sully Prudhomme	Literature	1956	André F. Cournand	Medicine
1903	Henri Becqueral	Physics	1957	Albert Camus	Literature
1903	Pierre Curie	Physics	1960	Saint-John Perse	Literature
1904	Frédéric Mistral	Literature	1964	Jean-Paul Sartre	Literature
1906	Henri Moissan*	Chem.	1965	François Jacob*	Chemistry
1908	Alphonse Laveran	Medicine	1965	André Lwoff*	Medicine
1908	Lippmann*	Physics	1966	Jacques Monod	Physics
1912	Victor Grignard	Chem.	1966	Alfred Kastler	Physics
1912	Paul Sabatier	Chem.	1970	Louis Néel	Physics
1912	Alexis Carrel	Medicine	1977	Roger Guillemin	Medicine
1913	Charles Richet	Medicine	1980	Jean Dausset	Medicine
1915	Romain Rolland	Literature	1987	Jean-Marie Lehn	Chemistry
1921	Anatole France	Literature	1988	Maurice Allais	Economics
1926	Jean Perrin	Physics	1991	Pierre de Gennes	Physics
1927	Henri Bergson*	Literature	1997	C. Cohen-Tannoudji*	Physics
1928	Charles Nicolle	Medicine	2005	Yves Chauvin	Chemistry
1929	Louis de Broglie	Physics	2007	Albert Fert	Physics
1935	Frédéric Joliot	Chemistry	2008	F. Barre-Sinoussi	Medicine
1935	Irène Joliot-Curie	Chemistry	2008	Luc Montagnier	Medicine
1937	Roger du Gard	Literature	2008	J. M. Le Clézo	Literature
1952	François Mauriac	Literature			

6. Fields Medallists and Wolf Prize winners

France has produced 17 of the mathematicians who have received the Fields Medal or the Wolf Prize awarded for outstanding work in mathematics. These are listed in Table 9.4. Five of these have been Jews.

Thus, Jews have produced 29 percent of top French mathematicians, giving them an Achievement Quotient of 36.

Table 9.4. French prizewinning mathematicians (Jews are asterisked)

Year	Field Medal	Year	Wolf Prize
1950	Laurent Schwartz*	1979	Jean Leray
1954	Jean-Pierre Serre	1979	Andre Weil*
1958	René Thom	1980	Henri Cartan
1974	Enrico Bombieri	1986	Albert Libchaber*
1978	Pierre Deligne	1993	Jacques Tits
1982	Alain Connes	2000	Jean-Pierre Serre
1984	Pierre-Louis Lions		
1994	Lean-Christophe Yoccoz		
1998	Maxim Kontsevich*		
2002	Laurent Lafforgue		
2006	Werner Wendelin		

7. Significant Figures

Charles Murray lists 188 Frenchmen (170 Gentiles and 18 Jews) in his roster of "significant figures" in world cultural and intellectual achievement (2003, p. 280). Thirteen of these are listed in Table 9.5. Murray's list is more comprehensive than Nobel Prize winners and includes painters, mathematicians, composers, philosophers and engineers. Only two French Nobel Prize winners appear in his list (Henri Bergson & André Lwoff). Murray explicates the numbers of Jewish and Gentile "significant figures" who were active between 1870 and 1950 and the ratio of Jewish to Gentile "significant figures" in relation to their numbers in the population. These calculations yield a Jewish Achievement Quotient of 19.1, remarkably close to the Jewish Achievement Quotient of 20.9 based on Nobel Prize winners.

128   THE CHOSEN PEOPLE

Table 9.5. French Jewish "Significant Figures"

Michel de Montaigne	Philosophy	1533–1592
Fromental Halévy	Music	1799-1862
Adolphe Adam	Music	1803-1856
Camille Pissarro	Art	1830-1903
Ludovic Halevy	Literature	1834-1908
Ferdinand Moissan	Technology	1852-1907
Henri Bergson	Philosophy	1859-1941
Jacques Hadamard	Mathematics	1865-1963
Paul Dukas	Music	1865-1935
Marcel Proust	Literature	1871-1944
Darius Milhaud	Music	1892-1974
André Lwoff	Biology	1902-1994

8. Bridge Champions

Not surprisingly, Jews are prominent in top-level bridge in France. The names of the 22 French Open World Bridge Champions recognised by World Bridge Federation in 2004 are given in Table 9.6. Five of them are Jews, denoted by asterisks.

Table 9.6. French open world bridge champions in 2004; (Jews are denoted by asterisks.)

Rene Bacherich	Pierre Ghestem	Gerard Bourchtoff
Paul Chemla*	Michel Lebel*	Claude Delmouly
Pierre Jais	Franck Multon	Albert Faigenbaum*
Alain Levy*	Philippe Soulet	Roger Lattes
Christian Mari	Henri Szwarc*	Dominique Pilon
Herve Mouiel	Pierre Adad	Bertrand Romanet
Michel Perron	Maurice Aujaleu	

Thus, Jews, who are about 0.86 percent of the French population at the beginning of the 21st century, contribute 23 percent of the top bridge players, giving them an Achievement Quotient of 27.

Chapter 10

Germany

1. Numbers of Jews
2. The 19th Century
3. 1900–1918
4. The Weimar Republic, 1918–1933
5. Nazi Germany, 1933–1945
6. Jewish Achievement in Chess
7. Nobel Prize winners
8. Mathematicians
9. Significant Figures

Jews are known to have lived in Cologne in western Germany between 300 and 600 AD. As described in the previous chapter, in an attempt to promote culture and learning throughout his vast territories, the emperor Charlemagne invited a group of Jews in Italy to relocate to France and the Rhineland. Those who settled in the German lands adopted the name "Ashkenazim." They were granted some basic liberties, but also forced to suffer under a number of restrictions: Ashkenazim were not permitted to own land; they were banned from the guilds; and they were heavily taxed. As elsewhere in Europe, a number of them adapted to their new environment by becoming money-lenders. They also had a virtual monopoly of the trade in Eastern goods such as spices and silk.

The Jewish experience in Germany certainly had its share of conflict and suffering. As discussed previously, the Crusades and the Black Death inspired outbreaks of anti-Jewish violence. The 15th century saw a growing wave of anti-Semitism throughout the German lands. In 1414, the Jews were expelled from Trier; in 1424, they were expelled from Cologne; in 1430, from Saxony; and in 1446, from Brandenburg. Most of them headed east to Prussia, Poland, and Russia. In the 16th century, expulsions of Jews continued from a number of the small German states, including Wurttemburg (1521), Saxony (1536), Upper and Lower Bavaria (1551), Brunswick, Hanover, and Luneburg (1553), the Palatinate (1556–1559), and Brandenburg (1573) (Blom, Fuks-Mansfeld & Schoffer, 1996, p. 45).

The year 1618 saw the beginning of the Thirty Years War and attendant deprivation and bloodshed. Many Jews migrated to Poland and the Ukraine; others moved to Amsterdam in the Netherlands, and some went to Hamburg, which was a free port in which there was a community of Sephardim, among whom the wealthiest was the da Costa family.

In the 18th century, Germany was still divided into a number of independent principalities and remained this way until Otto von Bismarck (1815–1898) united the states in 1867–1870. In virtually all of these principalities, Jews suffered varying degrees of discrimination and restrictions, but the severity of these varied in the different states. In Prussia, the largest of the German states, Jews were prohibited from the craft trades for which guild membership was necessary. Frankfurt required Jews to live in the ghetto, whose entrance was locked at night by soldiers and reopened in the morning. Jews were limited to 500 families and 12 marriages a year and were prohibited from farming, manufacture of handicrafts, and dealing in weapons, silk, and fruit.

In the 17th and 18th centuries, most Jews worked as petty traders, dealing largely in second-hand goods, especially clothes and household furniture, and operated pawn shops and took part in other forms of money-lending and exchange. A few Jews achieved high social positions as "Court Jews" who served as the financial agents of princes in the control of salt and tobacco monopolies, arranging army contracts, establishing industrial enterprises, founding banks, and granting loans to finance military and civil expenditures.

In the late 18th century, the two most prominent Jewish families were the Oppenheims and the Rothschilds. Mayer Rothschild, who began trading in old coins, founded the banking dynasty and became the financial agent of the Elector of Hesse-Kessel, the richest of the German princes. The Oppenheim family ran a bank in Cologne that has survived up to the present day as the largest private bank in Germany.

The Napoleonic wars in the first decade and a half of the 19th century saw an improvement in the position of the Jews in Germany. In 1812, Napoleon emancipated the Jews in southwestern Germany from numerous restrictions, though many of these freedoms were withdrawn in the 1830s. During the Napoleonic Wars, a number of Jews used their money to finance the armies and made substantial sums from interest. After the end of the conflict, they had capital to launch and fund commercial enterprises. Many of them did so successfully and rose to positions of economic power and social eminence. According to Werner E. Mosse (1987), who has written one of the most authoritative works on the economic and social rise of the Jews from the 19th century up to the accession to power of Hitler, there were some "peripheral prejudices" against Jews but overt anti-Jewish discrimination was largely absent in 19th-century Germany. On the contrary, Gentiles generally accepted socially the Jews who had acquired wealth. Most of the wealthy descendants of the successful Court Jews of the 18th century converted to Christianity, and many of them married into the Gentile upper-middle class and nobility. By the mid-19th century, many of them had become integrated into the upper echelons of Gentile society and had disappeared from Jewish economic life.

1. Numbers of Jews in Germany

The approximate numbers of Jews in Germany and their percentages of the population for various dates are given in Table 10.1. Between 1871 and 1910, Jews were approximately one percent of the German population. Although the numbers of Jews increased during this period, their percentage of the population fell slightly due to lower fertility and intermarriage with Gentiles, which resulted in a number of Jews becoming assimilated. From 1910 to 1935, these trends persisted, and the numbers of Jews and their percentage of the population continued to decline. The decline from 1935 to 1945 was due to emigration and the Holocaust in the years 1942–1945. (The figures for 1945 and 1985 are for East and West Germany combined; these became two independent states in 1945.) The increase from 1945 to 1985 was due to immigration, largely from Russia.

Table 10.1. Numbers and percentages of Jews in Germany

Year	N. Jews	% Population
1871	410,000	1.00
1910	615,000	0.95
1935	525,000	0.78
1945	26,603	0.04
1985	42,000	0.08
2002	95,000	0.11

Sources: Gordon, 1984, p. 8; American Jewish Yearbooks

2. The 19th Century

During the 19th century, the restrictions placed on Jews were gradually relaxed. Jews flourished, as indexed by their greater longevity than Gentiles. A study in Frankfurt in 1855 found that Jews had an average life span of 49 years; the Gentile average was only 37 years (Johnson, 2004, p. 356). This was offset, however, by low fertility. It has been estimated that the birthrate of Jews in Munich in 1875 was 20 percent below that of Catholics (Chiswick, 1988).

In 1848, Jews became entitled to vote. When Bismarck had completed the unification of the hitherto independent states in 1870, he gave the Jews full civil rights, though it was not until 1875 that Jews were permitted to marry Gentiles.

Throughout the century, Jews succeeded in a number of fields and by its closing decades they were prominent in banking, commerce, industry, the professions, the arts, and intellectual life. Jews were approximately one percent of the population, but they had much higher percentages on a number of indices of educational, social, and economic achievement, and social standing. Many of the most famous in Germany in the 19th century were Jews, including the poet and essayist Heinrich Heine (1797–1856), the political economist Karl Marx (1818–1883), the composers Felix Mendelssohn (1809–1847), Jacques Offenbach (1819–1880), and Giacomo Mayerbeer (1791–1864), and the physicist Albert Einstein (1879–1955), who was born in Bavaria although he was educated in Switzerland and took Swiss nationality in 1901.

The field in which Jews achieved their greatest prominence was banking. Besides the aforementioned Rothschilds of Frankfurt (later the Goldschmidt-Rothschilds) and the Oppenheims of Cologne, the most successful of banking families were the Kaskells, who founded the Dresdner Bank in 1872 (which still exists as Dresdner-Kleinwort-Benson); the Seligmans and the Hirsches, who founded the Bayerische Hypotheken und Wechselbank (still one of the largest banks in Germany); the Kaullas family, who founded the Wurttembergerische Hofbank in Stuttgart; the Pfeiffers, who with other small Jewish bankers, established the Wurttembergerische Vereinsbank; and the Warburgs, whose London banking dynasty is still going strong as of this writing.

Jews also established successful businesses in textile manufacture and distribution, chemicals, brewing and distilling, sugar refining, metallurgy, alum and lignite mining, and transport. The most prominent in textiles were the Meyers, Liebermanns, Reichenheims, Weigerts, Kauffmanns, Frankels, Pinkuses, and Goldschmidts. In chemicals: Heinrich Caro (1834–1910), Franz Oppenheim (1852–1929), Fitz Haber (1868–1934), the Berends, Beers, Goldschmidts, and Kunheims. In brewing, distilling and sugar-refining: the Bachers, Berends, and Beers. In metallurgy: the Harzes, Hirsches, and the Coppels. In alum and lignite mining: the Kunheims and the Henochs. In transport, consisting initially of horse-drawn carriages and later of railways: the Henochs, Guterbocks, and the Beers.

As mentioned above, in the 19th century, the Gentile business community generally accepted Jews socially who had established successful businesses. In Prussia, public recognition of successful and creditable businessmen was accorded by the conferment of the coveted titles of Kommerzenrat (KG) and the more prestigious Geheimer Kommerzenrat (GKG). These were analogous to the orders of nobility; the Geheimer Kommerzenrat was entitled to be addressed as Geheimrat.

There were rigorous selection procedures for the conferment of these titles that took account of income and wealth, economic services to the state, public service, charitable activities, standing among peers, and respectable lifestyle.

The numbers of Jews and Gentiles who were awarded the titles of KG and GKG during the period 1819 to 1900 have been given by Mosse (1987). From these, I have calculated the percentages of these who were Jews from the totals and broken these down into those who were bankers, merchants, and manufacturers for four periods spanning the 19th century. These figures are given in Table 10.2. Three points are particularly striking. First, the percentage of Jews in the population in Germany during the 19th century was approximately 1.0 percent, so Jews were hugely overrepresented among the economic elite on whom these titles were conferred, as they were overrepresented in all sectors of the economy and at all times. Second, the percentage of Jews among this business elite nearly doubled from the first half of the century (1819–1852), when it stood at 10 percent, to the second half (1861–1900), when it averaged 18 percent. Third, the percentage of Jews was much higher in banking, where they constituted about half of the bankers, rather less in merchandising, where they were around a quarter in the second half of the century, and lowest in manufacturing where they ranged between five and seven percent. Jews also made up seven percent of journalists in 1881 (Gordon, 1984, p. 14).

Table 10.2. Percentages of Jews among the economic elite in Germany in 1819–1900

Years	Total	Bankers	Merchants	Manufacturers
1819–1852	10	54	5	5
1861–1872	19	50	25	7
1879–1889	20	52	26	7
1890–1900	15	45	21	6

Inevitably, it took time for Jews to take advantage of these new opportunities, but they gradually did so. As the century progressed, an increasing number of Jews achieved eminence. Gerhard Falk and Vern Bullough (1987) have collected information about 375 Jews who achieved eminence in academe and the professions (but not business) and who were born in Germany between 1785 and 1884. They used the criteria of listing in *Die Neue Deutsche Biographie, The Dictionary of Scientific Biography, The Jewish Encyclopedia, The Universal Jewish Encyclopedia,* and *The Encyclopedia Judaica.* They found that the numbers of Jews who achieved eminence gradually increased over the course of the century. Their figures are shown in Table 10.3. We can see that during the century there was a more than fivefold increase in the numbers of Jews achieving eminence. This shows that it takes a couple of generations for an oppressed people to find their place in the socioeconomic hierarchy.

Table 10.3. Numbers of Jews who achieved eminence in Germany

1785–1804	1805–1824	1825–1844	1845–1864	1865–1884
25	59	67	87	137

Falk and Bullough (1987) have also analyzed the occupational distribution of Jews and Gentiles in Germany at the end of the 19th century. Their results for 1895 are shown in Table 10.4.

Table 10.4. Occupational distribution of Jews and Gentiles in Germany in 1895 (percentages)

Occupation	Jews	Gentiles
Prof/Civil Service	7.1	6.4
Business	59.8	5.3
Railroads	5.4	5.3
Manual	22.5	37.5
Domestic Service	3.6	8.0
Farming	1.6	37.5

It will be seen that Jews were slightly overrepresented in the professional and civil service category and were massively overrepresented as business proprietors. On the other hand, Jews were substantially underrepresented in manual occupations, domestic service, and farming. Their average position in the socioeconomic hierarchy was clearly substantially higher than that of Gentiles.

Many studies have shown that crime is predominantly committed by the less intelligent. Probably the main reasons for this are that the more intelligent have a better understanding of the costs of crime, and since they generally have better jobs and higher social status, the cost of crime is usually greater for them. It is therefore interesting to note that Jews have tended to have lower crime rates than Gentiles. Cesare Lombroso notes (1911, p. 37):

> The statistics of many countries show a lower degree of criminality for Jews than for their Gentile fellow-citizens.... In Bavaria one Jew is sentenced for every 315 of them in the population, and one Catholic for every 265. In Baden, Jewish criminality was 63.8 percent of Christian criminality.

F. Lenz (1930, p. 680) confirmed this for the last decade of the 19th century. His figures for conviction rates for all crime are 103 per 10,000 populations for Jews and 124 per 10,000 populations for Gentiles.

Infant mortality was lower among Jews in the 19th and early 20th centuries.

Table 10.5. Infant mortality per 1,000 live births

Years	Location	Jews	Gentiles	% Difference
1812–40	Prussia	129	174	35
1819–70	Westphalia	96	140	46
1827–56	Magdeburg	135	225	67
1857–73	Baden	185	276	47
1878	Bavaria	152	296	95
1891–1913	Frankfurt	67	146	118
1894–1905	Munich	87	264	203
1901–1912	Hesse	70	128	82
1906	Breslau	62	217	250

Studies showing this have been summarized by Gretchen Condran and Ellen Kramarow (1991) and are shown in Table 10.5, where it will be seen that the infant mortality of Gentiles was between 35 and 250 percent higher than that of Jews.

By the later decades of the 19th century, it was becoming recognized in Germany that the Jews are an exceptionally intelligent people. For instance, Heinrich von Treitschke (1834-1896) noted the overrepresentation of Jews in the higher classes in Berlin colleges; Friedrich Nietzsche (1844-1900) wrote of "the extraordinary intellectual resources of the Jews of the present day" (Baker, 1974, pp. 44–46).

3. 1900–1918

Jews prospered in Germany during the early years of the 20th century and a large percentage became quite wealthy. Mosse (1987, 1989) has published the statistics, derived from tax returns, for the economic success of Jews between 1908 and 1911; they are shown in Table 10.6. Jews were about 0.08 percent of the population at this time. Yet row 1 shows that 36 percent of prominent businessmen were Jewish (chairmen, managing directors, and directors of the 100 largest corporations). Row 2 shows that 21.7 percent of millionaires (worth five million marks or more) in Prussia (by far the largest state) in 1908 were Jewish. Row 3 shows that 31 percent of multimillionaires were Jewish (families worth 50 million marks or more: there were 29 such families of which nine were Jewish).

Table 10.6. Percentages of Jews among the wealthy in Germany in 1908–1911

The Wealthy	% Jews
Prominent businessmen	36.0
Millionaires	21.7
Multimillionaires	31.0

The names of the wealthiest families ranked in order of the value of their holdings are given in Table 10.7, in which Jewish families are asterisked. Of the 29 wealthiest families, 10 (31 percent) were Jewish.

Table 10.7. Wealthiest families in Germany in 1908–1911: Jews are asterisked

Haniel	Thyssen	Schottlander*
Rothschild*	Stumm	Ballestrem
Henckell	Tiele-Winckler	Dippe
Krupp	Arenberg	Henschel
Hohenlohe	Gans/Weinberg*	Simon*
Speyer*	Bleichroder*	Schichau/Ziese
Waldthusen	Guilleaume	Mosse*
Mendelssohn*	Oppenheim*	Borsig
Schaffgotsch	von Roth	Metzler
Pless	von Schwarzenstein	
Source: Mosse (1987)		

Statistics showing the overrepresentation of Jews in the higher socioeconomic strata of Germany for the years 1904–1910 are given in Table 10.8. During this period, Jews were approximately one percent of the population. Row 1 shows that in 1900, 50 percent of the doctors in Berlin were Jews. Row 2 shows that in 1904, 27 percent of the lawyers were Jewish. Rows 3, 4, 5, and 6 show that in 1910, Jews were seven percent of university professors, 25 percent of law and medical students, 5.4 percent of all university students in the country, and 17 percent of students at the University of Berlin.

Table 10.8. Jews in Germany 1904–1910

Years	Occupation	% Jews	AQ
1900	Berlin doctors	50	50
1904	Lawyers	27	27
1910	University professors	7	7
1910	Law & medical students	25	25
1910	University students	5.4	5.4
1910	Berlin University students	17	17
Sources: rows 1–2: Gordon, 1984; row 3–6: Slezkine (2004)			

During the early 20th century, the Jewish physician Martin Englander (1902, pp. 11–12) contended that Jews are on average more intelligent that Gentiles and have larger heads, though inferior physique. During World War I, the suggestion that Jews are more intelligent than Gentiles appeared to be confirmed with the publication of a study by Ottokar Nemeck (1916) in which he analyzed the scholastic records of 1,549 15-18-year-old school students. He reported that Jewish students were on average superior in all academic subjects, including mathematics, physics, chemistry, languages, history, and geography.

4. The Weimar Republic, 1918–1933

Between 1918 and 1933, it was quite widely recognized that Jews were on average more intelligent than Gentiles. For instance, Fritz Lenz, who held the Professorship of Racial Hygiene at the University of Munich, wrote,

> But when we compare the average German Jew with the average German Gentile we cannot doubt that the Jews excel in intelligence and alertness. In the higher schools, where the pupils represent a selection for talent, the proportion of Jewish children is many times as large as the proportion of Jews in the general population. In the elementary schools, the Jewish children on the average perform better than the Gentiles; Jews form an immoderately large proportion of undergraduates at the universities; at the Prussian universities in 1911–1912, Jews were 5.6 percent of the students [and only one percent of the population]. (1931, p. 670)

Jews remained prominent in the economic elite during the Weimar Republic. Mosse (1987, pp. 355, 362), the historian of the socioeconomic position of Jews in Germany, writes, "men of Jewish extraction were to be found in some 39 of the largest industrial companies...and down to 1931, there is little evidence of any significant overall decline of the role of Jews in German economic life." Mosse does not, however, provide any further statistics to substantiate these assertions. In these years, Jews were also becoming increasingly assimilated with Gentile society.From 1901 to 1905, 15 percent of Jews married Gentiles. Between 1926 and 1932, this figure rose to 36 percent, and by 1933, to 44 percent (Gordon, 1984, p. 17).

Statistics showing the percentages of Jews among the socioeconomic elite in the Weimar Republic are given in Table 10.9 (at this time, Jews were about 0.78 percent of the population). Rows 1–3 show that in 1925, 16 percent of the physicians, 15 percent of the dentists and 25 percent of the lawyers were Jews. Row 4 shows that in 1928, Jews occupied 80 percent of the leading positions in the Berlin stock exchange. Row 5 shows that in 1930, Jews held 43 percent of the leading positions in Jewish private banks. Row 6 shows that in the same year, Jews held six percent of the leading positions in non-Jewish banks. Row 7 shows that in the same year, 75 percent of the plays produced in Germany were written by Jews. Row 8 shows that in 1931, 50 percent of theatre directors were Jews. In addition, "a large number of prominent actors and actresses were Jewish" (Gordon, 1984, p. 14).

Child mortality was lower for Jews in the 1920s, at a mean of 10.3 percent for Jews in Berlin, as compared with 25.5 percent for the general population (Schmelz, 1971).

Table 10.9. Jews in Germany 1918–1933

Years	Occupation	% Jews	AQ
1925	Physicians	16	20
1925	Dentists	15	19
1925	Lawyers	25	32
1928	Berlin stockbrokers	80	102
1930	Private bankers	43	55
1930	Public bankers	6	8
1930	Playwrights	75	96
1931	Theatre directors	50	64
Sources: rows 1–3: Slezkine (2004); rows 4–8: Gordon (1984)			

5. Nazi Germany, 1933–1945

As Adolf Hitler came to power in 1933, one of his prime objectives was to rid Germany of the Jews. Hitler's motives for doing this appear to have been that he believed that the Jews are exceptionally talented and could take control of the world. He may also have believed that the Jews were parasitical and had certain poor character qualities. Be this as it may, he began to take measures against the Jews shortly after he acquired power. In 1935, the Nuremberg Laws deprived Jews of their citizenship and prohibited them from marrying Gentiles, from attending public schools, engaging in business or the professions, and owning land. In 1938, a pogrom destroyed synagogues; the state confiscated most Jews' financial assets; and all Jews were required to live in ghettos. In the 1930s, it seems that the Nazis thought the way to rid Germany of the Jews would be to encourage them to emigrate and between 1933 and 1945, approximately 300,000 Jews who had been robbed of their goods and property were allowed to leave the country. The Nazis also considered plans to resettle the Jews in other countries. Madagascar was considered as a possible place to send them (Gordon, 1984). It appears that it was not until late 1941 or early 1942 that the Nazis formulated and began to implement the plan of the extermination of the Jews. During the next three years, approximately 160,000 were killed in the gas chambers, while some 26,600 survived, a figure that includes those in mixed marriages.

6. Jewish Achievement in Chess

Jews have excelled at chess in a number of countries, and up to 1939, Germany was no exception. Table 10.10 gives the names of the top-rated German-Jewish and Gentile chess grandmasters for the years 1851 to 2000 (Rubinstein, 2004, p. 37). There were six Jews and seven Gentiles among grandmasters in the years between 1851 and 1939.

Table 10.10. Jewish and Gentile chess grandmasters

Year	Jews	Gentiles
1851–1899	Horowitz	von der Lasa
	Harrwitz	Anderssen
	Newmann	Paulsen
	Schwarz	von Minckwitz
	Tarrasch	von Bardelben
1900–1939	Lasker	Lipke
		Teichmann
1940–2000		Hubner

144   THE CHOSEN PEOPLE

The Germans have only produced one top-rated grandmaster since 1940. Thus, Jews, who were about one percent of the population between 1871 and 1914, were 46 percent of the top-rated German chess grandmasters, giving them an Achievement Quotient of 46.

7. Nobel Prize winners

A list of German Nobel Prize winners is given in Table 10.11 (the Prize winners listed are those born in Germany, a number of whom emigrated in the 1930s). Of the 89 Nobel Laureates, 21 have been Jewish. Thus, Jews, who were about 0.78 percent of the population in the 1930s, received 24 percent of the Nobel Prizes, giving them an Achievement Quotient of 31.

Table 10.11. German Nobel Prize winners (Jews are asterisked)

Year	Name	Subject	Year	Name	Subject
1901	Emil von Behring	Medicine	1953	Fritz Lipmann*	Medicine
1901	Wilhelm Rontgoen	Physics	1954	Max Born*	Physics
1902	Emil Fischer	Chemistry	1954	Walther Bothe	Physics
1902	Theodor Mommsen	Literature	1955	Polykarp Kusch	Physics
1905	Adolf von Baeyer*	Chemistry	1956	Werner Forssmann	Medicine
1905	Philipp Lenard	Physics	1961	Rudolf Mössbauer	Physics
1907	Eduard Buchner	Chemistry	1963	Karl Ziegler	Chemistry
1908	Rudolf Eucken	Literature	1963	M. Goeppert-Mayer	Physics
1908	Paul Ehrlich*	Medicine	1963	J. Hans Jensen	Physics
1909	Wilhelm Ostwald	Chemistry	1964	Konrad Bloch*	Medicine
1909	Ferdinand Braun	Physics	1964	Feodor Lynen	Medicine
1910	Otto Wallach*	Chemistry	1966	Nelly Sachs	Literature
1910	Paul Heyse*	Literature	1967	Manfred Eigen	Chemistry
1910	Albrecht Kossel	Medicine	1967	Hans Bethe*	Physics
1911	Wilhelm Wien	Physics	1969	Max Delbrück	Medicine
1912	Gerhart Hauptmann	Literature	1970	Bernard Katz*	Medicine
1914	Max von Laue	Physics	1971	Gerhard Herzberg*	Chemistry
1915	Richard Willstätter*	Chemistry	1972	Heinrich Böll	Literature

Year	Name	Subject	Year	Name	Subject
1918	Fritz Haber*	Chemistry	1973	Ernest Fischer	Chemistry
1918	Max Planck	Physics	1978	Arno Penzias*	Physics
1919	Johannes Stark	Physics	1979	Georg Wittig	Chemistry
1920	Walther Nernst	Chemistry	1984	Georges Kohler	Medicine
1921	Albert Einstein*	Physics	1985	Klaus von Klitzing	Physics
1922	Otto Meyerhof*	Medicine	1986	Gerd Binnig	Physics
1925	Richard Zsigmondy	Chemistry	1987	Georg Bednorz	Physics
1925	James Franck*	Physics	1988	Johann Deisenhofer	Chemistry
1925	Gustav Hertz	Physics	1988	Robert Huber	Chemistry
1927	Heinrich Wieland	Chemistry	1988	Hartmut Michel	Chemistry
1928	Adolf Windaus	Chemistry	1988	Jack Steinberger*	Physics
1929	Thomas Mann	Literature	1989	Hans Dehmelt	Physics
1930	Hans Fischer	Chemistry	1991	Erwin Neher	Medicine
1931	Otto Warburg	Medicine	1991	Bert Sakmann	Medicine
1931	Friedrich Bergius	Chemistry	1992	Rudolf Marcus	Chemistry
1931	Carl Bosch	Chemistry	1994	Reinhard Selten	Economics
1932	Werner Heisenberg	Physics	1995	C Nusslein-Volhard	Medicine
1935	Hans Spemann	Medicine	1998	Horst L. Störmer	Physics
1939	Adolf Butenandt	Chemistry	1999	Günter Grass	Literature
1939	Gerhard Domagk	Medicine	1999	Günter Blobel	Medicine
1943	Otto Stern*	Physics	2000	Jack S. Kilby	Physics
1945	Ernst B. Chain*	Medicine	2005	Robert Auman*	Economics
1946	Hermann Hesse	Literature	2005	Theodor Harsch	Physics
1950	Kurt Alder	Chemistry	2007	Peter Gruneberg	Physics
1950	Otto Diels	Chemistry	2007	Gerhard Ertl	Chemistry
1953	H. Staudinger	Chemistry	2008	Harald zur Hausen	Medicine
1953	Hans Krebs*	Medicine			

8. Mathematicians

Germany has produced seven mathematicians who have received the Fields Medal or the Wolf Prize awarded for outstanding work in mathematics. These are listed in Table 10.12. Three of these have been Jews. Thus, Jews who have been about

0.4 percent of the population during the second half of the 20th century have produced 43 percent of top mathematicians, giving them an Achievement Quotient of 107.

Table 10.12. German Mathematicians (Jews are asterisked)

Year	Fields Medal	Year	Wolf Prize
1958	Klaus Roth*	1978	Carl Siegel
1966	Alexander Grothendieck*	1984	Hans Lewy*
1986	Gerd Faltings	1988	Friedrich Hirzebruch
		1994	Jürgen Moser

9. Significant Figures

Charles Murray (2003, p. 280) has calculated the numbers of Jewish and Gentile "significant figures" (i.e. great names in science and the arts) in Germany whose careers came within the years 1870 to 1950. He finds 40 Jews and 155 Gentiles. Calculating the ratio of Jewish to Gentile "significant figures," he arrives at an Achievement Quotient (Jewish overrepresentation) of 22. This is not greatly different from the Jewish Achievement Quotient of 31 for Nobel Prize winners.

CHAPTER 11

Israel

1. The Population
2. Intelligence of Jews and Arabs
3. Intelligence of European and Oriental Jews
4. Education Attainment of European and Oriental Jews
5. Genetic Basis of European-Oriental IQ difference
6. Abilities of Jews and Arabs in Mathematics and Science
7. Education of European Jews, Oriental Jews, and Arabs
8. Socioeconomic status of European Jews, Oriental Jews, and Arabs
9. Nobel and Wolf Prize winners
10. Ethiopian Jews
12. Fertility of European Jews, Oriental Jews, and Arabs
13. Infant Mortality and Life Expectancy
14. Intelligence of Jews in Israel, Britain, Canada, and the United States
15. Conclusions

The contemporary state of Israel is approximately coterminous with the historic land of Palestine, the original homeland of the Jews, from which they were expelled on three occasions between the sixth century BC and the second century AD. A few remained or returned, but Arabs mainly occupied the land until the end of World War I. The Ottomans ruled it from 1516 until 1918, when the British took control of Palestine as a mandate, which was in effect a colony. In 1917, the British Foreign Secretary, Arthur Balfour, issued a statement that "His Majesty's Government views with favor the establishment in Palestine of a national home for the Jewish people and will use their best endeavors to facilitate the achievement of this object." This became known as the Balfour Declaration and encouraged the growth of the Zionist movement, whose objective was to establish a Jewish state in the territory. The British plan was to divide Palestine into two independent states, one Jewish and the other Arab. The British held discussions in an attempt to achieve this, but the Jews and Arabs could not agree on the details of the partition.

Nevertheless, during the 1920s and 1930s, a number of Jews, mainly from Russia and Eastern Europe, migrated to Palestine in the expectation that a Jewish state would eventually be established. From 1933 onward, a number of German Jews also migrated to Palestine to escape the Nazis. The 1922 census reports that 12.9 percent of the population were Jews. By 1929, this had increased, as a result of immigration, to 18.9 percent. By 1940, the census found that this had increased further to a third of the population, the remaining two thirds consisting largely of Arabs (both Christian and Muslim).

The Jewish aspiration for their own country remained unresolved until 1947, when the United Nations recommended that the British should withdraw; the country was finally partitioned into independent Jewish and Arab states. In 1948, the British did withdraw, but the Arabs refused to accept partition. In May of that year, the Jews proclaimed the establishment of the state of Israel. The Arabs objected, and the five neighboring Arab countries of Egypt, Jordan, Syria, Lebanon, and Iraq attacked in an attempt to restore the single state. The Israelis defeated them, and the state survived. However, Israel continued to be harassed by Arab and Egyptian terrorists. In 1956, to prevent incursions from Egyptian *fedayeen* (terrorists), who operated from Sinai, the Israelis invaded and occupied Egypt east of the Suez Canal. Later in the year, the Israelis withdrew and a UN international force policed the Sinai.

1. The Population

Following the establishment of Israel in 1948, a Law of Return was passed, giving all Jews worldwide the right to immigrate to the country. In the years 1948–1956, about 850,000 did so, mainly from Central and Eastern Europe, Yemen, Iraq, and North Africa. In 1956, the population consisted of 1,872,390, including about 200,000 Arabs. By 1990, the population had grown to 5,696,000 and by 2000, to approximately six million.

There are five ethnic subpopulations in Israel. These are:

(1) The Ashkenazim, mainly from Europe and the United States, and a smaller number from other countries such as South Africa. This group is about 40 percent of the population of Israel and numbers approximately 2.4 million. The Ashkenazim are sometimes called the "European Jews," but this is not accurate. The term "Ashkenazim" designates the Jews of Central and Eastern Europe and their descendants in Western Europe, North America, and elsewhere, whereas European Jews include Sephardim from the Balkans. Furthermore, the terms Ashkenazim and European Jews also include a number of Russians who pretended to be Jews in order to obtain permission to leave the Soviet Union (Abbink, 2002; Lazin, 2002). Israeli demographers estimate that only about half of the 1.8 million Russians who immigrated to Israel between 1985 and 2000 were actually Jewish (Tolts, 2003). Thus, of the 2.4 million classified as European Jews in Israel, about 1.4 million, or just about half, are Ashkenazim, about 900,000 are non-Jewish Russians, and about 110,000 are Sephardim, who escaped from the Balkans during the German occupation in the Second World War or survived the Holocaust and migrated to Israel after the end of the war.

(2) The Sephardic Jews, originally from Spain and Portugal, from which they were expelled in 1492 and 1497. Most of them settled in the Balkans, and a number also settled in the ports of the Levant (the littoral of the eastern Mediterranean). The term "Sephardim" is sometimes used to designate Jews from the Near and Middle East, but this is inaccurate. The term should be reserved for those originally from Spain and Portugal and more recently the Balkans.

(3) The Oriental Jews of Near and Middle Eastern and North African origins, most of whom migrated to Israel from Iraq and Iran, together with some from Syria, Yemen, and other countries in southwest Asia

and North Africa, largely between 1950 and 1958. In the last decade of the 20th century, these numbered approximately 2.4 million and were about 40 percent of the population. The Oriental Jews are sometimes designated the "Mizrahim," but are more commonly described as "Oriental." I shall use this term, even though it is inaccurate, as many of them came from North Africa.

(4) The Ethiopian Jews, sometimes known as the Black Jews or *Falashas*. Although they have no genetic affinity with other Jews, they were accepted as Jews by Israel in 1973 and hence acquired the right of abode in Israel. Most of them took advantage of this privilege, and by 2000, there were approximately 80,000 of them in Israel, about 1.3 percent of the population.

(5) The Arabs, who in the 1996 census, comprised 20 percent of the Israeli population and numbered approximately 1.2 million.

2. Intelligence of Jews and Arabs

There have been six studies comparing the intelligence and related cognitive ability of Jews and Arabs in Israel. These have shown that Jews have a higher IQ than Arabs by about 14 points. The studies are summarized in Table 11.1, in which the means obtained by the Arabs are expressed in relation to Jewish means set at 100 with a standard deviation of 15. Row 1 gives an IQ of 86 for Arabs in Israel, obtained in the late 1970s in the standardization sample of the Wechsler Intelligence Scale for Children-Revised (WISC-R). Rows 2 and 3 give IQs of 87 and 89 for two reasoning tests, the first nonverbal and the second verbal, for Jewish and Arab university applicants. Rows 4 and 5 give means of the same applicants of 92 for mathematics and 91 for English. These are selected samples and tend to understate the true difference; they are nevertheless closely similar to the difference shown in row 1. Row 6 shows the mean score of 87 on a test of general knowledge of osteoporosis of Arab and Jewish women who had attended an outpatient clinic for women's health and were surveyed in 1999. The result can be regarded as a test of general knowledge, which is an important component of intelligence. Only the study given in row 1 is based on a representative sample of the population; the IQ of 86 is therefore adopted as the best reading of the IQ of Israeli Arabs in relation to 100 for Jews.

Table 11.1. IQs of Jews and Arabs

Age	Test	N. Jews	N. Arabs	Arab IQ	Reference
6–16	WISC-R	2111	639	86	Leiblich & Kugelmass, 1981
20–24	Reasoning: NV	1778	1017	87	Zeidner, 1987a
20–24	Reasoning: V	1778	1017	89	Zeidner, 1987a
20–24	Mathematics	1778	1017	92	Zeidner, 1987a
20–24	English	1778	1017	91	Zeidner, 1987a
53	Knowledge	176	80	87	Werner, 2003

The lower IQ of Arabs compared with that of Jews is expressed in their higher rate of mental retardation (0.8 percent compared with 0.4 percent among Jews), and also in their overrepresentation in classes for slow learners. In the 1990s, Arabs were 20 percent of children in Israeli schools, but 25–30 percent of children in classes for slow learners (Dinero, 2002).

3. Intelligence of European and Oriental Jews

A number of studies have shown that European Jews have higher IQs than Oriental Jews. These are summarized in Table 11.2, which expresses the means obtained by the Oriental Jews in relation to a European Jewish mean of 100 with a standard deviation of 15. Row 1 gives an IQ of 84 for 5-year-old Oriental Jewish children on the Full Scale IQ of the Israeli standardization of the Wechsler Intelligence Scale for Children (WISC). Rows 2 and 3 give the verbal and performance IQs of 84 and 86, respectively, in the same study and show that the Oriental Jews were not significantly handicapped verbally. Rows 4 and 5 give smaller European-Oriental differences of 91 (verbal) and 94 (nonverbal) on the Milta test (an Israeli test). Row 6 gives results from the Israeli standardization of the Wechsler Preschool and Primary Test (WPPSI) for children aged 4–6 years and shows that Oriental Jewish children had an IQ of 87. These were children whose fathers had come from the Middle East or from North Africa. There was little difference in the IQs of the two groups, who obtained IQs of 88 and 86, respectively. Row 7 gives a verbal IQ of 84 for a small sample of 9-year-old Oriental Jewish children. Row 8 gives an IQ of 84 for a sample of 4-year-old Oriental Jewish children. Row 9 gives an IQ of 85, derived from the standardization sample of the WISC. Row 10 gives an IQ of 90 for 5-year-old Oriental children, but these were from high socioeconomic status families matched to Europeans, so the IQ difference is reduced. The studies are in close agreement. If the study in row 10 is discarded on the grounds the samples were not representative (as well as being very small), the median gap between European and Oriental Jewish children is 15 IQ points. Five of the studies (rows 4, 5, 6, 8, and 10) are on preschool children and show the same difference as in older children, suggesting that the lower IQ of Oriental children cannot be attributed to poorer schools.

Table 11.2. IQs of Oriental and European Jewish children

	Age	Test	N. European	N. Oriental	Oriental IQ	Reference
1	5	WISC: FS	75	138	84	Smilansky, 1957
2	5	WISC: Verb	75	138	84	Smilansky, 1957
3	5	WISC: Perf	75	138	86	Smilansky, 1957
4	3-6	Milta-Verbal	115	195	91	Ortar et al., 1966
5	3-6	Milta-N.Verbal	115	195	94	Ortar et al., 1966
6	4-6	WPPSI IQ	186	443	87	Leiblich et al., 1972
7	9	WISC: Verb	41	41	84	Gill, 1974
8	4	Stanford-Binet	187	450	84	Smilansky et al., 1976
9	6-16	WISC	363	715	85	Gafni, 1978
10	5	WPPSI IQ	36	27	90	Gross, 1978

Table 11.3 gives mean scores, calculated from Burg and Belmont (1990), on verbal, reasoning, numerical, and spatial abilities for 6-to-7-year-old children whose fathers had come from Europe, Iraq, North Africa, and Yemen. The scores are expressed in terms of means of 50 and standard deviations of 10 for the groups for each test. The children had all been born in Israel in 1964 and had attended kindergarten and primary

schools. There were 80 children in each of the four groups, of whom 40 came from middle class and 40 from lower-class families. The effect of this is that they were not representative of the four ethnic groups for socioeconomic status because European Jews have higher socioeconomic status than the three groups of Orientals. Matching the groups for socioeconomic status disguises the magnitude of the group differences present in representative samples. Nevertheless, the Europeans obtained generally higher scores and a higher overall mean than the other three groups, consistent with the results given in Table 11.2. The interest of the study lies in the size of the differences on verbal, reasoning, numerical, and spatial abilities. The Europeans scored much higher than the three groups of Orientals on verbal ability, somewhat higher on reasoning and numerical abilities, but not so much higher on spatial ability. In fact, on spatial ability, the Iraqis scored fractionally higher than the Europeans. This pattern of the abilities of European Jews is similar to that found in an American study, in which Jewish children in New York were compared with Chinese, Blacks, and Puerto Ricans (Lesser, Fifer, & Clark, 1965).

Table 11.3. Abilities of European and Oriental Jews

Group	Verbal	Reasoning	Number	Spatial	Mean
European	55.5	53.4	52.7	52.0	53.4
Iraqi	50.4	51.7	50.5	52.3	51.2
North African	47.5	46.5	48.9	48.8	47.9
Yemeni	46.6	48.4	47.6	46.8	47.3

Jewish children scored much higher than the other three groups on verbal ability, about the same as the Chinese on reasoning and numerical abilities, but below the Chinese on spatial ability. It appears, therefore, that the European Jews have particularly strong verbal ability and somewhat less strong reasoning and numerical abilities, but their spatial ability is not nearly so good, not only compared with Oriental Jews but also with other racial groups, namely, Chinese, Blacks, and Puerto Ricans. This pattern of European Jewish abilities confirms the theory that these abilities evolved because they found a niche in Europe as money-lenders and tax farmers, for which verbal, reasoning, and numerical abilities were required, and were excluded from the craft occupations for which spatial ability is required. (This theory is discussed further in Chapter 20.)

Table 11.4 gives IQs for reasoning and verbal ability and an EQ for mathematics and the Grade Point Average (GPA) obtained by European and Oriental Jewish applicants to university in 1983. These figures have been calculated from data published by Zeidner (1987b). The applicants had an average age of 24 years and were not representative of the populations because fewer Oriental Jews apply to university, making this group more exclusive and therefore reducing the differences between Oriental and European Jews. Thus, Orientals in the study are only four IQ points lower on reasoning and three EQ points lower on mathematics, although they were 13 IQ points lower on verbal ability. This confirms the results given in Table 11.3, showing that the European Jews are particularly strong on verbal ability. Row 4 gives the grade point average (GPA) of the Oriental Jews at the university and shows that this was lower than that of the European Jews by three points. The author notes that "the mean academic performance for the Oriental Jewish group was at least as low as predicted by test scores"; hence, "the cultural bias hypothesis–contending that standardized aptitude tests are systematically biased against minority groups–was once again disconfirmed" (Zeidner, 1987b, p. 47).

Table 11.4. Mean IQs and EQs of European and Oriental Jewish college applicants and students

Test	N. European	N. Oriental	Oriental IQ/EQ
Reasoning	773	503	96
Mathematics	773	503	97
Verbal	773	503	87
GPA	773	503	97

Further evidence on intelligence differences between European and Oriental university students at Technion, the Israeli University of Technology, has been published by Y. Rim (1983) and is summarized in Table 11.5. He provides scores for tests of verbal IQ, nonverbal reasoning (measured by the Dominos Test), mechanical ability and number series, a test of reasoning with numbers.

Table 11.5. Mean IQs of European and Oriental students at Technion

Tests	European	Oriental	Sig.
Number	180	144	-
Verbal IQ	52.52	48.41	0.01
Nonverbal IQ	33.41	32.26	0.05
Mechanical IQ	12.54	10.57	0.01
Number Series	7.54	6.52	0.01

The standard deviation of the verbal IQ is 10, so the difference between European and Oriental Jews is 0.411 standard deviations or the equivalent of 6.2 IQ points. The report does not give standard deviations for the remaining three tests, but the significance levels are lower than for the verbal IQ, so the European-Oriental Jewish differences are evidently a little smaller. Once again, the Europeans are particularly strong on verbal ability. These samples of university students are selected for high intelligence, so the IQ difference is less than in general population samples.

4. *Educational Attainment of European and Oriental Jews*

European Jews have higher educational attainment than Orientals, consistent with their higher IQs. Y. Dar and N. Resh summarized studies of the differences in educational attainment (1991). They are shown in Table 11.6, which gives Oriental educational quotients (EQ) in relation to European quotients of 100. The median EQ of the Orientals in the 12 studies is 88, fractionally higher than the median IQ of 85. This suggests that the lower IQ of the Oriental Jews is largely responsible for their lower educational attainment.

The evidence is conflicting on whether the gap in educational attainment between European and Oriental Jews decreases with assimilation in Israel. In her study of 13-year-olds on tests of geography, arithmetic, Bible studies, language, and history, Gina Ortar (1967) divided her sample into two groups: those whose fathers had been born in Israel and those who had been born outside Israel. Both groups of Oriental Jewish children had the same mean educational quotient, showing that being reared and educated in Israel had no advantageous effect on their educational attainment. However, among the European Jewish children, those born in Israel had an educational quotient five IQ points higher than those born outside Israel. The explanation for this may be that being reared and educated in Israel had an advantageous effect on their educational attainment. Alternatively, it may be that more recent immigrants had lower IQs than earlier immigrants and transmitted these to their children.

Table 11.6. Educational attainment (EQ) of Oriental Jewish children

Year	Age	Test	EQ	Reference
1954–1967	14	Seker	86	Ortar, 1967
1963	14	Language	85	Smilansly & Yam, 1969
1963	14	Mathematics	87	Smilansly & Yam, 1969
1969–1971	11	General	87	Levy & Chen, 1976
1971	7	Reading	85	Smilansly & Shefatiya, 1977
1972	15	English	88	Levi et al., 1978
1973	14	General	87	Chen et al., 1978
1975	6–12	Reading	90	Eshel, 1980
1980	14	General	91	Chen, 1983
1982	11	Science	93	Zuzovsky, 1987
1983	15	Science	91	Levin, 1988
1985	12	General	92	Chen, 1987

In contrast to Ortar's results, Avram Minkowitch, Dan Davis, and Joseph Bashi (1982) found that the gap in educational attainment between European and Oriental Jews decreased from the first to the second generation. Their sample consisted of 12-year-olds tested in reading, mathematics, and geography and the results are shown in Table 11.7. It will be seen that the attainment of the Oriental Jews improved in the second generation in reading and mathematics, though not in geography.

Table 11.7. Educational attainment of first and second-generation Oriental Jews

Generation	N.	Reading	Mathematics	Geography
First	2753	87	88	85
Second	423	90	93	85

5. Genetic Basis of European-Oriental IQ Difference

Summarizing research on the IQs of the European and Oriental Jews brought up from early infancy in the same kibbutzim, Miles Storfer presented evidence that there is a substantial genetic basis of the European-Oriental IQ difference (1990, p. 221). Children of European parents had much higher IQs than the children of Oriental parents, while the children of mixed European-Oriental parents had IQs intermediate between the two. Unfortunately, Storfer did not report mean IQs of the three groups but only the percentages of children with IQs above 128, 120, and 110. Furthermore, he reported the percentages for the three groups broken down by the fathers' educational level into high-school graduates (n=401) and those with elementary school only or less (n=268). Nevertheless, the results are informative and are shown in Table 11.8. We can see that at both educational levels the children with two European parents had substantially greater proportions at all three levels of intelligence; the children with one European parent came next, while the children with two Oriental parents had the smallest proportions. The average of the two percentages of children of European parents with IQs above 128 is 18.6, indicating that the mean IQ of these must have been about 115. The average of the two percentages of children of two Oriental parents with IQs above 128 is 2.7, indicating that the mean IQ of these must have been about 100. Thus the mean IQs of these two groups differ by about 15 points, virtually exactly the same as the differences shown in Table 11.2. Since these children were all brought up in the same kibbutzim environment, the only conclusion that can be drawn is that the IQ differences must be wholly genetically determined. The mean IQs of the total sample are evidently somewhat higher than 100 and appear to be approximately 107.5 (the average of the children of the High School graduates and Elementary School fathers). The reason for this is that the test used in the study was the 1947 American WISC, and the norms were outdated by the Flynn effect.

Table 11.8. IQs of kibbutzim children with European and Oriental parents (percentages)

High School Graduates	128+	120+	110+
Both Parents European	26.1	47.0	71.2
One Parent European	19.7	42.3	74.6
Both Parents Oriental	0.4	40.8	65.2
Elementary School			
Both Parents European	11.2	28.0	46.4
One Parent European	8.4	31.3	48.2
Both Parents Oriental	5.0	12.5	27.6

The greater proportion of children among those with high IQs whose fathers were High School graduates must also be a genetic effect. This result confirms several studies carried out in Britain and the United States, in which the intelligence of children brought up in orphanages were found to be related to the socioeconomic status of their fathers. In the first of these studies, D.C. Jones and A.M. Carr-Saunders (1927) in Britain reported that these children with professional fathers had an average IQ of 107; the IQs of the children fell with declining socioeconomic status of their fathers to 93 for the children of laborers. I have summarized several other studies showing the same phenomenon in my book *Dysgenics* (1996).

6. Abilities of Jews and Arabs in Mathematics and Science

The Third International Mathematics and Science Study consisted of the collection of scores on tests of 14-year-olds in 49 countries. The results are given for mathematics and for science by Martin, Mullis, Gonzales, and Chrostowski (2004). Among the countries were Israel and the Palestine National Authority (which was treated as a country for the study's purpose). The mean scores of the Israelis were substantially higher than those of the Palestinians. The means are given in Table 11.9, together with the standard deviations for the set of 49 countries. The bottom row gives the "ds," i.e. the differences between the Israelis and the Palestinians expressed in standard deviation units. The IQ difference between Jews and Arabs shown in Table 11.2 is 16 IQ points and is the equivalent of 10.7d. Thus, the advantage of the Israelis over the Palestinians is greater for mathematics but less for science, as compared with the IQ difference. However, the average of the mathematics and science (10.2d) is almost the same as the IQ difference.

Table 11.9. Abilities of Jews and Arabs in Math and Science

Country	Number	Math	Science
Israel	385	395.20	438.8
Palestine	504	492.40	489.0
SD	-	73.00	70.0
d	-	1.33	0.71

7. Education of European Jews, Oriental Jews, and Arabs

Education was made free and compulsory for all Israeli children between the ages of five and 13 by law in 1956. However, more European Jews have chosen to continue into secondary and tertiary education than Oriental Jews and Arabs. Studies showing this are summarized in Table 11.10. Rows 1 and 2 give results from the 1961 census for the percentages of Oriental and European Jews who had completed nine years of school; for both sexes, the percentage of Europeans with such educational attainment was about twice as high as that for Orientals. Row 3 gives the percentages of Oriental and European Jewish school students passing the matriculation examination in 1970 and shows a considerably greater rate of success for the Europeans than for Orientals (80.6 percent as compared with 58.4 percent).

Table 11.10. Education of European and Oriental Jews and Arabs

	Education	Year	European	Oriental	Arabs
1	9 Years school: men	1961	48.0	28.0	-
2	9 Years school: women	1961	38.0	13.0	-
3	Matriculation	1970	80.6	58.4	-
4	Years schooling: men	1974	11.1	8.1	5.9
5	Years schooling: men	1983	12.8	9.9	8.4
6	Years schooling: women	1983	13.3	10.1	10.6
7	University degree	1983	17.4	3.4	-
8	Years schooling: men	1993	14.2	11.7	9.6
9	University graduates: men	1995	31.0	10.0	-
10	University graduates: women	1995	47.0	20.0	-
11	University students	1998	40.3	27.1	-
12	Ph.D. students	1998	58.1	15.7	-

Sources: rows 1–2: Friedlander et al., 2002; row 3: Eisikovits, 1997; row 4: Kraus & Hodge, 1990; row 5–6: Neuman, 1998; 7: Schmelz, Della Pergola & Avner (1990); row 8: Haberfeld & Cohen, 1998; 9–10: Cohen & Haberfeld, 2004; 11–12: Yisraeli, 1998.

Row 4 gives the average years of education of men of the three groups found in 1974 and shows that the Europeans had the most years of education, followed by the Orientals; the Arabs had the least. Rows 5 and 6 give the average years of education of men and women of the three groups found in the 1983 census and show that for both men and women, Europeans had the greatest amount of education, followed among men by the Orientals; the Arabs had the least education. Among women, however, the Arabs had about five months more education than the Orientals. Row 7 shows that in 1983, a much higher percentage of Europeans (17.4) had university degrees than of Orientals (3.4: 3.8 percent from Asia and 3.0 percent from North Africa). Row 8 shows that in 1992, the same differences in years of education remained between the Europeans, the Orientals, and the Arabs.

Rows 9 and 10 give percentages from the 1995 census for third-generation Israelis who were university graduates. Three times as many European men as Orientals were graduates; among women, nearly two and a half times as many were graduates. These results revealed that even among those who are acculturated to Israeli society, a substantial gap in educational attainment remains between the Europeans and the Orientals. Rows 10 and 11 show that in 1998, the percentages of university students who were European were much higher than the percentages who were Oriental; among PhD students, the disparity was even greater. These figures are for those born in Europe and the Near East (including North Africa), respectively.

The percentages of Orientals among university students in different faculties in 1999 have been given by Hanna David (2003) and are shown in Table 11.11.

Table 11.11. Percentages of Oriental university students, 1999

Subject	% Oriental	Subject	% Oriental
Medicine	18	Engineering	22
Science/Math	19	Social Science	30
Law	21	Humanities	33

Arabs were 9.6 percent of all students and the remainders were European. It is apparent that the Europeans were most heavily overrepresented in the more prestigious faculties of medicine and science, together with math, law, and engineering, with about 80 percent of the students. They were considerably overrepresented, although less so, in the less prestigious faculties of social science and humanities. The percentages of Orientals are intermediate between the European Jews and the Arabs.

There is a widespread consensus among Israeli social scientists that the Oriental Jews have been disadvantaged and discriminated against by the Europeans and that with time they would gradually improve their position. Whether this has occurred has been investigated by Savit, Cohen, Steir, and Bolotin (1999), who examined the percentages of 30-to-34-year-olds in the 1946-1962 birth cohorts who became university graduates. They confined their analysis to those born in Israel and subdivided the Orientals into Asians (including Egyptians) and North Africans. Their results for men are shown in Table 11.12 and for women in Table 11.13. The percentage of European men who became university graduates remained stable at approximately 30 percent over the 16-year period. The percentage of Asians increased from 12 to 15 percent, and the percentage of North Africans also increased from one to seven percent. Table 11.13 shows similar trends for women. Oriental Jews improved their position relative to Europeans, and Asians have done considerably better than North Africans. Nevertheless, even among the youngest cohort, the Europeans were still much more successful academically than the Orientals.

Table 11.12. Percentages of male university graduates

Group	1946	1954	1962
European	30	28	31
Asian	12	10	15
N. African	1	5	7

Table 11.13. Percentages of female university graduates

Group	1946	1954	1962
European	26	27	30
Asian	4	5	13
N. African	3	4	6

Further data for the education of European and Oriental Jews and Arabs together with their average earnings were obtained in income surveys of representative samples in 1975 and 2001 and have been given by Yinon Cohen and Yitchak Haberfeld (2003). The data are for employed men aged 25–54 and are shown in Table 11.14. In both years, the Europeans had the most education and the highest average monthly earnings; the Orientals came next; and the Arabs were at the bottom in both categories. The gap in years of education was reduced over the quarter century, but the gap in earnings increased. For instance, Europeans earned slightly less than twice as much as Arabs in 1975, but in 2001, they earned more than twice as much. The authors attribute this to the increased demand for skilled men, which pushed up salaries. As European Jews have more skills than Oriental Jews and Arabs, their earnings have risen more. They do not mention that there has been an increased demand for those with higher IQs.

Table 11.14. Education and earnings of European and Oriental Jews and Arabs

Year	Measure	Europeans	Orientals	Arabs
1975	Years education	13.7	10.3	7.6
1975	Earnings	5,210	4,041	3,559
2001	Years education	14.8	12.9	11.8
2001	Earnings	13,103	9,077	5,854

8. Socioeconomic Status of European and Oriental Jews and Arabs

European Jews have acheived, on average, a higher socioeconomic status than Oriental Jews. In 1966, 38 percent of European Jews worked in white-collar occupations, compared with 16 percent of Oriental Jews. By 2004, 58 percent of European Jews worked in white-collar occupations, compared with 49 percent of Oriental Jews (Della Pergola, 2007). Thus the gap between European and Oriental Jews narrowed over these 42 years, but was not completely closed.

Arabs do less well than Jews in socioeconomic status. Differences in socioeconomic status of European Jews, Oriental Jews, and Arabs are shown in Table 11.15. Row 1 gives the percentages of the three populations working in professional occupations found in a labor force survey carried out in 1955; European Jews had the highest percentage (8.5), followed by the Arabs (4.6), while the Orientals had the lowest percentage (3.4). Row 2 gives similar data from a labor force survey in 1974, showing again that the Europeans had a much higher percentage in professional occupations (27.0) than the Orientals (7.8). Arabs had a slightly higher proportion

166   THE CHOSEN PEOPLE

in professional occupations (8.5) in this survey, as in 1955. Row 3 gives the percentages of the three populations working in unskilled and service occupations found in the labor force survey of 1974 and shows that Europeans had the lowest percentage (8.4), followed by the Orientals (21.1), while the Arabs had the highest percentage (23.3). Row 4 gives the percentages of the three populations working in professional occupations in the labor force survey in 1986 and shows once again that Europeans had the highest percentage (36.2), but this time the Orientals had the next highest percentage (14.6), while the Arabs had the lowest percentage (10.3). Evidently the Orientals had gained some ground as compared with the Arabs over the 31-year period 1955–1986.

Table 11.15. Socioeconomic status of Arabs and Jews

Socioeconomic Status	Year	Arab	Oriental	European
Professional %	1955	4.6	3.4	8.5
Professional %	1974	8.5	7.8	27.0
Unskilled & service %	1974	23.3	21.1	8.4
Professional %	1986	10.3	14.6	36.2
Low status: men %	1983	21.8	28.0	15.3
Low status: women %	1983	36.5	41.1	18.0
Hourly wage: men	1983	118.0	152	219.0
Hourly wage: women	1983	133.0	132	180.0
Sources: rows 1–4: Kraus & Hodge, 1990; rows 5–8: Neuman, 1998				

Rows 5 and 6 give socioeconomic data from the 1983 census for the percentages of men and women from the three groups engaged in low-status occupations. Among men (row 5), Europeans had the lowest percentage (15.3), followed by the Arabs (21.8), while the Oriental Jews had the highest percentage (28.0). The same gradient is present for women shown in row 6. Rows 7 and 8 give the average hourly wage in shekels of men and women of the three populations found in the 1983 census. For men and women, Europeans had the highest wages. Among men, the Europeans were followed by Orientals and then the Arabs. Among women, however, the Arabs had fractionally higher average wages than the Orientals. These results are consistent with the differences in education and demonstrate the association between education and earnings that has frequently been found.

9. Nobel and Wolf Prize winners

Six Israelis have won Nobel Prizes, and two have received the Wolf Prize for outstanding work in mathematics. This is quite an impressive record, working out to approximately 1.4 Nobel laureates per million Israelis, a rate considerably better than that of any other country. (Britain comes next in the second half of the 20th century with 58 Prize winners from a population of about 57 million.) The Israeli Prize winners are listed in Table 11.16. All of them are Ashkenazi.

Table 11.16. Israeli Nobel and Wolf Prize winners

Year	Name	Subject	Year	Name	Subject
1966	Samuel Agnon	Literature	2004	Avram Hershko	Chemistry
1990	I. Piatetski-Shapiro	Mathmatics	2005	Robert Aumann	Economics
1999	Daniel Kahneman	Economics	2007	Halkin Furstenberg	Mathematics
2004	Aaron Ciechanover	Chemistry	2009	Ada Yonath	Chemistry

10. Ethiopian Jews

The Ethiopian or Black Jews are Jewish by religion rather than by descent. They are not genetically related to the other Jews, but converted to Judaism many centuries ago. In Ethiopia, "[t]hey lived in small villages and made their living in agriculture and craftsmanship; most of the older generation were illiterate" (Ben-David & Ben-Ari, 1997, p. 511). The Israeli government recognized them as Jews in the 1970s and permitted them to migrate to Israel. By 1998, virtually all of them had done so. In the year 2000, the number of Ethiopian Jews in Israel was approximately 80,000, representing some 1.4 percent of the population.

There have been three studies of the intelligence of the Ethiopian Jews in Israel and these are summarized in Table 11.17. The first sample of

15-year-olds assessed by the Standard Progressive Matrices one year after they arrived in Israel obtained a British IQ of 68; a second sample of 14-16-year-olds, who had been in Israel for four or more years and were attending Israeli boarding schools, obtained a British IQ of 66. These IQs are about the same as those of sub-Saharan Africans throughout the continent (see Lynn, 2006). These results suggest that education in Western schools does not benefit the African IQ. Row 3 gives the results of the third study of the IQ of Ethiopian Jews consisting of a small sample of 29 6-7-year-olds tested with the Colored Progressive Matrices. These obtained a higher IQ of 86. Part of the explanation for this higher IQ is that the Colored Progressive Matrices gives higher IQs for young children because it measures visualization rather than problem-solving ability (Lynn, Allik and Irwing, 2004). Africans also typically perform better on visualization tasks. Further, it is a small sample of only 29 and therefore not very reliable. The weighted average of the three studies is an IQ of 69 and can be adopted as the best reading of the IQ of Ethiopian Jews in Israel.

Table 11.17. IQs of Ethiopian Jews in Israel

Age	N.	Test	IQ	Reference
15	250	SPM	68	Kaniel & Fisherman, 1991
14–16	46	SPM	66	Kozulin, 1998
6–7	29	CPM	86	Tuzuriel & Kaufman, 1999

The Ethiopian Jews in Israel have all the characteristics of a low IQ population. They are a social problem and "make up one of Israel's poorest communities" (Clayton, 2000, p. 12).

> Many are not equipped with sufficient language, professional and social skills for Israeli society. There is a large proportion of Ethiopians living in relative poverty, and many do not or cannot improve themselves; the number of high school drop-outs as well as crime figures among the young are rising significantly.... In the 1990s, Ethiopian youth gangs made their appearance, terrorizing shopkeepers and neighborhoods.

Ethiopian Jews identify with an "aggressive and semi-criminal African-American youth culture" and have become "a kind of ethnic underclass" (Abbink, 2002, p. 13).

A report on the social problems of the Ethiopian immigrants has been issued by the Brookdale Institute (2004) based on a survey of about 15,000 Ethiopians in eight Israeli cities. The principal findings were: (1) In 2004, Ethiopians accounted for 4.1 percent (933 of 22,839) of juvenile crimes—double the proportion of Ethiopians in Israel's youth population. (2) Each Ethiopian immigrant costs the taxpayers about $100,000 over the course of his or her lifetime. (3) Thirty percent of the Ethiopian family units are single-parent families compared with nine percent for Israel (Lazin, 2002). (4) Ethiopian Israelis have a school dropout rate of six percent, compared to four percent among the general Jewish population. (5) At age 17, some 25 percent of Ethiopians in 2002 were not in schools under the auspices of the Ministry of Education compared to about 15 percent of all 17 year-old Israeli youth. (This statistic is based on data from the Ministry of Education on the number of Ethiopian students in school and on estimates from the Central Bureau of Statistics on the size of the age cohorts.)

(6) Poor school achievement: according to the national achievement tests of the Ministry of Education in 2002, some 75–80 percent of the Ethiopian children in fifth and eighth grades were below the national average in English, Science, Mathematics, and Hebrew. A national study was conducted in 2000 for the Ministry of Education on achievements of Ethiopian children in fifth, eighth, and 11th grades. It found that the average achievement scores in Mathematics and Hebrew of Ethiopian children are 60–70 percent of the average of all Jewish children in the fifth grade and declined to 40–60 percent of the average in the 11th grade. Data from the national evaluation survey of 2003 found that the average scores of Ethiopian children aged three in language and basic concepts were some 70 percent of the scores of all Israeli children. At ages five, six, and eight, the average scores of Ethiopian children in language skills were 62 percent, 56 percent, and 43 percent of the average scores of Israeli children, respectively. In mathematics, the scores of Ethiopian children at ages five, six, and eight were 65 percent, 60 percent, and 39 percent of the average scores.

(7) High School Matriculation Exams: Ethiopians do poorly in the matriculation exams taken at the end of high school, which are the basis for acceptance to higher education. Table 11.18 shows pass

rates for 2003 for Ethiopian and for all Israeli 17-year-olds for the matriculation pass rate (Level 1) and the higher-level pass rate (Level 2) required for university entry. Thirty-one percent of Ethiopians achieved a Level 1 pass compared with 52 percent of all Israeli students, while 13 percent of Ethiopians achieved a Level 2 pass compared with 45 percent of all Israeli students.

Table 11.18. Matriculation pass rates in 2003

Pass rates	Ethiopians	All Israelis
Level 1	31	52
Level 2	13	45

Source: Myers-JDC-Brookdale Institute: analysis of Ministry of Education data

The authors of the report comment:

> These findings reinforce the need for a greater effort to enhance the educational achievement of Ethiopian Israelis and reduce the educational gaps. At the same time the findings also point to an opportunity. They reveal that there is a large group who has successfully passed the matriculation exams, yet not at the level that meets university requirements. There is a high probability that with extra assistance they can take this significant additional step ahead.

(8) Employment rates: in 2003, about 45 percent of Ethiopian men age 18–64 were employed. This is a decline from 54 percent in 1995–1996. This decline reflects the growing difficulties that unskilled workers have experienced in Israel in the last decade. Among women of the same ages, there was an increase in employment from 24 percent in 1995–1996 to 32 percent in 2003. This reflects a significant increase in the number of women looking for work, which is particularly influenced by their length of stay in Israel. Indeed, along with the increase in those employed, there was a significant increase in the percentage of Ethiopian women who were looking for work but still unemployed. The authors of the report comment: "There is a serious concern that the immigrants may develop a reliance on public assistance rather than becoming integrated into the labor force."

(9) Family structure and size: some 60 percent of Ethiopian families have five or more children (ages 0-18); 20 percent of families with children are single parent; a large percentage of single-parent families have three or more children.

(10) Hebrew proficiency: about 45 percent of Ethiopian parents are unable to hold a simple conversation in Hebrew, and most (about 75 percent) are unable to read or write simple Hebrew. This is true even of a large proportion of those who have been in the country for a relatively long time.

(11) Demographic status: some measures obtained in a 1995 survey of the socioeconomic status of Ethiopians compared with all Israelis are summarized in Table 11.19. Rows 1 through 4 show the low levels of education of the Ethiopians. Row 5 shows the higher percentage of single-parent families (18 percent compared with 10 percent). Row 6 shows that 41 percent of Ethiopian children were being raised in families without an earner and were therefore dependent on welfare support, compared with only nine percent of all Israeli children.

Table 11.19. Demographic status of Ethiopian and all Israeli children in 1995 (percentages)

Demographic status	Ethiopian Children	All Israeli Children
Father's education	-	-
No education	61.0	3.3
Education 1–8 years	20.0	14.7
Education 13+ years	5.6	35.0
Single–parent families	18.0	10.0
No earner	41.0	9.0
Source: Brookdale Institute, special analysis of 1995 National Census of the Central Bureau of Statistics		

(12) Delinquency: the most reliable data on the delinquency rate of Ethiopian children are for 1996, when a police file was opened for 2.6 percent of Ethiopian children, as opposed to 1.4 percent of non-Ethiopians. It was found that Ethiopian children become delinquent at an earlier age and have more offences on average than do non-Ethiopian offenders.

(13) Military service: the report notes, "the serious problems of Ethiopian families impact on Army service...and about 25 percent do not complete their Army service." (It does not give the corresponding figure for all Israelis.)

The authors of the report conclude:

> There are a number of worrying trends among Ethiopian youth. The special characteristics and challenges facing Ethiopian families place many of them in risk situations. About half the families are known to the social service departments and receive assistance for a variety of needs, ranging from household equipment to help with difficulties in the functioning of the family. Because of the difficulties facing the families, the percentage of Ethiopian children known to the social services is three times the percentage found in the general population, reaching a third of all Ethiopian children. In light of the special difficulties faced by the immigrants from Ethiopia, Israel adopted a strategy of affirmative action and from the beginning provided special assistance beyond that available to other immigrants. This is consistent with the overall framework of differential assistance to immigrant groups within absorption policy in Israel.

The authors of the report fail to note the low IQ of the Ethiopian immigrants and that this goes a long way toward explaining the social problems of poor educational attainment, high unemployment, single motherhood, and high rates of crime. There is considerable reluctance to acknowledge, or even mention, the low IQs of Ethiopian Jews in Israel. Girma Berhanu is an Ethiopian working at Göteborg University in Sweden who has attempted to analyze why the Ethiopian Jews do poorly at school. He contends that the problem is that "Ethiopian students are in a state of identity crisis as they grapple with two cultural systems and structures of meaning which confuse their sense of direction."

> In the process, meaningfully propelled learning dispositions and an affectively driven urge to achieve scholastic excellence deteriorate. Thus, the lagging academic performance of these children is partly caused by the school system, which has little knowledge of the way these children and their parents feel and think in terms of identity, belongingness and negotiation of meaning. It is not that Ethiopian students are unmotivated; they work hard to achieve excellence. It is more that the process of learning a new code of behavior, values

and school culture is taking place rapidly without the original culture's active participation as a basic link and a vehicle for further learning. (Berhanu, 2005, p. 51)

The Ethiopian Jews have several of the characteristics of the Black underclass in the United States and Britain, including low average IQs, poor educational attainment, and high rates of unemployment, single motherhood, crime, and HIV infection (Pollack, 1993). The Ethiopian Jews have become ghettoized because many white Jews prefer not to live in communities with a large number of black Jews (Lavin, 2000).

11. Fertility of European and Oriental Jews and Arabs

From the foundation of the state of Israel, the Oriental Jews have had higher fertility than the European Jews, and fertility has been still higher among the Arabs. These fertility differences are shown for the years 1950–2007 in Table 11.20.

Table 11.20. Fertility of the European and Oriental Jews and Arabs

Year	Jews born in Europe/ America	Jews born in Asia/ Africa	Jews born in Israel	Jews born in Israel; father, Europe/ America	Jews born in Israel; father, Asia/ Africa	Arabs
1950	3.28	5.69	3.94	-	-	
1960	2.38	5.10	2.76	-	-	9.31
1970	2.84	4.07	3.12	2.95	3.14	8.95
1980	2.75	3.04	2.76	2.68	2.79	5.98
1990	2.31	3.09	2.76	2.73	2.81	4.70
2000	2.25	3.20	2.78	2.58	2.62	4.74
2007	-	-	2.80	-	-	3.90

Source: Israel Central Bureau of Statistics; della Pergola (2009)

The fertility difference between the Europeans and Orientals has been partly due to the more efficient use of contraception by the Europeans. A survey carried out in 1988 found that 38 percent of unmarried European young women born in Israel used contraception during their first sexual experience, compared with only 20 percent of Orientals (Wilder, 2000). This is itself partly attributable to the difference in intelligence. The fertility of all three groups has declined over the 25 years and the differences have converged. The difference between the European and the Oriental Jews had virtually disappeared by the year 2000 for those born in Israel, although the fertility of those born in Asia and Africa was about 43 percent greater than of those born in Europe. By the year 2000, the fertility of the Arabs had also declined, but remained above that of the Jews.

12. *Infant Mortality and Life Expectancy*

Jews enjoy better health than Arabs, as indexed by rates of infant mortality and life expectancy. Differences between Arabs and Jews in infant mortality have been published for 1977 through 1999 by Dov Chernichovsky and Jon Anson (2005) and are shown in Table 11.21. Throughout the period, the rate of infant mortality of Arabs was more than double that of Jews. The Israeli National Health Insurance Act of 1995 gave free medical care to all Israeli residents, including Arabs, but this evidently did not reduce the different rates for Arabs and Jews.

Table 11.21. Infant mortality per 1,000 births

Year	Arabs	Jews
1977	32	14
1987	17	8
1999	9	4

Chernichovsky and Anson have also published life expectancy for Arabs and Jews from 1975 through 2001. The figures for these are shown in Table 11.22. Throughout this period, life expectancy was greater for Jews by three or four years. Life expectancy was greater for women than for men, as is invariably the case.

Table 11.22. Life expectancy of Arabs and Jews

Year	Sex	Arabs	Jews
1975	Men	68	71
1975	Women	71	74
1987	Men	73	75
1987	Women	75	78
2001	Men	68	78
2001	Women	78	82

13. Intelligence of Jews in Israel, Britain, Canada, and the United States

We now consider the question of how the intelligence of European and Oriental Jews in Israel compares with that of European Jews in Britain and the United States. There are no studies that give direct evidence on this question, but it can be answered indirectly. To do this, we need to look first at studies of intelligence in Israel in relation to the "Greenwich standard" IQ of 100 for intelligence in Britain. Eight such studies are summarized in Table 11.23.

Table 11.23. Intelligence in Israel

Age	N.	Test	IQ	Reference
13–14	200	WISC	95	Ortar, 1952
11–15	267	SPM	95	Moyles & Wolins, 1973
10–12	180	Lorge-Thorndike	97	Miron, 1977
10–12	268	SPM	95	Globerson, 1983
11	2,781	SPM	89	Lancer & Rim, 1984
5	52	CPM	96	Tzuriel & Caspi, 1992
9–15	1,740	SPM	90	Lynn, 1994
13	-	SPM	96	Kazulin, 1998

The IQs lie in the range of 89–97, with a median of 95. We can adopt this as the IQ of Israel. Approximately half of the Jews in Israel are European Jews; the other half are Orientals. Ten studies carried out in Israel summarized in Table 11.2 have found that the Orientals have a mean IQ approximately 15 IQ points lower than the European Jews. From these figures, it can be estimated that the European Jews in Israel have a mean IQ of 106; Oriental Jews have a mean IQ of 91 (15 IQ points lower). The combination of both groups gives an IQ of 98 for Jews in Israel.

Arabs make up approximately 20 percent of the population of Israel; their IQ of 84 is 14 points below that of Israeli Jews (as shown in Table 11.1, row 1). This is not surprising, since it is the same as the IQ of other southwest Asian, Arab peoples (see Lynn, 2006). The weighted mean of the IQs of the three groups gives the IQ of 95 for Israel.

The IQ of 106 calculated for European Jews in Israel is lower than the IQ of 110 of European Jews in Britain, Canada, and the United States, given in the chapters on these countries. The explanation for this is that the Jews in Britain, Canada and the United States are Ashkenazim, whereas not all of those classified as European in Israel are Ashkenazim. As noted in Section 1, of the 2.4 million Jews classified as European in Israel, approximately 1.4 million (58 percent) are Ashkenazim, about 900,000 are non-Jewish Russians, and about 110,000 are Sephardim from the Balkans. We can assign the Ashkenazim an IQ of 110 and the non-Jewish Russians and the Sephardim an IQ of 99 (see Lynn, 2006, and Chapter 17). Weighting these figures with their proportions among European Jews, we arrive at the IQ of 106 for European Jews in Israel.

14. Conclusions

In the early days after the foundation of the state of Israel, it was soon observed that European Jews did better than Orientals and Arabs in education, earnings, and occupational status. Virtually all Israelis believed that these differences would soon diminish and eventually disappear as the Orientals and Arabs became assimilated. The evidence has shown, however, that this has not happened. In fact, the earnings gap has become greater in the period 1975–1992 (Cohen and Haberfeld, 1998, p. 507).

We have seen that there is a gradient of intelligence in the four ethnic populations in Israel. Intelligence is highest in the European Jews (IQ=106), lower in the Orientals (IQ=90), lower still in the Arabs (IQ=84), and lowest in the Ethiopian Jews (IQ= 69). These IQ differences predict and largely explain the differences in educational attainment, earnings, and socioeconomic status. However, Israeli social scientists have been very shy about acknowledging this. A number of Israeli social scientists attribute the poor performance of the Orientals, the Arabs, and the Ethiopian Jews to "discrimination" by European Jews. For instance, Savit, Cohen, Steir and Bolotin (1999, p. 6) write that "the Israeli Arabs suffer from severe discrimination":

> Scholars agree that the social disadvantages of the Mizrahim have their roots in the way they were received by the Ashkenazim establishment during the early years of the state...inequality persists because the dominant ethnic group, the Ashkenazim, manages to perpetuate its privileges by excluding others from the higher and more selective educational tracks." (p. 18)

In a similar, if opaque, vein, Friedlander, Okun, Eisenbach, and Elmakias, (2002, p. 135) assert, "ethnic gaps are functions of political and economic historical factors and contextual factors."

Two other social scientists who believe that the poor performance of the Orientals, the Arabs, and the Ethiopian Jews is attributable to "discrimination" by European Jews against the other groups are Vared Kraus, a sociologist at the University of Haifa, and Robert Hodge, a sociologist at the University of Southern California (Kraus and Hodge, 1990). They have concluded that Israel is meritocratic insofar as the racial and ethnic differences in socioeconomic status are virtually wholly determined by the differences in education, so "the process of occupational attainment is basically egalitarian" (p. 179). Why, therefore, do the European Jews do so much better than the Orientals and the Arabs? Their explanation is that the Europeans discriminate against the Orientals and the Arabs and keep them in a socially subordinate position. They do this to maintain their own position and are particularly motivated to do so because they are aware of their low fertility and the threat this poses to their dominance. Thus, "the dominant European-American Jewish elements in the Israeli population sought, by means of established institutions of education, to control the flow of other ethno-religious groups into positions of power and prestige.

> Their scheme was ostensibly fair because it was meritocratically based; nevertheless, it effectively excluded Arabs and Asian-African Jews from the highest echelons of the nation's social institutions and economy because of their lack of access to educational opportunities. Thus, what appears to be a meritocratic system may also be construed as a system of social control based on their educational credentials by the dominant elite (European-American Jews) in order to exclude the educationally disadvantaged (Asian-African Jews as well as Arabs). (p. 175)

This is the standard sociological theory of racial and ethnic differences in educational attainment, earnings, and socioeconomic status. With few exceptions, it is axiomatic for sociologists that all groups are equal in intelligence, despite massive evidence to the contrary. Hence, ethnic differences in socioeconomic status must be caused by "discrimination" by the socially dominant group. But this explanation does not stand up to examination. How can the Europeans use their power to secure higher marks for their children than for the Oriental Jews and the Arabs in examinations at school and university? It is not suggested that the Europeans fake the marks, but how else can the better performance of the European children be explained? And if the Europeans used their power to exclude the Oriental Jews and the Arabs from higher education and higher socioeconomic status positions, they would surely have exercised this more strongly against the Arabs, who are widely perceived by Jews in Israel as enemies, than against their ethnic coreligionists, the Oriental Jews. Yet the Arabs do pretty much as well as the Oriental Jews in socioeconomic status, and even had higher percentages in the professional class in 1955 and 1974. Contrary to Kraus and Hodge's conspiracy theory, there is nothing to stop Oriental Jews and Arabs from entering the universities and the professions, except that fewer of them are able to pass the entrance examinations, and the reason they cannot do this is that they have lower IQs.

Other Israeli social scientists, including Cohen and Haberfeld, have concluded that the poor performance of the Orientals, the Arabs, and the Ethiopian Jews cannot be explained by "discrimination." Reviewing the studies, they write, "most previous research detected no differential labor market discrimination of Jews of Eastern origin" (1998, p. 510); their own studies have confirmed this conclusion. They believe much of the gap can be explained by "the increase of returns to college education" (p. 507), but they have no explanation to offer for why so many more European Jews have college education than Orientals and Arabs.

It is difficult to believe that these social scientists are unaware of the higher intelligence of the European Jews and that this can explain their better achievements. It can only be presumed that they have chosen not to mention it.

Chapter 12

Italy

1. 1859–1944
2. 1944–2006
3. Nobel Prize winners
4. Infant Mortality

There has been a Jewish community in Rome since the first century AD, when 30 Jewish families came from Palestine and settled in a ghetto in the Travevere district. In the late Roman Empire, the number is estimated at about 50,000 (Roth, 1946). At this time Jews do not appear to be in any way exceptional: "if there were any callings characteristic of the Italian Jews at this period, they were of the lowliest nature; there were Jewish butchers, tailors, tentmakers and other craftsmen" (Roth, 1946, p. 23). This substantiates the view that the early Jews did not have a high average IQ; this came later as a result of experiences in the Middle Ages.

In the early Middle Ages, "attitudes to Jews were fairly tolerant" (Johnson, 2004, p. 216). However, in the 1480s, when there were about 50,000 Jews in Italy, they were expelled from most of the northern cities, including Perugia, Parma, Milan, Lucca, Florence, and Venice. In 1493, they were expelled from the Kingdom of Sicily; in

1510, from the Kingdom of Naples; and in 1569, from the Papal States, with the exception of Rome and Ancona (Barnaav, 1998; Castello & Kagan, 1994).

During the period between 1480 and 1600, Jews were intermittently expelled and readmitted–and then expelled again–throughout the numerous independent states that existed in Italy until the country was unified in the mid-19th century. In the 1490s, a number of Sephardic Jews who had been expelled from Spain and Portugal moved to Italy. The descendants of these formed the great majority of Jews in Italy, although some Ashkenazim came to Italy from Germany in the 15th and 16th centuries. In 1541, Jews were expelled from Naples and in 1550 from Venice and Ancona, but in the later 1500s, they were readmitted to Venice and a number of other Italian cities (Barnaav, 1998; Castello and Kagan, 1994). In 1555, Pope Paul IV issued a Papal Bull *Cum Nimis Absurdum* that required the segregation of Jews into ghettos throughout his domains.

In the second half of the 16th century, "the position of the Jews was pitiable;

> The bulls of Paul IV and Pius V had reduced them to the utmost humiliation and had materially diminished their numbers.... In southern Italy there were almost none left; in each of Rome, Venice and Mantua, there were about 2,000, while in all Lombardy there were about 1,000. (Castiglioni, 1904, pp. 7,10)

From the 16th to the 18th centuries, throughout Italy, "generally speaking, Jews were not allowed to have shops outside the ghetto, or to engage in retail trade except among their coreligionists, or to practice any organized handicraft, or to follow any liberal profession, or to enter any branch of manufacture, or to employ Christians.

> [T]here was a small aristocracy of wholesale importers and textile magnates, but the vast majority were itinerant hawkers, rag-pickers and second-hand dealers. By and large, the economic history of Italian Jewry is a record of fruitless endeavors to extend the range of their activities, alternating with bursts of savage repression. (Roth, 1946, p. 373)

Napoleon liberated the Jews of Italy in 1796, but at the end of the Napoleonic Wars, "restrictions were re-imposed and until the Revolution of 1848, there was hardly a country in Europe where the restrictions placed on Jews were more galling.... [T]he liberty acquired under Napoleon was of short duration; it disappeared after his downfall. Pope Pius VII reinstalled the Inquisition.... he deprived the Jews of every liberty and confined them to the ghetto. (Castiglioni, 1904, p. 7)

In the early 19th century, Jews were severely discriminated against in most of Italy: "Students were expelled from all educational institutions, from the elementary and trade schools to the universities.... They were not allowed to become lawyers, notaries, apothecaries, or physicians, except for practice among their coreligionists" (Roth, 1946, p. 449). Jews were subjected to frequent intermittent persecution in Italy until the middle of the 19th century. Jews in Italy at this time seem to have had the low fertility typical of their people. It has been estimated the birthrate of Jews in Florence in the first half of the 19th century was 47 percent below that of Gentiles (Chiswick, 1988).

1. 1859–1944

In 1859, the numerous formerly independent Italian states were united to become the Kingdom of Italy, and the Jews obtained full emancipation. At the time, "most Italians could neither read nor write, whereas literacy in the Jewish community was nearly 90 percent" (Stille, 2005, p. 25). From 1859 until 1938, Jews enjoyed civic liberties in Italy and there was very little anti-Semitism: "there was no part of the world where religious freedom was more real or religious prejudice so small" (Michaelis, 1978, p. 3). Not surprisingly, Jews flourished during this period.

In the first House of Deputies (the Italian Parliament) of 1861, there were three Jewish deputies; this rose to 11 in 1871 and 15 in 1894. In 1906, Italy acquired a half-Jewish Prime Minister, Sidney Sonnino (1847–1922), and in 1910, a fully Jewish Prime Minister in the person of Luigi Luzzati (1841–1927). The most famous Italian Jews of this period were the forensic physician Cesare Lombroso (1836–1909), who claimed that criminals have smaller than normal brains, and the painter Amedeo Modigliani (1884–1929), who immigrated to Paris, where his frank nudes shocked even the French to such an extent that his first exhibition in 1918 was closed on the first day for indecency. Hardly less famous were Camillo Olivetti (1868–1943), who founded

Olivetti typewriters in 1911, and the novelist Alberto Pincherle (1907–1990), better known by his pen name Alberto Moravia, who was half-Jewish.

The approximate numbers of Jews in Italy and their percentages of the population between 1901–2001 are given in Table 12.1. The growth in numbers from 1901 is attributable to natural increase, although this was to some degree offset by Jews leaving the community. An estimated 44 percent of Jews married Gentiles during the interwar years, and many of these defected from Judaism (Zimmerman, 2005). The fall in numbers from 44,000 in 1940 to 29,000 in 1945 was a result of the killing of approximately 7,700 by the Germans in World War II and the emigration of around 6,000 to Switzerland and elsewhere (Michaelis, 1978; Sarfatti, 2006). The small increase from 1945 to 1965 was due to immigration (Johnson, 2004, p. 563), and the subsequent decline from 1965 to 2001 is attributable to below-replacement fertility.

Table 12.1. Numbers and percentages of Jews in Italy

Year	N. Jews	% Population
1800	34,000	0.20
1901	34,653	0.10
1940	44,000	0.10
1945	29,000	0.06
1965	32,000	0.07
2001	29,500	0.05

From 1900 to the 1930s, Jews were accepted and did well in Italy. In the 1901 census, it was found that 94.3 percent of Jews were literate, compared with 50.1 percent of the population (Sarfatti, 2006, p. 31). In 1904, King Victor Emmanuel III (1869–1947) asserted, "Jews may occupy any position, and they do.... Jews for us are full-blown Italians" (Johnson, 2004, p. 501). In World War I, the Italian foreign minister, Sidney Sonnino, was a Jew, and there were 11 Jewish generals in the army. Jews were also prominent in the socioeconomic elite:

> Jewish families played key roles in rural land development, the silk industry, and urban construction, and held substantial influence

in the insurance business; Jewish banking firms, such as Weil-Weiss and Malvano in Turin, Weil-Schott in Milan, and Treves in Venice, held key positions in the Italian banking industry; Jews were overrepresented among owners, editors, and journalists in the Italian newspaper industry, and the Jewish firms of Treves, Bemperad, Lattes, Formiggini, and Voghera stood out among Italy's major publishing houses; Jews were overrepresented within the Italian civil service, law, business, and academia. (Brunstein, 2003, pp. 253–4)

And in the period 1900–1939, Jews were highly overrepresented in the universities. "the number of outstanding Jewish scholars was disproportionately high.... [T]he number of Jewish university teachers continued to be disproportionately high, and so did the number of Jewish generals and admirals" (Michaelis, 1978, p. 51). The percentages are shown in Table 12.2. Jews, who were approximately 0.1 percent of the population, constituted between 6.4 and 8.0 percent of professors in the universities.

Table 12.2. Percentages of professors in Italian universities who were Jewish

Year	% Jews	Year	% Jews
1901	6.4	1928	6.7
1919	6.8	1938	8.0

Benito Mussolini (1883–1945) assumed power in 1922 and began to express some anti-Semitism. In 1926, he founded the Academia d'Italia as a national academy for the most distinguished academics and instructed that no Jews were to be elected members. However, in the early years of his dictatorship, he was not stridently anti-Semitic, possibly because both his Minister of Finance, Guido Jung (1876–1949), and his mistress, Margherita Sarfatti (1880–1961), were Jewish. Mussolini became more anti-Semitic in the mid-1930s and "saw to it that members of the Jewish community did not reach positions of control either in the government or in the party hierarchy" (Michaelis, 1978, p. 51).

The prosperous position of Jews was shown in the 1931 census, whose relevant results were summarized by Michele Sarfatti

(2006, p. 34) and are given in Table 12.3. Jews were more than five times overrepresented among professionals and were also significantly overrepresented among proprietors, managers, and shopkeepers. On the other hand, Jews were underrepresented among laborers and among agricultural workers (a category that includes agricultural laborers and proprietors).

Table 12.3. Percentages of Jews and Gentiles in different occupational categories, 1931

Occupation	Jews	Gentiles
Professions	10.8	1.9
Proprietors & Managers	11.1	4.9
Shopkeepers	34.3	6.1
Laborers	5.6	21.1
Agriculture	0.8	48.5

By 1938, "the Italian Jewish population had been highly integrated into general society and, on the whole, was solidly middle class" (Zimmerman, 2005, p. 4). This was shown in a further census of that year, which gave a statistical breakdown of the percentages of Jews and Gentiles in different occupational categories. This is shown in Table 12.4. The results are broadly similar to those in the 1931 census, although some of the categories differ. We can see that 8.8 percent of Jews, as compared with 0.6 percent of Italians, worked in the liberal professions of medicine, dentistry, law, architecture, engineering, and journalism (Zimmerman, 2005, p. 4). Jews were also about tenfold overrepresented in financial services, included banking and insurance, and in trade. In public administration, Jews were about 40 percent overrepresented, indicating very little anti-Semitic discrimination. In the other occupational categories of industrial workers, transportation and agriculture, Jews were underrepresented.

Table 12.4. Percentages of Jews and Gentiles in different occupational categories

Occupation	Jews	Gentiles
Professions	8.8	0.6
Finance	5.9	0.6
Public administration	11.6	7.5
Industry	22.1	29.3
Transportation	3.6	3.8
Trade	43.3	8.2
Agriculture	1.5	50.0

In the fall of 1938, Mussolini instituted more serious anti-Semitic measures. These laws prohibited the publication of Jewish periodicals, prohibited Jewish children from attending public and private schools, and expelled Jews from teaching positions in schools, universities, and learned societies. In the universities, 96 professors were dismissed, including Emilio Segrè (1905–1989), a physicist who moved to the United States and received the Nobel Prize in 1956, and Tullio Levi-Civita (1873–1941), the most distinguished Italian mathematician. These expulsions had a damaging effect on Italian academic work: "some branches of study, such as physiology, in which a majority of university chairs happened to be filled by Jews, seemed to be completely denuded" (Roth, 1946, p. 528). One of the most serious losses was Enrico Fermi (1901–1954). While a professor of physics at Rome University, Fermi had sucessfully split the atom, work for which he was later awarded the Nobel Prize. He left Italy for Columbia University in New York, where he shortly joined the Manhattan Project for developing the nuclear bomb. (Fermi was not Jewish himself, but had a Jewish wife.)

In addition to these expulsions, Mussolini introduced anti-Semitic laws that prohibited marriages between "Aryans" (i.e. White Gentiles) and Jews (and also between "Aryans" and Blacks). Jews were prohibited from entering the military and the civil service, from owning land of more than 50 hectares, and owning or managing enterprises employing more than 100 persons. Jews were expelled from the Fascist Party, a serious deprivation because membership was required for virtually all employment. They were expelled from all positions on the Stock Exchange, joint stock banks and insurance companies, and were forbidden to open new businesses; "Almost the only category of Italian Jews as yet unaffected was the proletariat of street peddlers, still common in Rome; but in the end they too were menaced" (Roth, 1946, p. 531). Italian citizenship granted to Jews after 1919 was revoked, and all foreign Jews, except those aged over 65, were ordered to leave the country. In 1939, a new law was passed imposing further restrictions of Jews, which included banning them from the professions of medicine, dentistry, law, architecture, engineering and journalism.

Despite these hostile measures against Jews, Mussolini did not order the killing of any of them: "the Fascist government was not in sympathy with the Nazi extermination policy.... But resolved to arrange for their evacuation" (Sarfatti, 2006, p. 146). But in July of 1943, Mussolini was removed from office, and the Germans acquired greater powers in Italy. Heinrich Himmler ordered the capture of Jews for execution. Most of the Italians were sympathetic to the Jews, and many of those who were given these orders were uncooperative: "many Italian police were not particularly eager to carry out the arrests of Jews and warned them beforehand so that they might flee" (Stille, 2005, p. 31). Many Italians helped Jews to escape deportation and gave Jews refuge in convents, monasteries, and private houses. Nevertheless, as noted above, an estimated 7,700 Jews were deported to concentration camps and killed during World War II.

2. 1944–2006

In the postwar period (1944 on), Jews recovered their position in Italy. In 1944, Jews who had been expelled from their university positions were reinstated. In the 1950s, 14 percent of Jews were university graduates, as compared with 1.4 percent of Gentiles (Encyclopedia Judaica, 1968). They had the low fertility and high longevity typical of Jews elsewhere. A study carried out in 1965 found that the birthrate of Jews in Italy was 11.4 per 1,000, compared with 18.3 for the population as a whole (Johnson, 2004, p. 563).

3. Nobel Prize winners

A list of Italian Nobel Prize winners is given in Table 12.5. Of the 17 Nobel Laureates, four have been Jewish. Thus, Jews, who comprised about 0.075 percent of the population during the century, produced 24 percent of the Nobel Prize winners, giving them an Achievement Quotient of 320.

Table 12.5. Italian Nobel Prize winners (Jews are asterisked)

Year	Name	Subject	Year	Name	Subject
1906	Giosuè Carducci	Literature	1969	Salvador Luria*	Medicine
1906	Camillo Golgi	Medicine	1975	Eugenio Montale	Literature
1909	Gugliemo Marconi	Physics	1975	Renato Dulbecco	Medicine
1926	Grazia Deledda	Literature	1984	Carlo Rubbia	Physics
1934	Luigi Pirandello	Literature	1985	Franco Modigliani*	Economics
1938	Enrico Fermi	Physics	1986	Rita Levi-Moltancini*	Medicine
1959	Quasimodo	Literature	1997	Dario Fo	Literature
1959	Emilio Segrè*	Physics	2002	Riccardo Giacconi	Physics
1963	Giulio Natta	Chemistry			

4. Infant Mortality

From the early 19th century, it has been found that Jews in Italy had lower infant mortality than Gentiles. Four studies showing this, Paul Johnson (2004), are shown in Table 12.6. It will be seen that the rate of infant mortality of Gentiles ranged between 45 and 146 percent higher than that of Jews.

Table 12.6. Infant mortality per 1,000 live births

Years	Location	Jews	Gentiles	% Difference
1818–1837	Florence	129	218	69
1838–1847	Florence	149	216	45
1851	Trieste	105	258	146
1901–1907	Rome	72	138	93

CHAPTER 13

Latin America

1. Argentina
2. Brazil
3. Chile
4. Mexico
5. Peru
6. Venezuela
7. Nobel and Wolf Prize winners

The history of Jews in the Americas dates back to Christopher Columbus (1451–1506) and his first Atlantic voyage in 1492, when he left Spain and "discovered" the New World. His date of departure was also the day on which the Catholic monarchs Isabella I of Castile (1451–1504) and Ferdinand II of Aragon (1452–1516) decreed that the Jews of Spain had to convert to Catholicism or be expelled from the country. Those who sincerely converted were known as *"Conversos"* or "New Christians"; those who converted nominally but continued to practice Judaism in secret ("crypto-Jews") were known by the pejorative *"Marranos."* There were at least seven Jews who sailed with Columbus in his first voyage including Rodrigo De Trianav (1469–?), who was the first to sight land, Maestre Bernal (?–?), who served as the expedition's physician, and Luis De Torres (?–1493), the interpreter, who spoke Hebrew and Arabic, which it was believed would be useful in the Orient (their intended destination).

In the 16th and 17th centuries, a number of Spanish and Portuguese Jews settled in Latin America, largely in Argentina, Brazil, Suriname, Peru, and Mexico. They were intermittently persecuted and put to death by the Inquisition. In his eyewitness account of the conquest of Mexico, Bernal Díaz del Castillo (1492–1585) describes a number of executions of soldiers in the forces of Hernán Cortés (1485–1547); they were killed because they were Jews. The Jewish communities that remained assimilated with local Gentile populations and had almost entirely disappeared by the end of the 19th century. From the 1880s on, there was an influx of Jews from Eastern Europe, principally to Argentina, where today about half of Latin American Jews live, and to Brazil, which accounts for 20 percent. The six Latin American countries containing the most Jews and their numbers and percentages of the population in 1982 have been summarized by U. O. Schmelz and Sergio Della Pergola (1985, p. 55) and are shown in Table 13.1.

Table 13.1. Jews in Latin America, 1982

Country	Number Jews	% Population
Argentina	233,000	0.80
Brazil	100,000	0.80
Chile	20,000	0.20
Mexico	35,000	0.05
Uruguay	30,000	1.20
Venezuela	20,000	0.14

1. Argentina

After their expulsion from Spain in 1492, a number of Jews settled in Argentina. Most of these immigrants assimilated into the general population and by the mid-1800s, Jews had virtually disappeared. Immigration of Jews on a significant scale began in the middle decades of the 19th century. The majority of these were Yiddish speakers from Poland, although there were also some from France, as well as some

Sephardim from the Ottoman Empire. Initially, they were denied a number of civil rights, including that of having Jewish marriages registered. This right was won in 1860, but it was not until 1888 that Jews were given full civil rights.

By the beginning of the 20th century, the Jewish immigrants were prospering: "their children and grandchildren often became professionals–lawyers, teachers, artists, and doctors" (Elazar & Redding, 1983, p. 95). They even secured control of more than half of the prostitution trade, hitherto in the hands of the French.

From 1881 onward, there was a third wave of immigrants fleeing poverty and pogroms in Russia and Poland. Baron Maurice de Hirsch (1831–1896) founded the Jewish Colonization Association that bought some 600,000 hectares of land in Argentina for Jews to settle as farmers. Between 1906 and 1912, Jewish immigration increased at a rate of 13,000 per year. Most of the immigrants were Ashkenazim from Europe, but there were also a number of Jews from Morocco and the Ottoman Empire. By 1920, more than 150,000 Jews were living in Argentina. By the year 2000, Argentina's Jewish community numbered about 250,000, with about 200,000 living in Buenos Aires and most of the remainder in provincial towns. About 85 percent are Ashkenazi. Recently, many young Jews have been migrating to other countries because of the poor state of the Agentine economy.

Anti-Semitism has not been particularly strong in Argentina, although Jews have been by convention excluded from work in the government, the judiciary and the officer corps of the military. Between 1918 and 1930, there was an increase of anti-Semitism, largely because Jews were perceived as Communists who had played a large part in the Russian Revolution. In 1919, there was a pogrom against the Jews in Buenos Aires, in which many were beaten and had their properties burned. There was a further outbreak of anti-Semitism in 1960–1961, as a result of the abduction of Adolf Eichmann from a Buenos Aires suburb by Israeli agents and his trial in Jerusalem.

Statistics for the educational attainment and socioeconomic status of Jews in Argentina in 1960 are given by Schmelz and Della Pergola (1984) and are shown in Tables 13.2 and 13.3. Table 13.2 shows that Jews were better educated than Gentiles. Fewer Jews had no education or only primary education, while more Jews had secondary and university education. The proportion of Jews with university education was more than four times that of Gentiles.

Table 13.3 gives the occupational distribution of Jews and Gentiles in Argentina in 1960 and shows that Jews had higher socioeconomic status than Gentiles in Argentina with approximately twice the proportion in professional occupations and more than three times the proportion in managerial occupations. In the lower socioeconomic status categories, there were lower proportions of Jews in blue-collar occupations, services, and agriculture.

Table 13.2. Education of Jews and Gentiles in Argentina in 1960 (percentages)

Education	Jews	Gentiles
None	5.3	10.5
Primary	51.3	71.6
Secondary	32.1	15.2
University	11.3	2.7

Table 13.3. Occupational distribution of Jews and Gentiles in Argentina in 1960 (percentages)

Occupation	Jews	Gentiles
Professional	11.1	6.5
Managerial	9.5	2.6
Clerical	13.2	11.9
Sales	37.2	10.3
Blue collar	22.3	34.1
Services	4.5	14.7
Agriculture	2.2	19.8

Jews in Argentina have had lower fertility than the general population. The 1960 census found that for ever-married women aged 45–64, the average number of children was 2.4 for Jews and 3.2 for the general population, while for ever-married women aged 65 and over, the corresponding figures were 3.6 and 4.1 (Schmelz & Della Pergola, 1984).

2. Brazil

Jewish history in Brazil dates back to 1500, when Gaspar da Gama (1444–c.1510-20), a Jew by birth, but later forcibly baptized, accompanied the Portuguese admiral Pedro Álvares Cabral (c.1468–c. 1520) when he landed in what is now Brazil. Following their expulsion from Portugal in 1497, Jews fled to places throughout the New World, including Brazil. They arrived in Brazil primarily as Catholic converts (*Conversos*), but many secretly practiced Judaism (*Marranos*). Despite continued persecution by the Brazilian Inquisition, the "New Christians" successfully established sugar plantations and mills. By the 1600s, approximately 50,000 Europeans lived in Brazil, with *Conversos* making up a significant percentage. Many of them settled in Sao Paulo. They were businessmen, importers, exporters, teachers, writers, and poets. In 1624, the Dutch established a colony in northeastern Brazil. The Dutch generally tolerated the Jews, who flourished in the sugar industry, tax farming, and the slave trade, buying slaves cheap and reselling them at a profit. In 1645, the Dutch Jewish population was 1,500, approximately half of the Gentile European population of about 3,000.

The Portuguese drove the Dutch out of Brazil in 1654, and the Jews who remained were subjected to the Portuguese Inquisition. In 1647, the Portuguese authorities arrested Isaac de Castro (1623—1647) for teaching Jewish rites and customs and sent him back to Portugal, where the Inquisition sentenced him to death and burned him at the stake. Portuguese anti-Jewish persecution led to a mass immigration to places like Curacao and New York, where they laid foundations for new Jewish communities, while others returned to Europe. Most who could not escape were killed, but some became "crypto-Jews," practicing Judaism in secret. They lived away from the authorities in the interior of Brazil, many becoming ranch hands or cowboys. The persecutions, arrests, confiscation of property and emigration of the Jews greatly damaged the Brazilian economy by bringing the manufacture and export of sugar to a near standstill and seriously disrupting trade between Portugal and Brazil.

In 1773, a Portuguese royal decree finally abolished legal discrimination against Jews and a number settled in Brazil. In 1822, Brazil gained independence from Portugal, and a number of Moroccan Jews arrived and settled in Belem in northern Brazil and Manaus, at that time a prosperous city on the Amazon. By World War I, there were approximately 7,000 Jews in Brazil.

Approximately 47,000 Western European Jews came to Brazil in the 1920s and 1930s. In the late 1950s, another wave of Jewish immigration brought more than 3,500 North African Jews to Brazil. By the 1960s, Brazilian Jewry was thriving. In the 1966 parliamentary elections, six Jews, representing various parties, won seats in the federal legislature. In addition, Jews served in state legislatures and municipal councils. By 1969, approximately 140,000 Jews lived in Brazil, mostly in the large cities: Rio de Janeiro (50,000), Sao Paulo (55,000), Porto Alegre (12,000), Belo Horizonte (3,000), Recife (1,600), and Belem (1,200).

From the end of World War II, Jews prospered in Brazil. The University of Sao Paulo has a Center for Jewish Studies. In 1969, 36 percent of Jewish men and 13 percent of Jewish women aged 15–29 had university degrees, compared with 6.4 percent of White Brazilians recorded in the 1980 census (Schmelz & Della Pergola, 1985). Jewish and Israeli film festivals are common in Sao Paulo and Rio de Janeiro. In 1994, Jaime Lerner (b. 1937) was elected head Jewish governor. In 1998, Professor Dr. Eva Alterman Blay (b. 1937) became the first Jewish woman to serve in Brazil's Senate. Jews have also served in the Cabinet. Jews have made a large contribution to the Brazilian economy. Jewish families own Brazil's two largest publishing and jewelry companies, the sixth largest bank, and are among the executives of several other large corporations.

In a total population exceeding 160 million people, the Jewish population has stabilized around 95,000. About half of these are in Sao Paulo. More than 8,000 Brazilian Jews have moved to Israel since 1948. By the end of the 20th century, about half of Brazilian Jewry was intermarrying with Gentiles.

3. Chile

Chile became a refuge for Russian Jews in the early part of the 20th century. More Jews came from Germany in the 1930s, and a number of Hungarian Jews entered the country following the Hungarian Revolution of 1956.

Jews have generally been treated well in Chile and have participated in business, politics, and the professions. Julio Bernstein started the first sugar refinery in Vino del Mar. Saloman Sack was a successful steel businessman and financed the University of Chile's School of Architecture. Under the Allende government (1970–1973), a number of Jewish individuals achieved high status. Among them were Jacques Chonchol, minister of agriculture; Jacobe Shaulson, a Radical Party member of parliament; Volodia Teitelbaum, senator and leader of the Communist Party; Oscar Weiss, editor of the government newspaper; Enrique Testa, professor of commercial law at the University of Chile and later the president of the State Defense Council. Others were prominent in the political opposition to the Allende government. These included Angel Faivovich, a former senator; Marcos Chamudes, who owned the opposition paper P. E. C; and Brigadier General Jose Berdichevsky Scher, who was one of the Air Force officers responsible for the bombing of the presidential palace where Allende died.

In the 1990s, Jews continued to be influential and active in the universities, politics, theatre, music, education, and the arts. These include Alejandro Lipschuetz, an anthropologist and endocrinologist who has acquired a reputation for his research on the American Indians; Dr. Abraham Horowitz, director of the Pan American Health Service; Efrain Freidmann, the director of the Chilean Atomic Research Committee; and Jaime Wisnaik, the director of the department of engineering at the Catholic University of Santiago. In theatre, prominent Jewish actors include Don Francisco (born Mario Kreutzberger in 1940), Alejandro Cohen, and Nissim Sharim, along with actresses Birginia Fischer, Jael Unger, and Anita Klesky. Vitor Tevah, a noted violinist and conductor, won the National Art Prize in 1980. Andy Pollack is a leading Jewish jazz musician.

4. Mexico

There have been Jews in Mexico since the early 1500s, when Hernando Cortez was accompanied by several *Conversos* in his conquest of the Aztecs. In the 1860s, a large number of German Jews settled in Mexico as a result of invitations from Maximilian I (1832–1867). Beginning in the 1880s, many Ashkenazi Jews fleeing pogroms in Russia, Poland, and Romania came to Mexico. Another large wave of immigration occurred in the 1920s, mainly from Turkey, Morocco, and France. Finally, a wave of immigrants fled the Nazi persecutions in Europe in the 1930s.

At the start of the 21st century, there were around 40,000 Jews in Mexico. About 37,000 live in Mexico City; there are also Jewish communities in Guadalajara, Monterrey, and Tijuana. The majority is Ashkenazi. There is a Mizrahi community of mainly Syrian immigrants and a Sephardic community primarily made up of descendants of Turkish and Spanish immigrants.

A survey in 1991 found that Jews in Mexico were almost entirely middle class. Only four percent worked in blue-collar occupations. The distribution of the remaining 97 percent who worked in white-collar occupations was 27 percent professional, 53 percent managerial, 11 percent clerical, and five percent sales (Della Pergola, 2007). Among the most successful of the Jews in Mexico was Isaac Saba Raffoul (1925–2008), who was the wealthiest man in the country.

5. *Peru*

In the 16th and 17th centuries, Lima was the capital of the Spanish colony in Latin America. The city contained a number of Sephardic Jews from Spain and Portugal who had converted to Christianity, or, more often, pretended to do so. These Jews were prominent in the commercial life of the colony: "by the 1630s, the 'New Christians' controlled much of the commerce in Latin America; large numbers of Jews were starting to acquire tremendous wealth and power" (Elazar and Medding, 1983, pp. 65-6):

> [F]rom brocade to sack-cloth, from diamonds to cumin-seed, everything passed through their hands; the Castilian who had not a Jewish partner could look for no success in trade.... They would buy cargoes of whole fleets with the fictitious credits they exchanged, thus rendering capital unnecessary, and would distribute the merchandise through the land by their agents who were likewise Jewish. (Cohen, 1971, p. 24)

By the 1630s, the commercial prominence of the Jews was beginning to excite envy. In 1639 the Inquisition ordered the burning of all Jews as heretics. A few escaped, but a large number were burned in Lima in the public ceremony of *auto da fe*, as a result of which the Jewish community in Lima and much of Spanish Latin America was virtually wiped out. The elimination of the Jews had the effect that "the entire viceroyalty of Peru went into an economic decline: the Inquisition had sequestered the property of the Jews so there was a scarcity of capital and no-one to carry on commerce on the scale heretofore handled by the Jews. (Elazar and Redding, 1983, p. 67)

6. Venezuela

A small Jewish community became established in Venezuela in the middle of the 19th century. By 1917, the number of Jews was only 475. In the 1920s and 1930s, the Jewish community increased with the arrival of North African and Eastern European Jews. Jewish immigration from Eastern and Central Europe, including Germany, increased after 1934. By 1950, in spite of immigration restrictions, the Jewish population grew to around 6,000. More immigrants arrived in 1967 after the Six-Day War, when a large influx of Jews from Morocco arrived. By 1982, the Jewish population in Venezuela reached about 20,000, largely centered in Caracas, but with smaller concentrations in Maracaibo. Most of Venezuela's Jews are either first or second generation. Intermarriage rates are low compared to the United States or Britain.

Living under the Hugo Chávez regime, Venezuelan Jews have experienced some anti-Semitism and, in many cases, have emigrated. The Latin American Jewish Congress estimated that some 22,000 Jews lived in Venezuela when Chávez took office in 1999; by 2007, the Jewish community had shrunk to between 12,000 and 13,000.

A survey in 1998 found that Jews in Venezuela were almost entirely middle class. Only three percent worked in blue-collar occupations. The distribution of the remaining 97 percent who worked in white-collar occupations was 17 percent professional, 28 percent managerial, 31 percent clerical, and 21 percent sales (Della Pergola, 2007). Among the most eminent of the Jews in Venezuela are Baruj Benacerraf (b. 1920), who won the Nobel Prize for medicine in 1980, and Manual Blum (b.1938), who won the Turing Award for computing in 1995.

7. Nobel and Wolf Prize winners

Latin America has produced eight Nobel Prize winners and one Wolf Prize winner for mathematics. These are listed in Table 13.4. Two of the Nobel Prize winners have been Jews. These are Baruj Benacerraf of Venezuela, and César Milstein (1927–2002) of Argentina, who won the prize for medicine in 1984. Thus, Jews, who are about 0.1 percent of the population of Latin America, have produced 22 percent of Latin American Nobel and Wolf Prize winners, giving them an astounding Achievement Quotient of 220.

Table 13.4. Latin American Nobel and Wolf Prize winners (Jews are asterisked)

Year	Name	Country	Subject
1945	Gabriela Mistral	Chile	Literature
1947	Bernardo Houssay	Argentina	Medicine
1967	Miguel Asturias	Guatemala	Literature
1970	Luis Leloir	Argentina	Chemistry
1971	Pablo Neruda	Chile	Literature
1980	Baruj Benacerraf*	Venezuela	Medicine
1982	Gabriel Marquez	Colombia	Literature
1984	César Milstein*	Argentina	Medicine
1989	Alberto Calderon	Argentina	Mathematics

Chapter 14

Poland, Lithuania, and Latvia

1. Numbers of Jews in Poland
2. 1800–1919
3. 1919–2010
4. Jews in Chess
5. Nobel and Wolf Prize winners
6. Lithuania and Latvia
7. Mixed marriages

Jews migrated into Poland from France and Germany following the pogroms against them during the First Crusade of 1095. As mentioned above, the French and Germans widely perceived the Jews as allies of the Moslems who occupied the Holy Land, and at the start of the First Crusade, there were massacres of Jews in France and Germany: "the ancient, rich and populous Jewish communities of the Rhineland were destroyed, most Jews being killed or dragged to fonts; others scattered" (Johnson, 2004, p. 208). Among those who escaped, most migrated east and settled in Poland. There were more attacks on Jews during the Third Crusade of 1189-90—"the preaching of a crusade always brought anti-Semitism to the boil" (Johnson, 2004, p. 210)—and again a number escaped to Poland. Further migrations into Poland took place following the expulsions of the

Jews from England in 1290, from France in 1396, and from a number of German states in the early decades of the 15th century including Trier in 1414 and Cologne in 1424.

In 1385, Poland was united with Lithuania, an arrangement that lasted until the late 18th century. In the 1400s, many Jews migrated into Poland-Lithuania, and by 1570, the number of Ashkenazim in the region is estimated at 385,000, 10 percent of the population. This was likely the largest community of Jews in the world (Sm, 1960, p. 216). In general, the Jews lived fairly safely in Poland-Lithuania, but in the 17th century, they were persecuted during the war against Sweden (1648–1650); some of them fled to the Netherlands, which had a flourishing Jewish community and had become a safe haven.

Between 1772 and 1795, Poland-Lithuania disappeared as an independent state. It was carved up between Russia, which took the whole of Lithuania and eastern Poland, the Austro-Hungarian Empire, which took southwestern Poland (Galicia), and Prussia, which took northwestern Poland. Poland regained independence through the Paris Peace Conference of 1919, which followed the First World War. Between 1939 and 1945, Poland was invaded by Nazi Germany and the Soviet Union, both of which inflicted great damage on the population during their occupations. Germany established many of its concentration camps in annexed Polish territories, including Auschwitz-Birkenau, where some 1 million Jews perished. After being integrated into the Soviet sphere during the Cold War, Poland and Lithuania gained independence as the Union collapsed in 1989.

1. Numbers and Percentages of Jews in Poland

Numbers and percentages of Jews in Poland at various dates are shown in Table 14.1.

Table 14.1. Numbers and percentages of Jews in Poland

Year	N. Jews	% Population
1570	385,000	10.0
1921	2,855,381	10.5
1931	3,110,933	9.8
1956	65,000	0.2
1985	5,000	0.0
2002	3,500	0.0

The figure for 1570 is for Poland-Lithuania. There were censuses in Poland in 1921 and 1931. Over this 10-year period, the numbers of Jews increased, but their percentage in the population declined from 10.5 to 9.8 percent. The principal reason for this is that Jews had lower fertility than Gentiles; in addition, there was some emigration.

2. 1800–1919

During the first two thirds of the 19th century, Jews suffered from a number of restrictions. They were emancipated in the 1860s and obtained equality of rights and were admitted to government schools and universities. They soon became a significant presence in the professions and the governmental bureaucracy. About half the Jews lived in the cities of Warsaw and Lodz, where "there emerged a wealthy Jewish industrial and commercial class...which played a key role in the development of the region" (Mendelsohn, 1983, p. 20). It is likely that at this time, Jews in Poland had higher IQs than Gentiles; Nathaniel Hirsch (1926) reported that in the United States, children of Jewish immigrants from Poland had an IQ 11.4 points higher than the children of non-Jewish Polish immigrants.

During this period, Jews became prominent in the professions, intellectual life, banks, commerce and industry. The most internationally famous of the Jewish Poles of this time was the composer Gustav Mahler (1860–1911), who was born in Kalist.

In the southern province of Galicia, Jews were more backward. They "were basically of the East European type, lower middle class, and proletarian, extremely conspicuous in local commerce" (Mendelsohn, 1983, p. 18). This region was a stronghold of the Hassidic Jews, whose men wore black coats, white stockings, and long side curls.

In the late 19th and early 20th centuries, the infant mortality of Gentiles was between two and 20 percent higher than that of Jews. Studies showing this have been summarized by Condran and Kramarow (1991) and are shown in Table 14.2.

Table 14.2. Infant mortality per 1,000 live births in Poland

Years	Location	Jews	Gentiles	% Difference
1851	Galicia	213	217	2
1891–1910	Lvov	160	167	4
1851–1909	Cracow	152	183	20

3. 1919–2010

Poland became independent after World War I, and Jews were given full civil rights and a share of public funds for their own schools. In practice, however, there was a great deal of discrimination against the Jews:

> [T]he government engaged in a tacit conspiracy to make the life of the Jew so unpleasant that he would be forced to migrate; Jews were kept out of the civil service, the co-operatives and the government monopolies; they were discriminated against in the licensing of traders and craftsmen, refused bank loans, limited in the practice of law and medicine, and in many instances were driven out of the universities. (Ms, 1960, p. 62)

In the early postwar years, there were a number of riots throughout Poland in which Jews were attacked and killed and their properties were damaged. Jews in the civil service were pensioned off and no more appointed. In the 1930s,

> violent anti-Semitism made a dramatic reappearance...Jewish doctors were not appointed in state hospitals, and Jewish lawyers were not employed in state institutions; Jewish professors in Polish universities were virtually unknown; there were hardly any Jewish officers (aside from doctors) in the Polish army. (Mendelsohn, 1983, pp. 42, 68)

In 1921, 24.6 percent of university students were Jews, but as the universities increasingly discriminated against Jewish applicants, by 1938, Jews were only 8.2 percent of students. Much of the anti-Semitism was fuelled by resentment of Jewish socioeconomic success. In 1935, the centrist Peasant Party issued a statement that demanded wealth redistribution along ethnic lines:

> The Jews as a middle class occupy a far more important position in Poland than in any other country, so that the Poles have no middle class of their own. It is vital for the Polish state that these middle class functions shall more and more pass into the hands of Poles. (Mendelsohn, 1983, p. 72)

To promote this objective there were widespread boycotts of Jewish shops and businesses, and there were numerous attacks on

Jews during the 1930s. The government made plans to expel the Jews to Palestine. A number of Jews thought it would be wise to go voluntarily: 139,756 migrated to Palestine during the years 1919–1942, from which many moved on to other countries. Among these were Maurice and Anne Charpak who moved to Paris in 1931. Their son Georges (1924–2010) survived the Holocaust and won the Nobel Prize for Physics in 1998.

The historian Ezra Mendelsohn describes the Jewish population in interwar Poland as largely "lower middle class and proletarian,"

> with a numerically small but important intelligentsia and wealthy bourgeoisie... [T]he typical Jewish worker was a shoemaker, bakers, a tailor who worked in a small shop, possibly with a few other journeymen, but often alone" (Mendelsohn, 1983, p. 27).

Jews were prominent in the intellectual and cultural life; these included two of the leading poets, Julian Tuwim (1894–1953) and Antoni Slonimski (1895–1976), the historian Szymon Ashkenazi (1866–1935) and the pianist Wanda Landowska (1879–1959); the latter was born in Warsaw, moved to Berlin, where she was appointed professor of music at the Berlin Hochschule, moved on to Paris, and in 1940 sought refuge in Switzerland. Mendelsohn comments:

> The presence of a small but important Polish Jewish cultural elite belies any meaningful comparison with other oppressed groups such as the American Blacks, whose contribution to the high culture of the majority is far less striking. (1983, p. 68)

Despite strong anti-Semitism, Jews were highly overrepresented in the professions. Statistics from the 1931 census, given in Table 14.3, bear this out. Jews, who were 10.2 percent of the population, were 56 percent of doctors in private practice, 43 percent of private teachers, 33 percent of lawyers, 24 percent of the pharmacists, and 22 percent of the journalists, publishers, and librarians. On the other hand, Jews were only 2.5 percent of state primary and secondary schoolteachers because they were normally debarred from appointment because of anti-Semitism.

Table 14.3. Jews in the Professions in Poland in 1931

Professions	Percent Jews	AQ
Doctors-private practice	56	5.6
Teachers-private schools	43	4.3
Lawyers	33	3.3
Pharmacists	24	2.4
Journalists & Publishers	22	2.2
State schoolteachers	2.5	0.25
Source: Slezkine (2004)		

Germany invaded Poland in September of 1939 and from 1940 on, began violently attacking Jews. Many of them were worked to death in forced labor camps. Others were sent straight to the concentration camps at Auschwitz, Sobidor, Belzec, and Treblinka. Of the 3,350,000 Jews in Poland in 1939, nearly 90 percent were killed during the war. About a quarter of a million escaped, leaving approximately 90,000 in 1945. After the war, anti-Semitism persisted, and in 1946, there was a pogrom in Kielce against Jews who had survived the war. Many of the 90,000 or so who survived emigrated, with the result that the numbers declined to 65,000 in 1965 and fell to 3,500 in 2002.

4. Jews in Chess

While the overrepresentation of Jews in the higher socioeconomic strata of Poland is remarkable, it is overshadowed by their prowess in chess. There have been six Polish players among top-rated chess grandmasters for the years 1851 to 2003 (Rubinstein, 2004). They are listed in Table 14.4. All six were Jewish.

Table 14.4. Polish top-rated chess grandmasters

Years	Chess Champions	Years	Chess Champions
1851–1899	Rosenthal	1900–1939	Rubinstein
	Zuckertort		Reshevsky
	Janowsky	1940–1969	Najdorf

5. Nobel and Wolf Prize winners

Poland has produced 9 Nobel Prize winners, of whom four have been Jewish, and two Wolf Prize winners for mathematics, both of whom were Jewish. They are listed in Table 14.5 (Marie Curie (née Sklodowska, 1867–1934) is one of the few who have been awarded the Nobel Prize twice, but is only counted once here). All six of the Jews escaped the Holocaust by emigrating from Poland. George Wald (1906–1997), Isaac Bashevis Singer (1902–1991), Roald Hoffman (b.1937), Samuel Eilenberg (1913–1998), and Benoît Mandelbrot (1924–2010) migrated to the United States, while Georges Charpak went to Switzerland. Thus, Jews, who comprised about five percent of the population of Poland during the 20th century, have produced 67 percent of the Nobel and Wolf Prize winners, giving them an Achievement Quotient of 10.

Table 14.5. Nobel and Wolf Prize winners (Jews identified by asterisks)

Year	Name	Subject	Year	Name	Subject
1903	Marie Curie	Physics	1980	Czeslaw Milosz	Literature
1905	Sienkiewicz	Literature	1981	Roald Hoffmann*	Chemistry
1911	Marie Curie	Chemistry	1982	George Stigler	Economics
1967	George Wald*	Medicine	1986	Samuel Eilenberg*	Mathematics
1977	Andrew Schally	Medicine	1992	Georges Charpak*	Physics
1978	Isaac Singer*	Literature	1993	Mandelbrot*	Mathematics

6. Lithuania and Latvia

Lithuania and Latvia have had Jewish populations from the 16th century, when these countries were united with Poland. In 1923, there were approximately 157,527 Jews, identified by religion, in Lithuania, comprising 7.3 percent of the population; of these, 54,600 lived in the capital city of Vilnius (Mendelsohn, 1983, p. 224; Sm, 1960, p. 218). The Jews occupied a similar socioeconomic position as they did in Poland and elsewhere in Eastern Europe. Jews comprised a lower middle class and proletarian community of small shop-keepers and artisans, with the usual thin but important stratum of wealthy businessmen, industrialists and professionals. The most internationally famous Lithuanian Jew of the early 20th century was Chaim Soutine (1893–1943), the expressionist painter who migrated to Paris.

> In commerce, 77 percent of the population were Jews and in industry, 21 percent; very important was the relatively large number of Jewish intellectuals in the community, particularly the teachers, but also the editors, journalists, writers and the like.... In 1922 Jewish students comprised 31.5 percent of the student body at the University of Kaunas (the second city of Lithuania), but by 1934 their percentage had fallen to 15.9 percent. (Mendelsohn, 1983, pp. 226, 237)

The decline in the percentage of Jewish students was a result of discrimination against Jewish applicants.

In Latvia, there were 95, 675 Jews recorded in the census of 1925, comprising 5.2 percent of the population. Forty-one percent lived in the capital city of Riga, where "over one fourth of all commercial and industrial enterprises were in Jewish hands, as were a number of banks, and Jews were conspicuous in the professions" (Mendelsohn, 1983, p. 244). Latvia has produced two of the top-rated chess grandmasters for the years 1851 to 2003 (Rubinstein, 2004). These were Aron Nimzovitch (1886–1935) in the 1930s and Mikhail Tal (1936–1992) in the 1960s. Both of them were Jewish.

Of the 253,203 Jews in Lithuania and Latvia in the 1920s, approximately 26,000 migrated to Palestine during the years 1925–1939. An estimated 200,000 perished in the Holocaust. By 2002, there were approximately 4,000 Jews in Lithuania (0.12 percent of the population), and about 9,000 in Latvia. The 2001 Lithuanian Census recorded the occupations of Jews and Gentiles; the results are given in Table 14.6. Notice that Jews were greatly overrepresented between the first two categories of legislators, senior officers and managers, and professionals; they were greatly underrepresented among the last six categories of skilled and unskilled blue-collar workers.

Table 14.6. Occupations of Jews and Gentiles in Lithuania in 2001 (percentages)

Occupation	Jews	Gentiles
Senior officers and managers	19.6	8.1
Professionals	28.6	15.0
Technicians and associate professionals	9.6	9.6
Clerks	2.7	4.4
Service workers, shop, and sales workers	7.4	11.2
Skilled agricultural and fishery workers	1.2	10.1
Craft and related trades workers	5.8	14.1
Machine operators and assemblers	3.2	11.5
Unskilled occupations	3.4	7.1
Other or not indicated	18.4	8.9

7. Mixed Marriages

In the second half of the 20th century, increasing numbers of Jews in the Baltic States married Gentiles. Statistics showing this for the years 1958-1993 are provided by Mark Tolts (2003) and are given in Table 14.7. The same trend has taken place in Russia, and in virtually all other countries. Typically, the children of mixed marriages are raised as Gentiles and lose their Jewish identity. It is likely that this will continue in the Baltic States.

Table 14.7. Percentage of children of mixed origin among children born to Jewish Mothers, 1958–1993

Republic	1958	1968	1988	1993
Latvia	14	27	40	48
Lithuania	12	19	32	
Estonia	34		63	67

Chapter 15

Russia

1. Numbers of Jews in Russia and the Soviet Union
2. 1800–1917
3. The Bolshevik Revolution and the Soviet Union, 1917–1939
4. Discrimination against Jews, 1939–1989
5. Jewish Achievement in Chess
6. Nobel Prize winners
7. Mathematicians
8. Lenin Prize winners
9. Jews in the Post 1989 Russian Federation
10. Mixed Marriages

The first significant settlement of Jews in Russia took place in 1396 as a result of their expulsion from France in that year. More came in the early decades of the 15th century, following their expulsion from a number of German states. There were massacres of Jews in the Ukraine in 1648–1650, when many of those who escaped fled to the Netherlands.

Throughout the 19th century, about 90 percent of Jews lived in the Pale of Settlement, an area in the southwest of the Russian Empire that included the eastern portions of present day Poland, Lithuania,

Byelorussia, and Ukraine. Jews were legally restricted to this region. They spoke Yiddish and lived largely in *shtels* (Jewish villages), although some lived in the major cities of Warsaw, Kiev, Lodz, and Vilna. They were prohibited from working in the civil service and on the railroads when these were being constructed in the middle decades of the century. Apart from these restrictions, Jews were fairly well treated and tolerated (until the series of pogroms from 1881 onward). Jews were successful and prominent in commerce:

> Jews dominated the commercial life of the Pale for most of the 19th century; Jewish banks in Warsaw, Vilna and Odessa had been among the first commercial lending institutions in the Russian empire.... Their representation in the wealthiest commercial elite was particularly strong.... [I]t was the initiative of Jewish contractors that accounted for the construction of fully three-fourths of the Russian railroad system. (Slezkine, 2004, pp. 118, 120)

By the end of the century, the Jewish Gintsburg family controlled a large portion of the Siberian gold mining industry; the Jewish Gessen brothers ran the main shipping business between the Baltic and Caspian seas; and Jews developed the Caucasus oil industry, financed by the Rothschilds.

In 1900, approximately 94 percent of Jews worked as traders; serving as middlemen between the farmers and the towns, they would buy agricultural produce, ship it to the towns, and resell it. Others provided credit; leased and managed estates and various processing plants, such as factories, tanneries, distilleries, and sugar mills; kept shops and inns; provided professional services, principally as doctors and pharmacists; and performed artisan work, such as tailors, blacksmiths, shoemakers, jewelers, and watchmakers (Slezkine, 2004, p. 105). Russian Jews lived in their own segregated quarters and spoke Yiddish. About four percent worked in factories or on farms. While Jews were approximately four percent of the population, they had much higher percentages on a number of indices of educational, economic achievement, and social standing.

It was well recognized at the time that Jews were generally intelligent. In 1874, Daniel Khvol'son, a professor at the University of St. Petersburg, published a pamphlet arguing that the Jews and the Hottentots represented the two extremes of high and low intelligence.

According to Maxim Gorky, Vladimir Lenin claimed, "a smart Russian is almost always a Jew or somebody with an admixture of Jewish blood." Lenin himself was a quarter Jewish through his maternal grandfather (Slezkine, 2004, p. 163).

1. Numbers of Jews in Russia and the Soviet Union

The approximate numbers of Jews in the Russian empire and the Soviet Union at various dates, and their percentages of the population, are given in Table 15.1. In 1800, there were approximately one million Jews in the Russian Empire, which at that time included Poland. Their numbers grew by natural increase to about 5.2 million by 1900, when they constituted about four percent of the population. By 1913, the number of Jews in Russia had increased to 6,946,000, 4.1 percent of a total population of 170,903,000 (Rubinstein, 2000). The increase in the number of Jews was partly due to their lower mortality. In the period 1880–1914, the age standardized death rate of Jews was 14.2 per 1,000 per year in European Russia, less than half of the 31.8 per 1,000 per year of Orthodox Russians (Johnson, 1987, p. 356).

Table 15. 1. Numbers and percentages of Jews in Russia and the Soviet Union

Year	N. Jews	% Population
1900	5,200,000	4.0
1913	6,945,000	4.1
1926	2,672,000	1.8
1939	3,000,000	1.8
1985	2,100,000	1.2
1989	550,000	0.4
2002	230,000	0.16

Sources: American Jewish Yearbooks

In 1926, the number of Jews in the Soviet Union had fallen to about 2.6 million. This was due to the loss of Poland and the Baltic States, which had become independent in 1918, and to deaths in World War I. By 1985, the number of Jews in Russia had fallen to about 2.1 million.

The explanation for this is that the Germans in World War II killed approximately 1.4 million Jews. The remaining loss of 0.6 million was due to deaths in the war and to emigration, much of it to Israel. The Soviet Union broke up in 1989; the figures for 1989 and 2002 are for the Russian Federation. The number of Jews in the Russian Federation was only 550,000 in 1989, falling to 230,000 in 2002 as a result of emigration.

2. 1800–1917

During the first two thirds of the 19th century, Jews generally did not excel in education, but by the end of the century, they had surpassed Gentiles. Some statistics showing this are given in Table 15.2.

Table 15.2. Jews in Russian universities and gymnasia 1840–1886

Years	Position	Percent Jews	AQ
1840	University students	0.5	0.12
1853	Gymnasium students	1.3	0.32
1878	Gymnasium students	19.0	4.75
1886	University students	14.5	3.60
1886	Kharkov: medicine/ law	40.0	10.00
Source: Slezkine (2004)			

Row 1 shows that in 1840, Jews were only 0.5 percent of university students in Russia and were therefore underrepresented in relation to their four percent of the population. Row 2 shows that in 1853, Jews were 1.3 percent of Gymnasium (elite high school) students and were again underrepresented in relation to their four percent of the population. However, row 3 shows that by 1878, Jews were 19 percent of Gymnasium students and thus overrepresented in relation to their four percent of the population by a factor of 4.75. Row 4 shows the same story for university students in 1886. Row 5 shows that in 1886, Jews were 40 percent of students in the faculties of medicine and law at the University of Kharkov. These figures demonstrate the rapid upward social mobility of Jews in Russia in the third quarter of the 19th century.

By the end of the 19th century and in the early years of the 20th, Russian Jews were prominent and successful in many aspects of society. The 1897 census showed that Jews were twice as literate as non-Jews (Levin, 2000). It is likely that at this time, Jews in Russia had higher IQs than Gentiles. N.D.Hirsch (1926) reported that in the United States, the children of Jewish immigrants from Russia had IQs 9.5 points higher than the children of non-Jewish Russian immigrants. Some statistics showing that at this time, Jews were overrepresented in the professions and business are given in Table 15.3. Rows 1 and 2 show that in 1889, Jews were 14 percent of certified lawyers in the Russian empire and 43 percent of apprentice lawyers (the next generation of professionals). Row 3 shows that in 1910, Jews comprised 35 percent of the mercantile class (Rubinstein, 2000). Row 4 shows that in 1914, Jews comprised 37 percent of the managers in Kiev (Slezkine, 2004).

Table 15.3. Jews in the professions and business 1889–1914

Years	Occupation	Percent Jews	AQ
1889	Certified lawyers	14	3.5
1889	Apprentice lawyers	43	10.7
1910	Mercantile class	35	8.7
1914	Kiev: managers	37	9.2
Source: Slezkine (2004)			

Jews were also prominent in the arts in the second half of the 19th century. The Gnesin sisters founded the first Russian music school for children; the Rubinstein brothers founded the Russian Music Society, the St. Petersburg conservatory, and the Moscow conservatory. In the visual arts, many of the leading painters were Jewish. They are not generally well known in the West except for Marc Chagall (1889–1980), the surrealist painter who migrated to Paris and then to the United States, and Leon Bakst (1866–1924, born Lev Rozenberg), the painter and premier stage designer who designed the décor and costumes for Sergei Diaghilev's ballet. In addition to these were Leonid Pasternak (1862–1945), the foremost portraitist; Mark Antokolsky (1843–1902), generally reckoned the greatest Russian sculptor of the 19th century; and Isaak Levitan (1860–1900), "who became, and still is, the most beloved of all Russian landscape painters" (Slezkine, 2004, p. 126).

Other famous Russian Jews include the novelist Boris Pasternak (1890–1960), author of *Doctor Zhivago* (and the son of Leonid Pasternak); the revolutionary communist Leon Trotsky (1879–1940, born Lev Bernstein), who together with Lenin was mainly responsible for organizing the Bolshevik Revolution of 1917 and served as Commissar for Foreign Affairs until Lenin's death in 1924; and the anthropologist Franz Boas (1858–1942), who emigrated to the United States, where he obtained the chair of anthropology at Columbia University, from which he did anthropology a huge disservice by divorcing it from biology.

There was a large Jewish community in the port city of Odessa on the Black Sea. Some statistics for the educational and commercial standing of Jews in the city are given in Table 15.4.

Table 15.4. Jews in Odessa 1878–1899

Years	Occupation	% Jews
1878	Gymnasium students	33
1886	University students	33
1886	Medicine/ law students	40
1886	Lawyers	49
1875–1899	Guild merchants	50
1875–1899	Factory output	57
1875–1899	Grain exports	70
Source: Slezkine (2004)		

Row 1 shows that in 1878, Jews were one third of all Gymnasium students in the city, and, according to a contemporary observer, they typically outperformed the Russians: "all the schools are filled with Jewish students from end to end and, to be honest, the Jews are always at the head of the class" (Slezkine, 2004, p. 124). Row 2 shows that in

1886, Jews were one third of students at the University of Odessa; row 3 shows that 40 percent of students in the faculties of medicine and law were Jews. Row 4 shows that Jews were 49 percent of lawyers in the city. Rows 5, 6, and 7 show that in the last quarter of the 19th century, 50 percent of the city's guild merchants were Jews, that 57 percent of factory output was produced by Jews, and that Jews were responsible for 70 percent of the grain exports.

Statistics for St. Petersburg tell the same story. St. Petersburg lay outside the Pale, and therefore Jews were not legally permitted to live in the city. Nevertheless, some Jews did live there illegally in the years from 1880 up to World War I. They comprised about two percent of the population and were massively overrepresented in the commercial and professional life of the city. Statistics showing this are given in Table 15.5.

Table 15.5. Jews in St. Petersburg 1881–1915

Year	Occupation	% Jews	AQ
1881	Stock brokers	43	21.5
1881	Pawnbrokers	41	20.5
1881	Business owners	27	13.5
1881	Brothel keepers	16	8.0
1881	Lawyers	32	16.0
1881	Doctors	11	5.5
1881	Dentists	9	4.5
1913	Doctors	17	8.5
1913	Dentists	52	21.0
1915	Stock Exchange Council	41	20.5
1915	Bank managers	40	20.0

Source: Slezkine (2004)

Rows 1 through 4 show that in 1881 Jews constituted 43 percent of stock brokers, 41 percent pawnbrokers, 27 percent all business owners, and 16 percent of the brothel keepers. Rows 5-7 show that in the same year Jews made up 32 percent of lawyers, 11 percent of the doctors, and nine percent of the dentists in the city. By 1913, these percentages had increased to 17 percent and 52 percent, respectively. Rows 10 and 11 show that in 1915, Jews were 41 percent of the members of the St. Petersburg Stock Exchange Council and 40 percent of joint-stock bank managers.

In the first half of the 19th century, Jews in Russia were tolerated without much overt discrimination. But by the 1870s, their success had begun to excite concern. The numbers of Jews among the socioeconomic elite worried Russian officials. In the 1880s, the universities introduced quotas restricting the numbers of Jews applying for places. Many Jews overcame this problem by attending universities abroad. V. D. Spasovich, then-chairman of the St. Petersburg bar, observed in 1889, "we are dealing with a colossal problem." V. Kokovtsev, then- Finance Minister of the Russian government, put it in 1906: "the Jews are so clever that no law can be counted on to restrict them" (Slezkine, 2004, p. 158).

In the last three decades of the 19th century, the commercial success of the Jews generated so much resentment that the Gentiles began a series of attacks on them known as pogroms. The first of these broke out in 1871 in Odessa, started by local Greeks who found themselves unable to compete with the Jews. In 1881, there were further pogroms against the Jews in a number of cities following the assassination of Tsar Alexander II, for which the Jews were widely blamed. These were followed by a series of further outbreaks. As a result of these many Jews emigrated. (Others left Russia, no doubt, to avoid conscription in the Russian Army and to seek a better life (Levin, 2000).) Between 1897 and 1914, approximately 1,288,000 left the Empire. About one million of these went to the United States and another 100,000, to Britain. There were more attacks on the Jews during the 1914–1918 War, when Jews were perceived as potentially or actually disloyal.

Infant mortality was lower among Jews in the late 19th and early 20th centuries. Studies showing this have been summarized by Condran and Kramarow and are shown in Table 15.6: infant mortality of Gentiles was between 106 and 213 percent higher than that of Jews.

Table 15.6. Infant mortality per 1,000 live births

Years	Location	Jews	Gentiles	% Difference
1896–1897	Russia	130	268	106
1900–1904	Russia	119	254	113
1905–1909	Leningrad	117	262	124
1910–1914	Leningrad	78	244	213
1922–1924	Leningrad	78	178	128

3. The Bolshevik Revolution and the Soviet Union, 1917–1939

Partly as a result of the series of attacks on Jews from the 1870s on, and the failure of the Tsarist state to protect them, many Jews joined the Bolshevik Party. Its objective was to overthrow the Russian state and replace it with a new communist order based on the ideals of ethnic equality and universal brotherhood. Jews were prominent among the Bolsheviks during the Civil War between the Red and the White Russians of 1917–1921. The Red Army was led by Trotsky, who was Jewish, and Jews were 40 percent of the top elected officials in the Army. At the First All-Russian Congress of Soviets in 1917, 31 percent of the Bolshevik delegates were Jews. In the Second Congress of Soviets, Jews were 37 percent of the Bolshevik delegates. The first two heads of the Soviet State–Lev Kamenev (born Rozenfeld, 1883–1936) and Yakov Sverdlov (1885—1919)–were both Jews, and so also were the first Bolshevik bosses of Moscow and Petrograd–Kamenev and Zinoviev. From 1919 to 1921, Jews were approximately 25 percent of the Party's Central Committee. When Cheka (the secret police) was set up in 1918, Jews were 19 percent of the investigators; they made up 50 percent of the investigators employed in the department for combating "counter-terrorism." In 1923, Cheka was replaced by OGPU; Jews composed 15 percent of the senior officials and half (four out of eight) of the governing Secretariat.

Put simply, Jews prospered in the Soviet Union in the period between the two World Wars: "there is no doubt that the Jews had a much higher proportion of elite members than any other ethnic group in the USSR" (Slezkine, 2004, p. 236). A higher percentage of Jews than Gentiles were literate: 85 percent in 1926, compared with 58 percent of Russians; 94 percent in 1939, compared with 83 percent of Russians. In 1939, 26.5 percent of Jews had a high-school education, compared with 7.8 percent of the population of the Soviet Union as a whole and 8.1 percent of Russians in the Russian Federation. Further statistics for the educational and socioeconomic standing of the Jews are given in Table 15.7.

During the period 1917–1939, Jews were approximately 1.8 percent of the population. Row 1 shows that in 1926, nine percent of the officers in military academies were Jews. Row 2 shows that at the First Congress of Soviet Writers in 1934, Jews made up 19 percent of the delegates. Row 3 shows that in 1934, when the OGPU was transformed into the NKVD, Jews made up 63 percent of the senior officials (37 out of 59).

Table 15.7. Jews in the Soviet Union 1926–1939

Years	Occupation	% Jews	AQ
1926	Military officers	9	5.0
1934	Writers	19	10.5
1934	NKVD	63	35.0
1939	University students	11	6.1
1939	University graduates	15	8.3
1939	Doctors	20	11.1
1939	University professors: Russia	14	7.7
1939	University professors: Belarus	33	18.3
1939	University professors: Ukraine	29	16.1
Source: Slezkine (2004)			

Row 4 shows that in 1939, Jews made up 11 percent of the university students and row 5, that Jews were 15 percent of the university graduates. Row 6 shows that in the same year Jews were 20 percent of the doctors. Rows 7 through 9 show that Jews constituted 14 percent of the university professors in Russia, 33 percent of the university professors in Belarus, and 29 percent of the university professors in the Ukraine.

In Moscow during the years 1926–1939, the number of Jews in the city was approximately 250,000 (6.0 percent of the total). In 1939, 40 percent of Jews were high school graduates as compared with 27 percent of the population of the city. Table 15.8 shows that in 1926. In 1939, Jews were 45 percent of the professors of music in Moscow, 17 percent of university students, and 24 percent of university graduates in the city.

Table 15.8. Jews in Moscow 1926–1939

Years	Occupation	% Jews	AQ
1926	Music professors	45	7.5
1939	University students	17	2.8
1939	University graduates	24	4.0
Source: Slezkine (2004)			

In Leningrad as well, Jews were prominent among elites. The number of Jews in the city increased from 35,000 (1.8 percent) in 1910 to 84,600 (5.28 percent) in 1926, and again to 201,500 (6.3 percent) in 1939. Jews were massively overrepresented in the professional life of the city. Statistics showing this are given in Table 15.9.

Table 15.9. Jews in Leningrad 1939

Occupation	% Jews	AQ
University students	19	3.0
Lawyers	45	7.1
Doctors	39	6.2
Dentists	69	11.0
Pharmacists	59	9.4
Journalists & writers	31	4.9
University professors	18	2.9
Artists	12	1.9
Actors & directors	12	1.9
Store managers	31	4.9
Source: Slezkine (2004)		

Row 1 shows that Jews were 19 percent of university students, 45 percent of lawyers, 39 percent of the doctors, 69 percent of the dentists, 59 percent of pharmacists, 31 percent of journalists and writers, 18 percent of university professors, 12 percent of artists, actors, and directors, and 31 percent of the store managers.

Jews assimilated well with Gentiles in the years between the two World Wars. There was an acceleration of mixed marriages between Jews and Gentiles, which between 1924 and 1936, increased from 17.4 to 42.3 percent in the Russian Republic. There was little overt anti-Semitism, but nevertheless, the authorities were at pains to defuse a certain degree of resentment about Jewish prominence among the elite. When it was discovered that Lenin's maternal grandfather was Jewish, Stalin decreed that this fact should be suppressed, lest it foster the notion that the Revolution had been engineered by Jews.

Between 1937 and 1938, what has come to be known as "The Great Terror" began: thousands of Army officers and professionals were executed or deported to the gulags. Jews, however, survived the purges fairly well. Only about one percent of all Soviet Jews were arrested for supposed political crimes, as compared with 16 percent of Polish Jews and 30 percent of Latvian Jews. In 1939, the proportion of Jews in the gulags was about 16 percent lower than their proportion in the population. The explanation for this is that Jews were nearly all loyal to the Soviet Union and the Marxist ideology. This is shown by the high proportion of Jews among the professors of Marxism-Leninism in the universities and the research institutes. Jews were 20 percent of these, and 25 percent in the elite universities of Moscow, Leningrad, Kiev, and Kharkov.

After the Second World War, Jews continued to be hugely overrepresented among the professional elite. Statistics showing this for 1949 are given in Table 15.10. At this time, Jews were about 1.8 percent of the population, yet they constituted 39 percent of the faculty at the Moscow Institute of Jurisprudence (row 1). Row 2 shows that Jews were 80 percent of the members of the Institute of Literature of the Academy of Sciences. Rows 3 through 6 show that they were between 39 percent and 51 percent of the directors of Moscow theatres, art galleries, popular music shows, and circuses. Row 7 shows that Jews were 33 percent of the chief engineers at

Soviet armaments plants. Row 8 shows that Jews were 23 percent of the top managers at the Telegraphic Agency of the Soviet Union (TASS).

Table 15.10. Jews among the professional elite in 1949

Position	% Jews	AQ
Moscow Institute of Jurisprudence	39	21.7
Institute of Literature	80	44.0
Directors, Moscow theatres	42	23.3
Directors, art galleries	40	22.2
Directors of popular music shows	39	21.7
Directors of circuses	51	28.3
Chief engineers	33	18.3
Telegraphic Agency	23	12.8
Source: Slezkine (2004)		

4. Discrimination against Jews, 1939–1989

In 1939, Joseph Stalin began to develop suspicions about the loyalty of the Jews. He put Molotov in charge of Soviet diplomacy and ordered him to remove the Jews from the Commissariat of External Affairs. The purge of the Jews increased during the war with Germany "and turned into an avalanche in 1949, when ideological contagion became the regime's chief concern and Jews emerged as its principal agents" (Slezkine, 2004, p. 301). In January 1948, one of the best known and high profile Soviet Jews, Solomon Mikhoels (1890–1948), was murdered on Stalin's orders. The establishment of the state of Israel in 1948 increased Stalin's growing paranoia about the Jews. Many Russian Jews welcomed the state of Israel; Stalin thought they would become more loyal to Israel than to the Soviet Union and that Jews and Jewish institutions were already subversive. During the years 1948–1952, all Jewish theatres and writers' organizations were closed and many Jewish writers were arrested. In 1952, 15 members of the former Jewish Anti-Fascist Committee were put on trial as "bourgeois nationalists," and all but one were shot. "By 1950 few Jews could make it to the top bureaucratic positions, though Jews continued to be widely represented in the Soviet academic, cultural and artistic elite" (Sacks, 1998, p. 249).

Stalin died in 1953, and the purges of the Jews ceased. From 1953 onward, "Jews returned to the top of the Soviet professional hierarchy; they remained by far the most successful of all Soviet nationalities" (Slezkine, 2004, p. 331). In 1955, the Soviet physicists, in a largely Jewish team led by Andrei Sakharov (1921–1989), successfully exploded the hydrogen bomb. Other brilliant Jewish scientists of this period included the physicists Igor Y. Tamm (1895–1971) and Lev Landau (1908–1968), the mathematicians Izrail Gelfand (1913–2009) and Leonid Kantorovich (1912–1986), and the novelist Boris Pasternak (1890–1960). However, despite the ending of overt discrimination against Jews, covert discrimination continued: "in the 1970s, career advancement and job appointments were limited by something akin to percentage quotas." Many Jews who found conventional careers blocked found new fields to work in:

> When access to top research institutions was restricted, Jews poured into the burgeoning fields of computer science and information services. Jews had specialized knowledge and experience that remained in short supply and this assured their entry into high status positions. (Sacks, 1998, p. 249)

Throughout the 1960s up to the 1990s, there remained a strong current of anti-Semitism throughout Russia, generated by resentment over the obvious and inescapable Jewish overrepresentation among the professional elite. By this time, Jews had so consolidated their positions to such an extent that they could be said to be "hereditary members of the cultural elite" (Slezkine, 2004, p. 335); these select lived in the affluent suburbs of Moscow and Leningrad and sent their children to the top schools and universities; their offspring who would, in turn, enter the elite. To combat this, the Soviet state put quotas on the numbers of Jews admitted to elite universities and prestigious professional positions. Many Jews, however, were able to overcome these "affirmative-action" programs directed against them. In some cases, the projects, such as the development of nuclear weapons, missiles, and space research, were too important, and Jewish scientists were appointed simply because they were the best. Some Jews changed their names to make them sound Russian.

Others took positions in less prestigious universities and research institutes and transformed them into first-rate institutions. Overall, the "anti-Jewish discrimination was not very successful (the enormous achievement gap between Jews and everyone else was narrowing very slowly)" (Slezkine, 2004, p. 337).

Nevertheless, despite the ability of many Jews to overcome the discrimination against them, many of them felt uncomfortable in the Soviet Union from the 1950s onward. The Jewish writer Mikhail Agursky (1933–1991) described the widespread Jewish sentiments of this period:

> Could one really expect that a nation [the Jews] that had given the Soviet state political leaders, diplomats, generals, and top economic managers would agree to become an estate whose boldest dreams would be to a position as head of a laboratory at the Experimental Machine-Tool Research Institute or senior researcher at the Automatics and Telemechanics Institute? The Jews were oppressed and humiliated to a much greater degree than the rest of the population. (Slezkine, 2004, p. 338)

Jews increasingly identified with Israel, especially after the victory in the Six-Day War of 1967, which established Israel in the eyes of Soviet Jews as a serious country of which they could be proud. The next year–1968–saw the Soviet invasion of Czechoslovakia. Many Soviet Jews disapproved of the brutal crushing of the incipient democracy and became further alienated from the Soviet Union.

The response of many Jews to this increasingly unfriendly and sometimes hostile atmosphere was to emigrate. Increasing numbers applied for exit visas. The government responded by further discrimination against Jews in education and employment and by raising the fee for an emigration visa, which further alienated the Jews. Between 1968 and 1994, about 1.2 million left the USSR and its successor states. Officially they applied to go to Israel, but many treated this as a staging post *en route* to the United States. By 1988, 89 percent of emigrants were going to the United States. To stem this outflow, the U.S. reduced its quota for Soviet Jews. By 1994, 63 percent of Jewish émigrés from the USSR had ended up in Israel and 27 percent in the United States (Slezkine, 2004, p. 358). The result of the extensive emigration of Jews in the 1960s, '70s, and

'80s was that their numbers in the Soviet Union fell precipitously. In 1973, there were approximately 3.5 million Jews in the Soviet Union out of a total population of approximately 200 million; they comprised approximately 1.7 percent of the population, as compared with about four percent during the 19th century.

Jews continued to be overrepresented among the professional elite during the post World War II years. Statistics showing this for 1959 and 1989 are given in Table 15.11. Rows 1 and 2 reveal that in 1959, 11.4 percent of Jews were college graduates, compared with 1.8 percent of Russians; 1.35 percent of Jews were employed as scientists, compared with 0.01 percent of Russians. Rows 3 and 4 show that in 1989, 64 percent of Jews were college graduates, compared with 15 percent of Russians; 5.3 percent of Jews were employed as scientists compared with 0.5 percent of Russians.

Table 15.11. Jews among the professional elite in 1959 and 1989 (percentages)

Year	Occupation	Jews	Russians
1959	College graduates	11.4	1.8
1959	Scientists	1.3	0.01
1989	College graduates	64.0	15.0
1989	Scientists	5.3	0.5
Sources: Altshuler, 1987; Sacks, 1998)			

5. Jews in Chess

It is well known that Russians have been preeminent at chess; less well known is the fact that Jews have been highly overrepresented among top Russian chess players. There is an annual Soviet chess championship tournament in which there are typically about 20 participants. In the Soviet championship tournaments for the years 1947–1949 and 1970–1976, there were 83 Jewish and 110 Gentile participants. In these years, Jews in the Soviet Union numbered about 2 million in a population of approximately 230 million. Jews were therefore 88 times overrepresented than Gentiles among these top Russian chess players.

Jews have been similarly overrepresented among Russian chess grandmasters. The top-rated Russian chess grandmasters for the years 1851 to 2003 are given by William Rubinstein (2004) and are listed in Table 15.12. There was only one Russian grandmaster (Carl von Jaenisch (1813–1872)) between 1851 and 1870. It was not until the 1870s that the first Russian Jew (Szymon Winawer (1838–1920)) appeared among the top-rated Russian chess grandmasters. In the whole period, there are 14.5 Jews and 18 Gentiles among the grandmasters. (Gari Kasparov (born Weinstein in 1963) is only half-Jewish, so he is counted as 0.5.) Hence, Jews have been 44 percent of the total.

Table 15.12. Top-rated Russian chess grandmasters (Jews are asterisked)

Years	Chess Champions	Years	Chess Champions
1851–1869	von Jaenisch	1940–1969	Spassky*
1870–1899	Chigorin		Korchnoi*
	Winawer*		Taimanov*
1900–1939	Bogolyubov	1970–2003	Polugayevsky*
	Bernstein*		Kasparov*
	Tartakower*		Gurevich*
	Nimzovitch*		Gelfand*
	Alekhine		Beliavsky
	Keres		Romanishin
	Lillienthal*		Ivanchuk
1940–1969	Smyslov		Salov
	Petrosian		Bareev
	Kholmov		Beliavsky
	Karpov		Kramnik
	Botvinnik*		Shirov
	Bronstein*		Morozevich
	Tal*		

It will be noted that in the period 1970–2003, the number of Gentile top-rated Russian chess grandmasters exceeded the number of Jews for the first time since 1900. This is explained by the massive emigration of Jews from the Soviet Union in these years. During this period, Jews were only approximately one percent of the population of the Soviet Union, as compared with about 2.5 percent during the first three quarters of the 20th century.

6. Nobel Prize winners

A list of the Russian Nobel Laureates is given in Table 15.13, with Jews identified by asterisks. Russia has produced 23 Nobel Prize winners, of whom 16 (70 percent) have been Jewish. Thus, Jews, who comprised about 2.1 percent of the population of the Soviet Union during the 20th century, have produced 70 percent of the Nobel Prize winners, giving them an Achievement Quotient of 47·

Table 15.13. Russian Nobel Prize winners (Jews are asterisked)

Year	Name	Subject	Year	Name	Subject
1904	Ivan Pavlov	Medicine	1971	Simon Kuznets*	Economics
1908	Ilya Mechnikov*	Medicine	1973	Wassily Leontief*	Economics
1933	Ivan Bunin	Literature	1975	Leonid Kantorovich*	Economics
1952	Selman Waksman*	Medicine	1977	Ilya Prigogine*	Chemistry
1958	Boris Pasternak*	Literature	1978	Pyotr Kapitsa	Physics
1958	Pavel A. Cherenkov	Physics	1982	Aaron Klug*	Chemistry
1958	Il´ja M. Frank*	Physics	1987	Joseph Brodsky*	Literature
1958	Igor Y. Tamm*	Physics	2000	Zhores Alferov*	Physics
1962	Lev Landau*	Physics	2003	Alexei Abrikosov*	Physics
1964	Nicolay G. Basov	Physics	2003	Vitaly L. Ginzburg*	Physics
1964	Alexander Prokhorov	Physics	2007	Leonid Hurwicz*	Economics
1970	Alexandr Solzhenitsyn	Literature			

7. Mathematicians

Russia has produced 14 mathematicians who have received the Fields Medal or the Wolf Prize. These are listed in Table 15.14. Ten of these have been Jews (Gregori Margulis (b. 1946) has been awarded the Wolf Prize as well as the Fields Medal, but is only counted once; Grigori Perelman (b. 1966) declined the Wolf Prize but is counted). Thus, Jews, who have been about 1.5 percent of the population during the second half of the 20th century, have produced 71 percent of top mathematicians, giving them an Achievement Quotient of 47.

Charles Murray (2003, p. 280) has calculated the numbers of Jewish and Gentile "significant figures" (i.e. great names in science and the arts) in Russia whose careers fell within the years 1870 to 1950. He finds nine Jews and 63 Gentiles. Calculating the ratio of Jewish to Gentile "significant figures," he arrives at an Achievement Quotient (Jewish overrepresentation) of 4.1.

Table 15.14. Russian Mathematicians (Jews are asterisked)

Year	Fields Medal	Year	Wolf Prize
1970	Serge Novikov	1978	Izrail Gelfand*
1978	Gregori Margulis*	1980	Andrei Kolmogorov
1990	Vladimir Drinfeld*	1981	Oscar Zariski*
1994	Efim Zelmanov*	1982	Mark Krein*
2002	Vladimir Voevodsky	1993	Mikhael Gromov*
2006	Andrei Okounkov	1996	Yakov Sinai*
		2001	Vladimir Arnold*
		2006	Grigori Perelman*

8. Lenin Prize winners

About 200 Lenin Prizes have been awarded annually for meritorious work. The numbers of these, and the numbers who have been Jews for the years 1967–1968 and 1971–1972, are shown in Table 15.15. Once again, Jews have been substantially overrepresented among the recipients of these prizes.

Table 15.15. Lenin Prize winners

Year	N. Prize winners	N. Jews	% Jews	AQ
1967	203	29	14	11.7
1968	192	30	16	13.3
1971	228	26	11	9.2
1972	185	21	11	9.2

9. Jews in the Post 1989 Russian Federation

In 1989, the Soviet Union disintegrated and its constituent republics became the independent states of the Russian Federation, Ukraine, Belarus, and so forth. Discrimination against Jews was relaxed, and it was made easier for Jews to emigrate. Large numbers of Jews took advantage of this opportunity. Between 1989 and 2002, more than 15 million Jews and their relatives emigrated from the former Soviet Union, mainly into Israel (about 940,000, or 62 percent), and the reminder largely to the United States and Germany. In the Russian Federation, Mikhail Gorbachev (b.1931) introduced a more liberal order and discrimination against Jews largely came to an end. Nevertheless, many Jews still felt uncomfortable and continued to emigrate. In 1989, there were 551,000 Jews in the Russian Federation. By the 2002 census, the number of Jews had approximately halved to 230, 000, and became only 0.16 percent of the population.

In the new Russian Federation, "Jews are still heavily concentrated at the top of the professional hierarchy" (Slezkine, 2004, p. 362). The 1989 census showed that 64 percent of employed Jews had a higher education, compared with only 15 percent of Russians. The percentages of Jews and Russians in the professions and as metalworkers are shown in Table 15.16.

By this time, Jews were 0.4 percent of the population, but 16.1 percent of employed Jews were graduate engineers as compared with 5.1 percent of Russians; 6.3 percent were employed as physicians, as compared with 0.9 percent of Russians (Sacks, 1998). Jews were similarly overrepresented in other professions. On the other hand, fewer Jews than Russians were employed as metalworkers.

Table 15.16. Jews and Russians in the professions and manual occupations in 1989 (percentages)

Occupation	Jews	Russians	AQ
Engineers	16.1	5.1	3.2
Physicians	6.3	0.9	7.0
Scientists	5.3	0.5	10.6
School teachers	5.2	2.2	2.4
Managers	3.3	0.6	5.5
University faculty	2.6	0.4	6.5
Metalworkers	2.6	7.2	0.4

In the Russian Federation, it continues to be widely recognized that the Jews are successful. In a poll conducted in 1997, 75 percent of the respondents said they believed that Jews are well brought up and well educated; 80 percent said they believed that Jews include a large number of talented people. It is remarkable, though perhaps unsurprising, that of the seven top multimillionaires who made huge fortunes when Russia privatized its oil and natural gas industries in the Yeltsin era, six were Jews: Pyotr Aven (b.1955), Boris Berezovsky (b.1946), Mikhail Fridman (b.1964), Vladimir Gusinsky (b.1952), Mikhail Khodorkovsky (b.1963), and Alexander Smolensky (b.1954). Jews, who at this time were about 0.2 percent of the population, produced 86 percent of the new plutocracy.

10. Mixed Marriages

In the second half of the 20th century, there has been an increasing trend for Jews to marry Gentiles. In 1988–1989, in the former Soviet Union as a whole, 58 percent of Jewish men and 47 percent of Jewish women had entered into mixed marriages (Altshuler, 1998; Tolts, 2003). The result of this has been that an increasing number of children born to Jewish mothers have Gentile fathers. Statistics showing this for the years 1958 through 1993 are provided by Mark Tolts (2003) and are given in Table 15.17.

Table 15.17. Percentage of children of mixed origin born to Jewish mothers in the FSU

Republic	1958	1968	1988	1993
FSU	19	...	41	...
Russia	27	40	58	68
Ukraine	17	30	42	69
Belarus	14	32	37	71
Moldavia	7	12	17	58

We see that in Russia, Ukraine, Belarus, and Moldova, the same trend has been present. An increase of mixed marriages has also taken place in the former Soviet Baltic states of Latvia, Lithuania, and Estonia (see chapter 14).

Typically, Jews who enter mixed marriages lose their Jewish identity and raise their children as Gentiles. This has occurred in Russia in about 84 percent of mixed-marriage couples (Altshuler, 1998; Tolts, 2003). Thus, most of the Jews that have chosen to remain in Russia have largely abandoned their Jewish identity and come to think of themselves as Russians. In a poll carried out in 1995, only 16 percent of Russia's ethnic Jews considered themselves as religious. It seems likely that the great majority of Jews who remain in Russia and the other states of the former Soviet Union will increasingly assimilate with the ethnic Russians through intermarriage and lose their Jewish identity. In the foreseeable future, Jews in the former Soviet Union are likely to disappear as a self-conscious ethnic group, much as did the Jews of Spain and Portugal who converted to Christianity in the late 15th century.

CHAPTER 16

South Africa

1. Numbers of Jews
2. Educational Attainment
3. Earnings and Socioeconomic Status
4. Nobel Prize winners
5. Fertility

In the 16th and 17th centuries, the Dutch East India Company established a settlement in Cape Town as a staging post en route to the Far East. A number of Jewish merchants in the Netherlands were involved in the Dutch East Indies trade, and a few of them settled in Cape Town. They were prohibited from further settlement in 1652, when the Company banned all settlers except Protestants. This prohibition lasted until 1806, when the British gained control of the province of South Africa and allowed Jews to settle. A number of mainly Dutch, British, and German Jews took advantage of this opportunity. From henceforth, "Jews had much to do with the development of South Africa" (Johnson, 1966, p. 272). Noteworthy among these were the De Pass brothers, who developed copper mining at Port Nolloth and sugar plantations in Natal, and the Mosenthals, who introduced to South Africa the Mohair goat and flourished in ostrich farming and sheep and cattle breeding.

Other South African Jews who have taken a prominent part in science, the legal profession, in political, philanthropic, industrial, and mining affairs have been Simeon Jacobs (a judge of the Supreme Court), the Mendelssohns, Papaports, Rabinowitzes, Solomons, Lilienfelds, Kisches, Neumanns, Moselys, Alfred Beit, Sir David Harris, Sir Lionel Phillips, and Sir George Albu.

Between 1860 and 1900, a number of Eastern European Jews migrated to South Africa to participate in the mining of diamonds, which had been unearthed in Kimberley in the 1860s, and gold, following discoveries in the Rand in the 1880s. During the last decades of the 19th century, "Jews played a notable part in the South African deep-level mines and in the financial system which raised the capital to sink them" (Johnson, 2004, p. 573). The foremost among these in the diamond industry was Sir Ernest Oppenheimer (1880–1957), the son of a German Jewish cigar manufacturer, who formed the Anglo-American Corporation of South Africa. By 1957, his firm controlled more than 95 percent of the world's supply of diamonds. He endowed several university chairs in South Africa.

In 1899, a British journalist, J. A. Hobson, visited South Africa and commented on the prosperity of the Johannesburg Jews, who numbered around 7,000 at the time: they were so powerful that the Johannesburg stock exchange was closed on the Day of Atonement. Hobson observed, "The shop fronts and business houses, the market place, the saloons, the "stoops" of the smart suburban houses are sufficient to convince one of the large presence of the chosen people." (Johnson, 2004, p. 573)

In 1930 a Quota Act was passed that effectively stemmed further immigration of Jews.

1. Numbers of Jews

Figures for the numbers of Jews in South Africa and their percentage of the White population are given in Table 16.1. Both figures are taken from Daniel Elazar and Peter Redding (1983) and the *American Jewish Yearbook*. The decline in numbers of Jews from 1970 to 2001 is largely a result of emigration. There has also been an increase in the number of Gentile Whites, due to immigration from Zimbabwe, which has contributed to the reduction in the percentage of Jews among the White population.

Table 16.1. Numbers and percentages of Jews in South Africa

Year	N. Jews	% Population
1904	38,101	3.41
1926	62,103	4.09
1936	90,645	4.52
1946	104,156	4.39
1960	114,762	3.70
1970	118,200	3.15
1991	100,000	2.00
2001	79,000	1.30

2. Education

Jews in South Africa have a high level of educational attainment as compared with White Gentiles. Statistics showing this are given by Dubb (1984, 1991) and are shown in Table 16.2.

Table 16.2. Education of Jews and Whites in South Africa (percentages)

Year	Measure	Jews	Whites	AQ
1970	Matriculation	56	23	2.4
1970	University degree	10	4	2.5
1970	Doctorate	0.2	0.1	2.0
1980	University degree	15.7	7.1	2.2
1991	Matriculation	93.0	23.4	4.0
1991	University degree	22.6	10.1	2.2

Row 1 gives figures, from the 1970 census, for the percentages of Jews (56 percent) and Whites (23 percent) who passed the matriculation examination taken by school-leavers. Row 2 shows that 10 percent of Jews and four percent for Whites had university degrees in 1970. Row 3 reveals that the percentage of Jews with doctorates in that year was nearly double that of Whites. Row 4 gives the percentages that had university degrees in the 1980 census: the percentage for Jews had increased to 15.7 percent, while that for White Gentiles had risen to only 7.1 percent. Row 5 gives the matriculation rate of 93 percent for Jews, found in a survey of a representative sample of 1,000 Jews carried out in 1998 and published by Barry Kosmin, Jacqueline Goldberg, Milton Shain, and Shirley Bruk (1999); a corresponding figure for Whites, taken from the 1991 census, was 23.4 percent. Row 6 shows that according to 1991 census, 22.6 percent of Jews had university degrees, as compared with 10.1 percent of Gentile Whites.

3. Income and Socioeconomic Status

Jews in South Africa have higher average incomes than White Gentiles. Sergio Della Pergola and Allie Dubb (1988) have calculated that in 1980, the median income of Jews was 8,323 Rand, approximately 25 percent greater than the 6,139 Rand of White Gentiles.

Jews in South Africa also have higher socioeconomic status than White Gentiles. The percentages of Jews and White Gentiles in six socioeconomic status categories in 1936, 1960, 1970, 1980, and 1991, obtained from census returns, have been given by Marcus Arkin (1984), Della Pergola and Dubb (1988), and Dubb (1994). The occupational distributions for 1936, 1960, and 1970 are shown in Table 16.3.

In 1936, Jews were slightly overrepresented in the professions and in clerical and sales, but underrepresented in administrative and managerial occupations and among blue-collar workers and in agriculture. By 1960, the position of the Jews had improved. They were now considerably overrepresented in the professions, administrative and managerial occupations, and clerical and sales, and again underrepresented in blue-collar occupations and agriculture. The occupational distribution for 1970 is similar, except that Jews had become somewhat underrepresented in clerical and sales occupations.

Table 16.3. Socioeconomic Status of Jews and whites in South Africa, 1936–1970 (percentages)

Occupation	1936 Jews	1936 Whites	1960 Jews	1960 Whites	1970 Jews	1970 Whites
Professional	9.7	8.2	20.0	12.3	22.7	15.4
Admin/managerial	2.0	12.7	19.7	5.2	17.5	5.3
Clerical & sales	53.5	23.1	49.7	33.3	20.7	26.7
Services	5.3	5.7	1.8	5.3	4.0	6.8
Blue collar	17.6	47.1	7.5	33.5	5.3	26.1
Agriculture	1.9	3.2	1.3	10.4	1.0	3.0

Table 16.4 gives the occupational distributions for 1980 and 1991 and shows that these were similar to those in 1970.

Table 16.4. Socioeconomic Status of Jews and whites in South Africa, 1980–1991 (percentages)

Occupation	1980 Jews	1980 Whites	1991 Jews	1991 Whites
Professional	28.7	19.8	29.8	18.5
Admin/managerial	17.1	7.3	22.0	11.5
Clerical & sales	20.0	36.8	32.4	32.6
Services	4.3	7.9	3.2	7.9
Blue collar	7.1	28.2	12.6	29.5
Agriculture	1.5	1.6	-	-

4. Nobel Prize winners

South Africa has produced five Nobel Prize winners for science and literature, which is respectable for a White population of around 3.7 to 5 million. They are listed in Table 16.5. It is remarkable that two of the five have been Jews, who were 3.1 percent of the population in 1970 and 2.0 percent of the White population in 1991. Thus, Jews, who comprised about 2.5 percent of the White population of South Africa in the second half of the 20th century, have produced 40 percent of the Nobel Prize winners, giving them an Achievement Quotient of 16.

Table 16.5. Nobel Prize winners (Jews are asterisked)

Year	Name	Subject	Year	Name	Subject
1951	Max Theiler	Medicine	2002	Sydney Brenner*	Medicine
1979	Allan Cormack	Medicine	2003	J. M. Coetzee	Literature
1991	Nadine Gordimer*	Literature			

5. Fertility

Della Pergola and Dubb (1988) have published the fertility rates of Jews and Gentile Whites in South Africa for 1940 through 1970. Their figures for these are shown in Table 16.6. The fertility rates of Jews have been consistently lower than those of White Gentiles, as has been the case, almost invariably, in Western countries in the 20th century. Nevertheless, in the period 1950–1970, the Jewish fertility rates have been comfortably above the 2.1 required for replacement.

Table 16.6. Fertility rates of Jews and Gentiles

Year	Jews	Gentiles
1940	2.1	3.1
1950	3.0	3.4
1960	3.0	3.5
1970	2.7	3.2

Chapter 17

Switzerland

1. Numbers of Jews in Switzerland
2. The 19th Century
3. 1900–1945
4. Intellectual Achievement
5. Nobel Prize winners
6. 1945–2010: Business, Finance, and the Professions

Switzerland has had a settled Jewish community since the 13th century. The first recorded mention of Jews in Switzerland came in 1213 in Basel, when the country hosted one of the largest Jewish communities in Europe, made up mostly of Jews from Germany and France. Jews settled in Bern by 1259, St. Gall in 1268, Zurich in 1273, and Schaffhausen, Diessenhofen, and Luzerne in 1299. The Jewish community in Basel flourished until 1348, when during the Black Death, they were accused of poisoning wells. As a result, 600 Jews were burned at the stake on an island in the Rhine in 1349, although their children were spared and forcibly baptized. At about the same time, the Jews in Bern were accused of murdering a Christian boy named Rudolf (Ruff) and were expelled from the city. The public animosity toward the Jews was so great that in 1349, they were expelled from

Switzerland. However, they were permitted to return to Zurich in 1352 and to Basel in 1361.

In the 14th century, Jews from Alsace, Ulm, Nuremberg, France, and various southern German cities began to settle in Neuchâtel, Biel, Vevay, Pruntrut, Solothurn, Winterthur, Zofingen, and various places in Aargau and Thurgau. At this time, the Jews of Switzerland were regarded as *"Kammerknechte"* ("chamber farmhands") of the Holy Roman Empire and were under its protection as long as they paid an annual tribute. Some towns exercised the *"Judenregal,"* the right to protect the Jews and impose taxes on them; foreign Jews had to pay fees to the municipality in order to be allowed to remain even for a few days.

As in most of Europe during the Middle Ages, Jews were almost exclusively confined to peddling second-hand goods and to money-lending; there were also a few Jewish physicians. They were subjected to many restrictions. Jews were ostracized and required to wear the *"Judenhut"* ("Jew's hat"), although Jewish physicians were sometimes exempted. Jews were required to live in designated neighborhoods, and their infrastructure, such as slaughterhouses, synagogues, mikvot (ritual purification baths), and cemeteries were located in these ghettos. Jews had to pay high taxes for these privileges, particularly for their cemeteries. As the Jews' principal occupation was money-lending, when the Christians were in debt, they blamed Jews collectively for their hardships, and often tortured or attacked them. Expulsions and persecutions ocured repeatedly. Because of Christians' prohibition against usury, the absence of Jews due to expulsion would swiftly have an adverse effect on the economic functioning of society. Simply put, the Jews were needed, as they advanced funds to all strata. Thus, after various expulsions, the Jews were often allowed to return and continue their money-lending activities.

The 1400s saw further persecutions and expulsions of the Jewish communities. In 1401, all of the Jews living at Schaffhausen were accused of blood libel and condemned to death; 30 were burned alive. In the same year, 18 men and women were burned at the stake in Winterthur. The Jews of Zurich, though, were safeguarded. In Basel in 1434, a church edict required Jews to attend Christian church services and listen to proselytizing sermons; rather than comply, most Jews left the city and did not return until the 1800s. Jews were banished from the city and canton of Bern in 1427, from Freiburg in 1428, from Zurich in 1436, from Schaffhausen in 1472, from Rheinau in 1490, from Thurgau in 1494, and from Basel in 1543. Despite these expulsions, a number of Jews found their way back into Switzerland during these years. A few were admitted in the 16th century when Christian printers in Basel began printing Hebrew texts. They needed Jews to proofread these texts and therefore acquired hundreds of residency permits for them.

At the end of the 18th century, a Jewish community was established in Geneva, after a number of Jews from Lorraine settled in the suburb of Carouge. Up to the end of the 1700s, Jews in Switzerland did not enjoy full civil rights, but were considered resident aliens. They required special permission to marry, and their business activities were heavily regulated. They did not obtain the same type of financial assistance for their schools that the rest of Swiss society received. In the Great Council of Helvetia of 1798–1799, which ocured under French revolutionary occupation, prominent Swiss liberals advocated that Jews be granted full civic equality, and some rights were conferred on them in concordance with treaties with Britain, France, and the United States. However, the Jews of Switzerland would have to wait until the late 19th century before they were treated as citizens.

1. Numbers of Jews in Switzerland

The numbers of Jews in Switzerland recorded in censuses from 1850 through 2000 are shown in Table 17.1. The numbers approximately quadrupled from 1850 to 1900 as a result of natural increase and immigration. There was a further increase from 1900 to 1950, largely resulting from immigration. From 1970 to 2000, the Jewish population has been sustained by immigration, which has offset declining numbers due to low fertility and the many mixed marriages, whose offspring typically abandon Jewish identity.

Among the Cantons of Switzerland, only Zurich, Basel-City, Geneva, and Vaud have a Jewish community exceeding 1,000 people. One third of Swiss Jews reside in the Canton of Zurich (6,252 people). The percentage of Jews in the population has fallen considerably from 1950 to 2000, largely as a result of an increase of the Swiss population through immigration.

Table 17.1 Numbers and percentage of Jews in the population

Year	Jewish population	% of total
1850	3,145	0.1
1900	12,264	0.4
1950	19,048	0.4
1970	20,744	0.3
2000	17,914	0.2

2. The 19th Century

Emancipation came to the Jews of Switzerland in the 19th century, as in most of Europe. During the Napoleonic period, Jews in Geneva obtained full civil rights, but these were revoked on November 14, 1816, when a new law forbade them from owning land in the canton. It was not until 1841 that they were again granted civic equality. In 1843, Jews in Geneva were naturalized and granted full religious liberty; these right were granted to Jews in other parts of the country only in 1874 with the establishment of the Swiss Federal Constitution. Switzerland was thus one of the last Western European countries to treat its Jews as citizens.

Following emancipation, Jews prospered in Switzerland. The most famous Swiss Jew of the 19th century was Meyer Guggenheim (1828–1905), who was born in Aargan. He migrated to the United States and made a fortune in mining and smelting. He established a family dynasty that founded museums and art galleries, first in New York and later in Venice, Bilbao, Berlin, Guadalajaro, Abu Dhabi, Budapest, and Vilnius.

3. 1900–1945

Jews continued to do well in Switzerland in the early decades of the 20th century (Kamis-Mueller, 1992). From 1933 onward, many German Jews sought refuge in Switzerland in response to the increasing anti-Semitism of the National Socialist government. The Swiss government was not particularly welcoming, perhaps through fear of offending Hitler. In 1938, Swiss government made an agreement with Germany to limit the numbers of Jews permitted to enter the country. German authorities stamped "J" on the passports of Jews, making it easier for the Swiss to refuse them entry. Nevertheless, in the 1930s and during World War II, Switzerland gave refuge to about 23,000 Jewish refugees.

Many more Jews were turned away, however. In 1942, the Swiss police issued a regulation that denied refugee status to "refugees only on racial grounds, e.g. Jews." By the end of the war, more than 30,000 Jews had been refused entry. Furthermore, the Swiss government decreed that Jews would not be permitted permanent residence and that Switzerland would serve only as a country of transit. The Jewish refugees did not receive the financial support from the government that non-Jewish refugees received, and most of them left Switzerland at the end of the war.

In 1996, Swiss President Kastar Villiger formally apologized to world Jewry for the 1938 accord with the Nazis and Switzerland's wartime actions against the Jews. At the same time, however, he downplayed economic cooperation between Switzerland and Nazi Germany. It transpired that numerous documents relating to Jewish property in Swiss banks disappeared during the 1940s and '50s, and there was significant pressure in the 1990s and early 21st century to rectify and compensate Holocaust victims and their heirs who were denied their assets in Swiss banks.

In 1956, after the Sinai campaign and the Hungarian uprising, the Swiss Federation of Jewish Communities admitted Jewish refugees from Egypt and Hungary. In 1968, it also looked after Jews who fled to Switzerland from Czechoslovakia. Switzerland has generally been supportive toward Israel, while maintaining its neutrality. This support was strengthened by an Arab terrorist attack on an El Al plane in Zurich in 1969 and an act of sabotage on a Swissair plane bound for Israel in 1970. However, as in some other European countries, reports of anti-Semitism and anti-Israeli sentiment in Switzerland have increased since 2000.

4. Intellectual Achievement

From emancipation onward, Switzerland became a major haven for Russian Jewish intellectuals. One of these was Chaim Weizmann (1874–1952), first president of the state of Israel, who wrote of his university days in 1898,

> If Russian Jewry was the cradle of my Zionism, the Western universities were my finishing schools. The first of these schools was Berlin, with its Russian-Jewish society; the second was Berne, the third Geneva, both in Switzerland.

Around this time, prominent Jews who would become leaders of the Bolshevik Revolution, such as Georgi Valentinovich Plekhanov (1857-1918), Marxist philosopher and leader of the Russian Social Democratic movement, and Leon Trotsky, were also resident in Switzerland. Albert Einstein (1879–1955) attended school and college in Switzerland and became a Swiss national in 1901. He received his doctorate from the Federal Polytechnic Academy in Zurich and worked in the Swiss patent office 1902–1905, where he wrote his groundbreaking papers on special relativity in 1905. In 1909, a professorship was created for him at Zurich, where he remained until 1914, when he moved to Berlin as director of the Kaiser Wilhelm Institute of Physics.

5. Nobel Prize winners

A list of the Swiss Nobel Laureates is given in Table 17.2, with Jews identified by asterisks.

Table 17.2. Swiss Nobel Prize winners (Jews are asterisked)

Year	Name	Subject	Year	Name	Subject
1909	Theodor Kocher	Medicine	1958	Daniel Bovet	Medicine
1913	Alfred Werner	Chemistry	1978	Werner Arber	Medicine
1919	Carl Spitteler	Literature	1986	Heinrich Rohrer	Physics
1920	Charles Guillaume	Physics	1987	Karl Müller	Physics
1937	Paul Karrer	Chemistry	1991	Richard Ernst	Chemistry
1948	Paul Muller	Medicine	1992	Edmond Fischer*	Medicine
1952	Walter Hess	Medicine	1996	Rolf Zinkernagel	Medicine
1957	Tadeus Reichstein*	Medicine	2002	Kurt Wüthrich	Chemistry
1958	Felix Bloch*	Physics			

Switzerland has produced 17 Nobel Prize winners, of whom three have been Jewish (the list does not include Einstein who was born in Germany). Jews, who comprised about 0.3 percent of the population during the 20th century, have produced 18 percent of the Nobel Prize winners, giving them an Achievement Quotient of 60.

6. 1945–2010: Business, Finance, and the Professions

Despite their small numbers, Jews play a fairly important role in the textile and clock-making industries, as well as in manufacturing and wholesaling. Switzerland's Jews are not prominent in the big banks. They do, however, own several private banks, including the Dreyfus Bank in Basel, the Julius Bar in Zurich (both founded in the 19th century), the Republic National Bank of New York, and the Discount Bank & Trust Company. Jews are well represented in the professions as doctors, dentists, pharmacists, lawyers, engineers, academics, and artists, although there are few in the public service and press (Kamis-Mueller, 1992). At the beginning of the 21st century, Jews in Switzerland lived in prosperous communities and were "concentrated in white collar jobs" (Encyclopedia Judaica, 2007, vol.19, 343). The most well known Jewish figure in Switzerland in recent years is Ruth Dreifuss (b.1940), who entered the federal government in 1993 and became Switzerland's first female president in 1999.

CHAPTER **18**

The Balkans

1. Jews in the Ottoman Empire
2. Bulgaria
3. Greece
4. Romania
5. Turkey
6. Yugoslavia
7. Nobel Prize winners and Chess Champions
8. Intelligence of the Sephardic Jews
9. Conclusions

Jews settled in the Balkans in the first century AD, following the destruction of Jerusalem in 70 AD by the Romans. This original population is known as the Romaniot. In AD 330, the Roman emperor Constantine established the city of Constantinople on the Bosphorus Strait as the "New Rome" and capital of the empire. The city became the center of what historians would later call the Byzantine Empire, which extended across the Balkans and Asia Minor. The Roman Empire in the east survived for the next 11 centuries, during which "the Jews faced severe persecution under Byzantine rule" (Goffman, 2000, p. 16). As Paul Johnson bluntly puts it, "the treatment of Jews was always bad" (Johnson, 2004, p. 205).

In the 14th century, the Turks began to conquer parts of the southern Balkans and incorporate them into the Ottoman Empire. The Turks welcomed Jewish refugees from other domains and "offering a place of refuge, attracted many Jews" (Benbassa and Rodrigue, 1995, p. 4). In 1361, they conquered the city of Edirne (Adrianople) and welcomed Jewish refugees from Hungary, from which they had been expelled in 1376, from Spain, fleeing the massacres of 1370, and from France, from which they had been expelled in 1394. In the census of 1477, 1,647 Jewish households were recorded in Edirne, comprising about 8,000 individuals, roughly 11 percent of the population of the city.

In 1453, the Turks captured Constantinople, which they renamed Istanbul, and which they made the capital of the Ottoman Empire. They welcomed the Jews and a number of the Romaniot Jews moved to the city where "they worked mainly in trade." The Istanbul Jews were also prominent in "farming taxes, the collection of custom dues, and the mint; they controlled all major tax farming in the Istanbul region in 1470-80" (Benbassa & Rodrigue, 1995, p. 6). More Jews arrived after being expelled from Spain and Portugal in 1492 and in 1497, respectively. The Sultan of the Ottoman Empire invited them to come to Istanbul because he needed competent people to populate the city; somewhere between 50,000 and 100,000 took up this invitation to settle in Istanbul and other towns in the Balkans. Others settled in North Africa and the Levant (the eastern Mediterranean littoral) and a smaller number went to the Netherlands. These refugees from Spain and Portugal became known as the Sephardim. At the time of the expulsions, the Jews in Spain and Portugal were given the option of leaving or converting to Christianity. About 80,000 to 120,000 chose to convert. But as discussed in a previous chapter, many of these continued to practice Judaism in secret, coming to be known as the "Marranos." The Spanish and Portuguese suspected this and from time to time had them investigated by the Inquisition, which ordered the convicted to be burned. As a result of this continued persecution, waves of *Marranos* left Spain, most ending up in the Balkans.

From 1500, the Turks gradually colonized the whole of the Balkans, until by 1683, their Empire included southeast Europe, comprising Greece, what would become Yugoslavia, Bulgaria, Romania, and Hungary. In 1687, they reached the outskirts of Vienna and laid siege to the city, though they were never able to capture it. During this time, large colonies of Turks were settled in the Balkans, which began forming a Turkish-European ethnic mix with an average IQ of about 92, slightly higher than the IQ of Turks in Turkey, 90 (see Lynn, 2006). The cities with the greatest Jewish populations in the Balkans during Turkish rule were Istanbul and Salonica, but Jewish communities were found in towns throughout the Balkans.

There were three groups of Jews in the Balkans. The first of these were the Romaniot (the original population). Second, there were the Sephardic Jews, who immigrated following their expulsion from Spain in 1492 and from Portugal in 1497. Most of these settled in Istanbul, but some went to other cities in the Balkan Ottoman Empire, particularly Salonica and Edirne. After a century or so, the Romaniots "completely assimilated into the Sephardi group. " According to Esther Benbassa and Aron Rodrigue (1995, p. 14), there were fewer Sephardim but they "succeeded in dominating the Romaniots" because of "the weight of their scholars, their culture, and the dynamism of many of their rabbis."

The third group of Jews in the Balkans were the Ashkenazim from Central and Northern Europe, who from time to time moved to the Balkans because they were expelled or were being persecuted. A number of these came from Hungary after they had been expelled in 1360. Most of the Ashkenazim settled in Romania but some settled in other parts of the Balkans, especially in Bosnia-Hertzegovina. However, these were quite few compared with the Sephardim-Romaniots, who were by far the largest group of Jews in the Ottoman Empire in the Balkans, except in Romania where the Ashkenazim were the majority. It is estimated that in 1900, there were approximately 400,000 Sephardic Jews in the Balkans (Montgomery, 1902).

1. Jews in the Ottoman Empire

The Ottoman Empire provided a benign environment for the Jews, which is why so many of them who had been persecuted in Spain, Portugal, and Northern Europe sought refuge there. The Ottomans "success in government largely consisted in the wise policy of toleration which they practiced toward Jews..." (Fisher, 1936, p. 138). And without question, "the Ottoman takeover significantly ameliorated the Jews' condition" (Goffman, 2000, p. 16). In the early 1400s, there were prosperous Jewish communities in the Balkan cities of Edirne and

Salonica (Inalcik, 2000, p. 4). Moreover, "[u]nder Moslem rule, it was easier for Moslems and Jews to live side-by-side without disturbance than in Christian lands" (Roberts, 1996, p. 159). Jews were granted much greater liberty in the Ottoman Empire than in Northern Europe and were allowed to work as craftsmen and shopkeepers. Most Jews "were engaged in food processing, soap making, tanning, and a host of other artisanal occupations..." On top of this,

> a smaller elite emerged that became significant in often interlocked areas such as finance, international commerce and brokerage, and the manufacture and marketing of textiles. (Benbassa and Rodrigue, 1995, p. 36, 41)

The Sultan Mohammed the Conqueror (1451–1481) also welcomed the Jews. His minister of Finance (Ya'kub) and his physician (Moses Hamon) were both Jews.

Around 1510 the Jews of Salonika wrote to the Jews who were being expelled from France: "Come and join us in Turkey and you will live in peace and freedom as we do" (Benbassa & Rodrigue, 1995, p. 8). Many of them did so, and by 1529 Jews were about 55 percent of the population of the city, which became one of the most important Jewish centers in the world.

Many authorities have testified that the benign toleration of Jews in the Ottoman Empire contrasted with the frequent persecutions of Jews in Central, Northern and Eastern Europe. Thus, "Jews fleeing from Spain and other European countries found in the Ottoman Empire a secure and friendly haven."

> What makes their experience unique—especially when compared with that of European Jewry—is that over a period lasting five centuries, in good times and bad, Jews were never singled out for persecution or oppression because of their religion. In fact for much of the period they enjoyed the status of a favored minority. (Levy, 2002, p. xix)

And the Ottoman bureaucracy "demonstrated particular sympathy towards the Jews" (Inalcik, 2000, p. 6). Indeed, Jews in the Ottoman Empire occupied more prominent positions than Jews in Central and Northern Europe:

> In the fifteenth and sixteenth centuries they were instrumental in developing and expanding the Ottoman administration and

economy, and they continued to maintain a prominent role in those areas for a long time thereafter. Jews performed important services as government advisers, ambassadors, tax farmers, financial agents, scribes, international and interregional traders, and in a wide range of urban industries and trades. They also made significant contributions to Ottoman society in science, medicine, technology, culture, and entertainment. (Levy, 2002, p. xix)

In the court of Sultan Sulaiman the Magnificent (1520–1566), "Jews held positions of trust and honor, and took part in diplomatic negotiations.... Commerce was largely in their hands... In Constantinople they owned beautiful houses and gardens on the shores of the Bosporus." Into the 19th century as well, "the attitude of the government [towards Jews] was uniformly kind"(Montgomery, 1904, pp. 280–4).

One of the major reasons for the greater acceptance of Jews in the Ottoman Empire than in Europe was that for some five centuries, from around 1400 up to 1918, the Muslim Ottoman Empire was in conflict and frequently at war with Christian Europe for control of the Balkans. To be sure, there was a "clash of civilizations" between the two cultures, divided by religion and ethnicity. The Jews were conscious of being persecuted in Europe, and the Ottomans and Jews regarded each other as ethnic allies in what was widely regarded as a holy war. It may also be that Jews and Turks are of the same race (South West Asians) and are thus more compatible than Jews and Europeans, in accordance with the principles of Genetic Similarity Theory (see Rushton, 1989).

Whatever the case, the Jews prospered in the benign environment provided in the Ottoman Empire, and "they flourished more within the Ottoman economy and society than any other group."

> In the late fifteenth and sixteenth centuries, Jews instituted tremendous innovations in commerce between the Ottoman Empire and Europe. Their situations as bankers, industrialists, and especially Ottoman officials helped propel that empire beyond military dominance into economic distinction as well. (Levy, 2002, p. 33)

The leading Jewish family in the empire was the house of Mendes, "which controlled a large share of the international spice trade and had accumulated enormous capital in Europe" (Inalcik, 2000, p. 10).

Some four centuries later a descendant of the same family, Pierre Mendes-France, became Prime Minister of France.

It was not only in commerce that the Jews flourished: "the Ottoman Jewish communities became the most important centers of Jewish scholarship and learning in the world, a position they maintained for a long time" (Levy, 2002, p. xix). Jews were also prominent among doctors in the Ottoman Empire from 1450 up to 1900; their "primacy... within the medical profession was unchallenged" (Murphey, 2000, p. 73). The apogee of the profession was the palace corps of physicians, who looked after the sultan and his household. In 1548, there were 30 of these, among whom 14 were Jews; by 1609, the number had risen to 62, among whom 41 (66 percent) were Jews (Murphey, 2000, pp. 65, 73).

In the 18th century, however, Jewish prominence within the empire began to wane. "The sixteenth century saw the heyday of their role [in the economy], which went into a relative decline in the following century until the modern period, without ever being effaced completely" (Benbassa and Rodrigue, 1995, p. 36). This decline was evident on the cultural front as well. While at the beginning of the 16th century there is evidence for a highly literate Jewish culture in the Ottoman Empire, this culture gradually disappeared after the 16th century, so that from the mid-18th century until the intervention of the European powers in the 20th century, there was "an unmistakable picture of grinding poverty and ignorance" (Lewis, 1984, 164) among Jews in the Muslim world.

Kevin MacDonald writes,

> Jews became increasingly degraded in the Ottoman Empire, and their decline was far more extreme than can be explained solely by the economic fortunes of the Ottoman Empire, since it affected them far more than their Muslim and Christian co-residents. (MacDonald, 1994, p. 197).

Apparently, the position of the Jews declined because they could not withstand the competition of other ethnic groups: "other minorities simply out competed [them]." MacDonald attributes this not to "deficits in the capabilities of Jews" but to Christians networking skills (MacDonald, 1994, p. 197). "Muslim Turks, Armenians, and especially Greeks were also active in customs and tax collection and often outshone the Jews" (Benbassa & Rodrigue, 1995, p. 37). However, according to MacDonald, there was "a resurgence of Ottoman Jews in the 19th century," as a result of patronage and protection from European Jews, once again a flowering of a highly literate culture, including secular schools based on European models. (MacDonald, 1994, p. 198)

Also in the 19th century, Turkey began to lose control of its territory in the Balkans. Greece achieved independence in 1830, and the largely Jewish city of Salonica became part of Greece in 1913. In 1875, the provinces of Bosnia, Hertzegovina, Serbia, and Bulgaria rebelled. Bosnia-Hertzegovina was annexed by Austria-Hungary in 1878, while Serbia and Bulgaria achieved independence. Turkey retained Macedonia, but lost this and all her remaining territory in the Balkans in 1918, except for Istanbul and the hinterland which she retains to this day.

Infant mortality was lower among Jews in the late 19th and early 20th centuries. Studies showing this have been summarized by Gretchen Condran and Ellen Kramarow and are shown in Table 18.1. The infant mortality of Gentiles was between 20 and 50 percent higher than that of Jews.

Table 18.1. Infant mortality per 1,000 live births

Years	Location	Jews	Gentiles	% Difference
1851	Buscovina	143	198	25
1851	Transylvania	89	178	50
1896–1905	Serbia	140	170	20

2. Bulgaria

Jews enjoyed a dominant position in the Third Bulgaria State, which achieved independence in 1878. Before World War I, Jews,

> controlled 90 percent of the country's exports of cereals, tobacco, fruit and dairy produce–a proportion which fell to 60–70 percent in 1932.... They controlled between 30 and 40 percent of the imports of soap, oil and colonial produce. (Benbassa & Rodrigue, 1995, p. 95)

These are impressive figures, especially considering that the Jews were about 0.9 percent of the population. In the 1920s and

1930s, about half of the Jews lived in the capital Sophia. They "were composed of small businessmen, merchants, and artisans and did not face any significant threat to their existence until the Second World War" (Benbassa and Rodrigue, 1995). Between the World Wars, anti-Semitism was not particularly rife in Bulgarian society. In 1941, Bulgaria joined Germany as an ally, and as a result, German troops occupied the country. Berlin pressured the Bulgarian government to transport the Jews to concentration camps. The Bulgarians were reluctant to comply, but they did hand over about 11,300 foreign Jews to the Germans, many of whom were transfered to Treblinka. Apart from these, Bulgaria's Jews almost entirely escaped the Holocaust.

The numbers of Jews in Bulgaria and their percentages in the population between 1881 and 1949 are given in Table 18.2.

Table 18.2. Numbers and percentages of Jews in Bulgaria

Year	Jewish population	% of total
1881	20,503	0.90
1900	33,663	0.90
1934	48,398	0.80
1945	41,000	0.58
1949	6,000	0.08
2001	2,500	0.03

Sources: Benbassa & Rodrigue, 1995, pp. 190, 256–7; American Jewish Yearbook, 2004

As mentioned above, Jews were approximately 0.9 percent of the population between 1881 and 1900. By the 1934 census, the numbers of Jews had increased, but their percentage in the population had fallen to 0.8 percent. It fell further by around 7,398 by 1945, largely as a result of Germany's anti-Semitic policies. By 1949, it had fallen again to about 6,000. The reason for this is that most of the Jews felt uncomfortable in Bulgaria after the end of World War II and thought they could have better and safer futures in Israel. Approximately 35,000 of them migrated there between 1945 and 1949, leaving only a remnant in Bulgaria.

Bulgaria is the only country in the Balkans for which it has proved possible to find statistics for the numbers of Jews in the two major professions of medicine and law. These are shown in Table 18.3 where we see that in 1940, Jews were 4.6 percent of the doctors and 3.0 percent of the lawyers. As Jews were 0.80 percent of the population, they had Achievement Quotients of 5.75 and 3.75, respectively.

Table 18.3. Percentages of Jewish doctors and lawyers in Bulgaria

Year	Occupation	% Jews	AQ
1940	Doctors	4.6	5.75
1940	Lawyers	3.0	3.75
Source: (Benbassa & Rodrigue)			

3. Greece

Numbers and percentages of Jews in Greece are shown in Table 18.4. Of the 79,950 Jews in 1940, an estimated 62,573 were deported to Nazi concentration camps, leaving 10,371 in 1947. Over the next 12 years, about half of these emigrated, largely to Israel, leaving only 5,260 in 1959.

Table 18.4. Numbers and percentages of Jews in Greece

Year	Jewish population	% of total
1928	92,020	1.50
1940	79,950	1.10
1947	10,573	0.13
1959	5,260	0.07
Source: Benbassa & Rodrigue, 1995, p. 25		

4. Romania

The Jews of Romania were partly Ashkenazim and partly Sephardim, unlike in most other parts of the Balkans where the Sephardim predominated. They were treated more harshly under

Ottoman rule than were Jews in the rest of the empire. According to historians, "The story of the Romanian Jews in the Turkish provinces of Moldavia and Wallachia in the nineteenth century is a story of cruel, brutal mistreatment" (Ms, 1960, p. 59). "In 1870, the Romanian government introduced a series of harsh anti-Jewish restrictions and even tacitly encouraged mob attacks on Jews" (Sachar, 1992, p. 83). Despite all this, on the eve of World War I, Jews in Romania were 36 percent of the doctors, dentists, and veterinary surgeons (Brunstein, 2003).

At the end of the war, Romania achieved independence from Turkish rule, and Jews were given full civil liberties. However, anti-Semitism remained strong: "Romania had a well-deserved reputation for being, along with Russia, the most anti-Semitic country in Europe" (Mendelsohn, 1983, p. 174). Nevertheless, Jews found a way to flourish. According to Ezra Mendelsohn (1983, pp. 179, 189), "The number of Jewish students far exceeded the Jewish percentage in the population.... [T]hough on the whole very poor, [Jews] played a dominant role in commerce, crafts and the professions." The occupational distribution of Jews and Gentiles in the 1930 census is shown in Table 18.5. Jews were effectively debarred from the civil service, so the 2.7 percent of Jews in row 1 were virtually all in the professions. The great majority (73.7 percent) of Gentiles were peasant farmers, while the great majority of Jews (81.1 percent) worked in commerce, industry, and crafts.

Table 18.5. Occupations of Jews and Gentiles in Romania, 1930

Occupation	Jews	Gentiles
Civil Service/ professions	2.7	3.1
Commerce	48.3	4.2
Industry/ crafts	32.8	11.3
Transportation	2.4	2.3
Army	1.9	2.9
Agriculture	4.1	73.7

The percentages of Jews in various occupations in Romania in 1937 have been given by William Brustein and Ryan King (2004, p. 696) and are shown in Table 18.6. The Jewish population in the 1930 census numbered 756,930 and was 4.2 percent of the population. It will be seen that Jews were greatly overrepresented among Army doctors, engineers in the textile industry, journalists, lawyers, stockbrokers, and university students.

Table 18.6. Percentages of Jews in occupations in Romania, 1937

Occupation	% Jews	AQ
Doctors – Army Medical Corps	50	11.9
Engineers – textile industry	80	19.0
Journalists	70	16.7
Lawyers	40	8.5
Stockbrokers	99	23.6
University students	15	3.6

Anti-Semitism increased from the late 1930s onward. In 1937, the premier, Octavian Goga (1881–1938), disenfranchised the Jews and deprived them of citizenship, as a result of which they were not allowed to work. In 1940, following Romania's loss of territory in arbitration between then-allies Germany and the Soviet Union, the combined forces of the fascistic Iron Guard and Ion Antonescu (1882–1946) took power in a *coup*. The new government sought an alliance with the Axis Powers and intensified anti-Semitic policies within the country: Jewish property was confiscated and Jewish shops boycotted. Between 1941 and 1944, about 261,300 Jews were killed in the concentration camps. Approximately 346,440 survived the war (Mendelsohn, 1983, p. 210). Afterwards, many Jews emigrated to Israel. In 1965 the dictator Nicolae Ceausescu (1918–1989) struck a deal with the United States whereby American Jews paid $8,000 for every Jew permitted to emigrate. Between 1967 and 1989, 165,000 departed for Israel, leaving around 20,000 in Romania (Sachar, 1992).

5. Turkey

In 1900, there were some 400,000 Jews in the Ottoman Empire; about 320,000 of these were in Europe (Levy, 2002). As a result of the loss of most of its territory in the Balkans at the end of World War I, there were, according to the 1927 census, 81,872 Jews in Turkey. Most lived in Istanbul and Edirne (in Europe) and in Izmir (in Asia Minor). When the Germans began to persecute the Jews from 1933 onward, Turkey admitted 300 distinguished Jewish doctors, scientists, and intellectuals. Many of these found positions in universities. But Turkey refused to admit others who lacked specialist qualifications. In 1942, heavy taxes were imposed on Jews of 179 percent of their annual income. About 40 percent of them emigrated to Israel as soon as this became possible in 1949. Jewish demographics in Turkey are given in Table 18.7.

Table 18.7. Numbers and percentages of Jews in Turkey

Year	N. Jews	% Population
1927	81,872	0.6
1945	76,963	0.4
1955	45,995	0.2
1990	19,000	0.02
Source: Benbassa and Rodrigue		

In 1988, 94 percent of Jews in Istanbul worked in white-collar occupations (11 percent professional, 15 percent managerial, seven percent clerical, and 61 percent sales). The remaining six percent were blue-collar laborors (Della Pergola, 2007).

6. Yugoslavia

Yugoslavia, the Kingdom of Serbs, Croats, and Slovenes, was an invention of the victorious Allies in the postwar Paris Peace Conference of 1919. The numbers of Jews in Yugoslavia are shown in Table 18.8. In the 1931 census, there were 68,405 Jews, of whom 57 percent were Ashkenazim and 38 percent, Sephardic; five percent defined themselves as Orthodox. Much as in Bulgaria, anti-Semitism was not common during the interwar years (Benbassa & Rodrigue, 1995, p. 95).

Table 18.8. Numbers and percentages of Jews in Yugoslavia

Year	Jewish population	% of total
1931	68,405	0.49
1940	82,242	0.50
1945	15,000	0.10
2002	3,400	0.00
Source: (Benbassa & Rodrigue, 1995, p. 93, 256–7)		

The number of Jews increased to 82,242 in 1940, though after the Axis invasion, approximately 62,000 of these were killed during the Holocaust. About 20,000 survived by going into hiding or escaping to Switzerland or the Italian controlled west of the country. Many of these later went to Israel.

7. Nobel Prize winners and Chess Champions

The Balkans have produced seven Nobel Prize winners; they are listed in Table 18.9. One of these, Elias Canetti (1905–1994), was Jewish; though he was born in Bulgaria, Canetti migrated to Britain. The remaining six were Gentiles, of whom George Palade (1912–2008) emigrated to the United States, and Vladimir Prelog (1906–1998), to Switzerland. Thus, Jews, who constituted about 0.6 percent of the population in the Balkans, have produced 14 percent of the Nobel Prize winners, giving them an Achievement Quotient of 23.

Table 18.9. Nobel Prize winners (Jews are asterisked)

Year	Name	Country	Subject
1961	Ivo Andric	Yugoslavia	Literature
1963	Giorgos Seferis	Greece	Literature
1974	George Pelade	Romania	Medicine
1975	Vladimir Prelog	Bosnia	Chemistry
1979	Odysseus Elytis	Greece	Literature
1981	Elias Canetti*	Bulgaria	Literature
2009	Herta Müller	Romania	Literature

There have been three top-rated chess champions from the Balkans from 1851 to 2000 (Rubinstein, 2004); one of whom, Milan Vidmar (1885–1962) of Yugoslavia, was Jewish. Thus, Jews, comprising about one percent of the population in the Balkans in the period between 1851 and 1940, produced a third of top-rated chess champions. The sample is small, but the striking overrepresentation of Jews in top class chess is consistent with their overrepresentation among Nobel Prize winners.

8. Intelligence of the Sephardic Jews

There have been no studies of the intelligence of the Sephardic Jews in the Balkans. Nevertheless, it is possible to make an approximate estimate of their intelligence. Generally, there is little doubt that the intelligence of the Sephardim is (1) higher than that of Gentiles in the Balkans, (2) lower than that of the Ashkenazim of Central, Eastern and Northern Europe, and (3) higher that that of Mizrahim Jews from the Middle East and North Africa. The following considerations point to this conclusion:

(a) When the Sephardim were expelled from Spain in 1492 and from Portugal in 1497, some of them settled in North Africa. The Sephardim quickly came to dominate the local Jews and "rapidly became dominant in the economy as well as in rabbinic learning" (Benbassa & Rodrigue, 1995, p. 4). It can be inferred that they had higher intelligence. When the Balkans were occupied by the Turks from the late 15th century, it was observed that "The Turks were good soldiers but they were unsuccessful as businessmen, and accordingly they left their commercial occupations to other nationalities.... Hence the Jews soon became the business agents of the country" (Montgomery, 1902, p. 280). This again suggests that the Sephardic Jews had higher intelligence than the Turks.

(b) Numerous authorities have testified that the Sephardim as a group had a higher socioeconomic status than the Gentile communities among whom they lived and were overrepresented among physicians, merchants, and professionals. It can be inferred from this that they were more intelligent.

(c) In the 19th century, the Ashkenazim "regarded Eastern Sephardi Jewry as exotic and backward" (Benbassa & Rodrigue, 1995, p. 113), which they undoubtedly were compared with the Jews of Central, Eastern, and Northern Europe. This suggests that the Ashkenazim were more intelligent than the Sephardim.

(d) In Yugoslavia in the 1920s and 1930s, there were both Ashkenazi and Sephardic communities. The Ashkenazi were more prosperous: they lived in "the most urbanized and westernized areas in the north," whereas the Sephardim "settled in the poorer zones in the south and east of the country" (Benbassa and Rodrigue, 1995, p. 144). The Ashkenazim had fewer children than the Sephardim (Benbassa and Rodrigue, 1995, p. 91), which is generally a sign of higher intelligence (Lynn, 1996).

(e) In Israel, Jews form an ethnic status hierarchy such that "the Sephardim show a position midway between the Ashkenazim and Mizrahim (Benbassa and Rodrigue, 1995, p. 191). This hierarchy is based on differences in intelligence. It is shown in Chapter 11 on Israel that European Jews in Israel have an average IQ of 106 and Mizrahim, an average IQ of 91. Hence, as the Sephardim fall midway between the other two groups, they should have an IQ of about 98.

(f) In Britain, Jews are overrepresented among doctors by a factor of 6.6 and among lawyers by a factor of 9.0. Bulgaria is the only country in the Balkans for which there are comparable statistics, and here Jews in 1940 were overrepresented among doctors by a factor of 5.75 and among lawyers by a factor of 3.75. The overrepresentation in the two professions in Britain averages 7.8, while in Bulgaria it averages 60 percent of this: 4.75. In Britain, Jews have an average IQ of 110 as compared with 100 for Gentiles. It can be reasonably assumed that in Bulgaria, Jews had about 60 percent of this 10 IQ point advantage over Gentiles, i.e. an IQ of 106 compared with 100 for Gentiles in Bulgaria. Two studies of the IQ of Gentiles in Bulgaria have given IQs of 91 and 94, which can be averaged to 92.5 (Lynn, 2006). Hence the IQ of Bulgarian Jews should be approximately 98.5 (92.5 + 6.0 = 98.5). This is virtually identical to the estimate of 98 given in the last paragraph.

(g) The Sephardim of the Balkans have only produced one Nobel Prize winner (Elias Canetti from Bulgaria) from a population in 1940 of about 288,000, estimated by adding the populations in Bulgaria, Greece, Yugoslavia, and Turkey. This is a rate of 3.5 per 1 million. The Ashkenazim have produced 120 Nobel Prize winners from a population in 1940 of about 18 million, a rate of 6.7 per 1 million. Thus, the Ashkenazim have produced approximately double the rate of Nobel Prize winners as the Sephardim of the Balkans. This provides further confirmation that the intelligence level of the Ashkenazim is higher than that of the Sephardim.

(h) In the United States, three studies have found that Ashkenazic children obtain higher IQs than Sephardic children. In the first of these, Riverda Harding Jordan (1921) reported that Romanian Jewish children obtained a nonverbal IQ 4.7 points lower than Russian Jewish children. This was confirmed in two further studies by Morris Gross (1967, 1986), who found that Ashkenazic 6-year-olds obtained higher IQs than Sephardic children. In the first study of 90 children, the Ashkenazic children outscored the Sephardic on vocabulary by 17 IQ points. In the second study, the Ashkenazic children outscored the Sephardic by 12 points (Gross, 1986). The Ashkenazim in the United States do better socially than the Sephardim. From 1890 to 1930, some 30,000 Sephardim from the Levant migrated to the United States, where about 90 percent settled in New York. They did not do nearly so well as the Ashkenazim:

> Essentially without marketable skills, living in the wretchedest of Lower East Side tenements, the newcomers eked out their existence as bootblacks, as candy and ice-cream vendors in nickelodeons, as cloakroom attendants or waiters. Others worked for starvation wages in the cigarette factory of their 'kinsmen,' the Schinasi brothers. The women, all but illiterate found intermittent employment in the garment industry but more commonly as maids or laundresses. Alcoholism, prostitution, and wife abandonment were far more extensive among them than among Ashkenazi immigrants. Few shared the Russian-Jewish passion even for functional education. (Sachar, 1992, p. 338)

9. Conclusions

Four salient points stand out in this chapter. First, the Sephardim of the Balkans did better socioeconomically and in the medical and legal professions than the Gentile communities they lived amongst. This can be attributed to their higher intelligence. Second, the intelligence of the Sephardim in the Balkans can be estimated at an IQ of 98, as compared with that of 92 of Gentiles in the Balkans, and 100 of Gentiles in Central and Northern Europe. Third, the IQ of 98 of the Sephardim is well below the IQ of 110 of the Ashkenazim of Britain, Canada, and the United States (see the chapters on the Jews of these countries). Fourth, this difference can be attributed to the Sephardim in the Balkans having been generally free from persecution over the course of approximately five centuries when they were in the Ottoman Empire, to which numerous authorities cited in this chapter have testified. This contrasts with the repeated pogroms against the Ashkenazim of Central, Eastern, and Northern Europe. As discussed further in Chapter 21, the effect of these pogroms of the Ashkenazim will have been to selectively eliminate the less intelligent, leaving those with higher intelligence as survivors.

Chapter 19

United States

1. Numbers in the Population
2. Intelligence
3. The Jewish Intelligence Profile
4. Literacy, 1880–1910
5. Overrepresentation in Ivy League Universities
6. Anti-Semitism
7. Education
8. Earnings and Wealth
9. Socioeconomic Status
10. Eminence
11. The Academic Elite
12. Nobel Prize winners
13. Mathematicians
14. Chess
15. Bridge
16. Pulitzer Prizes
17. Music and Hollywood
18. The Media
19. Sport
20. Fertility and Infant Mortality
21. Crime

The first Jews to come to the United States in the 1660s settled in Newport, Rhode Island, and in New York. They were Sephardim, and by the 1770s, they numbered approximately 2,500 in the 13 colonies out of a population of approximately 3.75 million (Kosmin & Lachman, 1993). Between 1830 and 1881, a number of Ashkenazim from Eastern Europe and Germany arrived, and by 1860, they numbered about 275,000. From the 18th century, Jews had greater freedom in the United States than anywhere else in the world, including the right to engage in all trades, own property, and attend universities. Many of them prospered; some became exceptionally wealthy, such as the the Speyer and Seligman banking families. The third wave of Jewish immigration began in 1881 from Russia and Poland, as Ashkenazi Jews fled the pogroms. By 1924, approximately 2.5 million of these had arrived. A further 150,000 or so came to the United States in the 1930s as refugees from Germany; approximately 100,000 Holocaust survivors entered after the end of World War II.

1. Numbers in the Population

The numbers of Jews and their percentages in the population are given in Table 19.1. Howard Sachar provides the figures for 1927 (1992, p. 372). The 1957 figure is derived from a Census Bureau survey of 35,000 households that were asked their religion, of whom 3.2 percent were Jewish. The figures for 1957 and 1980 are given by Paul Johnson (2004) and for 1990 and 2002, by the *American Jewish Yearbooks*.

Table 19.1. Jews in the population of the United States

Year	Jewish Population	% of total
1780	2,500	0.0007
1927	4,228,000	3.55
1957	4,824,000	3.2
1970	5,420,000	2.7
1990	5,515,000	2.2
2002	5,700,000	2.0

The 1924 Immigration Act severely restricted immigration; between 1931 and 1941, only 580,207 immigrants entered the United States. Remarkably, 161,262 of these were Jews. The number of Jews in the U.S. increased during the 20th century, but their percentage of the population declined during the period 1927–2000. The reasons for this lie in the lower fertility of Jews than of the rest of the population and the immigration of Hispanics, Asians, Caribbeans, and Africans. (These figures are for what are called "core Jews," i.e. those who identify themselves as Jews.)

2. Intelligence

The first studies of Jewish intelligence in the United States were published by Henry Herbert Goddard (1913, 1917) and were based on Binet tests given to samples of immigrants at Ellis Island. In the 1917 paper, Goddard stated, "83% of the Jews, 80% of the Hungarians, 79% of the Italians, and 87% of the Russians were 'feeble-minded'" (p. 424). This conclusion was based on small numbers of 35 Jews, 22 Hungarians, 50 Italians, and 45 Russians, who were said to be typical. He did not, however, conclude that these low IQs were genetic, writing:

> Assuming that they are morons, we have two practical questions: first, is it a hereditary defect or, second, apparent defect due to deprivation? If the latter, as seems likely, little fear may be felt for the children. (p. 243)

In another early study, Carl Brigham (1923) reported on the IQs of the military servicemen of different national origins in World War I. Stephen Jay Gould (1996, pp. 195–8, 255–8) asserted that this study reported that Jews have low IQs. This is incorrect, as noted by J. Phillipe Rushton (1997). Brigham gave data for the mental ages of a number of racial and national groups and reported these as 13.3 years for native-born White draftees, 13.4 for foreign-born English-speaking Nordics, 12.6 for non-English speaking Nordics, 11.7 for Alpines (Central Europeans), 11.5 for Mediterraneans and Russians, and 10.7 for Blacks. Brigham asserted that 50 percent of the Russians were Jews and suggested that the data did not support the idea that Jews have a high IQ, but he did not give a breakdown of the scores of Jewish and non-Jewish Russians because these were not available. Thus, the result does not tell us anything about the intelligence of Jews.

Studies of the intelligence of Jews in the United States compared with Gentile Whites from 1920 to 2008 are summarized in Table 19.2. (These studies have been obtained through a computerized literature search using PsychINFO, PsychNet, ISI Web of Science, and Web of Knowledge.) The Jews' IQs are calculated in relation to the Gentile White mean set at 100, with a standard deviation of 15. Many of these studies compared Jews with Gentile Whites who were tested at the same time, but others report Jewish means compared with standardization test norms. In these studies, the Jewish means are adjusted for the "Flynn effect" (the name given to the secular increase of intelligence, which means that IQs need adjustment for the year when the test was standardized). Wechsler IQs have been increasing at about three points a decade, verbal IQs, at about two points a decade, and nonverbal (performance) IQs, at about four points a decade. Stanford-Binet IQs have been increasing at about 2.5 IQ points a decade (Flynn, 1984). Hence, Jewish IQs obtained later than the standardization have been adjusted down to allow for this.

Row 1 gives the first of the post-World War I studies. The study was carried out in New York City schools. Jews obtained an IQ one point higher than native-born Whites, but 21 IQ points higher than ethnic Italians, who were also included in the study. Row 2 gives the IQs of native-born White and Russian Jewish primary school children, in which Jews obtained an IQ one point higher than Whites on a nonverbal test. However, in this study, the Jewish children scored lower than the Whites on a language test. The explanation for this is likely that many of the Jewish children spoke Yiddish as their first language. The parents of the Jewish children were of lower socioeconomic status; only 2.8 percent had fathers working in the professions, compared with 18.1 percent of the Whites. This study also reported results for a sample of 99 Romanian Jewish children, who obtained a nonverbal IQ of 96.3, i.e. 4.7 points lower than Russian Jewish children. Row 3 gives the Binet IQs of native-born White and Jewish 5–7-year-olds. Both groups obtained the same average IQ. Some of these Jewish children spoke Yiddish as their first language. As the Binet test is largely verbal, the Jewish children would have been handicapped.

Table 19.2. IQs of Jews in the United States

	Age	N Jews	N Gentiles	Test	IQ	Reference
1	9–15	500	500	Pressy	101	Murdoch, 1920
2	6–10	81	129	Trabue	101	Jordan, 1921
3	5–7	79	367	Binet	100	Pintner & Keller, 1922
4	10	100	200	Binet	109	Bere, 1924
5	12–18	872	1,442	Army Alpha	99	Feingold, 1924
6	12	800	-	NIT	102.5	Seago & Koldin, 1925
7	6	47	60	Binet	106	Graham, 1925
8	9–13	702	1,030	PCPM	101.5	Hirsch, 1926
9	6–11	55	500	DAM	106	Goodenough, 1926
10	8–13	445	8,130	NIT	99	Rigg, 1928
11	7–8	174	811	Dearborn/Otis	100	Easterbrooks, 1928
12	13	378	-	Terman Group	114	Franzblau, 1934
13	10–15	91	-	Pintner	103	Pintner & Artensian, 1937
14	11	2,999	-	NIT	101	Pintner & Maller, 1937
15	6	335	334	S. Binet	111	Brown, 1944
16	-	2,453	-	Binet/Otis/Pintner	111	Nardi, 1948
17	14	246	160	Pintner	107	Solomon, 1956
18	4–5	2,083	-	S. Binet	110	Levinson, 1957a
19	5	1,451	-	S. Binet	107	Levinson, 1957b
20	Adult	49	1,414	Vocabulary	117	Miner, 1957
21	Adult	64	-	WAIS	116	Levinson, 1958
22	5	117	-	WISC	103	Levinson, 1959
23	10–13	47	-	WISC	106	Levinson, 1960a
24	16	65	2,171	Quick	110	Bachman, 1970
25	12–18	720	-	Otis	115	Romanoff, 1976
26	4–6	400	-	S. Binet	111	Levinson & Block, 1977
27	6	324	-	S. Binet	116	Gross, 1986
28	14–23	98	9,426	AFQT	112.6	Herrnstein & Murray, 1994

	Age	N Jews	N Gentiles	Test	IQ	Reference
29	14	397	9,658	Math	113	Fejgin, 1995
30	14	397	9,658	Reading	107	Fejgin, 1995
31	18–70	150	5,300	Vocabulary	107.5	Lynn, 2004
32	18–70	433	17,335	Vocabulary	109	Lynn & Kanazawa, 2008

Row 4 gives the Binet IQs of Jewish, Italian, and Bohemian children, in which Jews obtained an IQ nine points higher than the Italians and Bohemians, who, one should keep in mind, were likely not representative of the United States. Row 5 gives the IQs of native-born White and first-generation Jewish high-school students, in which Jews obtained an IQ one point lower than Whites on the verbal Army Alpha test. Again, many of the first-generation Jewish children would have spoken Yiddish as their first language and been handicapped on the test. Row 6 gives the IQs for Jewish and Italian children of foreign-born parents in New York for the National Intelligence Test, which contains items of arithmetic, sentence completion, synonyms/antonyms, "logical selection" (not defined), and digit symbol; it is largely a verbal test of general intelligence. On the test norms, the Jewish children obtained a mean IQ of 102.5 and the Italian children, a mean IQ of 90.4. As both groups were recent immigrants and were handicapped by an imperfect command of English, it is considered that the best reading of the results is to take the 12 IQ point advantage of the Jewish children as the best estimate of the Jewish IQ in relation to European Gentiles.

Row 7 shows an IQ of 106 for Jewish children attending clinics for problem children in Massachusetts, as compared with Italian children. Row 8 gives results for 9–13-year-old native White American, Polish Jewish, and Russian Jewish children who took the Pintner-Cunningham Primary Mental Test. In relation to a White mean of 100, 75 Polish Jews obtained an IQ of 104.5 and 627 Russian Jews, an IQ of 101.2, giving a weighted average of 101.5.

Row 9 shows an IQ of 106 for Jewish children in California, compared with European-American children. Row 10 gives an IQ of 98.7 for Jewish children on the National Intelligence Test. In this study the Jewish children scored 3.1 points higher than Gentile Whites on an arithmetic test, but 2.5 points lower on a reading test, suggesting they were handicapped in English. Row 11 gives an IQ of 100 for Jewish children at schools near Boston. Row 12 gives an unusually high IQ of 114 for Jewish adolescents. Row 13 gives results for second-generation Jewish children in New York public schools. This study gave IQs for bilingual children brought up by parents whose first language was Yiddish and monolingual children whose parents spoke English. The bilingual children scored two IQ points lower than the monolinguals on verbal IQ, but only 0.64 points lower on nonverbal IQ. The IQ for the monolinguals is entered in the table, with a one-point deduction for the Flynn Effect because the test was standardized approximately three years before the study. Row 14 gives an IQ of 101 for another sample of Jewish children in New York public schools. Row 15 gives an IQ of 111 for second-generation Jewish and Scandinavian children in Minneapolis public schools tested with the 1916 Stanford-Binet. Jews scored one Binet IQ point higher than Scandinavians (108.3 vs. 107.3) and 1.5 IQ points higher on vocabulary. Row 16 gives results for school students (ages not given) attending nine Hebrew schools on the 1916 Stanford-Binet. Their mean IQ was 118.6. Adjusting for the secular rise of intelligence at 2.5 IQ points a decade brings the mean IQ down to 111. Row 17 gives an IQ of 107 for Jewish high-school students who obtained an IQ seven points higher than a sample of 160 Gentiles attending the same school. Row 18 gives results for 4–5-year-olds applying for New York Yeshiva schools who took the 1937 Stanford-Binet. Their mean IQ was 114.9. Adjusting for the secular rise of IQ brings the mean IQ down to 110.

Row 19 gives an IQ of 107 for Jewish 5-year-olds in New York. (This is a confusing paper with inconsistent data; the IQ entered is for samples A and C.) Row 20 gives a vocabulary IQ of 117 for a sample of Jewish adults. Row 21 gives an IQ of 116 for another sample of Jewish adults. Row 22 gives an IQ of 103 for a sample of 5-year-olds applying for New York Yeshiva schools. Row 23 gives an IQ of 106 for 11–13-year-old Jewish children in New York schools. Row 24 gives an IQ of 110 for a vocabulary test (the Quick Test) obtained by Jews in the Youth in Transition study. Row 25 gives an IQ of 115 for a sample of adults tested with the largely verbal Otis test. Row 26 gives an IQ of 111 obtained by a sample of adults on the Stanford-Binet. Row 27 gives an IQ of 116 for 6-year-old Ashkenazi children entering Jewish parochial schools. This study also reported an IQ of 104 for Sephardic children, confirming other studies showing that the Ashkenazim have a higher IQ than the Sephardim. Row 28 gives an IQ of 112.6 for Jews put forth by Richard Herrnstein and Charles Murray (1994) in *The Bell Curve*, a figure derived from the National Longitudinal Study of Youth. The test was the Armed Forces Qualification Test (AFQT), which consists of subtests of word knowledge, verbal comprehension, arithmetical reasoning, and mathematics. This figure is in relation to 100 for Whites, not for the whole American population including Blacks and Hispanics, in comparison with whom, the Jewish IQ is 115.

Rows 29 and 30 give means of 113 for mathematics and 107 for reading from the NELS national sample of eighth graders, aged approximately 14 and tested in 1988. These results are treated here as IQs. Row 31 gives an IQ of 107.5 for Jewish adults given a 10-word vocabulary synonyms test in which a word is presented and the task is to identify the synonym from five alternatives. Vocabulary is a good measure of general intelligence. The test was given in the General Social Surveys of representative samples from continental United States (i.e. excluding Alaska and Hawaii); results presented were for the years 1990–96. The IQ is a little lower than in the other recent studies, possibly because the test is short and thus has reduced reliability. Row 32 gives an IQ of 109 for Jewish adults calculated from a more extensive analysis of the 10-word vocabulary test in the General Social Surveys spanning the years 1972 through 2004.

It can be seen from inspection of the table that the IQs obtained by Jews have tended to increase during the course of the 20th century and into the early 21st. In the first 14 studies published between the years 1920–1937, Jewish children obtained a median IQ of 101.5. In the next nine studies published between 1944 and 1960, Jews obtained a median IQ of 107. In the last nine studies published between 1970 and 2008, Jews obtained a median IQ of 111. The correlation between the year of publication and IQ is 0.59 and is statistically significant at p<0.01, showing that Jewish IQs have increased significantly over this period. It appears that in the earlier studies, Jews were handicapped, probably largely because many of them were relatively recent immigrants who were impoverished, had poor nutrition and health, and spoke Yiddish as their first language. Apparently, in the 1950s, some of them were still handicapped by speaking Yiddish;

Boris Levinson (1959) reported that Jewish children who spoke only English obtained an IQ six points higher than those who were bilingual in English and Yiddish.

In addition to these general population studies, there have been four studies of Jewish college students compared to Gentiles at the same college. These are shown in Table 19.3, in which the Jewish IQs are given in relation to White Gentile college students' mean of 100 (Sds 15). In the first of these, Irma Cohen (1927) published a study of the intelligence of native-born Jews and White Gentiles at Ohio State University. Comparing 193 freshmen from each group, she found that Jews had an average IQ 4.7 points higher than Gentiles; she also noted that Jews were three percent of the population of the state but seven percent of the student body. The two next studies also found Jewish students obtained higher average IQs than White Gentiles. However, the last study by A.M. Shuey (1942) for native-born Jews and Gentiles at Washington Square College in New York showed virtually no difference. She also presented data that included foreign-born subjects with approximately the same negligible difference. Possibly, the more intelligent Jews in New York secured admission to more prestigious colleges.

Table 19.3. IQs of Jewish college students in the United States

College	N Jews	N Gentiles	Test	IQ	Reference
Ohio State	193	193	OSUPE	104.7	Cohen, 1927
Columbia	82	65	Thorndike	113.7	Garrett, 1929
Pittsburgh	158	158	ACPE	102.7	Held, 1941
Washington Sq	1171	538	ACPE	100.8	Shuey, 1942
OSUPE: Ohio State University Psychological Examination; ACPE: American Council Psychological Examination					

All these studies, which consistently show that Jews have higher average IQs than European Gentiles, are corroborated by further evidence that Jews are underrepresented among the mentally retarded and overrepresented among the gifted. In a study of military servicemen in World War I, Pearce Bailey (1922) reported that 17.2 percent of the Jews were "mentally retarded," compared with 29.2 percent of the whole of the draft, suggesting that Jews had above-average IQs with fewer at the lower end of the distribution. (Obviously, Bailey used a much broader definition of "mental retardation" than that which is currently accepted. Today, two per cent of the population is considered mentally retarded, defined as having an IQ below 70.)

Similar results were reported in a 1931–1932 study of the intelligence and educational progress of various racial and ethnic groups in New York City schools by Julius Maller (1933). He reported that Jews had the lowest percentage of slow educational progress at 25.7 percent, compared with 29 percent for the whole of the city. As for the gifted, in 1921, Lewis Terman collected data on 1,528 children (on average, 11 years old) with IQs above 140. He reported that 10.6 percent of them were Jewish, about twice the proportion for Gentiles in the cities from which the samples were recruited (Terman, 1925, p. 56). In another early study, Bertha Luckey (1925) reported that in a sample of 3,779 children, 11.9 percent of Jews had IQs above 120, compared with 9.8 percent of native-born Whites. In a later study, Paul Sheldon (1954) identified all the children in the New York City public school system with IQs of 170 or higher. He found there were 28; 24 of them were Jews.

3. The Jewish Intelligence Profile

Jews have higher verbal than visualization-spatial IQs. Seven studies where these two abilities have been measured are summarized in Table 19.4. The first four are based on general population samples. The fifth is based on Yeshiva college students, who had a WAIS verbal IQ of 123 and a performance IQ of 101. The sixth is based on a sample of 216 older Jews (average age of 69) who attended Department of Welfare day centers in New York City and whose WAIS verbal IQ was 99.3 and performance IQ was 91.5. This study is not given in Table 19.2 because most of the 192 subjects were foreign born and were "not claimed as representative" (Levinson, 1962, p. 57).

The last study in Table 19.4 by Gerald Lesser, Gordon Fifer, and Donald Clark (1965) requires some explanation. The study tested the abilities of Jewish, Chinese, Black, and Puerto Rican 6–7-year-olds in New York, with 80 children in each group. The absence of a White group makes it difficult to make the usual comparison of the Jewish

IQ with the White "Greenwich standard." However, the scores of the Black sample can be used as an alternative. It has long been known that Blacks in the northern states have a higher average IQ than those elsewhere; Alan Kaufman and Jerome Doppelt (1976) report an average IQ of 93 for Blacks in the northeastern region. Adopting this figure, the Jewish sample in this study obtained a higher verbal IQ than the Black group by 16.5 points, giving them a verbal IQ of 109.5 in relation to a White IQ of 100; a higher numerical IQ by 13.5 points, and therefore a numerical IQ of 106.5 in relation to the White mean; a higher nonverbal reasoning IQ of 9.5 points, and therefore a nonverbal reasoning IQ of 102.5 in relation to Whites; and a higher spatial IQ by 8.2 points, and therefore a spatial IQ of 101.2 in relation to Whites.

Table 19.4. Verbal and visualization-spatial IQs of Jews in the United States

Age	Test	Verbal	Visual-spatial	Diff	Reference
Adult	WAIS	125	105	20	Levinson, 1958
5	WISC	106	103	3	Levinson, 1959
10–13	WISC	115	94	21	Levinson, 1960a
5	WISC	103.5	100.4	3	Levinson, 1960b
20	WAIS	123	101	22	Levinson, 1960b
69	WAIS	99.3	91.5	8	Levinson, 1962
6–7	-	109.5	101.2	7	Lesser et al., 1965
Mean	-	111.6	99.5	12	-

It will be seen that in all the studies summarized in Table 19.4, Jews had higher verbal than visualization-spatial IQs. The average disparity is 12 IQ points. It appears from these studies that the high Jewish intelligence is verbal and their visualization-spatial intelligence is about the same as that of Gentile Europeans.

A further study finding the same Jewish ability profile is Margaret Backman's (1972) analysis of the data in Project Talent, a nationwide American survey of the abilities of 17-year-olds carried out in 1960. The study was based on 1,236 Jewish and 1,051 non-Jewish Whites, in addition to 488 Blacks and 150 Orientals.

IQs were calculated for six abilities. The mean IQs of the Jews in relation to the non-Jewish White mean of 100 and standard deviations of 15 were as follows: verbal knowledge (described as "a general factor, but primarily a measure of general information" and identifiable with Carroll's (1993) verbal comprehension factor): 107.8; English language: 99.5; mathematics: 111.0; visual reasoning (a measure of reasoning with visual forms): 91.3; perceptual speed and accuracy: 102.2; memory (short-term recall of verbal symbols): 95.1. These are consistent with the other reports that Jews perform well on tests of verbal ability (though not always of the English language) and mathematics but less well on visual and spatial tests. Nevertheless, the IQ of 91.3 for visual reasoning is remarkably low. These differences were calculated on Jews and Gentiles matched for socioeconomic status. Because Jews have a higher average socioeconomic status than Gentiles, the reported differences are not an accurate measure of the true differences, and there is no way of estimating the Jewish IQ from this study.

4. Literacy, 1889–1910

The percentages of Jews, Whites, and Blacks that were literate, obtained in the censuses of 1880, 1900 and 1910, are given by Darity, Dietrich, and Guilkey (1997) and are shown in Table 19.5.

Table 19.5. Racial and ethnic differences in literacy 1880–1910 (percentages)

Group	1880	1900	1910
Whites	95	99	99
Jews	83	79	79

During this period, Whites were nearly all literate. (These figures are for the ethnic English; non-English speaking Whites were counted as illiterate if they could not read English, and this applied to 14–20 percent of them in the given period.) But in 1880, only 83 percent of Jews were literate. This is because 17 percent of them still spoke Yiddish or German and were not counted as literate in English. The percentage of literate Jews fell to 79 in the 1900 and 1910 censuses due to the immigration of large numbers of Jews from Russia, among whom a significant number continued to speak Yiddish and was illiterate in English.

5. Overrepresentation in Ivy League Universities

As early as the 1910s, people began to comment on the high intelligence and educational attainment of Jewish children. An Industrial Commission Report of this period noted, "In the lower schools the Jewish children are the delight of their teachers for cleverness at their books, obedience and general good conduct" (Steinberg, 1974, p. 9). By 1910, Jews began to outperform Gentiles in the entrance tests for universities, which were first constructed by the College Entrance Examination Board in 1899.

Some figures for the percentages of Jews in the Ivy League colleges are shown in Table 19.6.

Table 19.6. Percentages of Jews at Ivy League colleges and other universities

Year	College	% Jews
1908	All Ivy League	7
1909	Harvard	6
1919	Harvard	20
1919	Yale	13
1919	Brown	20
1919	Pennsylvania	25
1919	Columbia	40
1920	NY City College	90
1920	Hunter College	90
1952	Harvard	24
1957	Ivy League	23
1957	Seven Sisters	16

Rows 1 and 2 show that in 1908 and 1909, the percentages of Jews in all the colleges and at Harvard were seven and six percent, respectively. Rows 3 through 7 show that by 1919, this had increased to 20 percent of the students at Harvard and about the same figure at Yale, Brown, and Pennsylvania; at Columbia, 40 percent of the students were Jewish (Slezkine, 2004). Rows 8 and 9 show that in 1920, 90 percent of the students in the two colleges in New York (City College and Hunter College) were Jewish. Rows 10, 11 and 12 show that in the 1950s, Jews were slightly more overrepresented at Ivy League colleges than in 1919. For instance, Jews were 20 percent of students at Harvard in 1919; this rose to 24 percent in 1952. In 1957, Jews were 23 percent of students at all Ivy League universities, a little higher than in 1919 (except in the case of Columbia). The Ivy League universities were for men only at this time, but there were the "seven sister" elite colleges for women (Radcliffe, Smith, Bennington, Vassar, etc.) and in 1957, 16 percent of the students at these were Jewish (Moynihan & Glazer, 1970).

The large numbers of Jews who were gaining admission to the Ivy League colleges alarmed the WASPs who made up most of the administration and faculty. They devised ways to restrict the numbers of Jews, which have been described by Steven Farron (2005). To keep the numbers of Jews down, the Ivy League colleges introduced selection procedures using "character" tests for "manliness, uprightness, cleanliness and native refinement" and by regional quotas to combat what became known as "the Jewish invasion." Regional quotas limited the number of Jews, who lived mainly in New York. Columbia University had a particularly large Jewish intake as it is situated in Manhattan. In 1919, it introduced a new application form that asked applicants about extracurricular activities, required essays and letters of recommendation, the purpose of which was to legitimize taking Gentile applicants with lower examination marks than Jews. In 1922, Harvard tried a different strategy of limiting the intake of Jews to 15 percent. The problem here was that Jews did not always admit to being Jewish and anglicized their names to conceal their ethnic identity. To overcome this problem, Harvard's application form asked, "What change, if any, has been made since birth in your name or that of your father?" Harvard, Yale, and Princeton also introduced selection procedures that favored applicants who were the children of alumni (Karabel, 1984).

These strategies kept the numbers of Jewish students down to more or less acceptable limits, except at Columbia, New York City College, and Hunter College.

6. *Anti-Semitism*

The restriction on the numbers of Jews admitted to universities was one expression of the anti-Semitism that was widespread in the United States at this time. It developed following the immigration of large numbers of Jews from Russia from 1881 onward. Anti-Semitism was probably a significant factor in the 1924 Immigration Act, which fixed quotas for the numbers of immigrants from different countries in order to restrict the entry of Jews from Eastern Europe. According to Daniel Moynihan and Nathan Glazer, these sentiments persisted into the 1930s, when "anti-Semitism was becoming a major issue in American life.... Jews were excluded from social clubs, preparatory schools, better neighborhoods, the organized institutions of high society, and the occupations associated with high status." After World War II, discrimination declined and "in New York City only social and golf clubs and high society remained rigorously closed to Jews" (Moynihan & Glazer, 1970, pp. 156,160).

Although Jews comprised about 20 percent of the students at Ivy League and other major universities in the 1920s and 1930s, they were only rarely appointed to the teaching faculty. It was not until 1946 that the first Jew was appointed to the faculty at Yale. With the decline of anti-Semitism after 1945, Jews began to be appointed more frequently, and by 1970 they were 22 percent of the faculty at Yale (Hollinger, 2002, p. 149). By 1998, the presidents of Harvard, Yale, and Princeton were all Jewish.

7. *Education*

In the second half of the 20th century, Jews had more education than White Gentiles. Statistics showing this from 1957 through 1990 are given in Table 19.7. In 1957, a survey by the Bureau of the Census of the years of education of different religious groups aged 25 and over found that Jews had an average of 12.3 years of education as compared with 10.7 for Protestant Whites, 10.4 for Catholics, and

10.6 for the total White population (Chiswick, 1985). In the same year, Jews also had a higher percentage of those aged 25 and over who had obtained college degrees at 19.6 compared with 9.4 (Goldstein, 1971). The greater education of Jews was found again in the censuses of 1980 and 1990, when higher percentages of Jews than Whites had completed high school and had been awarded high-school diplomas (Darity, Dietrich & Guilkey, 1997). In the 1990 census, the percentage of Jews with college degrees again was more than twice that of American Whites.

Table 19.7. Years of education and percentages of Jews and Gentiles with High School Diplomas and College Degrees

Group	Years Education 1957	College Degree 1957	HS Diploma 1980	HS Diploma 1990	College Degree 1990
Jews	12.3	19.6	92	97	47
Whites	10.6	9.4	79	91	21

8. Earnings and Wealth

Average annual earnings (in thousands of U.S. dollars) for Jewish and White Gentile men for 1957 through 1990 are given in Table 19.8. Column 1 gives the median annual earnings for 1957 of men aged 14–64 obtained in the 1957 Bureau of the Census study (Chiswick, 1985). Column 2 gives the average annual earnings, for 1970, of men aged 25–64 obtained in that year's census (Chiswick, 1985). The figure for Jews is for native-born men of foreign parentage who reported Yiddish, Hebrew, or Latino as their mother tongue (defined as the language spoken in the home as a child). The figure for White Gentiles is also for native-born men of foreign parentage. The mean earnings of Whites with native-born parents were a little lower at $9,441. Similar data from the General Social Surveys are given by Wade Clark Roof (1979).

Column 3 shows the average annual earnings (thousands of U.S. dollars) for native-born men aged 25–54 given in the Bureau of the Census's Public Use Microdata, a one-percent sample from the 1980 census. The figure of those who identified themselves as ethnic Russians are presented for Jews, because virtually all of them were Jewish. Column 4 gives the median annual household earnings (thousands of U.S. dollars) for 1990 found in the National Survey of Religious Identification (Kosmin and Lachman, 1993, p. 260). The figures for the Gentiles are for Whites from the major religious denominations. Inclusion of Blacks would lower these by $1-2,000. In all four years, Jews had higher average earnings than White Gentiles; the magnitude of this advantage remained about the same, at approximately 130 percent of the average earnings of White Gentiles.

Table 19.8. Incomes ($ 1000) of Jewish and White Gentile men

Group	1957	1970	1980	1990
Jews	4,900	16,176	32,400	36,700
Gentile Whites	3,608	10,431	23,400	28,080

By the 1990s, Jews were hugely overrepresented among the very wealthly. Steve Silbiger (2000) has reported that Jews comprised more than a quarter of the people on the *Forbes Magazine* list of the richest 400 Americans, 45 percent of the top-40 richest Americans, and a third of all American multimillionaires. These figures have been confirmed for 2009 by Jacob Berkman (2009), who estimates that 130 of the *Forbes Magazine* richest four hundred Americans were Jewish (32 percent).

9. Socioeconomic Status

The socioeconomic status of Jewish and White Gentiles calculated from census data from 1880 to 1990 has been provided by William Darity, Jason Dietrich and David Guilkey (1997). Socioeconomic status was calculated by the Duncan Socioeconomic Index, which gives a score to each occupation (e.g. physicians: 100, laborers: 1, etc.). These scores were then averaged to give a mean for Jews and for the English and Scots-Irish as White Gentile comparison groups. The results are given in Table 19.9. It will be seen that in 1880, the Jews scored higher than the English and the Scots-Irish. At this time the Jews were predominantly German Ashkenazim who were established in the United States. In 1900 and again in 1910, the Jews scored a little lower than English and the Scots-Irish. This reflects the large influx of impoverished Jewish immigrants from Russia between 1881 and 1914, many of whom worked in low socioeconomic-status occupations such as the garment industry. By 1980 and 1990, the Jews had established themselves in the United States and were well ahead of the English and the Scots-Irish.

Table 19.9. Socioeconomic status of Jewish and White Gentiles, 1880–1990

Group	1880	1900	1910	1980	1990
Jews	27.41	26.93	29.10	59.65	60.97
English	24.38	28.14	30.39	45.17	47.61
Scots-Irish	22.57	27.62	31.64	46.09	46.73

Barry Kosmin and Seymour Lachman (1993) determined the numbers and percentages of Jews who were considered "upper class" by the American Institute of Public Opinion in a survey carried out in 1945. They also enumerated the Jews in the U.S. Senate from 1989 to 1991 and Justices in the Supreme Court from 1900 to 1990. They comment that there is "a marked overrepresentation (given their numbers in the population) of Jews" (p. 253). Their results are given in Table 19.10.

Table 19.10. Percentages of Jews in high status groups

Group	Year	% Jews	AQ
Upper Class	1945	22	7.3
U.S. Senate	1989–1991	8	3.6
Judges	1900–1990	9	3.0

The percentage of Jews in the United States was approximately three percent for the 20th century and 2.2 percent for 1990.

Adopting these figures gives Jewish Achievement Quotients of 7.3, 3.6, and 3.0 for these three elite positions in American society. The occupational distribution of Jews as compared with the general population for the years 1954 through 2000 is shown for men in Table 19.11.

Table 19.11. Occupations of Jewish and White men in 1945 through 2000 (percentages)

	1945		1957		1990		2000	
Occupation	Jews	Pop.	Jews	Whites	Jews	Whites	Jews	Whites
Professional	14.4	10.5	20.3	9.9	42.3	19.0	53.0	19.7
Managerial	21.7	8.5	35.1	13.3	16.5	13.1	14.8	15.1
Sales	-	-	14.1	5.4	18.3	11.4	18.5	10.4
Clerical	-	-	8.0	6.9	7.9	7.1	3.1	6.0
Service	4.3	11.2	2.3	6.1	5.4	8.8	3.8	9.1
Farm laborers	-	-	0.1	2.5	0.0	1.3	0.2	0.9
Construction	-	-	-	-	4.8	16.6	2.8	18.7
Transportation	-	-	-	-	1.7	13.3	2.1	9.0
Production	-	-	-	-	2.8	9.3	1.7	11.0

The figures for 1945 are derived from an Office of Public Opinion Research survey of 12,000 respondents and show that the percentages of Jews in professional and managerial occupations were higher than those in the general population, while the percentage in service occupations were lower (Information Service, 1948). The figures for 1957, 1990, and 2000, compiled by Sidney Goldstein (1971) and Barry Chiswick (1985, 2005), compare Jews with White 25-64-year-olds. The data are taken from the Bureau of the Census surveys.

The most salient feature of the results is the overrepresentation of Jews in the professions in all these years and the increase of this overrepresentation from 1945 to 1957, from 1957 to 1990, and again from 1990 to 2000. In 1945, 14.4 percent of Jewish men were in professional occupations compared with 10.5 percent of the general population. By 1957, 20.3 percent of Jewish men were in professional occupations compared with 9.9 percent of Whites (the definition of professional occupations may have changed in this year compared with that in the 1945 survey). In 1970, 27 percent of Jewish men were in professional occupations compared with 15.0 percent of Whites. In 1990, 42.3 percent of Jewish men were in professional occupations, compared with 19.0 percent of Whites. In 2000, the percentage of Jews in professional occupations had increased to 53.0 percent, while the percentage of Whites had barely increased at all (from 19.0 to 19.7 percent). Jews were also overrepresented in managerial positions in 1957, 1970, and 1990, though not in 2000. Evidently, Jews, who in the earlier years were managers, became professionals in the later years. Further, Jews continued to improve their socioeconomic position in the last decade of the 20th century. Jews are also conspicuously underrepresented in the last four blue-collar occupations in the table (farm laborers, construction, transportation, and production; farm owner and managers are classified as "managerial").

The occupational distribution of Jewish women given by Goldstein (1971) and Chiswick (1985, 2007) for the years 1957 to 2000 is shown in Table 19.12.

Table 19.12. Occupations of Jewish and White women in 1957 through 2000 (percentages)

	1957		1990		2000	
Occupation	Jews	Whites	Jews	Whites	Jews	Whites
Professional	15.5	12.2	41.8	23.4	51.4	28.5
Managerial	8.9	5.5	14.0	10.2	15.9	11.0
Sales	14.4	6.9	9.8	12.1	12.9	11.1
Clerical	43.9	30.3	24.7	15.4	12.1	25.1
Service	5.1	22.7	5.9	8.8	4.7	15.4
Farm laborers	0.0	3.0	0.0	0.4	0.0	0.3
Construction	-	-	1.9	2.3	1.7	0.8
Transportation	-	-	0.8	2.1	0.6	2.3
Production	-	-	1.0	6.6	0.3	5.8

In all the years, Jewish women were overrepresented in the professions and management, and this overrepresentation increased throughout the period. In 1957, 15.5 percent of Jewish women were in professional occupations, compared with 12.2 percent of Whites. In 1990, 41.8 percent of Jewish women were in professional occupations, compared with 23.4 percent of Whites. In 2000, the percentage of Jewish women in professional occupations had increased to 51.4 percent, while the percentage of Whites had only increased from 23.7 to 28.5 percent. Thus, Jewish women, like Jewish men, were continuing to improve their socioeconomic position up to the last decade of the 20th century. Jewish women, like Jewish men, are also conspicuously underrepresented in the last four blue-collar occupations in the table (farming, construction, transportation, and production).

A breakdown of the professions in which Jews are overrepresented has also been presented by Chiswick (2007). His figures for men are given in Table 19.13. We see here that Jews are between 2.1 and 5.3 times overrepresented in the major professions of medicine (including dentistry), law, and academics. They are only about two times overrepresented in the minor professions aggregated as "Other."

Table 19.13. Professional occupations of Jewish and White men in 1990 and 2000 (percentages)

Profession	1990			2000		
	Jews	Whites	AQ	Jews	Whites	AQ
Medicine	3.4	1.0	3.4	4.8	0.9	5.3
Law	2.9	1.1	2.6	5.3	1.1	4.8
University	3.7	0.8	4.6	1.9	0.9	2.1
Other	32.4	16.1	2.0	41.0	16.8	2.4

Table 19.14 gives the same breakdown for women and shows similar differences, except that Jewish women were slightly underrepresented among university faculties in 2000.

Table 19.14. Professional occupations of Jewish and White women in 1990 and 2000 (percentages)

Profession	1990			2000		
	Jews	Whites	AQ	Jews	Whites	AQ
Medicine	0.4	0.2	2.0	2.1	0.4	5.2
Law	2.3	0.6	3.8	3.3	0.5	6.6
University	2.3	0.6	3.8	0.8	0.9	0.8
Other	36.8	22.4	1.6	45.1	26.7	1.7

10. Eminence

The first study of the proportion of Jews to achieve eminence in the United States was made by Nathaniel Weyl (1966). He used seven reference books as sources of eminence (e.g. *Who's Who in America, American Men and Women of Science, Who's Who in Finance and Industry*, etc.), and he counted the numbers in these with identifiable ethnic and racial names. (For instance, Cole and Spence are the commonest English names; Schmid and Wagner are the commonest German names; and Cohen and Rosenberg are the commonest Jewish names.) Next, he expressed the frequency of ethnic and racial names in the reference books as a ratio of their frequency in the general population taken from Social Security rolls. The ratios for Jews and White Gentiles were finally multiplied by 100 to give an "occupational performance coefficient." Thus, a performance coefficient of 100 is the average for the total population and also the average for White Gentiles, who formed the great majority of the population at this time. He found that Jews had a performance coefficient of 448 (i.e. Jews were overrepresented by a factor of 4.48).

A similar study was made by Stanley Lieberson and Donna Carter (1979) for the years 1924–1925, 1944–1945, and 1974–1975; Monica McDermot (2002) has updated their analysis for the years 1994–1995. They took *Who's Who in America* as their source for eminence and followed Weyl in categorizing those listed into ethnic groups on the basis of their names. Thus, the names Bell, Bennet, etc. were classified as English; Amato, Basso, etc. as Italian; Carlson, Dahl, etc., as Scandinavian; and Abraham, Abrams, etc. as Jewish.

The frequencies of the names in the general population were taken from Social Security records. The rates of inclusion of the names in *Who's Who in America* were then calculated as rates per 10,000 of the names in the general population. The results for Jews and for the total population are shown in Table 19.15. We see that in the years 1924–1925 the Jewish index of 1.59 was significantly lower than the 2.27 for the total population. In 1944–1945, the Jewish index of 1.79 was still significantly lower than the 2.48 for the total population. However, by 1974–1975, their index was more than twice as high (8.39) as the 3.42 for the total population. By 1994–1995, it (16.62) was more than four times higher than that of the total population. The increasingly high Jewish indices reflect the two or three generations it took for impoverished immigrants from Eastern Europe in the period 1880–1924 to establish themselves in the United States and get the college education that is generally required to achieve the degree of eminence for inclusion in *Who's Who in America*.

Table 19.15. Rates of inclusion in **Who's Who in America** *(per 10,000 population)*

Group	1924–1925	1944–1945	1974–1975	1994–1995
Jews	1.59	1.97	8.39	16.62
Total	2.27	2.48	3.42	3.55

In a further study of Jews and eminence, Charles Murray (2003, p. 280) calculated the numbers of Jewish and Gentile "significant figures" (i.e. great names in science and the arts) in the United States whose careers fell in the years 1870-1950. He found 48 Jews and 261 Gentiles. Calculating the ratio of Jewish to Gentile "significant figures," he arrived at an Achievement Quotient (Jewish overrepresentation) of 5.1. This is about the same as the Jewish Achievement Quotients in the professions shown in Tables 19.13 and 19.14.

Jews have also become highly overrepresented among the business elite. In 1982, *Forbes* magazine reported a survey that listed the 40 richest individuals in the United States. Forty percent of these were Jews.

Jews are not equally overrepresented in all occupations, however. Weyl (1966) has analyzed Jewish Achievement Quotients for a number of occupations for around the year 1960. His results are shown in Table 19.16. Jews have high Achievement Quotients ranging between 3.3 and 5.8 for psychiatrists, dentists, mathematicians, doctors, writers, and lawyers. Achievement Quotients are substantially lower, ranging between 0.5 and 1.7, for architects, engineers, artists, and military officers. The most likely explanation for these differences is that the professions for which Jews have higher Achievement Quotients require strong verbal and mathematical abilities, which Jews possess, while the professions for which Jews have lower Achievement Quotients require strong visualization and spatial abilities (architecture, engineering, painting), with which Jews are less often endowed (see Table 19.3). The lowest Jewish Achievement Quotients is for the military, among whose ranks, Jews are underrepresented. One explanation for this is that Jews may sense (rightly or wrongly) that there could be an element of anti-Semitism in the military and that this would hinder their advancement.

Table 19.16. Jewish Achievement Quotients for different professions, 1960

Occupation	AQ	Occupation	AQ
Psychiatrists	5.8	Lawyers	3.3
Dentists	4.0	Architects	1.7
Mathematicians	3.8	Engineers	1.1
Doctors	3.7	Artists	1.4
Writers	3.4	Military	0.5

11. The Academic Elite

In 1969, a survey was carried out of the number of Jews among 60,000 American academics. Harriet Zuckerman (1977) analyzed the results and calculated that Jews were approximately three times overrepresented among university faculty, and seven times overrepresented among university faculty in elite colleges. His figures for the percentages of Jews in the faculties of the 17 most prestigious universities are shown in Table 19.17. Achievement Quotients are calculated on the basis of Jews being 2.7 percent of the population at this time. Jews were massively overrepresented in all areas.

Table 19.17. Jews in elite university faculties in 1969 (percentages)

Faculty	% Jews	AQ
Law	36	13.3
Sociology	34	12.6
Economics	28	10.4
Physics	26	9.6
Political Science	24	8.9
History	22	8.1
Philosophy	20	7.4
Mathematics	20	7.4

A similar study of top American intellectuals in 1970 has been published by Charles Kadushin (1974). The results are summarized in Table 19.18. Row 1 shows that Jews were 50 percent of top American intellectuals identified as those who published in the top twenty intellectual journals. Rows 2 and 3 show that Jews were 56 percent of top social scientists and 61 percent of those in the humanities.

Table 19.18. Jews in the academic elite in 1970

Group	% Jews	AQ
Intellectuals	50	18.5
Social scientists	56	20.7
Humanities	61	22.6

12. Nobel Prize winners

It will come as no surprise to learn that Jews are overrepresented among American Nobel Prize winners. A list of all United States Nobel Prize winners is given in Table 19.19; Jews are denoted by asterisks. The list includes those born in the United States, and therefore excludes a number of those, like Einstein, who emigrated and made their homes in America later in life. Of the 200 American Nobel Prize winners, 62 have been Jewish (31 percent). Jews were about three percent of the population during the 20th century, giving them an Achievement Quotient of 10. Jews were much less prominent in the first half of the 20th century, when they were only two out of 19 Prize winners (10.5 percent) than in the second half and up to 2008, when they were 60 out of the 181 Prize winners (33 percent). During this latter period, Jews, who have been about 2.2 percent of the population, had a Nobel Prize Achievement Quotient of 15.

This greater representation of Jews among Nobel Prize winners in the second half of the 20th century is consistent with other results such as the increasing overrepresentation of Jews in the higher socioeconomic status occupations (see Table 19.9). This trend is not surprising, since most of the Jews arrived penniless during the years 1881–1924 and made a living in skilled manual work like tailoring. It took a generation for them to learn English and establish themselves to the extent that they could give their children the education necessary to do work meriting a Nobel Prize. These prizes are normally awarded to those in later middle age for work done a number of years previously that is widely accepted as being important. Thus, an immigrant arriving in, say, 1890 might have a child born in 1900 who would be accepted at a good university in 1918. He (or, more rarely, she) might do brilliant work in the 1930s and 1940s and be award a Nobel Prize in recognition of this in the 1950s and 1960s. Thus, the much greater number and percentage of Jewish Nobel Prize winners in the second half of the 20th century than in the first half is to be expected.

Table 19.19. Nobel Prize winners (Jews are asterisked)

Year	Name	Subject	Year	Name	Subject
1914	Theodore Richards	Chemistry	1985	Michael Brown*	Medicine
1930	Sinclair Lewis	Literature	1985	Joseph Goldstein*	Medicine
1932	Irving Langmuir	Chemistry	1986	Herschbach	Chemistry
1936	Carl D. Anderson	Physics	1986	James Buchanan	Economics
1937	Clinton Davisson	Physics	1986	Stanley Cohen*	Medicine
1938	Pearl Buck	Literature	1987	Donald J. Cram	Chemistry
1939	Ernest Lawrence	Physics	1987	Robert M. Solow*	Economics
1943	Edward A. Doisy	Medicine	1987	Gertrude Elion*	Medicine
1944	Joseph Erlanger*	Medicine	1988	George Hutchings	Medicine
1944	Herbert S. Gasser	Medicine	1988	Leon Lederman*	Physics
1946	John H. Northrop	Chemistry	1988	Melvin Schwartz*	Physics
1946	Wendell M. Stanley	Chemistry	1989	Thomas R. Cech	Chemistry
1946	James B. Sumner	Chemistry	1989	J. Michael Bishop	Medicine
1946	Hermann Muller*	Medicine	1989	Harold Varnus*	Medicine
1946	Percy Bridgman	Physics	1989	Norman Ramsey	Physics
1949	William F. Giauque	Chemistry	1990	Elias Corey	Chemistry
1949	William Faulkner	Literature	1990	Markowitz*	Economics
1950	Philip S. Hench	Medicine	1990	Merton Miller*	Economics
1950	Edward C. Kendall	Medicine	1990	William F. Sharpe	Economics
1951	Edwin McMillan	Chemistry	1990	Joseph E. Murray	Medicine
1951	Glenn T. Seaborg	Chemistry	1990	E. Donnall Thomas	Medicine
1952	E. M. Purcell	Physics	1990	Jerome Friedman*	Physics
1954	Linus Pauling	Chemistry	1990	Harry Kendall	Physics
1954	Ernest Hemingway	Literature	1992	Gary S. Becker*	Economics
1954	John F. Enders	Medicine	1992	Edwin G. Krebs	Medicine
1954	Frederick Robbins	Medicine	1993	Kary B. Mullis	Chemistry
1954	Thomas H. Weller	Medicine	1993	Robert W. Fogel	Economics
1955	Vincent du Vigneaud	Chemistry	1993	Douglass North	Economics
1955	Willis E. Lamb	Physics	1993	Toni Morrison	Literature
1956	Dickinson Richards	Medicine	1993	Phillip A. Sharp	Medicine
1956	John Bardeen	Physics	1993	Russell A. Hulse	Physics
1956	Walter H. Brattain	Physics	1993	Joseph H. Taylor	Physics

Year	Name	Subject	Year	Name	Subject
1958	George Beadle	Medicine	1994	John F. Nash	Economics
1958	Joshua Lederberg*	Medicine	1994	Alfred G. Gilman*	Medicine
1958	Edward Tatum	Medicine	1994	Martin Rodbell*	Medicine
1959	Arthur Kornberg*	Medicine	1994	Clifford Schull	Physics
1959	Owen Chamberlain	Physics	1995	F. Rowland	Chemistry
1960	Willard F. Libby	Chemistry	1995	Frederick Reines*	Physics
1960	Donald A. Glaser*	Physics	1995	Eric F. Wieschaus	Medicine
1961	Melvin Calvin*	Chemistry	1996	Robert Curl	Chemistry
1961	Robert Hofstadter*	Physics	1996	Richard Smalley	Chemistry
1962	John Steinbeck	Literature	1996	David M. Lee*	Physics
1962	James Watson	Medicine	1996	Douglas Osheroff	Physics
1964	Charles H. Townes	Physics	1996	Robert Richardson	Physics
1965	Robert B. Woodward	Chemistry	1997	Paul D. Boyer	Chemistry
1965	Richard P. Feynman*	Physics	1997	Robert C. Merton	Economics
1965	Julian Schwinger*	Physics	1997	Stanley Prusiner*	Medicine
1966	Robert S. Mulliken	Medicine	1997	Steven Chu	Physics
1966	Charles B. Huggins	Chemistry	1997	William Phillips	Physics
1966	Peyton Rous	Medicine	1998	Robert Furchgott*	Medicine
1967	Haldan K. Hartline	Medicine	1998	Louis J. Ignarro	Medicine
1968	Robert W. Holley	Medicine	1998	Ferid Murad	Medicine
1968	Marshall Nirenberg*	Medicine	1998	Robert Laughlin	Physics
1968	Luis Alvarez	Physics	2000	Alan Heeger*	Chemistry
1969	Alfred D. Hershey	Medicine	2000	James J. Heckman	Economics
1969	Murray Gell-Mann*	Physics	2000	Daniel McFadden	Economics
1970	Paul Samuelson*	Economics	2000	Paul Greengard*	Medicine
1970	Julius Axelrod*	Medicine	2000	Herbert Kroemer	Physics
1971	Earl Sutherland	Medicine	2001	William Knowles	Chemistry
1972	Christian Anfinsen*	Chemistry	2001	K. Barry Sharpless	Chemistry
1972	Stanford Moore	Chemistry	2001	George Akerlof	Economics
1972	William H. Stein*	Chemistry	2001	Michael Spence	Economics
1972	Kenneth Arrow	Economics	2001	Joseph Stiglitz*	Economics
1972	Gerald Edelman*	Medicine	2001	Leland Hartwell	Medicine
1972	John Bardeen	Physics	2001	Eric A. Cornell	Physics
1972	Leon N. Cooper*	Physics	2001	Carl E. Wieman	Physics

Year	Name	Subject	Year	Name	Subject
1972	Robert Schrieffer	Physics	2002	John B. Fenn	Chemistry
1975	David Baltimore*	Medicine	2002	Vernon L. Smith	Economics
1975	Howard M. Temin*	Medicine	2002	Robert Horvitz*	Medicine
1975	James Rainwater	Physics	2002	Raymond Davis	Physics
1976	William Lipscomb	Chemistry	2003	Peter Agre	Chemistry
1976	Milton Friedman*	Economics	2003	R. MacKinnon	Chemistry
1976	Baruch Blumberg*	Medicine	2003	Robert F. Engle	Economics
1976	Carleton Gajdusek	Medicine	2003	Paul C. Lauterbur	Medicine
1976	Burton Richter*	Physics	2004	Irwin Rose*	Chemistry
1977	Rosalyn Yalow*	Medicine	2004	Edward Prescott	Economics
1977	John H. van Vleck	Physics	2004	Richard Axel*	Medicine
1978	Herbert Simon*	Economics	2004	David J. Gross*	Physics
1978	Daniel Nathans*	Medicine	2004	David Politzer*	Physics
1978	Robert Wilson	Physics	2004	Frank Wilczek	Physics
1979	Theodore Schultz	Economics	2004	Linda B. Buck	Medicine
1979	Sheldon Glashow*	Physics	2005	Robert Grubbs	Chemistry
1979	Steven Weinberg*	Physics	2005	Thomas Schelling	Chemistry
1980	Paul Berg*	Chemistry	2005	Roy Glauber*	Physics
1980	Walter Gilbert*	Chemistry	2005	John Hall	Physics
1980	Lawrence Klein*	Economics	2006	Roger Kornberg*	Chemistry
1980	George D. Snell	Medicine	2006	Edmund Phelps	Economics
1980	James Cronin	Physics	2007	Eric Maskin*	Economics
1980	Val Fitch	Physics	2007	Roger Myerson*	Economics
1981	James Tobin	Economics	2007	Mario Capecchi	Medicine
1981	Roger W. Sperry	Medicine	2008	Paul Krugman*	Economics
1981	Arthur Schawlow	Physics	2008	Martin Shalfie	Chemistry
1982	George J. Stigler	Economics	2008	Roger Tsien	Chemistry
1982	Kenneth G. Wilson	Physics	2009	Carol Greider	Medicine
1983	B.McClintock	Medicine	2009	Thoms Steitz	Chemistry
1983	William A. Fowler	Physics	2009	George Smith	Physics
1984	Bruce Merrifield	Chemistry	2009	Elinor Ostrom	Economics
1985	Herbert Hauptman*	Chemistry	2009	O. Williamson	Economics
1985	Jerome Karle*	Chemistry			

13. Mathematicians

The William Lowell Putnam Competition is an annual event sponsored by the American Mathematical Society and is the most prestigious mathematical competition for undergraduates in the United States. Each year, there are about 3,000 contestants. During the years 1994-2002, there were 242 participants who received a prize or an honorable mention, of whom 51 (21 percent) were Jewish. During these years Jews were approximately 2.1 percent of the population, so they were 10 times overrepresented among these gifted young mathematicians.

The United States has produced 16 of the world-class mathematicians who have received the Fields Medal or the Wolf Prize (Stephen Smale (b.1930) has been awarded both prizes, but is only counted once.) These are listed in Table 19.20. Six of the 16 have been Jews. Thus, Jews, who comprised about 2.2 percent of the population during the second half of the 20th century, have produced 37.5 percent of top mathematicians, giving them an Achievement Quotient of 16.

Table 19.20. United States Mathematicians (Jews are asterisked)

Year	Fields Medal	Year	Wolf Prize
1936	Jesse Douglas*	1982	Hassler Whitney
1962	John Milnor	1996	Joseph Keller*
1966	Paul Cohen*	2002	John Tate
1966	Stephen Smale	2007	Stephen Smale
1970	John Thompson	2008	Phillip Griffiths
1978	Charles Fefferman*	2008	David Mumford
1978	Daniel Quillen		
1982	William Thurston		
1986	Michael Freedman*		
1990	Edward Witten*		
1998	Curtis McMullen		

14. Chess

Although the United States has not produced many top-rated chess players, Jews have been prominent among them. In William Rubinstein's (2004) list of the 141 top-rated chess grandmasters for each decade spanning the years 1851–2000, only five have been American. Table 19.21 gives their names and dates.

Table 19.21. Chess grandmasters (Jews are asterisked)

Years	Name	Years	Name
1851–1910	Morphy	1930–2000	Kashdan*
	Pillsbury		Fine*
			Fischer*

In the first period from 1851 to 1910, the United States produced two top-rated grandmasters; both were Gentiles. It would not be expected that Jews would have made much of a showing in these years, because most Jews were recent immigrants and were too busy making a living to master serious chess. There were no top-rated American grandmasters between 1910 and 1930. The next top-rated American grandmaster, Issac Kashdan (1905–1985), appeared in the 1930s, followed by Reuben Fine (1914–1993) in the 1940s, and Bobby Fischer in the 1970s. All three were Jewish. Thus, Jews, who were 3.55 percent of the population in 1927, produced 60 percent of the top-rated chess players over the period 1851–2000, giving them an Achievement Quotient of 16.9.

15. Bridge

In contrast to chess, the United States has produced many top-rated bridge players. In 2004, 55 of the 156 top-rated bridge players among the Open World Champions have been American. The names of these are given in Table 19.22. Eighteen of the 55 are Jews (33 percent). Thus, Jews, who were about two percent of the population at the beginning of the 21st century, have produced 33 percent of top bridge players, giving them an Achievement Quotient of 16.

Table 19.22. United States Open World Bridge Champions in 2004 (Jews are asterisked)

Bob Hamman	Eddie Kantar*	Ed Manfield*
Bobby Wolff*	Bob Lipsitz*	Lew Mathe
Billy Eisenberg*	Nick Nickell	Rose Meltzer
Chip Martel*	Steve Robinson	Don Oakie
Jeff Meckstroth	Alan Sontag*	Steve Parker
Eric Rodwell*	Peter Weichsel*	Mike Passell
Lew Stansby	Russ Arnold	Eric Paulsen
Paul Soloway*	Roger Bates	Peter Pender*
John Crawford	Mike Becker	Bud Reinhold
Bobby Goldman*	Clifford Bishop	William Rosen
Jim Jacoby	Peter Boyd	Michael Rosenberg*
Mike Lawrence	Malcolm Brachman	Ira Rubin*
George Rapee	Milton Ellenby	Ronnie Rubin*
Hugh Ross	Charles Goren	Sidney Silodor
Howard Schenken*	Fred Hamilton	John Solodar
Samuel Stayman	Gaylor Kasle	Douglas Steen
B J Becker	Kyle Larsen	John Swanson
Seymon Deutsch	Bobby Levin*	
Dick Freeman*	Theodore Lightner	

16. Pulitzer Prizes

The Pulitzer Prizes were established in 1917 by Joseph Pulitzer (who was Jewish) and is widely regarded as the most prestigious American award prize for literature. Prizes are normally given annually for nonfiction, fiction, poetry, drama, history, and biography. Jews have won 52 percent of the prizes for nonfiction, 15 percent of the prizes for fiction, 20 percent of the prizes for poetry, and 34 percent of the prizes for drama (it has not proved possible to find the ethnic identity of the winners for history and biography). The Jewish winners for nonfiction are listed below.

Theodore H. White (1962), *The Making of the President, 1960*

Barbara Tuchman (1963), *The Guns of August*

Richard Hofstadter (1964), *Anti-Intellectualism in American Life*

David Brion Davis (1967), *The Problem of Slavery in Western Culture*
Ariel Durant (1968), *Rousseau And Revolution*
Norman Mailer (1969), *The Armies Of The Night*
Erik Erikson (1970), *Gandhi's Truth*
Barbara Tuchman (1972), *Stilwell and the American Experience in China*
Robert Coles (1973), *Children of Crisis*
Ernest Becker (1974), *The Denial of Death*
Carl Sagan (1978), *The Dragons of Eden*
Douglas Hofstatder (1980), *Gödel, Escher, Bach: An Eternal Golden Braid*
Carl Schorske (1981), *Fin-De-Siècle Vienna: Politics And Culture*
Susan Margulies Sheehan (1983), *Is There No Place on Earth for Me?*
Paul Starr (1984), *The Social Transformation Of American Medicine*
Studs Terkel (1985), *The Good War: An Oral History of World War II*
Joseph Lelyveld (1986), *Move Your Shadow: South Africa, Black and White*
J. Anthony Lukas (1986), *Common Ground: A Turbulent Decade in the Lives of Three American Families*
Daniel Yergin (1992), *The Prize: The Epic Quest for Oil, Money, and Power*
David Remnick (1994), *Lenin's Tomb: The Last Days of the Soviet Empire*
Jonathan Weiner (1995), *The Beak of the Finch: A Story of Evolution in Our Time*
Tina Rosenberg (1996), *The Haunted Land: Facing Europe's Ghosts After Communism*
Richard Kluger (1997), *Ashes to Ashes: America's Hundred-Year Cigarette War, the Public Health, and the Unabashed Triumph of Philip Morris*
Jared Diamond (1998), *Guns, Germs, and Steel*
Herbert Bix (2001), *Hirohito and the Making of Modern Japan*
Anne Applebaum (2004), *Gulag: A History*
Saul Friedlander (2008), *The Years of Extermination: Nazi Germany and the Jews, 1939–1945*

17. Music and Hollywood

From the 1920s on, Jews have dominated American music in three areas: popular songs, musicals, and Classical. In the golden age of "Tin Pan Alley" (1920 to 1960), about half the leading songwriters were Jews. Luminaries of the genre included George Gershwin (1898–1937), Jerome Kern (1885–1945), Richard Rodgers (1902–1979), and Irving Berlin (1888–1989). The other half of the leading songwriters were Gentiles, e.g. Cole Porter (1891–1964), Harry Warren (1893–1981), Vincent Youmans (1898–1946), Duke Ellington (1899–1974) (Rubinstein, 2004, p. 41). Perhaps the greatest of this group was Irving Berlin, who was born in Russia as Israel Baline and brought to the United States at the age of five. He later expressed his gratitude for this by writing the song "God Bless America." Further Jewish musicians who have been successful worldwide in popular music including pioneer jazz clarinetist Benny Goodman (born Gutman, 1909–1986), Bob Dylan (born Zimmerman, 1941), unquestionably the greatest songwriter and social commentator of the 1960s and '70s, and songwriters/musicians Paul Simon (b.1941), and Randy Newman (b.1943).

William Rubinstein writes, "the Hollywood musical was almost entirely a product of Jews" (2004, p. 41). Perhaps the most famous and enduring are *Show Boat* (1927) written by Jerome Kern, with lyrics by Oscar Hammerstein (1895–1960), and George Gershwin's *An American in Paris* (1928) and *Porgy and Bess* (1935).

In Classical music, Jews have produced the composers Aaron Copland (1900–1990) and Leonard Bernstein (1918–1990); a number of the greatest virtuosi, including the pianists Artur Schnabel (1882–1951), Vladimir Horowitz (1903–1989), and Artur Rubinstein (1887–1982); and the violinists Jascha Heifetz (1901–1987), Nathan Milstein (1904–1992), Isaac Stern (1920–2001), and Yehudi Menuhin (1916–1999).

A quantification of the numbers of Jews in music in the early decades of the 20th century was undertaken by Keith Sward (1933), and his results are summarized in Table 19.23.

Table 19.23. Jewish musicians, 1922–1932

Specialism	N	% Jews	AQ
Players	1,048	26	7.2
Conductors	37	46	12.8
Virtuosi	145	37	10.0
Composers	42	24	6.7
Amusement	586	36	10.0

Row 1 gives number of players in the 12 leading American symphony orchestras in the years 1922–1932 and shows that 26 percent were Jews. Row 2 shows the number of conductors in the 12 leading American symphony orchestras in 1932 and reveals that 46 percent of these were Jews. Row 3 gives the number of violin, piano, and cello virtuosi in the 12 leading American symphony orchestras in 1932 and shows that 37 percent were Jews. Row 4 gives the number of composer-artists who appeared in the four leading American symphony orchestras (Boston, New York, Chicago, and Philadelphia) in 1922–1932 and shows that 24 percent were Jews. Row 5 gives the number of players in 23 "amusement orchestras" in 1922–1932 and shows that 36 percent were Jews. The achievement quotients are calculated on the basis of Jews being 3.6 percent the population in 1927 and give Jews an average achievement quotient of 9.4.

In the same study, Sward carried out exams to determine whether Jews have a particularly strong musical ability, but he found no difference between Jewish and Gentile 11-year-olds matched for IQ on the Seashore and other tests of simple musical ability.

Jews played a major role in the development of Hollywood and have continued to predominate in the film industry. Adoph Zukor (1873–1976) and William Fox (1879–1952) immigrated from Hungarian shetls to become the leaders of Paramount and Fox Pictures. Carl Laemmle (1867–1939) came from Southern Germany and founded Universal Studio in 1884, and Samuel Goldwyn (formerly Goldfish) came from Warsaw around 1885. Throughout the 20th century, Jews were prominent in Hollywood as both producers and stars: "any list of the most influential production executives at each of the major movie studios will produce a heavy majority of recognizably Jewish names" (Medved, 1999). Among the best known that have retained their Jewish names are the actors Barbra Streisand (b.1942), Deanna Durbin (b.1921), Victor Borge (1909–2000), the Marx Brothers, Paul Newman (1925–2008), and Dustin Hoffman (b.1937), as well as the producer and director Steven Spielberg (b.1946). But most have adopted English sounding names. These include Woody Allen (Konigsberg), Douglas Fairbanks (Ullman), Danny Kaye (Kaminsky), Binnie Barnes (Gittel), Tony Curtis (Schwartz), Lili Palmer (Peiser), Melvyn Douglas (Hesselberg), John Garfield (Garfinkle), Hedy Lamarr (Keisler), Judy Holiday (Tuvim), Paul Muni (Weisenfreund), Edward Robinson (Goldenberg), Sylvia Sidney (Koskow), Jack Benny (Kubelsky), Benny Baker (Zifkin), Judy Garland (Gumm), Mary Livingston (Marks), George Burns (Birnbaum), Edward Bromberg (Bromberger), and Sue Carol (Lederer).

On December 19, 2008, Joel Stein wrote in the *Los Angeles Times*: "How deeply Jewish is Hollywood?":

> When the studio chiefs took out a full-page ad in the *Los Angeles Times* a few weeks ago, to demand that the Screen Actors Guild settle its contract, the open letter was signed by: News Corp. President Peter Chernin (Jewish), Paramount Pictures Chairman Brad Grey (Jewish), Walt Disney Co. Chief Executive Robert Iger (Jewish), Sony Pictures Chairman Michael Lynton (surprise, Dutch Jew), Warner Bros. Chairman Barry Meyer (Jewish), CBS Corp. Chief Executive Leslie Moonves (so Jewish his great-uncle was the first prime minister of Israel), MGM Chairman Harry Sloan (Jewish) and NBC Universal Chief Executive Jeff Zucker (mega Jewish). If either of the Weinstein brothers had signed, this group would have not only the power to shut down all film production but to form a *minyan* with enough Fiji water on hand to fill a *mikvah*.

18. The Media

Jews have been prominent among the owners and senior employees of American TV, radio, and newspapers. Three companies broadcast most of the television news and entertainment: American Broadcasting Company (ABC), Columbia Broadcasting System (CBS), and National Broadcasting Company (NBC). William Paley (1901–1990), whose parents were immigrant Jews from Russia, ran CBS for more than half a century. In 1928, Paley bought United Independent Broadcasters and renamed it Columbia Broadcasting System. He took the position of president, became chairman of the board in 1946, and held that post until his partial retirement in 1983. In 1986, Laurence Tisch (1923–2003) became the chairman and CEO of CBS. NBC was formerly a subsidiary of Radio Corporation of America (RCA). From 1930 to 1970, NBC was controlled by David Sarnoff (1891–1971), who was of Russian Jewish origin. Following his death in 1970, his son Robert (1918–1997) took over the corporation. In 1986, General Electric Co. merged with RCA, and now NBC is a wholly owned subsidiary of GE. In 1990, Steve Friedman (b.1950) became executive producer of NBC Nightly News and was succeeded in 1993 by Jeff Zucker (b.1965).

In May 1990, *American Film* magazine listed the top 10 U.S. entertainment companies (in terms of gross revenues in the previous year) and their CEOs and ranked them by size. These were Time Warner Communications (Steven J. Ross (1927-1992)), Walt Disney Co. (Michael D. Eisner (b.1942)), NBC (Robert C. Wright (b.1943)), Paramount Communications (Martin S. Davis (1927-1999)), CBS (Laurence Tisch), 20th Century Fox (Barry Diller (b.1942)), Columbia Pictures Entertainment (Victor A. Kaufman (b.1942)), Viacom (Sumner Redstone (b.1923)), Capital Cities/ ABC (Thomas Murphy (b.1925)), and MCA Inc. (Lew Wasserman (1913–2002)). The CEOs of eight of these top 10 entertainment companies—Ross, Eisner, Davis, Tisch, Diller, Kaufman, Redstone, and Wasserman—were Jewish.

The newspapers, too, have become largely owned by Jews. Two of the most prestigious and influential, the *New York Times* and the *Washington Post*, have been owned and largely staffed by Jews. Two Gentiles, Henry J. Raymond (1820–1869) and George Jones (1811–1891), founded the *New York Times* in 1851. After their deaths, a wealthy Jewish publisher, Adolph Ochs (1858–1935), purchased it in 1896. It remained in the family, and his great-grandson, Arthur Ochs Sulzberger Jr., became the publisher and CEO. As of this writing, the Sulzberger family still controls the *Times* and also owns 33 other newspapers, including the *Boston Globe*, purchased in June 1993; 12 magazines, including *McCall's* and *Family Circle*, with circulations of more than five million each; seven radio and TV broadcasting stations; a cable-TV system; and three book publishing companies.

The *Washington Post* was established in 1877 by Stilson Hutchins (1838–1912); purchased in 1905 by John R. McLean; and later inherited by Edward B. McLean (1889–1941). These were all Gentiles. In 1933, the newspaper was forced into bankruptcy. It was purchased by Eugene Isaac Meyer (1875–1959), a Jewish financier, and was successively run by his daughter, Katharine Meyer Graham (1917–2001), and grandson, Donald (b. 1945). The Washington Post Co. has a number of other media holdings in newspapers, television, and magazines.

The *Wall Street Journal* is another influential paper and was founded by Clarence Barron (1855–1928), a Gentile. It has remained largely owned by the Barron family until Rupert Murdoch (b.1931) bought it in 2007.

The three largest circulation news magazines–*Time, Newsweek*, and *U.S. News & World Report*–are largely owned and run by Jews. *Time* is published by a subsidiary of Time Warner Communications, the media conglomerate formed by the 1989 merger of Time Inc. with Warner Communications. The Washington Post Co. publishes *Newsweek*. *U.S. News & World Report* is owned, edited, and published by Mortimer Zuckerman (b.1937), who also publishes New York's tabloid the *Daily News* and once owned *The Atlantic Monthly*. "The most widely-read American journals like *Commentary, The Public Interest, The New York Review of Books, New Republic*, and *Partisan Review* are either explicitly Jewish or contain a disproportionately Jewish input" (Rubinstein, 1982, p. 64).

A quantification of the proportion of Jews among the media elites is given in Table 19.24. Row 1 shows the proportion of Jews among the media elite in 1975 at 26 percent (Rubinstein, 1982, p. 61). Row 2, 3, and 4 give the results of a study published by *Forbes* magazine in 1982. It estimated that Jews were 30 percent of media elite, defined as those working on the news divisions of the three television networks and the Public Broadcasting Service (PBS), the three leading news magazines (*Time, Newsweek,* and *U.S. News & World Report)*, and the four top newspapers. Rows 3 and 4 show that Jews were 46 percent of the directors and producers of Hollywood TV and 66 percent of the directors and producers of Hollywood movies. Row 5 gives the results of a *Vanity Fair* article of 1994 that published profiles of the 23 most influential media people. It was described as "the new establishment" and consisted of "men and women from the entertainment, communications, and computer industries." Eleven of these (48 percent) were Jews.

Table 19.24. Media Elites

Year	Group	% Jews	AQ
1975	Media elite	26	10.0
1980	Media elite	30	13.6
1980	Hollywood movies	66	30.0
1980	Hollywood TV	46	20.9
1994	"New establishment"	48	21.8

19. Sport

Although it appears that Jews are good at almost everything, there is a common stereotype that they do not fare well at sport. In 1921, Henry Ford opined,

> Jews are not sportsmen.... Whether this is due to their physical lethargy, their dislike of unnecessary physical action or their serious cast of mind, others may decide.... It may be a defect of character; it is nevertheless, a fact which discriminating Jews unhesitatingly acknowledge. (Hoberman, 1991, p. 39)

This verdict was not, however, entirely correct. On the contrary, in the first half of the 20th century, Jews excelled at basketball and boxing:

> Jewish players dominated the American Basketball League in numbers and accomplishments. Almost half the league (45 of 91 players) was Jewish in the 1937–1938 season. Even a decade later in the 1945-1946 season, almost 45 percent (71 of 159) of the players were Jewish. (Klein, 2000, p. 216)

310   THE CHOSEN PEOPLE

Jews were also prominent in boxing: "between 1910 and 1939, the presence of Jewish fighters grew until they became the dominant force.... In 1933, Jews held four of the eight division titles" (Klein, 1999, p. 216). In the 1930s there were 60 World Boxing Champions, and 15.9 percent of them were Jewish (Riess, 1998).

After World War II, the Jewish presence in basketball and boxing declined to insignificance. The most likely explanation for the success of Jews in these sports in the first half of the century is that these did not require years of investment in education. After World War II, most Jewish families had succeeded to the extent that they could give their children the education needed to enter the professions and management, and these were more attractive career options. By this time, "Jews are not a major sporting success story because they don't need to be" (Klein, 2000, p. 221).

20. Fertility and Infant Mortality

Jews in the United States, as elsewhere, have had low fertility in the 20th century. Table 19.25 gives statistics, from a Bureau of the Census survey of 1957, for this phenomenon expressed as children ever born per 1,000 women aged 44 and over (see Chiswick, 1988a). It will be seen that Jewish women had substantially fewer children than all other women. Chiswick notes that as early as the 1930s,

> A survey of contraceptive practices indicated that a higher proportion of Jews used contraceptives, planned their pregnancies, used more efficient methods of birth control, and began to use contraception earlier in their marriages than Protestants and Catholics. (Chiswick, 1988a, p. 587)

The table also gives identical birth rates for Jews and almost identical birth rates for Whites for 1989, which were obtained in a survey carried out by the Bureau of the Census (Goldstein, 1993). (The comparison group for 1989 is Whites, while that for 1957 is for the total population.)

Table 19.25. Children ever born per 1,000 women aged 44+

Group	1957	1989
Jews	2.2	2.2
Non-Jews	2.8	2.7

Infant mortality was lower among Jews in the late 19th century and early 20th century. Studies showing this are summarized in Table 19.26, where it will be seen that between 1885 and 1915, the infant mortality of White Gentiles was approximately twice as high as that of Jews. Infant mortality rates of Jews compared with Italians in New York in the early 1930s again shows lower rates among Jews.

Table 19.26. Infant mortality per 1,000 live births

Years	Jews	Gentiles	Reference
1885–1889	81	167	Condran & Kramarow, 1991
1911–1915	54	108	Condran & Kramarow, 1991
1930–1934	39	56	Pintner & Maller, 1937

According to Preston, Ewbank, and Hereward (1994), the low Jewish rate of infant mortality is attributable to "unmeasured child care practices, having mostly to do with feeding practices and general hygienic standards." These are attributable to higher Jewish IQs.

21. Crime

It is well known that crime is associated with low intelligence, so we would expect that Jews would have low rates of crime. We noted some evidence for this in the chapter on Germany. Low Jewish crime rates have also been found in the United States. Statistics for the percentages of criminals in the population and in reformatories and jails in three locations have been given by Hans von Hentig (1948, pp. 337–8) and Calvin Goldscheider and Jon Simpson (1967) and are shown in Table 19.27.

Table 19.27. Percentages of Jews and other denominations in the population and among criminals

	Location	Group	Jews	Protestants	Catholics	Others
1a	Massachusetts	Population	6.7	25.2	66.4	1.7
1b	Massachusetts	Criminals	3.9	28.6	66.3	1.2
2a	Pennsylvania	Population	4.3	27.8	23.3	44.6
2b	Pennsylvania	Criminals	1.2	64.3	33.0	1.5
3a	Allegheny	Population	4.1	20.4	25.2	49.3
3b	Allegheny	Criminals	1.3	49.6	46.0	2.3
4a	Los Angeles	Population	6.6	57.8	21.5	2.7
4b	Los Angeles	Criminals	2.7	-	35.2	-

Von Hentig gave data for three locations, in all of which Jews were considerably underrepresented among criminals as compared with their representation in the population. Rows 1a and 1b give the percentages of Jews, Protestants, Catholics, and Others in the population and the percentages in reformatories. This shows that Jews were 6.7 percent of the population but only 3.9 percent in reformatories. The other three groups have about the same percentages in the population and in jails. There is a somewhat greater underrepresentation of Jews among adult criminals in the other two locations shown in rows 2a and 2b, and in rows 3a and 3b. The disparities in "Others" is due to the fact that this category included "None"; many criminals claim to belong to religious denominations hoping to be recommended for clemency by prison chaplains (von Hentig, 1948, pp. 335, 342). Goldscheider and Simpson (1967) have confirmed the underrepresentation of Jews among juvenile delinquents in Los Angeles in 1960. Their results are given in rows 4a and 4b, showing that Jews were 6.6 percent of the population but only 2.7 percent of juvenile delinquents.

CHAPTER 20

Theories of Jewish Intelligence

1. Intelligence of the Four Jewish Peoples
2. Achievements of the Four Jewish Peoples
3. The Jewish Intelligence Profile
4. Genetic Basis of Jewish Intelligence
5. The Eugenic Hypothesis
6. The Persecution Hypothesis
7. The Discrimination Hypothesis
8. The Miscegenation Hypothesis
9. The Apostasy Hypothesis
10. Genetics of the High Jewish IQ

We have seen in the body of this book that the Ashkenazim have a high level of intelligence, but that there are four Jewish peoples and that the other three—the Mizrahim, the Sephardim, and the Ethiopians—are not remarkable in this regard. We begin this chapter by summarizing these conclusions and then consider the theories that attempt to explain how these differences have arisen.

1. Intelligence of the Four Jewish Peoples

The IQ of the Ashkenazim has been examined in Britain, Canada, the United States, and Israel, where it has been calculated at 110, 109, 110, and 110. From these results, we conclude that the Ashkenazi Jews have an average IQ of 110 in relation to a European Gentile mean of 100 (standard deviation of 15). This 10-point advantage should give Ashkenazi Jews approximately four times the percentage of individuals with an IQ of 130 and above and approximately six times the percentage of individuals with an IQ of 145 and above. The effect of this should be that Ashkenazi Jews should be considerably overrepresented among the highly successful. We have seen that this is the case in all of the 17 countries and regions we have considered. Everywhere, Jews are considerably overrepresented in the professions, among the wealthy, and among intellectual elites.

The IQs of the four Jewish peoples are shown in Table 20.1. Also shown for comparison are the IQs of the Gentiles among whom these Jewish peoples have lived. The detailed evidence for the derivation of these figures is set out for the Ethiopian Jews and for the Mizrahim in the chapter on Israel, for the Sephardim in the chapter on the Balkans, and for the Ashkenazim in the chapters on Britain, Canada, the United States, and Israel. The evidence for the derivation of the IQs for the Gentile peoples is given in my *Race Differences in Intelligence* (Lynn, 2006).

Table 20.1. IQs of Jews and Gentiles

Jews	IQ	Gentiles	IQ	IQ Difference
Ashkenazim	110	European Gentiles	100	10.0
Sephardim	98	Balkans Gentiles	92.5	5.5
Mizrahim	91	Arabs	84	7.0
Ethiopian Jews	68	Negroids	67	1.0

Looking at these paired comparisons, we see that the IQs of the Ashkenazim, Sephardim, and Mizrahim are all higher than those of the Gentile communities among whom they have lived. The Ashkenazim have a 10-point advantage over the Northern and Central European Gentiles, with IQs of 110 and 100, respectively. The Ashkenazi Jews were originally an Arab people, which does not appear to have been exceptionally intelligent and presumably had the same average IQ (84) as other Arab peoples. Over the course of some 2,000 years, they gained 26 IQ points (from 84 to 110) on their former Arab kinsmen and 10 points on Central and Northern Europeans.

The second of the paired comparisons is between the Sephardic Jews and the Balkan Gentiles among whom most of them have lived for approximately the last 500 years (1492 to the 20th century.) Their IQs are 98 and 92.5, respectively. Thus, the Sephardic Jews, also originally Arabs, have gained 14 IQ points (from 84 to 98) on their former Arab kinsmen, and 5.5 IQ points on their Gentile neighbors in the Balkans. This is the second problem that requires explanation.

The third of the paired comparisons is between the Mizrahi Jews and the Arabs among whom they have lived. Their IQs are 91 and 84, respectively. The Mizrahi Jews were originally an Arab people and are still closely related to Arabs genetically; they have lived among Arabs for 2,000 years or more and interbred with them. Yet, the Mizrahim's average IQ is six points higher than the Arabs'. How this has occurred is a further problem that requires explanation.

Finally, looking at the last of the paired comparisons between the Ethiopian Jews and the Negroids (sub-Saharan Africans), we see that their IQs are virtually identical at 69 and 67, respectively. The IQ of the Negroids is derived as the median of 57 studies collected in my *Race Differences in Intelligence* (2006). No significance can be attached to the two IQ point difference between the two groups. Their IQs are the same. This is what would be expected, because the Ethiopian Jews are a Negroid people and have no genetic affinity with the Semitic Jews. Nevertheless, there is a problem: the other three Jewish peoples have all made intelligence gains on their Gentile host communities, while this has not occurred in the case of the Ethiopian Jews. Why?

2. Achievements of the Four Jewish Peoples

The different IQs of the four Jewish peoples are consistent with each one's educational attainment, earnings, socioeconomic status, and intellectual achievements. The Ashkenazim, with their IQ of 110, have done much better in all these respects than the Gentiles in all of the 17 countries and regions we have studied in Chapters 3 through

19. The Sephardim did better in the Balkans than their Gentile host communities. In Israel, parallel gradients of intelligence, educational attainment, earnings, and socioeconomic status run from the Ashkenazim to the Mizrahim, and then to the Ethiopian underclass.

The differences in intelligence among these four Jewish peoples are also consistent with the extent to which they have produced outstanding individuals. It is only the Ashkenazim that have produced a large number of exceptionally talented people. In the 20th century, there have only been two Sephardim among the 143 Jewish Nobel Prize winners; these are the Bulgarian Elias Canetti, who won the Nobel Prize for literature in 1981, and the English Harold Pinter (of the Da Pinta Portuguese Jewish family), who won the Nobel Prize for literature in 2005. None of the numerous Jewish chess champions and top grandmasters from 1851 up to the present has been Sephardic; William Rubinstein notes, "One can think of virtually no Sephardi Jew who demonstrated great chess ability" (Rubinstein, 2004, p. 40). It is the same in the world of business. The big Jewish banking and financial houses—the Rothschilds, Dresdner-Kleinworts, and Goldman-Sachs—are all Ashkenazi.

The Sephardim have not produced anything like the huge number of highly talented individuals that have come from the Ashkenazim. Nevertheless, they have produced a handful of distinguished individuals. The Sephardic Jews produced a number of moderately gifted scholars in Spain during the period of Arab rule that lasted from 711 until 1492. David E. Smith (1958) has written, in his *History of Mathematics*, "The most learned scholars in Spain at the close of the 11th century...were not Mohammedans" but Jews (p. 206). He gives the four most important Jewish mathematicians in Spain during Arabic rule as Savasorda (1065–1145), who produced the *Liber Embadorum*, a treatise on geometry, and a mathematical encyclopedia; Abraham ben Ezra (1089–1164), who wrote on the theory of numbers, the calendar, and astronomy; Avenpace (1095–1138), who wrote on geometry; and Averroes (1126–1198), who wrote on astronomy and trigonometry (although it is not certain that he was Jewish). He also lists a number of other lesser figures. However, none of these made any significant advances in mathematics. They were compilers and commentators on the work of the Greeks.

The only significant Sephardic Jews up to the end of the 19th century have been Moses Maimonides—"the one Jewish philosopher produced by the Spanish Jews" (Russell, 1961, p. 420); Michel de Montaigne, the French philosopher, who was half-Jewish; Baruch Spinoza, the philosopher in the Netherlands; David Ricardo, the English economist; and Benjamin Disraeli, the British prime minister. It has also been claimed that Miguel de Cervantes (1547–1616) was descended from a family of Jewish *conversos*. This is quite an impressive achievment, but considering that the Sephardim were the majority of Jews until the middle of the 19th century, it is not so impressive as the record of the Ashkenazim. In the 19th and 20th centuries, "nearly every prominent Jew is Ashkenazi" (Rubinstein, 1985, p. 14). Nevertheless, in the 16th century, the Sephardic Jews were prominent in commerce and medicine in the Balkans, and in the 17th century, they excelled in commerce in the Netherlands and Latin America. This suggests they were at least as intelligent as European Gentiles of the period.

The Mizrahim have produced fewer people of any great intellectual or other kind of distinction. Nevertheless, as early as the ninth century AD, some moderately gifted Mizrahi Jewish mathematicians appeared in Baghdad. These were Sahl ibn Bishr (786–845?), who wrote on algebra and astronomy, and Abu'l Taiyib, who wrote on trigonometry and compiled a set of astronomical tables. In the next century, another gifted Mizrahi Jewish mathematician, Sa'adia ben Joseph (892?–942), appeared in Egypt (Smith, 1958). But the non-Jewish Arabs, too, produced some gifted mathematicians about this time, so the Mizrahi Jews were not remarkably superior. In contemporary times, the contribution of the Mizrahim to world civilization has been quite modest. It is confined to Siegfried Sassoon (1886–1967), the poet of First World War, and Charles and Maurice Saatchi (b.1943, 1946), the British advertising tycoons. The families of these originally came from Baghdad. Nevertheless, the Mizrahim did better in Arab countries than their Arab hosts, as would be expected from their seven IQ point advantage:

> Beginning in the eighteenth century, the Middle East's indigenous Jews came increasingly to dominate the most lucrative sectors of the local economy...[e]specially in new economic sectors, including banking and insurance, they became decidedly more competitive than the region's Muslims. (Kuran, 2004, p. 72)

It has not proved possible to find anyone of any distinction produced by the Ethiopian Jews.

3. The Jewish Intelligence Profile.

In addition to their high IQs in relation to Gentiles, the Ashkenazim in the United States, Canada, and Israel have a distinctive pattern or profile of intelligence consisting of strong verbal and mathematical abilities and weaker visualization-spatial abilities. (This profile is not present in the Mizrahim in Israel (see Chapter 11).) Naturally, this profile should cause the Ashkenazim to excel particularly in fields requiring strong verbal and mathematical abilities, but to do less well in fields requiring strong visualization-spatial abilities. It has from time to time been observed that this is the case. Writing in Germany in 1930, Fritz Lenz (1930, p. 672) maintained that Jews are highly intelligent and good at most things, but added the proviso that "very few distinguished painters have been Jews, and scarcely any great sculptors or architects. The visualising and technical ability of the Jews is comparatively small." This observation seems to be right. There were no Jews among the numerous great painters in Renaissance Italy or in the Netherlands in the 17th century, although Jews were prominent in banking and medicine in these countries during this period. In more recent times, in the studies reviewed in Chapter 1, Colin Berry (1999) found that in the years 1830–1929, Jews had Achievement Quotients of 10.0 in mathematics (requiring strong verbal and mathematical abilities) but only 1.6 in engineering and 6.7 in painting (requiring strong visualization-spatial abilities). Charles Murray (2003), in an independent analysis for the years 1870–1950, found similar results: Jews obtained Achievement Quotients of 12.0 in mathematics and 12.0 in philosophy (*par excellence*, the subject requiring strong verbal ability) but only 3.0 in engineering and 5.0 in painting. Similar differences in achievement in different fields were shown by Asher Tropp (1991) in 20th-century Britain, where Jews obtained Achievement Quotients of 12.5 as barristers (a profession requiring strong verbal ability) but only 3.6 as architects and 2.2 as chartered surveyors (requiring strong visualization-spatial abilities). Nevertheless, Jews have done better than Gentiles even in engineering, architecture, and painting. There have certainly been a handful of Jewish painters of moderate distinction, including Marc Chagall, Chaim Soutine, Camille Pissarro, and Amedeo Modigliani (1884–1929). The explanation for the achievements of Jews in these fields is probably that it is only the average that does not seem to have a natural aptitude for this kind of work, but there are some who do. They also apply their general intelligence to achieve success.

In the 20th century, the Jews' strong verbal and weaker visualization-spatial abilities are expressed in the extent to which they are overrepresented in different professions. Typically, Jews are highly overrepresented among doctors and lawyers (requiring strong verbal ability), but much less overrepresented among architects and engineers (requiring visualization-spatial ability). Some figures showing this are given in Table 20.2 for Britain, Canada, Russia, and the United States. (The doctors category includes dentists.) It will be seen that Jewish Achievement Quotients are consistently about twice as great for the "verbal professions" of medicine and law as for the "visualization-spatial" of architecture and engineering.

Table 20.2. Jewish Achievement Quotients for doctors, lawyers, architects, and engineers

Year	Country	Doctor	Lawyer	Architect	Engineer
1985	Britain	7.4	9.5	3.6	-
1991	Canada	9.2	4.5	1.1	1.1
1989	Russia	7.0	-	-	3.2
1960	United States	3.8	3.3	1.7	1.1

4. Genetic Basis of Jewish Intelligence

The differences in the intelligence of the four Jewish peoples, as well as between them and their respective Gentile hosts, are considerable. The difference of 41 IQ points between the Ashkenazim (110) and the Ethiopian Jews (69) is huge. To put this difference in comparative perspective, it is virtually three times as great as the 15 IQ-point difference between Whites and Blacks in the United States and Britain.

There are environmental and genetic theories of the high IQ of the Ashkenazim, as for other ethnic and racial differences. On the environmental side, Christopher Jencks (1969, p. 28) has written, "Jewish children do better on IQ tests than Christians at the same socioeconomic level, but very few people conclude that Jews are genetically superior." Jencks does not mention the case for a genetic basis for the high Ashkenazi IQ that had been made six years previously by Nathaniel Weyl and Stefan Possony (1963). Nearly all sociologists and economists who have documented the high achievements of the Jews follow Jencks in failing to consider the possibility that Jews could have a genetic advantage. Many rule this out as too disreputable even to consider. Thus, Paul Burnstein (2007, p. 214) writes, "there are three major reputable social-scientific explanations of why Jews do so well—I emphasize 'reputable' and 'social-scientific' to exclude genetic explanations."

But as Arthur Jensen (1973, p. 60) observed in a response to Jencks:

> The fact that very few people might suggest a genetic factor in the Jewish vs. non-Jewish IQ difference (which averages about 8–10 IQ points)...does not make it an unreasonable hypothesis that genetic factors are involved in this subpopulation difference.

A strong genetic component to the high Ashkenazi IQ has more recently been argued by Kevin MacDonald (1994), as well as Gregory Cochran, Jason Hardy, and Henry Harpending (2006).

There are five reasons to believe that there must be a substantial genetic basis for the intelligence differences among the four Jewish peoples. First, numerous twin studies have been carried out in Europe, India, and Japan, and on Blacks and Whites in the United States; all have found a high heritability of intelligence in national populations. (These are reviewed in my *Race Differences in Intelligence*.) It is highly improbable that intelligence would be heritable in populations around the world, but not among Jews.

Second, the four Jewish peoples in Israel occupy a similar environment, with the same access to healthcare and education, but the intelligence differences between them are pronounced. We noted in Chapter 11 that Jewish children with European parents and with Mizrahim parents who were brought up in the same kibbutzim have approximately the same 15-IQ-point difference as those raised separately. Similarly, each of the pairs of Jews and Gentiles shown in Table 20.1 has lived in the same societies and are therefore matched for environmental inputs. From this, it can be reasonably assumed that the IQ differences between the pairs are largely genotypic.

Third, it is doubtful whether any environmental theory can explain the remarkable achievements of the Ashkenazim. Much has been made of the importance attached by Jews to education, but Boris Levinson and Zelick Block (1977) found that 400 Jewish 4–6-year-olds in the United States had an IQ of 111, just about the same as that of Jewish adults. If education were a factor responsible for the high Ashkenazi IQ, their IQ advantage should become greater after several years in school. But it does not.

Environmentalists such as Miles Storfer (1990) have argued that the high intelligence of the Ashkenazi Jews is attributable to the better infant care and stimulation provided by Jewish mothers. It may well be that Jewish mothers provide an excellent environment for nurturing the intelligence of their children, as suggested by their low rates of infant mortality. However, this does not mean that the high IQ of the Ashkenazim can be attributed to this favorable early environment. There is now widespread acceptance of the principle of genotype-environment co-variation, which states that the genes for high intelligence tend to be associated with favorable environments for the optimum development of intelligence (Plomin, 1994). Thus, intelligent women who are pregnant typically refrain from smoking, drinking alcohol excessively, and taking drugs, because they are aware that these are likely to impair the growth of the brain and subsequent intelligence of their babies. Intelligent parents tend to provide their children with good-quality nutrition because they understand the general principles of what constitutes a healthy diet, and a healthy diet is a determinant of intelligence. Intelligent parents are also more likely to give their children cognitive stimulation, which is widely believed to promote the development of the intelligence of their children. This principle operates for populations. The populations with high intelligence (such as the Ashkenazim) provide their children with the double advantage of transmitting favorable genes to their children and of providing them with a favorable environment with good nutrition, healthcare, and cognitive stimulation that enhances the development of their children's intelligence. Conversely, the children of the less intelligent populations tend to transmit the double disadvantage of poor-quality genes and poor-quality environment. Thus, the principle of genotype-environment co-variation implies that differences in intelligence between the populations for which the immediate cause is environmental are also attributable to genetic factors that contribute to the environmental differences.

Fourth, other environmentalists, such as Kevin Majoribanks (1972), have argued that the high intelligence of the Ashkenazi Jews is attributable to the typical "pushy Jewish mother." In a study carried out in Canada, he compared 100 Jewish boys aged 11 years with 100 Protestant White boys and 100 White French Canadians and assessed their mothers for "Press for Achievement," i.e. the extent to which mothers put pressure on their sons to achieve. He found that the Jewish mothers scored higher on "Press for Achievement" than Protestant mothers by five SD units and higher than French Canadian mothers by eight SD units; he argued that this explains the high IQ of the children. But this inference does not follow. There is no general acceptance of the thesis that pushy mothers can raise the IQs of their children. Indeed, the contemporary consensus is that family environmental factors have no long-term effect on the intelligence of children (Rowe, 1994).

Fifth, a final pointer to a genetic basis for the high Ashkenazi IQ is their high prevalence of myopia (short-sightedness), an error of refraction in which near objects can be seen clearly but distant objects appear blurred. It has been shown in a number of twin studies that myopia is largely genetically determined (Post, 1962; Sorsby, 1951). There is a correlation of around 0.20 to 0.25 between myopia and intelligence. This correlation has been found in many studies reviewed by Sanford Cohn, Catherine Cohn, and Arthur Jensen (1988), who also show that this is an intrinsic correlation that is present within families, such that adolescents with high IQs have a greater prevalence of myopia than their siblings with lower IQs. Jensen proposes that the reason for this relationship is *pleiotropy*, i.e. a gene or genes that are responsible for myopia also increase intelligence. Consistent with this theory is the fact shown by Richard Post (1962) that the prevalence of myopia is highest in East Asians (Chinese and Japanese), intermediate in Europeans, and lowest in Blacks. Hence, the prevalence of myopia in these three major races runs parallel to the differences in intelligence.

The significance of the association between myopia and intelligence is that there is a high prevalence of myopia among the Ashkenazim. This association was found by Karl Pearson and Margaret Moul (1927) in London schoolboys, among whom myopia was present in 13.3 percent of a sample of 900 Jews but only 2.3 percent in a sample of 10,416 Gentiles. This result was confirmed in another British study by A. Sourasky (1928), who reported that 43.2 percent of a sample of 1,649 Jewish boys aged 6–14 failed a reading test, as compared with only 21.7 percent in a sample of 600 Gentiles. The main reason for the difference was "the rather higher incidence of myopia among the Jewish children" (p. 211). He noted that the higher incidence of myopia among the Jewish children was present among 6-year-olds, and did not increase with age so that "it is apparently not produced by the excessive amount of close work done by Jewish boys."

It can be inferred from these studies that the gene or genes responsible for myopia and high intelligence are more frequent in Ashkenazi Jews than in European Gentiles. It would be useful and interesting to know whether the association between myopia and intelligence is present within Jewish populations and whether Ashkenazi Jews have a higher incidence of myopia than the Sephardim and Mizrahim.

For all these reasons, it is impossible to avoid the conclusion that there must be a substantial genetic basis for the intelligence differences among the four Jewish peoples and between the Jews and the Gentiles among whom they have lived. There is no reason to suppose that the intelligence of the original Jews who lived in Palestine was any different from that of the other Arab peoples of the Near East. The high intelligence of the Ashkenazim and the lesser intelligence of the Sephardim and Mizrahim must have evolved as a result of their different experiences after the Diasporas.

5. The Eugenic Hypothesis

There are three problems that require explanation. First, what has brought about these different IQs of the Ashkenazim, the Sephardim, and the Mizrahim? Second, why have these three subpopulations of Jews developed higher IQs than the Gentiles among whom they have lived? Third, why have the Ashkenazim acquired their pattern of high verbal, mathematical, and reasoning abilities but weaker visual and spatial abilities? We consider now the main theories that have been or can be advanced to explain these problems.

The Eugenic Hypothesis states that the Jews in general, and the Ashkenazim in particular, have practiced eugenics, and it is this that has been responsible for raising their intelligence. Eugenics consists of customs and practices that promote a greater number of surviving children of the more intelligent (and of those with other desirable qualities such as good health and sound moral character), as compared with the less intelligent. The greater reproductive success of the more intelligent can occur in two ways. First, by differential birth rates such that the more intelligent have greater numbers of children than the less intelligent. Second, by the children of the more intelligent surviving to adulthood in greater numbers than the children of the less intelligent. If either of these two conditions is present, the more intelligent will have more children surviving to adulthood than the less intelligent, who would be more likely to reproduce and transmit their genes for high intelligence to the next generation. The effect of these factors is to increase the proportion of genes for high intelligence in the population.

A good case for the eugenic hypothesis as an explanation for the high Jewish IQ has been made by MacDonald (1994, pp. 184–8). He notes, first, that Judaism has had a long tradition of according high status to scholars and wealth, and that the wealthy have been enjoined to marry their daughters to scholars. Thus, the Mishnah advises, "under all circumstances a man should sell everything he possesses in order to marry the daughter of a scholar, as well as to give his daughter to a scholar in marriage.... Never should he marry his daughter to an illiterate man" (see MacDonald, 1994, p. 184). These "eugenic marriages" brought wealth and intelligence together and normally produced relatively large numbers of surviving children, because historically the wealthy had greater numbers of surviving children than the poor, largely because they were able to provide them with better nutrition and healthcare. The effect of this would have been that the more intelligent would have had more surviving children than the less intelligent, and hence the intelligence of the Jews would increase over the generations.

Second, Jews also practiced negative eugenics, the limitation of the reproduction of the less intelligent, insofar as at some times they restricted the marriages of the poor. This occurred when the Gentiles among whom the Jews lived placed a limit on the numbers of Jewish marriages allowed each year, which was widespread throughout Austria and Germany in the 18th century. A third factor mentioned by MacDonald (1994, p. 184) is that poor (and less intelligent) Jews were more likely to defect from Judaism, thereby raising the average level of intelligence of the remaining community. A fourth eugenic factor may have been the requirement of Christian clergy to be celibate for much of the last two thousand years. It is a reasonable assumption that the Christian clergy had above average IQs, and especially higher verbal IQs, since the Catholic church was the principal avenue of advancement for intelligent children, through which they were able to acquire positions of considerable power as bishops, abbots, and so on. However, clerics were required to be celibate, and this obligation (although not always observed, as in the cases of Abelard and Heloise, a few of the popes, and a number of more lowly priests) would have reduced the intelligence of the Gentiles because a high proportion of the most intelligent were childless in each generation. In contrast, Jewish rabbis were encouraged to marry young and have children, which would have increased the intelligence of the Jews relative to that of Gentiles. A fifth factor may have been that the intelligent rabbis were frequently physicians and with their medical knowledge, would have been better able to care for the health of their children.

The eugenic hypothesis seems to provide a persuasive explanation for the high IQ of the Ashkenazim as compared with their Gentile neighbors. The effect of Jewish eugenic customs would only need to be quite small in each generation to explain the Ashkenazim IQ of 110. These eugenic customs appear to have been in place for some 2,000 years, during which they would have had to raise the Jewish IQ from 84 (the average IQ of Arabs in the Near East given in Lynn, 2006) to 110, i.e. 26 IQ points. This works out to an increase of 1.25 IQ points per century and 0.3 IQ points per generation. The impact of eugenic customs in producing IQ gains of this magnitude seems quite plausible.

The eugenic hypothesis also seems to provide a reasonable explanation for the high verbal IQ and more moderate visualization-spatial IQ of the Ashkenazim. The scholars and rabbis to whom wealthy Jews were enjoined to marry their daughters would have had the high verbal IQs required to master the Torah and other sacred Jewish texts, but would not have had high visualization-spatial IQs. Hence, the genes for high verbal intelligence would have been increased, but not the genes for high visualization-spatial intelligence, bringing about the high verbal/lower visualization-spatial IQ profile typical of Ashkenazim. It is known that there are some genes that determine general intelligence and other genes that determine verbal ability and visualization-spatial ability (e.g. Kovas, Harlaar, Petrill, and Plomin, 2005). It would have been the genes that determine general intelligence and verbal ability that would have been especially enhanced by Jewish eugenic customs.

However, the eugenic hypothesis may have difficulty in explaining why the Ashkenazim have a substantially higher average IQ than the Sephardim, Mizrahim, and Ethiopian Jews. MacDonald (1994, p. 186) states that "wealthy men would marry their daughters to promising scholars and support the couple to adulthood. This practice became a religiously sanctioned policy and persisted both among the Ashkenazim and the Sephardim." How, therefore, did this eugenic custom raise the intelligence of the Ashkenazim so much higher than that of the Sephardim? Possibly, these eugenic customs were less complied with among the Sephardim, but it has not proved possible to find any evidence for this theory. There is the further problem of the low IQ of the Mizrahim and Ethiopian Jews. MacDonald (1994, p. 198) offers an explanation for the low IQ of the Mizrahim in Yemen. He suggests that Yemen was so poor and rural that there were too few Mizrahim for them to form a class of money-lenders and tax farmers, and that they suffered intense persecution "generally considered to have been the most extreme in the Muslim world." He does not mention less adherence to eugenic customs among this group or among the much more numerous and wealthy Jewish community of Baghdad, which numbered around 40,000 in 1170 and from the eighth century on, provided court doctors and officials. It may be that for some reason, eugenic customs were practiced less among the Mizrahim, or that some other explanation is required such as that they were less persecuted and discriminated against than the Ashkenazim. The Ethiopian Jews have essentially the same IQ as other Negroid peoples. The most likely explanation for this is that they did not practice the eugenic customs of the other Jews at all.

6. The Persecution Hypothesis

The Persecution Hypothesis states that Gentiles have persecuted Jews for some 2,000 years; that in these persecutions, Jews were frequently killed; and that it can be surmised that the more intelligent Jews have been able to avoid being killed by foreseeing the danger in good times and moving to more friendly countries, by going into hiding, or by paying ransom to their persecutors. The less intelligent Jews have been eliminated. MacDonald has discussed this theory in detail (1994, p. 192), although he prefers to call it the Gentile Selection Hypothesis.

There is no doubt that Jews have frequently been persecuted and killed by Gentiles in Europe in large numbers and on numerous occasions (see Costello & Kagan, 1994 and Barnaav, 1998). In 1012, the Jews were expelled from Mainz, and those who remained were burned at the stake. Similar expulsions and retribution for those who failed to leave took place in Bavaria and Austria in 1298, when it is estimated that approximately 100,000 Jews were killed. In the 14th century, Jews were expelled from France (1394). In the first half of the 15th century, Jews were expelled from Austria (1422), Cologne (1426), and Brandenburg (1446). In the second half of the 15th century, Jews were expelled from Spain (1492), Naples (1493), and Portugal (1496). In the 16th century, Jews were expelled from most of Italy, beginning with their expulsion from the Kingdom of Naples in 1510. Pope Pius V expelled the Jews from all the Papal States, except Rome, in 1569. In 1571, Jews were expelled from Tuscany except for the ghettos in Florence and Sienna; in 1597, the Jews were expelled from Milan. The persecution of the Jews in Russia began in 1881, following the assassination of the Tsar. One of the assassins was identified as a Jewish woman, and the act was widely believed to be a Jewish conspiracy. The final major persecution of the Ashkenazi Jews occurred in the 1930s in Germany and in the early '40s in German-occupied Europe.

While it is difficult to show conclusively that the more intelligent Jews have tended to survive these persecutions, it is a reasonable conjecture that this is likely to have been the case. And there are occasional instances where this has been recorded. For example, Bernard Weinryb (1972) states that in the Cossacks' attacks on the Jews in Russia in 1648, it was the poor Jews who were unable to flee or pay ransom and were thus disproportionately killed. The hypothesis rests on the assumption that the rich Jews who survived were more intelligent than the poor Jews who were killed; this is a reasonable conjecture considering the association between intelligence and earnings that has frequently been found (for a review, see Lynn and Vanhanen, 2006). In recent times, there is a fair amount of evidence that during World War II, there was a tendency for the more intelligent Jews to avoid being sent to concentration camps. The Germans allowed Jews to emigrate in the 1930s on payment of large sums, and these could have been paid more easily by the more intelligent. Blom, Fuks-Mansfeld, and Schoffer (1996) note that during the Nazi occupation of the Netherlands in World War II, about 25,000 Jews escaped deportation to the concentration camps and that these were largely middle class. A number of countries such as Turkey, Britain, and the United States accepted only or mainly qualified professionals and academics as refugees. Other Jews escaped the concentration camps by getting to neutral Spain, Switzerland, and Turkey, by going into hiding, or by forging Gentile identity papers. All these actions require intelligence.

The Persecution Hypothesis provides a reasonable explanation of why the Ashkenazim have acquired higher IQs than the Sephardim, Mizrahim, and Ethiopian Jews: the Sephardim, Mizrahim, and Ethiopian Jews were not persecuted as much as the Ashkenazim. During their sojourn in Spain and Portugal, and their five centuries in the Ottoman Empire, the Sephardic Jews were well treated. As we have seen in the chapter on the Balkans, "the fate of the Jews in the hands of Islam had on the whole been far more tolerable than in other parts of Europe" (Silvera, 1995, p. 56); and in the Ottoman Empire, the reign of Sultan Murad II (1421–1451) "began a period of prosperity that lasted for two centuries and which is unequalled in their history in any other country." Jews had influential positions at court; they engaged in unrestricted trade and commerce; they dressed and lived as they pleased; and they traveled at their pleasure in all parts of the country. Murad II had a Jewish physician-in-chief, and this marked the beginning of a long line of Jewish physicians who obtained power and influence at court. The condition of Jews about the middle of the 15th century was so prosperous and in such contrast to the hardships endured by their fellow Israelites in Germany and Europe generally that Isaac Zarfati was moved to send a circular letter to all the Jewish communities in Germany and Hungary inviting their members to immigrate to Turkey. This letter caused an influx of Ashkenazi Jews (Montgomery, 1902, pp. 279–291).

The Mizrahim were also fairly well treated in the Near East and North Africa. As Bertrand Russell noted:

> Throughout the Middle Ages, the Mohammedans were more civilized and more humane than the Christians. Christians persecuted Jews, especially at times of religious excitement; the Crusades were associated with appalling pogroms. In Mohammedan countries, on the contrary, Jews were not in any way ill-treated. (Russell, 1945, p. 323)

Similarly, in contrast to their frequent persecutions in Europe, "the Jews found it easier to live and prosper in Islamic territories" (Johnson, 2004, pp. 176, 181). Nevertheless, over the course of 2,000 years, the Sephardim and the Mizrahim did suffer some persecution, sufficient to raise their IQs somewhat higher than those of the Gentiles among whom they lived. It can be posited further that the Ethiopian Jews were not persecuted by their African neighbors, their IQ thus remained the same as that of other Negroid peoples.

The Persecution Hypothesis can also explain why the Ashkenazi Jews have acquired their pattern of high verbal, mathematical, and reasoning abilities but weaker visual and spatial abilities. Those with high verbal IQs were the ones that acquired status and wealth, and they would have been able to use these to avoid being killed during pogroms, because they would have had the money and connections enabling them to escape.

7. *The Discrimination Hypothesis*

The Discrimination Hypothesis states that Gentiles in Europe discriminated against Jews by limiting the kinds of occupations they were permitted to pursue. Cochran, Hardy, and Harpending have set out the theory (2006). It states that Jews were generally not allowed to own land and work as farmers, or to work in the craft trades such as stone masons, blacksmiths, carpenters, thatchers, wheelwrights, cart wrights, coopers (barrel makers), fletchers (arrow makers), etc. The discrimination against Jews largely began around the 13th century. Until then "they suffered from no explicit economic restrictions; they were farmers, laborers, craftsmen, merchants, artisans, peddlers; if any occupation was characteristic of them it was wholesale trade and certain branches of the textile industry" (Roth, 1946, p. 103). From the 13th century, Jews were excluded from the craft trades that were controlled by the guilds. The guilds were religious as well as trade associations, and this excluded Jews on religious grounds and as unwelcome competitors. Jews were allowed to be money-lenders, to open banks and charge interest on loans, which was prohibited for Christians, to work as tax collectors and import-export merchants, and to deal in second-hand goods as peddlers. Those who were money-lenders, tax collectors, and import-export merchants made a reasonable living and were able to rear children who survived to adulthood. Those who worked as peddlers would have found it hard to make much of a living and would have been less able to rear children. Throughout historical times and up to around 1880, people had high birth rates and high infant and child mortality rates, and in general, the more affluent and more intelligent had more children who survived to adulthood. This selection differential would likely have been greater for Jews.

Although difficult to prove, the Discrimination Hypothesis is plausible. There is no doubt that Jews have frequently been discriminated against in Europe for some 2,000 years. This discrimination has been described for many countries in the body of this book. Even a small tendency for the more intelligent Jews to overcome this discrimination would have been sufficient to increase the average Ashkenazim IQ to the level of around 110 that it has become in the 20th century. The Discrimination Hypothesis also provides a plausible explanation of why the Ashkenazi Jews have acquired their pattern of high verbal, mathematical, and reasoning abilities but weaker visual and spatial abilities. To succeed as money-lenders, tax farmers, and import-export merchants, Jews would have needed strong verbal, mathematical, and reasoning abilities to assess risk and make calculations. The greater survival of Jews who had these abilities would have increased the genes responsible for them. These Jews would not have needed strong visual and spatial abilities. By contrast, the many Gentiles who worked as craftsmen would have needed strong visualization and spatial abilities. Hence there would have been selection pressure for strong visual and spatial abilities in Gentiles but not in Jews, bringing about the distinctive cognitive profiles of the two peoples.

Cochran, Hardy, and Harpending:

> The Jews of Islam, although reproductively isolated, seem not to have had the necessary concentration of occupations with high IQ elasticity. Some had such jobs in some of the Arab world, in some periods, but it seems it was never the case that *most* did. In part this was because other minority groups competed successfully for these jobs—Greek Christians, Armenians, etc., in part because Moslems, at least some of the time, took many of those jobs themselves, valuing non-warrior occupations more highly than did medieval Christians. In fact, to a large extent, and especially during the last six or seven hundred years of relative Moslem decline, the Jews of Islam tended to have "dirty" jobs. These included such tasks as cleaning cesspools and drying the contents for use as fuel—a common Jewish occupation in Morocco, Yemen, Iraq, Iran, and Central Asia. Jews were also found as tanners, butchers, hangmen, and other disagreeable or despised occupations. Such jobs must have had low IQ elasticity; brilliant tanners and hangmen almost certainly did not become rich.
>
> The suggested selective process explains the pattern of mental abilities in Ashkenazi Jews—high verbal and mathematical ability but relatively low spatial-visual ability. Verbal and mathematical talent helped medieval businessmen succeed, while spatial-visual abilities were irrelevant. (Cochran, Hardy & Harpending, 2006).

Overall, the Discrimination Hypothesis plausibly explains high Ashkenazi IQ *vis-à-vis* the Sephardim and Ethiopian Jews; it also dovetails, in many ways, with the Persecution Hypothesis discussed above. Cochran and Harpending have developed these ideas further in their book *The 10,000 Year Explosion* (2009).

8. The Miscegenation Hypothesis

A further factor that has contributed to the explanation of the differences in intelligence between Ashkenazim, Sephardim, Mizrahim, and the Ethiopian Jews arises from interbreeding with the Gentile communities among whom they lived, that is, miscegenation. Despite strict Jewish prohibitions on exogamy, there has always been some intermarriage and interbreeding between Jews and non-Jews living in the same localities. Even a small amount of miscegenation over many generations has been sufficient to introduce significant proportions of Gentile genes into the Jewish gene pool. The effects of this are visible in Ashkenazi Jews, a number of whom have fair hair and blue eyes. We have noted that Fisberg (1904) summarized a dozen studies of a total of 75,377 Ashkenazi Jews in Germany carried out at the end of the 19th century and found that approximately 47 percent had the dark hair and dark eyes of the original southwest Asian stock, 42 percent had mixed hair and eye color (fair hair with dark eyes or dark hair with blue eyes), while 11 percent had fair hair and blue eyes. Thus, at least 53 percent of German Jews had some Northern European ancestry. The average IQ of Gentiles in Central and Northern Europe is 100 (Lynn, 2006). If it is assumed that all Jews began with an IQ of 84, typical of the Near East, the effect of miscegenation with Northern Europeans would have increased their IQ to about 90, assuming the proportions of Northern European ancestry reported by Fisberg (1904). Clearly, miscegenation with Northern Europeans is nowhere near sufficient to explain the IQ of 110 of Ashkenazi Jews. It should only have raised their IQ by about six points, leaving the additional 20 IQ points to be explained by one or more of the other hypotheses. Nevertheless, miscegenation with Northern Europeans may explain about one fifth of the the 26-point increase (from 84 to 110) of Ashkenazi Jews during the course of some 2,000 years.

One factor contributing to the IQ differences between the Ashkenazi, Sephardic, and Mizrahi Jews is likely that there was less miscegenation with local host populations among the Ashkenazim. As Jon Entine notes:

> There are fewer genetic disorders specific to Sephardic Jews, Oriental Jews, and other small Jewish populations, probably

because they intermingled more with gentiles than did European Jews. Consequently, they often manifest the same genetic disorders that occur in the non-Jewish population of their native countries. (Entine, 2007, p. 276)

In addition, miscegenation would have reduced the IQs of the Sephardi and Mizrahim more than of the Ashkenazim because the local populations with whom they interbred had lower IQs. The Sephardic Jews that were expelled from Spain and Portugal in the 1490s mainly moved to the Balkans, where the average IQ of Gentiles is approximately 92, while in the Near East, the IQ of the indigenous populations is approximately 84. Although there was, no doubt, some miscegenation of the Ethiopian Jews with local Negroid peoples, this would not have had any effect on their IQ, since both populations have the same intelligence.

9. *The Apostasy Hypothesis*

The Apostasy Hypothesis of the high Jewish IQ has been proposed by Charles Murray (2007). He notes that in 64 AD, the Jewish High Priest Joshua ben Gamala issued an ordinance requiring all boys to attend school from the age of about six. The ordinance was implemented, and within about a century, the Jews had established universal male literacy and numeracy. Jewish education involved the study of the Torah and the Talmud. These are difficult texts, and only those with high verbal intelligence would have been able to cope with them. The result of this was that many Jews who did not possess high verbal ability became discouraged and renounced their faith. Murray suggests that this explains why the number of Jews fell from about 4.5 million in the first century AD to about one to 1.5 million in the sixth century. He concedes that some of this decline was due to about one million Jews being killed in the revolts against the Romans in Judea and Egypt; that there were some forced conversions from Judaism to other religions; and that some of the reduction may be associated with a general drop in population that accompanied the decline and fall of the Roman Empire. Nevertheless, there was a huge number of Jews who just disappeared. These, Murray suggests, were predominantly those with lower verbal abilities who abandoned the faith. He proposes that by around the year 1,000 AD, all Jews had a higher verbal IQ than Gentiles. During the next millennium, the IQs of the Ashkenazi were maintained or perhaps increased by discrimination and persecution, while the IQ of the Oriental Jews living in the Islamic world declined, possibly because they were less subjected to discrimination and persecution, or through intermarriage with Gentiles.

It is difficult to find definitive evidence for or against the five theories to explain the evolution of the different IQs of the four Jewish peoples (the Eugenic, Persecution, Discrimination, Miscegenation, and Apostasy Hypotheses). It may well be that several or all of these factors played important roles in the differentiation of Jewish intelligence.

10. Genetics of the High Jewish IQ

There are two genetic processes that may have occurred in the evolution of high intelligence in the Ashkenazim and, to a lesser extent, in the Sephardim and Mizrahim, but not in the Arabs. The first of these is that differences in the frequencies of the alleles for high and low intelligence may have evolved in the three populations; the second is that new alleles for high intelligence may have appeared as mutations in Ashkenazim but not in the Sephardim, Mizrahim, Ethiopian Jews, and Arabs.

The first of these processes is quite straightforward. It posits that the more intelligent of the Ashkenazim more often survived, and had more surviving children, because they had the most eugenic customs, were the most persecuted, discriminated against, etc. The result of this would have been that alleles for high intelligence became more frequent in the Ashkenazim population. Many of the less intelligent Ashkenazim carrying the alleles for low intelligence would have been unable to survive and rear children because of the eugenic customs, persecution, discrimination, etc.; this would have reduced the alleles for low intelligence in the Ashkenazi population. The Sephardim, Mizrahim, Ethiopian Jews, and Arabs had weaker eugenic customs, were less persecuted, less discriminated against, etc.; so more of those with lower intelligence survived and had surviving children (as compared with the Ashkenazim); and more of the alleles for low intelligence remained in the populations.

A second genetic process in the evolution of higher intelligence in the Ashkenazim may have been in the appearance of one or more new alleles for high intelligence as mutations in Ashkenazim but not in the Sephardim, Mizrahim, Ethiopian Jews, and Arabs (or fewer of them appeared in these populations, or they appeared in these but were not selected for). Cochran, Hardy, and Harpending advance this theory (2006). They propose that the clusters of Ashkenazi genetic diseases—the sphingolipid cluster (Tay-Sachs, Gaucher, Niemann-Pick, and mucolipidosis type IV) and the DNA repair cluster in particular, and possibly also dystonia and the disorders of steroid synthesis—increase intelligence in heterozygotes (those with one copy of the gene). The authors cite direct evidence for this in the case of Gaucher disease. They argue that the high prevalence of these diseases of biochemically related mutations is extremely unlikely to have occurred by chance or by genetic drift and that the existence of these categories or disease clusters among the Ashkenazi Jews suggests selective forces at work. This process is similar to the sickle-cell anemia disorders prevalent in Africa and around the Mediterranean, which are known to confer resistance to malaria in heterozygotes, although the disease also impairs homozygotes. Thus, the more numerous heterozygotes have an advantage. In the case of the Ashkenazim, the theory is that high intelligence was selected for because of the social niche they found in cognitively demanding occupations of money-lenders and tax farmers. This brought about an increase in the alleles for these intelligence-enhancing mutations in the Ashkenazim but not in their host populations of Gentiles, or in the Sephardim, Mizrahim, Ethiopian Jews, or Arabs.

Cochran, Hardy, and Harpending (2006) provide additional evidence in support of this theory for Gaucher disease. They cite evidence on the occupations of 302 Gaucher patients in Israel. These are virtually all the Gaucher patients in the country. Of the 255 patients who were employed, 81 were high-IQ occupations. There were 13 academics, 23 engineers, 14 scientists, and 31 in other high-IQ occupations like accountants, physicians, or lawyers. In Israel at large, 1.35 percent of the working-age population are engineers or scientists, while in the Gaucher-patient sample, 37 of the total of 255 (15 percent) were engineers or scientists. They assert that Ashkenazim make up 60 percent of the workforce in Israel, so a conservative base rate for engineers and scientists among Ashkenazim is 2.25 percent, assuming that all engineers and scientists are Ashkenazi. With this rate, six in the sample would be expected, but the actual number was 37. The chance of 37 or more scientists and engineers appearing in the sample is a highly improbable overrepresentation. They also found that there were five physicists and five unskilled workers in the sample and note that in the United States, the fraction of people with undergraduate or higher degrees in physics is one per thousand. Assuming that this fraction applies approximately to Israel, the expected number of physicists in the sample would be 0.25, while the observed number is five, i.e. twenty times the expected number. They conclude, "Gaucher patients are clearly a very high IQ sub-sample of the general population."

They advance similar arguments for the intelligence-enhancing properties of the second major cluster of Ashkenazi mutations, namely the DNA repair cluster, involving BRCA1, BRCA2, Fanconi's anemia, and Bloom syndrome. These diseases all affect a group of functionally related proteins involved in DNA repair. This is mainly an Ashkenazi cluster, though a common Ashkenazi BRCA1 mutation, 187delAG, is also common in Sephardim. They show that microcephalin, a gene controlling human brain size, has evolved rapidly throughout the primate lineage leading to humans and that this evolutionary process exhibits strong signs of positive selection.

Cochran, Hardy, and Harpending argue further that the time of the appearance of the Ashkenazi mutations is consistent with their theory. It would be expected that the IQ-increasing mutations with the highest frequency today should have originated shortly after conditions began favoring high IQ among the Ashkenazim, that is, shortly after they began to occupy their niche as money-lenders. Mutations that came into existence earlier, when IQ did not have an unusually high reproductive payoff, would have very likely disappeared by chance. It might be that a mutation would have side effects that would, in the absence of high payoffs to IQ, actually reduce carrier fitness. This must be the case for torsion dystonia. IQ-increasing mutations could have originated later, but would not have had as many generations in which to spread through the population. This implies that almost all of this class of mutations should have originated after the Ashkenazim began to occupy their niche as money-lenders, perhaps 800 years ago, with the most common mutations originating early in this period. They cite evidence that seven of the most common Ashkenazi mutations seem to have originated around that time.

Once a new mutant allele for higher intelligence had appeared, it would have conferred a selection advantage and would have spread through the Ashkenazim. The frequent migrations of the Ashkenazim to escape persecution would have provided ideal conditions for the spread of one or more new mutant alleles for higher intelligence that conferred a selection advantage.

Chapter 21

Conclusions

1. Jewish cultural values
2. Jewish motivation for achievement
3. Three troubling conclusions
4. The future of the Jewish people

We have seen in the body of this book that in all countries and regions that have been considered, the Ashkenazim have been far more successful than their Gentile hosts in education, earnings, and socioeconomic status, among chess grandmasters and top bridge players, and in the highest levels of intellectual achievement, indexed by the award of Nobel Prizes, Fields Medals, and Wolf Prizes for outstanding work in mathematics. We have also seen that the Ashkenazim have a high IQ; this book has argued that this goes some way toward explaining their remarkable achievements. In this concluding chapter, we consider whether the high Ashkenazi IQ is sufficient to explain their high achievements or whether they have some other traits that contribute to their successes. We also discuss some implications of the high IQ and achievements of the Ashkenazim, and consider finally the future of the Jewish peoples.

1. Jewish Cultural Values

Many of those who have discussed the success of the Ashkenazim have not considered their high intelligence but have attributed their achievements to other qualities, such as their cultural values regarding the importance of success and their strong motivation for achievement or work ethic. Thus, Gary Becker, the Nobel Prize winner for economics, concluded "the high achievement and low fertility of Jewish families are explained by high marginal rates of return to investments in the education, health, and other human capital of their children that lower the price of quality relative to quantity" (Becker, 1981, p. 110). Another economist, Barry Chiswick, has also noted that Jews do better than would be predicted from the amount of education they receive and wondered how this can be. He suggests,

> Jews may learn more in school or on the job because of supplemental training received in the home or in the Jewish community prior to or concurrent with schooling. Or it may be that there are cultural characteristics that enable Jews to be more productive in the labor market with the human characteristics embodied in them."

Chiswick concludes somewhat lamely, "the reasons for ethnic group differences in rates of return on human capital warrant further study."

It is likely that the Ashkenazim do have some motivational qualities that contribute to their high achievement. Although their high intelligence is undoubtedly an important factor, it is doubtful whether the Ashkenazic IQ of 110 is sufficient to explain their successes. This problem can be usefully considered in the following way. A population of Gentiles with an average IQ of 100 has 16 percent of individuals with an IQ of 115 and above, which is about the minimum required to become a physician, lawyer, or other major professional. The Ashkenazim, with an average IQ of 110, should have approximately double the proportion of individuals with this IQ. Consequently, if their high intelligence was the only factor involved in their high achievement, they should have about double the proportion of physicians, lawyers, and other major professionals, as compared with Gentiles. In fact, however, we have seen that in all the countries we have examined, the proportion of Ashkenazim has been more than double in these professions and in most countries, considerably more than double. These results are brought together for physicians and lawyers in Table 21.1 in which Jewish overrepresentation is expressed as Achievement Quotients (calculated by dividing the percentage of Jewish achievements by their percentage in the population). The median of the Jewish Achievement Quotients is 9.2, more than four times greater than the 2.0 that would be predicted from the higher Ashkenazim IQ. This suggests that the success of the Ashkenazim is attributable to more than just their high IQs and that they also possess strong motivational and work-ethic qualities.

Table 21.1. Jewish Achievement Quotients for physicians and lawyers

Country	Years	Physicians	Lawyers
Austria	1883–1910	14.7	17.7
Benelux	1930	2.7	2.3
Britain	1985	6.6	9.5
Canada	1991	9.2	4.5
Germany	1918–1933	16.0	25.0
Hungary	1920	12.0	10.1
Poland	1931	5.6	3.3
Soviet Union	1928–1939	11.1	-
United States	2000	5.3	4.8

We can apply the same argument to the large number of Jewish Nobel Prize winners. It is reasonable to suppose that an IQ of at least 130 is required for the work meriting the award of a Nobel Prize. A Gentile population with an IQ of 100 will have approximately two percent with IQs above this level, while the Ashkenazim, with an IQ of 110, will have about nine percent, four and a half times more. If their high intelligence were the only factor involved in the Ashkenazim high achievement, we would expect that they would be around four and a half times overrepresented among Nobel Prize winners. Ashkenazim Achievement Quotients for Nobel Prize winners are shown for 16 countries in Table 21.2. The median Jewish Achievement Quotient is 24.5, much greater than would be predicted from the Jewish IQ.

It may be considered that for the very high level of intellectual achievement represented by a Nobel Prize, the minimum IQ is greater than 130. The minimum IQ required for winning a Nobel Prize may be more like 145. In Gentile populations with an average IQ of 100, this is possessed by approximately 0.13 percent of individuals, while the Ashkenazim have approximately 0.98 percent at this level, 7.5 times as many. It would therefore be expected that the Ashkenazim would be around 7.5 times overrepresented among Nobel Prize winners. Yet, we see in Table 21.2 that the actual Jewish Achievement Quotients for Nobel Prize winners in all the countries except Britain is greater than this; in most countries, it is considerably greater. We are drawn to the same conclusion for the Jewish overrepresentation among physicians and lawyers. Jews are so hugely overrepresented among Nobel Prize winners that it would seem that there must be something more involved in their remarkable achievement than their high IQs.

Table 21.2. Jewish achievement quotients for Nobel Prize winners

Country	Nobel AQs	Country	Nobel AQs
Austria	24	Hungary	25
Balkans	23	Italy	320
Benelux	22	Latin America	220
Britain	6	Poland	8
Canada	35	Russia	33
Denmark	270	South Africa	16
France	19	Switzerland	60
Germany	31	United States	10

Several times, it has been suggested that Jews have cultural values that promote success. It is asserted that a high valuation of success has become a cultural norm in Jewish families, in which parents bring up their children to achieve and socialize them to value success.

> Success is so vitally important to the Jewish family ethos that we can hardly overemphasize it.... We cannot hope to understand the Jewish family without understanding the place that success for men (and recently for women) plays in the system. (Herz and Rozen, 1982, p. 306)

The historian Stephan Thernstrom and his wife assert that the achievements of the Jews are "the product of cultural values that they have brought with them and transmitted from generation to generation over a very long time" (Thernstrom and Thernstrom, 2003, p. 98).

There may be some plausibility in the theory that Jews have cultural values that promote achievement and that this is a major factor responsible for their success, but these assertions do not have a strong empirical base. I have therefore (in collaboration with Satoshi Kanazawa) examined this theory by looking at some data collected by the American National Opinion Research Center (NORC). This organization carries out annual or biannual surveys on approximately 1,500 individuals in the continental United States (i.e. excluding Hawaii and Alaska). These are known as the General Social Surveys (GSS). The surveys were first carried out in 1972. The samples are representative of the adult population of those aged 18 years and over, except that they exclude those who cannot speak English and in institutions such as prisons and hospitals.

Some of the GSS surveys have collected information about the respondents' cultural values, measured by their responses to a question on the values parents would most like in their children. The surveys have given 13 values and ask respondents to identify the one that they would most like their children to possess, as well as their top three choices. These values are as follows: (1) Success: "that he tries hard to succeed"; (2) Studiousness: "that he is a good student"; (3) Amicability: "that he gets along well with other children"; (4) Cleanliness: "that he is neat and clean"; (5) Considerateness: "that he is considerate of others"; (6) Control: "that he has self-control"; (7) Honesty: "that he is honest"; (8) Interest: "that he is interested in how and why things happen"; (9) Judgment: "that he has good sense and sound judgment"; (10) Manners: "that he has good manners"; (11) Obedience: "that he obeys his parents well"; (12) Responsibility: "that he is responsible" (13) Sex role: "that he acts like a boy (she acts like a girl)." For an analysis of whether Jews attach greater value than Gentiles to their children's success, the GSS samples have been analyzed for the years 1972 through 2004. This gives a total sample of 10,700, of whom there are 228 who identified themselves as Jews. These are 2.1 percent of the sample, which is about the percentage of Jews in the American population.

The differences between the Jews and non-Jews in the value they would most like their children to have are shown in Table 21.3. This gives the percentages of the respondents selecting each of the 13 values they would most like their children to have, for five religious categories. The right-hand column gives the values of t for the statistical significance of the different percentages of Jews compared with the remainder of the sample selecting each value as the most desired in their children (minus signs indicate that Jews attach less importance to these values). There are only two values in which Jews are significantly different from others. These are honesty, which Jews desire in their children less than do others, and judgment, which Jews desire in their children more than do others.

Table 21.3. Most important values: percentages

Values	Jews	Prot.	Cath.	None	Other	t
Numbers	228	6774	2736	781	181	-
Success	1.8	2.7	3.7	2.9	5.0	-1.14
Studiousness	0.0	0.8	1.2	0.9	2.2	-1.49
Amicability	1.8	1.7	2.3	2.3	0.6	0.11
Cleanliness	0.1	0.7	0.8	0.9	0.6	-0.51
Considerateness	9.2	5.8	9.0	13.1	9.9	1.14
Control	0.9	2.7	3.0	2.6	5.5	-1.77
Honesty	26.3	37.8	33.8	27.5	29.3	-2.96*
Interest	3.5	2.7	3.0	8.8	6.6	0.21
Judgment	32.0	16.9	17.3	20.4	12.7	5.82***
Manners	1.3	3.3	2.9	2.4	6.1	-1.57
Obedience	11.8	16.8	13.2	8.5	12.2	-1.39
Responsibility	10.1	7.1	9.0	9.0	9.4	1.28
Sex role	0.0	0.8	0.7	0.8	0.0	-1.31

* and *** denote statistically significant differences at $p<0.05$ and $p<0.001$, respectively

Table 21.4 gives similar results for values being one of the three most important that the respondents would most like their children to possess. The right-hand column gives the values of t for the statistical significance of the different percentages of Jews compared with the remainder of the sample selecting each value as the one of the three most desired in their children. There are eight values in which Jews are significantly different from others. Jews attach less importance to cleanliness, honesty, manners and obedience, but they attach more importance to considerateness, interest in how and why things happen, judgment and responsibility. (Fuller details of this study are given in Lynn and Kanazawa (2008).)

Table 21.4. One of three most important values: percentages

Values	Jews	Prot.	Cath.	None	Other	t
Numbers	228	6774	2736	781	181	-
Success	10.5	14.4	15.6	15.0	17.7	-1.81
Studiousness	5.3	6.2	8.1	5.9	11.0	-0.90
Amicability	14.9	12.2	14.7	12.7	13.8	0.91
Cleanliness	3.9	8.3	6.2	5.5	3.3	-1.99*
Considerateness	41.2	27.1	30.7	36.0	34.3	4.07***
Control	13.2	17.3	15.5	12.9	21.0	-1.36
Honesty	58.8	67.6	63.6	58.8	55.8	-2.16*
Interest	27.6	15.0	16.3	34.4	23.8	4.26***
Judgment	52.2	36.9	37.1	43.1	35.4	4.55***
Manners	10.5	24.4	23.3	16.9	22.7	-4.60***
Obedience	19.7	35.0	29.2	17.8	24.3	-3.94***
Responsibility	39.0	30.7	35.5	36.1	34.8	2.11*
Sex role	1.8	4.0	3.4	3.7	1.1	-1.59

* and *** denote statistically significant differences at p<0.05 and p<0.001, respectively

The results evidently provide no support for the theory that Jews attach more importance to success or to studiousness than non-Jews. In fact, Jews attach less importance to success and to studiousness than non-Jews, although the differences are not statistically significant. Jews do attach more importance to four values than non-Jews. These are considerateness, interest in how and why things happen, judgment, and responsibility, but it is not easy to see how these would contribute to the success of Jews in virtually all walks of life. The results that Jewish parents are more likely to foster interest in how and why things happen suggest that this might contribute to the high Jewish achievement in science, but Jews have been equally successful in law, the humanities, and business, for which an interest in how and why things happen would not seem to confer any obvious advantage. In general, the results show that Jews do not differ much from Gentiles in the values they would most like their children to have. Jews and non-Jews attach most importance to their children being considerate, honest, and responsible, and Jews and non-Jews attach least importance to their children valuing cleanliness and appropriate sex-role behavior.

2. Jewish Motivation for Achievement

Although Jews do not seem to attach more importance to success than do non-Jews, it is possible that Jews possess some kind of strong motivational or work ethic advantage that contributes to their achievements. This theory has been proposed by several scholars including Francis Hsu (1972), E. Kallen (1976), and James Flynn (1991). There is some evidence in support of the theory. For instance, Bernard Rosen (1959) proposed that the racial and ethnic populations in North America differed in what he called an "achievement syndrome" consisting of "achievement motivation," "value orientation," and "educational-occupational aspiration." He showed in an empirical study that Greeks, Jews, and White Protestants had a strong "achievement syndrome" and argued that this was responsible for their educational and socioeconomic achievements; Blacks, Catholic Italians, and Catholic French-Canadians had a weaker "achievement syndrome," and this was responsible for their lower educational and socioeconomic success. In support of this thesis, Richard Carney and Wilbert McKeachie (1962) have reported a study finding that Jewish college students had higher achievement motivation than those of any other denomination. The strong Jewish achievement motivation/work ethic theory received some further confirmation from a study carried out in the United States by Gerhard Lenski (1963), from which he concluded that Jews have done well because they have a strong form of the Protestant work ethic. He concluded that Jews are like White Protestants in possessing "individualistic, competitive patterns of thought and action linked with the middle class and historically associated with the Protestant ethic or its secular counterpart, the spirit of capitalism." Catholics and Blacks, he argued, have "the collectivist, security-oriented working class patterns of action, historically opposed to the Protestant ethic."

Some further supporting evidence for strong Jewish motivation for achievement was found by J. Kosa (1969) in a study of 2,630 American medical students. They were divided into Jews, Protestants, Catholics, and agnostics and were asked how much importance they attached to having a high income and high prestige. The results are given in Table 21.5 and show a higher percentage of Jews attached importance to having a high income and high prestige compared to the other three groups.

Table 21.5. Jewish-Gentile differences in importance they attached to having a high income and high prestige (percentages)

	Jews	Protestants	Catholics	Agnostics
High income	30	19	20	26
High prestige	44	35	28	23

A study carried out by Naomi Fejgin (1995) suggests the same differences. She analyzed the 1988 data of the American NELS national sample of eighth graders, aged approximately 14. These students were tested in mathematics and reading, on both of which they scored higher than White Gentiles (see Table 19.2). They also reported having higher educational aspirations ($0.71d$), doing more homework ($0.20d$), and watching less television ($0.47d$) than White Gentiles. The results are shown in Table 21.6. All three differences suggest Jews have stronger motivation for achievement.

Table 21.6. Jewish-Gentile differences in measures of motivation (sds in brackets)

Measure	Jews	Whites
Number	431	10,625
Educational aspirations	5.53 (2.28)	3.88 (2.37)
Homework (hours per week)	5.29 (2.72)	4.75 (2.66)
TV watching (hours per day)	2.01 (1.49)	2.71 (1.53)

Yet another study showing higher motivation for achievement in Jews compared samples in Israel, the United States, and Germany and found that Israelis had higher achievement motivation than both Americans ($d=0.41$) and Germans ($d=0.51$) (Byrne, Mueller-Hanson, Cardador, Thornton, Schuler, Frintrup, & Fox, 2004).

The results of all these studies suggest that Jews have stronger motivation for achievement than Gentiles. The high achievements of the Jews can be understood in terms of the formula IQ x Motivation x Opportunity = Achievement. It is the multiplicative interaction of IQ with motivation and opportunity that explains the huge overrepresentation of the Ashkenazim in all indices of high achievement. A Jewish advantage of around 0.4d to 0.5d in motivation interacting multiplicatively with a 0.67d (10 IQ points) advantage in IQ is sufficient to explain the huge Jewish advantage in achievement. Notice also that if any of the terms in the equation is zero, there can be no achievement. This was the case with Jews before their emancipation in the 19th century. They must have possessed their high IQ and motivation because these will have evolved over centuries, but they generally achieved little because they were denied the opportunity, except in a few places like Britain and the Netherlands. Once the Jews were emancipated, all three components of the equation for achievement were present and the Jews rapidly outperformed Gentiles in all areas.

The high Jewish motivation for achievement, together with high intelligence, most likely has a genetic basis, brought about through having been selected for by eugenic customs, persecution, and discrimination.

3. Three Troubling Conclusions

Studies reporting the high intelligence and achievements of the Ashkenazim that have been reviewed in this book have been around for many decades. The high intelligence of the Ashkenazim was first found in the 1920s in the United States and Britain. Over the next decades these high IQs were confirmed by many more studies published in the United States, two more studies in Britain, and two studies in Canada published in 1968 and 1973 that reported Jewish IQs of 107.1 and 110.5.

Strangely, however, the high intelligence of the Ashkenazim is hardly ever mentioned by social scientists. Of the several hundred social scientists who have documented the high achievements of the Jews and whose work has been summarized in this book, only Weyl and Possony (1963), Weyl (1989), Storfer (1990), MacDonald (1994), Herrnstein and Murray (1994), and Cochran, Hardy, and Harpending (2006) have noted and discussed the high Jewish IQ. All others have ignored it. For instance, the Harvard sociologist Stanley Lieberson and his colleague Donna Carter, who showed the remarkable overrepresentation of Jews in *Who's Who in America,* make no mention of the high Jewish IQ as a likely explanation (Lieberson & Carter, 1979). There is no mention of the high IQ of the Jews in discussions of Jewish successes by Harvard historians Thernstrom and Thernstrom (2003), or by the economists Gary Becker (1981) and Barry Chiswick (1985, 1988, 1999, 2007), the latter having devoted a quarter of a century to considering why Jews have done so well. The British sociologist Asher Tropp (1991), whose book documents the overrepresentation of Jews in the professions in Britain, curiously fails to make any mention of the studies showing that Jews have high IQs. There is also no mention of the high IQ of the Jews by the Canadian sociologist Edward Herberg (1990a, 1990b), who has documented the economic and professional achievements of Jews in Canada.

Nor is there any mention of the high IQ of the Jews in textbooks of sociology (e.g. Giddens, 1993) or of psychology (too numerous to cite), or even in textbooks on intelligence, such as Nathan Brody's *Intelligence* (1992), Nicholas Mackintosh's *IQ and Human Intelligence* (1998), Robert Sternberg's *Handbook of Intelligence* (2000), and Earl Hunt's *Human Intelligence* (2011). In 1994, the American Psychological Association set up a committee of experts on intelligence to produce a report on all the important facts that are known about intelligence.

This report included a discussion of the heritability of intelligence, the high IQ of the Chinese and Japanese, and the low IQ of Blacks (Neisser et al., 1996: *Intelligence: Knowns and Unknowns*). Strangely, absent in all these works has been any mention of the high IQ of the Jews.

How can this silence about the high IQ of the Jews be explained? While some of the historians, sociologists, and economists who have published studies documenting the Jews' high educational attainment, high earnings, high socioeconomic status, and remarkable intellectual achievements are, no doubt, ignorant of the high Jewish IQ, others must surely be aware of it and how it must be a major factor in Jewish successes. The contribution of intelligence to educational and socioeconomic status is quite well known in the social sciences as a result of the work of the sociologist Christopher Jencks (1972), and the well-publicized work of Herrnstein and Murray (1994) in the United States, and that of the sociologists Bond and Saunders (1999) in Britain. It is difficult to avoid the conclusion that sociologists know about high Jewish IQ, but have chosen to ignore it. It is certainly well known in psychology that intelligence is a major determinant of educational and socioeconomic achievement (see, e.g. Brand, 1996; Lynn, 1988; Nettle, 2003). The psychologists who are experts on intelligence must be aware of the studies of the high IQ of the Jews, but have likewise opted to ignore these.

Why should this be? Possibly, the reason for this omission is that the high IQ of the Jews raises three awkward problems: (1) the high IQ of the Jews must have a genetic basis; (2) Jewish eugenic customs have contributed to the high Jewish IQ, and hence eugenic practices are effective in raising the intelligence of a people; and (3) a minority ethnic group with a high IQ succeeds despite discrimination.

The first troubling conclusion raised by the high Jewish IQ is that it is difficult to avoid the conclusion that their high IQ must have a genetic basis. Five reasons for the inescapability of this conclusion have been given in Chapter 20. How else can we explain the extraordinary achievements of these peoples throughout the United States, Britain, Continental Europe, Canada, and elsewhere from the later decades of the 19th century onward? Jews arrived in these foreign countries as penniless refugees, and yet their children and grandchildren obtained higher average IQs (where this has been tested) than their Gentile hosts, outperformed them in educational attainment, earnings, socioeconomic status, and in intellectual achievements.

It is impossible to avoid the conclusion that a significant factor in these Jewish achievements is their high IQ and that this must have a substantial genetic basis. Once this conclusion has been reached, it inevitably invites the question of why other ethnic and racial groups, notably Blacks, American Indians, and Hispanics in the United States, Canada, and throughout Latin America, have failed to achieve equality with Whites, and why Blacks, North Africans, and South Asians have likewise failed to achieve equality with Whites in Britain and Continental Europe. If the Jews have done better than White Gentiles because they have a higher IQ, we are drawn to the conclusion that Blacks, American Indians, non-white Hispanics, and South Asians have failed to succeed because they have lower IQs. This was the conclusion drawn by Herrnstein and Murray (2004) in *The Bell Curve*, whose publication was met by a barrage of attacks. Most social scientists are reluctant to spell out this conclusion, either because they are ideologically committed equalitarians on race differences, or because they fear the criticisms they would be certain to incur.

The second troubling conclusion that has to be drawn from the high IQ of the Jews is that it seems to have been a eugenics success story. We have seen that there is a strong case that the eugenic customs and practices of the Ashkenazim (according high status to intelligent rabbis and other scholars and promoting their marriage to the daughters of wealthy merchants) seem to have been a major factor responsible for the evolution of their high intelligence. But who wants to admit that eugenics works and has contributed to the high intelligence and achievements of this extraordinarily gifted people? Evidently not those who have written textbooks on psychology, sociology, and intelligence.

The high IQ and achievements of the Jews lead to a third troubling conclusion. This is that an ethnic group with a high IQ succeeds despite discrimination, and this raises the question of why other ethnic groups have failed to succeed. The standard explanation of why Blacks, non-white Hispanics, and American Indians do poorly in IQ, education, earnings, and socioeconomic status is that Whites discriminate against them. The same explanation is routinely advanced to explain why Mestizos and indigenous peoples do poorly throughout Latin America, why Aborigines do poorly in Australia, and why Maoris do poorly in New Zealand. Yet, the Jews have suffered a great deal of discrimination over the last 2,000 years, and it has apparently not had an adverse effect on their intelligence or their achievements. How can this be explained? Jews have everywhere experienced anti-Semitism and discrimination, yet they have invariably done better in earnings, socioeconomic status, and intellectual achievement than Europeans. The only possible inference that can be drawn is that an ethnic group with a high IQ succeeds despite discrimination. This, in turn, discredits the theory that Blacks, Hispanics, and American Indians have failed to achieve equality with Whites because of discrimination. Those such as Sandra Scarr (1995), who maintain that racial discrimination is an important cause of Blacks' low IQ, have a problem explaining the high IQ of the Jews. Why Jews have succeeded where Blacks, Hispanics, and Native American Indians have failed poses a problem that many social scientists find hard to explain, and thus prefer not to address. It is difficult to avoid the conclusion that this is another of the reasons why a discreet veil of silence has been drawn over the high Jewish IQ.

4. The Future of the Jewish People

The Jews are unique in having survived as a people for around 2,000 years without a homeland and despite numerous persecutions. Normally, immigrant peoples become assimilated with their host populations within a century or two. The Normans who conquered England in 1066 preserved their French language and names for about 200 years, but after this, became assimilated with the native English, intermarried with them, adopted the English language, and disappeared as an ethnic group. The French established and ruled a colony around Istanbul in 1204 following the Fourth Crusade, but within two centuries they became assimilated. The Jews, on the other hand, have preserved their identity for 2,000 years. There are indications, however, that their continued survival as minority groups in Western countries and in Israel is in jeopardy.

The three major bonds through which the Jews have preserved their identity throughout the centuries have been their religion, their language, and their prohibition on marrying Gentiles. The strength of all three of these began to weaken in the 19th century, a process that was accelerated in the 20th. The first to go was the language. Until the 19th century, virtually all the Ashkenazim lived in Russia, Poland, Germany, and the Austro-Hungarian Empire, where they spoke Yiddish. In the 19th century, Jews in Germany and the Austro-Hungarian Empire gave up Yiddish and adopted the German or Hungarian languages. This facilitated their assimilation and successful Jews began to mix socially with Gentiles and intermarry with them. The proportion of Jews marrying Gentiles gradually increased until by the 1930s, it reached about half in Germany, Austria, and Hungary.

The future numbers of the Jewish people throughout the world, assuming the continuation of medium fertility, have been estimated by Sergio Della Pergola, Uzi Rebhun, and Mark Tolts (2000) for the years 2030 and 2080. Their estimates together with their figures for the year 2000 are given in Table 21.7. We see that they project declines in the numbers of Jews throughout the world, except in Israel, where the numbers of Jews is expected to increase and more than double from 2000 to 2080.

Table 21.7. Population projections for the Jewish people (thousands)

Region	2000	2030	2080
Total world	13,109	14,125	15,574
Israel	4,874	6,876	10,558
North America	6,065	5,763	4,094
Latin America	420	335	199
Europe	1,125	962	609
Former Soviet Union	413	22	0
Asia, Africa, Oceania	212	168	114

The projected decline in the numbers of Jews throughout the world (except in Israel) is attributed to four factors: continued migration to Israel, intermarriage with Gentiles, loss of faith, and below-replacement fertility. They assume continued anti-Semitism will likely be responsible for significant numbers of Jews migrating to Israel. Intermarriage with Gentiles reduces the numbers of Jews because most couples in these mixed marriages bring up their children as Gentiles and became assimilated into their host communities. In the 20th century, increasing numbers of Jews married Gentiles, but the extent of intermarriage varied in different countries. In Canada, only 12.9 percent of Jews had married Gentiles in 1991, but in the United States the 1990 National Jewish Population Survey showed that 52 percent of Jews had married non-Jews, and only 25 percent of children reared in Jewish-Gentile mixed marriages were being raised as Jews (Kosmin & Lachman, 1993). In the Netherlands between 1946 and 1999, 54 percent of Jews married Gentiles (Kalmijn, Liefbroer, van Poppel, & van Solinge, 2006), almost exactly the same as the 52 percent in the United States.

As significant numbers of Jews have lost their faith, they have ceased to accept the injunction against marrying Gentiles and instead have assimilated with them. This has been a major factor responsible for Jewish assimilation into Gentile communities that began throughout Europe in the middle decades of the 19th century and spread to the United States in the 20th. For instance, a survey of students at UCLA carried out in 1991 found that 17 percent of Jewish students had abandoned their parents' religion; this percentage was expected to increase as they grew older (Kosmin & Lachman, 1993). It seems likely that this trend will continue throughout the country. Indeed, many ethnically conscious Jews have perceived this and are concerned about it, but it is doubtful there is anything they could do to reverse it.

In addition to increasing assimilation with Gentiles, Jews have been having relatively few children. We have seen this in Canada, where in 1981, Jewish women aged 44 and over had an average of 2.24 children, barely two thirds of the 3.30 for the whole population. In the United States, as early as 1957, Jewish women aged 44 and over had an average of 2.22 children, significantly fewer than the 2.80 for the whole population. At the end of the 20th century, the fertility of Jewish women in the United States had fallen to 1.86, well below the 2.1 figure needed for replacement (Wertheimer, 2005). This is an expression of the general tendency for fertility to be below replacement present throughout economically developed countries, particularly among the better educated and the more intelligent.

The result of emigration to Israel, the lessening of religious commitment to Judaism, increasing rates of intermarriage with Gentiles, and below replacement fertility has been that the Jewish populations have declined significantly in Western countries. For instance, in Britain, the number of Jews declined from 360,000 in 1970 to 267,000 in 2001. The absolute number of Jews in a country is a critical factor determining whether they retain their identity. Where there are relatively few Jews, as in Britain, Continental Europe, and most of the rest of the world, it is difficult for Jews to find suitable Jewish marriage partners, so many of them marry Gentiles and lose their Jewish identity. This has been happening on an increasing scale even in the United States, where about half the Jewish population marry Gentiles, and almost three quarters of the children of these marriages are raised as Gentiles (Wertheimer, 2005).

It seems probable, even inevitable, that these trends will continue and that Jews as an ethnic group will continue to decline in numbers throughout Western countries up to the end of the 21st century. To estimate the extent of this decline in the United States, we can take Jewish fertility at 1.86 per woman, of whom half are born to Gentile partners of whom three quarters lose their Jewish identity. The effect of this is a replacement of 1.16 Jewish children per Jewish woman. This will result in an approximate halving of the Jewish population in each generation.

Despite this reduction in numbers, Jews are likely to remain an influential force in the United States by virtue of their high IQs, power, and wealth; it is also likely there will be a sufficient number for them to retain their identity and remain a significant element in the population, at least until the end of the 21st century.

Only in Israel is the number of Jews projected to increase. But the Jews in Israel face two problems. The first is the implacable hostility of their Arab neighbors. In the second half of the 20th century, the Jews in Israel did not have much difficulty in containing this by virtue of their higher intelligence, but whether they will be able to continue to do this if and when one or more of their neighbors secure nuclear weapons is questionable. A second problem lies in the differences in the fertility of the European Jews, the Mizrahim, and the Arabs. As we saw in Chapter 11, the European Jews are the elite with the highest IQs and educational achievement, and they form the majority of the professional and middle class. Yet, their numbers of children have been below those of the Mizrahim and the Arabs. In 2000, the fertility difference between the European Jews and Mizrahim had narrowed, especially for those born in

Israel, among whom fertility had become almost the same at 2.58 and 2.62, respectively. However, the fertility of the Arabs has been much greater than that of the Jews. In 1960, the average number of children of the Arabs was 9.31, compared with 3.94 for Jews born in Israel. This fertility difference has narrowed until by the year 2007, it reached 2.8 for Jews born in Israel and 3.9 for Arabs. It may be that the fertility of the Arabs will continue to decline until it becomes the same as that of the Jews. It seems more likely that the Arabs will continue to have more children than the Jews, with the result that they become an increasing proportion of the population. Arabs could even become the majority toward the end of the 21st century, raising the possibility that Jews could be displaced in their own country.

A pessimistic view of the future of Israel was taken by the U.S. Central Intelligence Agency in a report issued in March 2009. It predicted that Israel and Palestine would merge in a "one-state solution" and that the fertility of the Palestinians would be so much greater than that of Jews that they would inevitably become a majority of the population. Jews would then find Israel uncomfortable, and large numbers would emigrate. Even if this does not take place, increasing numbers of Jews will likely leave Israel. Many Jews already foresee these alarming potential possibilities and are considering emigration. The CIA report notes, "Over 500,000 Israelis have American passports and those who do not have American or Western passports, have already applied for them." The study further predicts the return of over 1.5 million Israelis to Russia and other parts of Europe. The report concluded that Israel may well not survive as a Jewish state beyond the next 20 years. Even if this timescale is excessively short, it is difficult to be optimistic about the survival of Israel as a Jewish state over the longer term.

For all these reasons, it is impossible to be other than pessimistic about the survival of the Jews as an ethnic group in the medium term. Israel will likely be lost as the Jewish homeland, as the numbers of Arabs increase and Jews emigrate. Elsewhere, apart from a small number of Hasidim, it seems likely that increasing numbers of Jews will lose their faith, marry non-Jews, and raise their children as Gentiles; more and more Jews will be assimilated with their Gentile host communities and lose their Jewish identity. This will be bad news for Jews who value their genetic and cultural heritage. On the other hand, it will be good news for Gentiles, who will benefit from an infusion of Jewish genes that have contributed so much to world culture.

References

Abbink, J.G. (2002). Ethnic trajectories in Israel. *Anthropos*, 97, 3–19.

Altschuler, M. (1998). *Soviet Jewry on the Eve of the Holocaust: A Social and Demographic Profile*. Jerusalem: Center for Research of East European Jewry, The Hebrew University.

Arkin, M. (1975). *Aspects of Jewish Economic History*. Philadelphia: Jewish Publication Society of America.

Arkin, M. (1984). *Economic activities*. In Arkin, M. (Ed.) South African Jewry. Oxford: Oxford University Press.

Bachman, J.G. (1970). *Youth In Transition Vol. 2: The Impact of Family Background and intelligence on Tenth Grade Boys*. Ann Arbor: University of Michigan.

Backman, M.E. (1972). Patterns of mental abilities: Ethnic, socioeconomic and sex differences. *American Educational Research Journal*, 9, 1–12.

Bailey, P. (1922). A contribution to the mental pathology of races in the United States. *Mental Hygiene*, 6, 370–391.

Baker, J.R. (1974). *Race*. Oxford: Oxford University Press.

Barnaav, E. (1998). *The Historical Atlas of the Jewish People*. London: Kuperard.

Baron, S.W. (1952). *A Social and Religious History of the Jews*. New York: Columbia University Press.

Becker, G. (1981). *Human Capital.* Chicago: University of Chicago Press.

Behar, D.M., Garrigan, D., Kaplan, M. E., Mobasher, Z., Rosengarten, D., Karafet, T. M., Quintana-Murci, L., Ostrer, H., Skorecki, K., and Hammer, M. F. (2004). Contrasting patterns of Y chromosome variation in Ashkenazi Jewish and host non-Jewish European populations. *Human Genetics,* 114, 354–365.

Benbassa, E. and Rodrigue, A. (1995). *The Jews of the Balkans.* Oxford: Blackwell.

Ben-David, A. and Ben-Ari, A.T. (1998). The experience of being different. *Journal of Black Studies,* 27, 510–527.

Ben-Shakhar, G. and Beller, M. (1983). On the cultural fairness of psychological tests. *Megamot Behavioral Sciences Quarterly,* 28, 42–56.

Bere, M. (1924). A comparative study of the mental capacity of children of foreign parentage. *Teacher's College Contributions to Education,* No.154.

Berhanu, G. (2005). Normality, Deviance, Identity, Cultural Tracking, and School Achievement: The case of Ethiopian Jews in Israel. *Scandinavian Journal of Educational Research,* 49, 51–82.

Berkman, J. (2009). At Least 139 of the Forbes 400 are Jewish. Weblog entry. Jewish Telegraphic Agency. http://blogs.jta.org/philanthropy/article/2009/10/05/1008323/at-least-139-of-the-forbes-400-are-jewish. 5 October 2009. Accessed 6 July 2011.

Berry, C. (1999). Religious tradition as contexts of historical creativity: patterns of scientific and artistic achievement and their stability. *Personality and Individual Differences,* 26, 1125–1135.

Birnbaum, P. (1996). *The Jews of the Republic: A Political History of State Jews in France from Gambetta to Vichy.* Stanford: Stanford University Press.

Blom, J.C.H., Fuks-Mansfeld, R.G. and Schoffer, I. (1996). *The History of the Jews in the Netherlands.* Oxford: Littman.

Bodmer, W.F. and Cavalli-Sforza, L.L. (1976). *Genetics, Evolution, and Man.* San Francisco, California: Freeman.

Bond, R. and Saunders, P. (1999). Routes of success: influences on the occupational attainment of young British males. *The British Journal of Sociology,* 50, 217-240.

Bonger, W.A. (1943). *Race and Crime.* New York: Columbia University Press.
Bonnie-Tamir, B. (1991). Genetic affinities of Ethiopian Jews. *Israel Journal of Medical Sciences,* 27, 245–151.
Brand, C.B. (1996). *The g Factor.* New York: John Wiley.
Brasz, F.C. (1996). After the Second World War. In J. C. Blom, R. G. Fuks-Mansfeld and I. Schoffer (Eds.) *The History of the Jews in the Netherlands.* Oxford: Littman.
Brigham, C.C. (1923). *A Study of American Intelligence.* Princeton: Princeton University Press.
Brigham, C.C. (1937). Intelligence tests of immigrant groups. *Psychological Review,* 37, 158–165.
Brody, N. (1992). *Intelligence.* San Diego, California: Academic Press.
Brook, S. (1990). *The Club: the Jews of Modern Britain.* London: Constable.
Brook, K.A. (2006 [1999]). The Jews of Khazaria. Lanham, MD: Rowman and Littlefield Publishers, Inc.
Brookdale Institute (2004). *Ethiopian Integration-Education and Employment.* Jerusalem: Brookdale Institute.
Brown, F. (1944). A comparative study of the intelligence of Jewish and Scandinavian kindergarten children. *Journal of Genetic Psychology,* 64, 67–92.
Brustein, W.I. (2003). *Roots of Hate.* Cambridge: Cambridge University Press.
Brustein, W.I. and King, R.D. (2004). Anti-Semitism as a response to perceived Jewish power. *Social Forces,* 83, 691–708.
Brym, R.J., Shaffir, W. and Weinfeld, M. (1993). *The Jews in Canada.* Toronto: Oxford University Press.
Buckser, A. (2003). *After the Rescue: Jewish Identity and Community in Contemporary Denmark.* New York: Palgrave Macmillan.
Burg, B. and Belmont, I. (1990). Mental abilities of children from different cultural backgrounds. *Journal of Cross-Cultural Psychology,* 21, 90–108.
Burnstein, P. (2007). Jewish educational and economic success in the United States: a search for explanations. *Sociological Perspectives,* 50, 209–228.

Byrne, Z.S., Mueller-Hanson, R. A., Cardador, J. M., Thornton, G. C., Schuler, H., Frintrup, A., and Fox, S. (2004). Measuring achievement motivation: tests of equivalency for English, German and Israeli versions of the achievement motivation inventory. *Personality and Individual Differences*, 37, 203–217.

Canter, D. (1985) (Ed.). *Facet Theory: Approaches to Social Research*. New York: Springer-Verlag.

Carney, R.E. and McKeachie, W.J. (1962). Religion, sex, social class, probability of success, and student personality. *Journal for the Scientific Study of Religion*, 2, 32–42.

Carroll, J.B. (1993). *Human Cognitive Abilities*. Cambridge: Cambridge University Press.

Castello, E.R. and Kagan, U. M. (1994). *The Jews and Europe*. Edison, New Jersey: Chartwell.

Castiglione, V. (1904). Italy. *Jewish Encyclopedia*, 7, 1–10: New York: Funk and Wagnalls.

Cavalli-Sforza, L. L., Menozzi, P., and Piazza, A. (1994). *The History and Geography of Human Genes*. Princeton, New Jersey: Princeton University Press.

Chamberlain, H.S. (1912). *Foundations of the Nineteenth Century*. New York: John Lane.

Chen, M. (1983). *Inter-ethnic integration, heterogenic educational attainment and the advancement of students*. Lecture held at the Institute for promotion of integration in the educational system, Bar Ilan University, Ramat Gan, Israel (in Hebrew).

Chen, M. (1987). *Discipline, educational attainment, and students' expectations in the secular and state-religious educational systems*. TAU Seminar on Social Mobility: The Interplay of Class, Ethnicity and Schooling, 31.5–2.6, Tel Aviv University.

Chen, M., Levi, A., and Kfir, D. (1977). The possibilities of interethnic group contact in the junior high schools: Implementation and results. *Megamot*, 23, 101–123 (in Hebrew).

Chernichovsky, D. and Anson, J. (2005). The Jewish-Arab divide in life expectancy in Israel. *Economics and Human Biology*, 3, 123–137.

Chiswick, B.R. (1985). The labor market status of American Jewry. *American Jewish Yearbook*, 85, 131–152.

Chiswick, B.R. (1988). Labor supply and investment in child quality: A study of Jewish and Non-Jewish women. *Contemporary Jewry*, 9, 35–61.

Chiswick, B.R. (1988a). Differences in education and earnings across racial and ethnic groups: tastes, discrimination and investments in child quality. *Quarterly Journal of Economics*, 103, 571–599.

Chiswick, B.R. (1999). The occupational attainment and earnings of American Jewry, 1890–1990. *Contemporary Jewry*, 20, 68–98.

Chiswick, B.R. (2007). The occupational attainment of American Jewry, 1990 to 2000. *Contemporary Jewry*, 27, 112–136.

Chiswick, B.R. and Huang, J. D. (2008). The earnings of American Jewish men: human capital, denomination, and religiosity. *Journal for the Scientific Study of Religion*, 47, 694–709.

Clayton, J. (2000). A land of promise for Ethiopia's Jews. *The Times* (London), 28 January, p. 12.

Cochran, G. and Harpending, H. (2009). *The 10,000 Year Explosion*. New York: Basic Books.

Cochran, G., Hardy, J., and Harpending, H. (2006). The natural history of Ashkenazi intelligence. *Journal of Biosocial Science*, 38, 659–693.

Cohen, I. and Loeb, H. (1927). *The Intelligence of Jews as compared with non-Jews*. Columbus: Ohio University Press.

Cohen, M.A. (1972). *The Jewish Experience in Latin America*. New York: Ktav Publishing.

Cohen, Y. and Haberfeld, Y. (1998). Second generation Jewish immigrants in Israel: have the gaps in schooling and earnings declined? *Ethnic and Racial Studies*, 21, 507–523.

Cohen, Y. and Haberfeld, Y. (2003). *Gender, Ethnic, and National Earnings Gaps in Israel: The Role of Rising Inequality*. Israel: Sapir Center, Tel Aviv University.

Cohen, Y. Haberfeld, Y., and Kristal, T. (2004). *Ethnicity and mixed ethnicity: educational gaps among Israeli-born Jews*. Israel: Sapir Center, Tel Aviv University.

Cohn, S.J., Cohn, C.M.G., and Jensen, A.R. (1988). Myopia and intelligence: a pleiotropic relationship? *Human Genetics*, 80, 53–58.

Condran, G.A. and Kramarow, E.A. (1991). Child mortality among Jewish immigrants to the United States. *Journal of Interdisciplinary History*, 22, 223–254.

Cranberg, L.D. and Albert, M. L. (1988). The chess mind. In K. L. Obler and D. Fein (Eds.) *The Exceptional Brain: Neuropsychology of Talent and Special Abilities*. New York: Guilford Press.

Dar, Y. and Resh, N. (1991). Socioeconomic and ethnic gaps in academic achievement in Israeli junior high schools. In: N. Bleichrodt and P. J. D. Drenth (Eds.) Contemporary *Issues in Cross-Cultural Psychology*. Amsterdam: Swets and Zeitlinger.

Darity, W.A., Dietrich, J., and Guilkey, D.K. (1997). Racial and ethnic inequality in the United States: a secular perspective. *American Economic Review*, 87, 301–305.

David, H. (2003). The influence of gender, religion and grade in mathematical learning in Israeli junior high schools. *Ph.D. thesis*, University of Ludwig-Maximilians, Munich.

David, H. and Lynn, R. (2007). Intelligence differences between European and Oriental Jews in Israel. *Journal of Biosocial Science*, 39, 465–473

Davies, M. and Hughes, A. G. (1927). An investigation into the comparative intelligence and attainments of Jewish and non-Jewish school children. *British Journal of Psychology*, 18, 134–146.

Della Pergola, S. (1993). Jews in the European Community. *American Jewish Yearbook*, 93, 25–84.

Della Pergola, S. (2007). "Sephardic and Oriental" Jews in Israel and Western Countries: Migration, Social Change, and Identification. *Studies in Contemporary Jewry*, 22, 1–43.

Della Pergola, S. (2009). Actual, intended, and appropriate family size among Jews in Israel. *Contemporary Jewry*, 29 (to appear).

Della Pergola, S. and Dubb, A.A. (1988). South African Jewry. *American Jewish Yearbook*, 88, 59–142.

Della Pergola, S., Rebhun, U., and Tolts, M. (2000). Prospecting the Jewish future: population projections, 2000–2080. *American Jewish Yearbook*, 100, 103–146.

Dinero, S.C. (2002). Special education use among Negrev Bedouin Arabs of Israel. *Race, Ethnicity and Education*, 5, 375–396.

Dorfman, D.D. (1982). Henry Goddard and the feeble-mindedness of Jews, Hungarians, Italians, and Russians. *American Psychologist*, 37, 96–97.

Dubb, A. (1984). Demographic picture. In Arkin, M. (Ed) *South African Jewry*. Oxford: Oxford University Press.

Dubb, A.A. (1991). *The Jewish Population of South Africa*. Cape Town: Kaplan Center

Easterbrooks, G.H. (1928). The relation between cranial capacity, relative cranial capacity and intelligence in school children. *Journal of Applied Psychology*, 12, 524–529.

Ecklund, E.H. and Scheitle, C. (2007). Religion among academic scientists: distinctions, disciplines, and demographics. *Social Problems*, 54, 289–307.

Eisikovits, R.A. (1997). The educational experience and performance of immigrant and minority students in Israel. *Anthropology and Education Quarterly*, 28, 394–410.

Daniel J. and Medding, P.Y. (1983). *Jewish Communities in Frontier Societies: Argentina, Australia, and South Africa*. New York: Holmes and Meier.

Encyclopedia Judaica. New York: Macmillan and Jerusalem: Keter.

Englander, M. (1902). *Die auffallend häufigen Krankheitserscheinungen der jüdischen Rasse*. Vienna: L. Pollak.

Entine, J. (2007). *Abraham's Children: Race, Identity, and the DNA of the Chosen People*. New York: Grand Central Publishing.

Eshel, Y. (1980). Antecedents of academic success and failure: Re-examination of prevailing disadvantage criteria. *Megamot* 31, 143–156 (in Hebrew)

Eysenck, H.J. (1995). *Genius: The Natural History of Creativity*. Cambridge University Press, Cambridge.

Falk, G. and Bullough, V. (1987). Achievement among German Jews born during the years 1785–1885. *Mankind Quarterly*, 27, 337–365.

Farron, S. (2005). *The Affirmative Action Hoax*. New York: Seven Locks Press.

Franzblau, A. N. (1934). Religious belief and character among Jewish adolescents. *Teachers College, Columbia University Contributions to Education*, No 634.

Feingold, G. A. (1924). Intelligence of the first generation of immigrant groups. *Journal of Educational Psychology*, 15, 65–83.

Fejgin, N. (1995). Factors contributing to the academic excellence of American Jewish and Asian students. *Sociology of Education*, 68, 18–30.

Feldman, D. (1994). *Englishmen and Jews: Social Relations and Political Culture, 1840–1914*. New Haven, Connecticut: Yale University Press.

Fisberg, M. (1904). *Germany*. London: Jewish Encyclopedia.

Fisher, H. A. (1936). *A History of Europe*. London: Edward Arnold.

Flynn, J.R. (1984). The mean IQ of Americans: massive gains 1932 to 1978. *Psychological Bulletin*, 95, 29–51.

Flynn, J.R. (1987). Massive IQ gains in 14 nations: what IQ tests really measure. *Psychological Bulletin*, 101, 171–191.

Flynn, J.R. (1991). *Asian Americans: Achievement Beyond IQ*. Hillsdale, New Jersey: Erlbaum.

Fraenkel, J. (1967). *The Jews of Austria*. London: Zed Books.

Fraser, J. (1915). *The Conquering Jew*. London: Cassell.

Friedlander, D., Okun, B. S., Eisenbach, Z., and Elmakias, L. L. (2002). Immigration, social change and assimilation: educational attainment among birth cohorts of Jewish ethnic groups, 1925–29 and 1965–69. *Population Studies*, 56, 135–151.

Frydman, M. and Lynn, R. (1992). The general intelligence and spatial abilities of gifted young Belgian chess players. *British Journal of Psychology*, 35, 233.

Gafni, N. (1978). *The relation between ethnic origin, social class, and gender in the level and structure of intelligence*. Master's thesis, the Hebrew University of Jerusalem (Hebrew).

Galton, F. (1883). *Enquiries into Human Faculty*. London: Dent.

Garrett, H.E. (1929). Jews and others. *Personality Journal*, 7, 341–348.

Giddens, A. (1997). *Sociology*. Cambridge, United Kingdom: Polity Press.

Gill, R. (1974). *Wechsler verbal intelligence and Bender gestalt performance of nine-year-old children of Western and Oriental origin from the upper and lower socioeconomic levels.* M. A. Thesis, Bar Ilan University, Ramat Gan.

Gillin, J.L. (1945). *Criminology and Penology.* New York: Appleton-Century.

Gilman, S.L (1996). *Smart Jews.* Lincoln, Nebraska: University of Nebraska Press.

Gobineau, A. de (1853). *Essai sur L'inegalite des Races Humaines.* Paris, France: Didot.

Globerson, T. (1983). Mental capacity and cognitive functioning: developmental and social class differences. *Developmental Psychology,* 19, 225–230.

Goddard, H.H. (1913). The Binet tests in relation to immigration. *Journal of Psycho-Aethenics,* 18, 105–107.

Goddard, H.H. Mental tests and the immigrant. *Journal of Delinquency,* 1917, 2, 243–277.

Godley, A. (Gra). *The History of Ethnic Entrepreneurship.* Princeton, New Jersey: Princeton University Press.

Goffman, D. (2000). Jews in early modern Ottoman commerce. In A. Levy (Ed.) *Jews, Turks, Ottomans.* Syracuse, New York: Syracuse University Press.

Goldman, M. (1980). *Society in Israel: statistical highlights.* Jerusalem: Central Bureau of Statistics.

Goldscheider, C. and Simpson, J.E. (1967). Religious affiliation and juvenile delinquency. *Sociological Inquiry,* 37, 297–310.

Goldstein, D.B. (2008). *Jacob's Legacy: A Genetic View of Jewish History.* Yale: Yale University Press.

Goldstein, S. (1969). Socioeconomic differentials among religious groups in the United States. *American Journal of Sociology,* 74, 612–631.

Goldstein, S. (1971). American Jewry, 1970. *American Jewish Yearbook,* 71, 3–88.

Goldstein, S. (1993). *Profile of American Jewry.* New York: Mandell Berman Institute.

Goodenough, F. L. (1926). Racial differences in the intelligence of school children. *Journal of Experimental Psychology*, 9, 388–397.

Gordon, S. (1984). *Hitler, Germans, and the Jewish Question*. Princeton, New Jersey: Princeton University Press.

Gould, S.J. (1996). *The Mismeasure of Man*. New York: Norton.,

Graham, D. and Waterman, S. (2005). Underenumeration of the Jewish Population in the UK 2001 Census. *Population, Space and Place*, vol. 11, 89-102.

Graham, V. T. (1925). The intelligence of Italian and Jewish children in the Habit clinics of Massachusetts division of mental health. *Journal of Abnormal and Social Psychology*, 20, 271–277.

Gross, M. (1967). *Learning Readiness in Two Jewish Groups*. New York: Center for Urban Education.

Gross, M. (1978). Cultural concomitants of preschoolers' preparation for learning. *Psychological Reports*, 43, 807–813.

Gross, M. (1986). Cultural concomitants of preschoolers' preparation for learning. *Psychological Reports*, 58, 774.

Haberfeld, Y. and Cohen, Y. (1998). Earnings of native-born Jewish and Arab men in Israel, 1987–1993. *Research in Social Stratification and Mobility*, 16, 69–88.

Halevi, I. (1987). *A History of the Jews*. London: Zed Books.

Halkin, H. (2008). Jews and their DNA. *Commentary*, 126, 37–43.

Hammer, M.F., Redd, A. J., Wood, E. T., Bonner, M. R., Jarjanazi, H., Karafet, T., Santachiara-Benerecetti, S., Oppenheim, A., Jobling, M. A., Jenkins, T., Ostrer, H., and Bonné-Tamir, B. (2000) Jewish and Middle Eastern non-Jewish populations share a common pool of Y-chromosome biallelic haplotypes. *Proceedings of the National Academy of Sciences*, 97, 6769–6774.

Held, O.C. (1941). Comparative study of the performance of Jewish and gentile college students on the American Council Psychological Examination. *Journal of Social Psychology*, 13, 407–411.

Heller, C. (1987). *On the Edge of Destruction: Jews in Poland between the Two World Wars*. New York: Columbia University Press.

Herberg, E.N. (1990a). The ethno-racial hierarchy in Canada: theory and analysis of the New Vertical Mosaic. *International Journal of Comparative Sociology*, 31, 206–221.

Herberg, E.N. (1990b). *The ethno-racial hierarchy in Canada: theory and analysis of the New Vertical Mosaic*. Unpublished.

Herrnstein, R.J. and Murray, C. (1994). *The Bell Curve: Intelligence and Class Structure in American Life*. New York: Free Press.

Herz, F.M. and Rozen, E.J. (1982). Jewish families. In McGoldrick, J. K. Pearce and J. Giordano (Eds.) *Ethnicity and Family Therapy*. New York: Guilford Press.

Herzog, M. (2001). *The Language and Culture Atlas of Ashkenazi Jewry*. Cambridge: Cambridge University Press.

Higley, J., Deacon, D., and Smart, D. (1979). *Elites in Australia*. London: Croom Helm.

Hirsch, N.D. (1926). A study of natio-racial differences. *Genetic Psychology Monographs*, No.1.

Hoberman, J. (1991). Why Jews play sports. *Moment*, April, 1–12.

Hollinger, D.A. (2002). Why are Jews pre-eminent in science and scholarship? The Veblen thesis reconsidered. *Adelph*, 2, 145–162.

Hsu, Francis I.K. (1972). *Challenge of the American Dream: the Chinese in the United States*. San Francisco, California: Wadsworth.

Hunt, E. (2011). *Human Intelligence*. Cambridge: Cambridge University Press.

Ifrah, A. (1999). *Health Status in Israel*. Jerusalem: Israel Center for Disease Control.

Inalcik, H. (2000). Foundations of Ottoman-Jewish Co-operation. In A. Levy (Ed.) *Jews, Turks, Ottomans*. Syracuse, New York: Syracuse University Press.

Information Service (1948). *Christianity and the Economic Order*. Washington, D. C.: Office of Public Opinion Research.

Irwing, P. and Lynn, R. (2006). The relation between childhood IQ and income in middle age. *Journal of Social, Political and Economic Studies*, 31, 191–196.

Jacobs, J. (1919). *Jewish Contributions to Civilization*. Philadelphia: Jewish Publication Society

Janos, A.C. (1982). *The Politics and Backwardness of Hungary, 1925–1945*. Princeton, New Jeresy: Princeton University Press.

Jencks, Christopher. (1969). Intelligence and race: what color is IQ? *New Republic*, Nos. 10–11, 25–29.

Jencks, C. (1972). *Inequality*. London: Penguin.

Jensen, A.R. (1998). *The g Factor: The Science of Mental Ability*. Westport Connecticut: Praeger.

Johnson, P. (2004 [1988]). *A History of the Jews*. London: Phoenix.

Johnston, H.H. (1930). *A History of the Colonization of Africa by Alien Races*. Cambridge, United Kingdom: Cambridge University Press.

Jones, D.C. and Carr-Saunders, A.M. (1927). The relationship between intelligence and social status among orphan children. *British Journal of Psychology*, 17, 343–364.

Jordan, R.H. (1921). *Nationality and School Progress; A Study in Americanisation*. Bloomington, Ill: Public School Publishing.

Kadushin, C. (1974). *The American Intellectual Elite*. Boston: Little, Brown

Kallen, E. (1976). Family lifestyles and Jewish culture. In K. Ishwaran (Ed) *The Canadian Family*. Toronto: Holt, Rinehart, and Winston.

Kalmijn, M., Liefbroer, A.C., van Poppel, F., and van Solinge, H. (2006). The family factor in Jewish-Gentile intermarriage: a sibling analysis of the Netherlands. *Social Forces*, 84, 1347–1357.

Kamis-Mueller, A. (1992). *Vie Juive en Swisse*. Zurich: Chronos.

Kaniel, S. and Fisherman, S. (1991). Level of performance and distribution of errors in the Progressive Matrices test: a comparison of Ethiopian immigrant and native Israeli adolescents. *International Journal of Psychology*, 26, 25–33.

Karabel, J. (1984). Status group struggle, organizational interests, and the limits of institutional autonomy: the transformation of Harvard, Yale, and Princeton, 1918–1940. *Theory and Society*, 13, 1–40.

Kaufman, A.S. and Doppelt, J.E. (1976). Analysis of WISC-R standardization data in terms of the stratification variables. *Child Development*, 47, 165–171.

Kaufman, A.S. and Kaufman, N.L. (1996). *Kaufman Assessment Battery for Children (K-ABC). Israeli version of interpretive manual*. Jerusalem: Ministry Education, Culture, and Sports.

Kazemipur, A. and Halli, S.S. (2000). *The New Poverty in Canada*. Toronto: Thompson.

Kazemipur, A. and Halli, S.S. (2001). The changing color of poverty in Canada. *Canadian Review of Sociology and Anthropology*, 38, 217–238.

Kazulin, A. (1998). Profiles of immigrant students' cognitive performance on Raven's Progressive Matrices. *Perceptual and Motor Skills*, 87, 1311–1314.

Khvol'son (Chwolson), D. (1874). *The Semitic Nations*, trans E. E. Epstein. Cincinnati: Block.

Klein, A. (2000). Anti-Semitism and anti-somatism: seeking the elusive sporting Jew. *Sociology of Sport Journal*, 17, 213–228.

Kobyliansky, E., Micle, S., Goldschmidt-Nathan, M., Arensburg, B., and Nathan, H. (1982). Jewish populations in the world: genetic likenesses and differences. *Annals of Human Biology*, 9, 1–34.

Kosa, J. (1969). The medical student: his career and religion. *Hospital Progress*, 50, 51–53.

Kosmin, B.A., Goldberg, J., Shain, M., and Bruk, S. (1999). *Jews in the New South Africa*. London: Institute for Jewish Policy Research.

Kosmin, B.A. and Lachman, S.P. (1993). *One Nation under God*. New York: Crown.

Kovas, Y., Harlaar, N., Petrill, S.A., and Plomin, R. (2005). Generalist genes and mathematics in 7-year-old twins. *Intelligence*, 33, 473–489.

Kraus, V. and Hodge, R.W. (1990). *Promises in the Promised Land: Mobility and Inequality in Israel*. New York: Knofp.

Krause, E. (1969). The Edgware survey: occupation and social class. *Jewish Journal of Sociology*, 11, 75–96.

Kugelmass, S., Lieblich, A., and Bossik, D. (1974). Patterns of intellectual ability in Jewish and Arab children in Israel. *Journal of Cross-Cultural Psychology*, 5, 184–198.

Kuran, T. (2003). Why the Middle East is economically underdeveloped: historical mechanisms of institutional stagnation. *Journal of Economic Perspectives*, 18, 71–90.

Kushner, A. (2009). *Anglo-Jewry since 1066*. Manchester: University Press.

Lancer, I. and Rim, Y. (1984). Intelligence, family size and sibling age spacing. *Personality and Individual Differences*, 5, 151–158.

Landau, J.M. (2000). Changing patterns of community structures. In A. Levy (Ed.) *Jews, Turks, Ottomans.* Syracuse, New York: Syracuse University Press.

Lazin, F.A. (2002) Israel and Ethiopian Jewish immigrants. *Society*, 39, 55–62.

Lehman, H.C. (1947). National differences in creativity. *American Journal of Sociology*, 52, 475–488.

Lenski, G. (1963). *The Religious Factor.* New York: Simon and Schuster.

Lenz, F. (1931). The inheritance of Intellectual Gifts. In E. Baur, E. Fischer and F. Lenz (Eds) *Human Heredity.* London: George Allen and Unwin.

Leroy-Beaulieu, A. (1893). *Israel chez les Nations.* Paris: Calmann Levy.

Lesser, G.S., Fifer, G., and Clark, D.H. (1965). Mental abilities of children from different social class and cultural groups. *Monographs of the Society for Research in Child Development*, 30, 4.

Levin, D. (2000). *The Litvaks.* Jerusalem: Yad Vashem.

Levin, M. (1997). *Why Race Matters.* Westport, Connecticut: Praeger.

Levin, T. (1988). Learning processes, teaching and educational attainment in the Israeli education system in eighth grade science. In P. Tamir, T. Levin, A. Lewy, D. Chen, and R. Zuzovsky (Eds.) *Teaching science in Israel in the eighties* (pp. 53–112). Jerusalem, Israel: The Israeli Center of Science Teaching (in Hebrew).

Levinson, B.M. (1957). The intelligence of applicants for admission to Jewish day schools. *Jewish Social Studies*, 19, 129–140.

Levinson, B.M. (1957b). A comparative study of the intelligence of Jewish preschool boys and girls of orthodox parentage. *Journal of Genetic Psychology*, 90, 17–22.

Levinson, B.M. (1958). Cultural pressure and WAIS scatter in a traditional Jewish setting. *Journal of Genetic Psychology*, 93, 277–286.

Levinson, B.M. (1959). A comparison of the performance of bilingual and monolingual native born Jewish preschool children of traditional parentage on four intelligence tests. *Journal of Clinical Psychology*, 15, 74–76.

Levinson, B.M. (1960a). A comparative study of the verbal and performance ability of monolingual and bilingual native born Jewish preschool children of traditional parentage. *Journal of Genetic Psychology*, 97, 93–112.

Levinson, B.M. (1960b). Subcultural variations in verbal and performance ability at the elementary school level. *Journal of Genetic Psychology*, 97, 149–160.

Levinson, B.M. (1962). Jewish subculture and WAIS performance among Jewish aged. *Journal of Genetic Psychology*, 100, 55–68.

Levinson, B.M. and Block, Zelick. (1977). Goodenough-Harris drawings of Jewish children of orthodox background. *Psychological Reports*, 41, 155–158.

Levy, A. (2002). Introduction. In A. Levy (Ed.) *Jews, Turks, Ottomans*. Syracuse, New York: Syracuse University Press.

Lewis, B. (1984). *The Jews of Islam*. Princeton, New Jersey: Princeton University Press.

Lewy, A. and Chen, M. (1976). Closing or widening of the achievement gap: a comparison over time of ethnic group achievement in the Israeli elementary school. *Studies in the Organization and Administration of Education*, 4, 3–52 (in Hebrew).

Lewy, A., Rapaport, H. and Riemer, M. (1978). *Aspects and achievements in the Israeli education system: a comparative international study*. Ramot: Tel Aviv University (in Hebrew).

Lieberson, S. and Carter, D. (1979). Making it in America: differences between eminent blacks and white ethnic groups. *American Sociological Review*, 44, 347–366.

Lieblich, A. (1973). *WPPSI-Wechsler Preschool and Primary Scale of Intelligence*. Jerusalem: Psychological Corporation and Hebrew University.

Lieblich, A. (1983). Intelligence patterns among ethnic and minority groups in Israel. In M. Nisan and U. Last (Eds.) *Between Education and Psychology* (pp. 335–357). Jerusalem: Magnes Press (in Hebrew).

Lieblich, A. (1985). Sex differences in intelligence test performance of Jewish and Arab school children in Israel. In M. Safir, M.T. Mednick, D. Israeli, and J. Bernard (Eds.) *Women's worlds: From the New Scholarship*. New York: Praeger.

Lieblich, A., Ben-Shachar, S., and Ninio, A (1976). WISC-R Hebrew Manual Psychological Corporation and Israeli Ministry of Education (in Hebrew).

Lieblich, A., Ben-Shahar, S. and Ninio, A. (1980). WISC-R Manual for Arabic Examiner (in Arabic). Jerusalem: Psycho-Counselling Services.

Lieblich, A. and Kugelmass, S. (1981). Patterns of intellectual ability of Arab school children in Israel. *Intelligence*, 5, 311–320.

Lieblich, A., Kugelmass, S., and Ehrlich, C. (1975). Patterns of intellectual ability in Jewish and Arab children in Israel. *Journal of Cross-Cultural Psychology*, 6, 218–226.

Lieblich, A., Ninio, A., and Kugelmass, S. (1972). Effects of ethnic origin and parental SES on WPPSI performance of pre-school children in Israel. *Journal of Cross-Cultural Psychology*, 3, 159–168.

Lombroso, C. (1911). *Crime: Its Causes and Remedies*. London: William Heineman.

Luckey, B.M. (1925). Racial differences in mental ability. *Science Monthly*, 20, 245–248.

Lynn, R. (1979). The social ecology of intelligence in the British Isles. *British Journal of Social and Clinical Psychology*, 18, 1–12.

Lynn, R. (1988). Multivariate analyses of the sociology of intelligence. In J. R. Nesselroade and R. B.Cattell (Eds.) *Handbook of Multivariate Experimental Psychology*. New York: Plenum.

Lynn, R. (1994). The intelligence of Ethiopian immigrant and Israeli adolescents. *International Journal of Psychology*, 29, 55–56.

Lynn, R. (1996). *Dysgenics: Genetic Deterioration in Modern Populations*. Westport, Connecticut: Praeger.

Lynn, R. (2004). The intelligence of American Jews. *Personality and Individual Differences*, 36, 201–206.

Lynn, R. (2006). *Race Differences in Intelligence: An Evolutionary Analysis*. Augusta, Georgia: Washington Summit Publishers.

Lynn, R. and Kanazawa, S. (2008). How to explain high Jewish achievement: the role of intelligence and values. *Personality and Individual Differences*, 44, 801–808.

Lynn, R. and Longley, D. (2006). On the high intelligence and cognitive achievements of Jews in Britain. *Intelligence*, 34, 541–548.

Macartney, C. A. (1969). *The Hapsburg Empire, 1790–1918*. New York: Schribner.

MacDonald, K. (1994). *A People That Shall Dwell Alone*. Westport, Connecticut: Praeger.

Mackintosh, N.J. (1998). *IQ and Human Intelligence*. Oxford, United Kingdom: Oxford University Press.

Madood, T. and Berthoud, R. (1997). *Ethnic Minorities in Britain*. London: Policy Studies Institute.

Majoribanks, K. (1972). Ethnic and environmental influences on mental abilities. *American Journal of Sociology*, 78, 323–337.

Maller, J.B. (1933). Economic and social correlatives of school progress in New York City. *Teachers College Record*, 34, 655–670.

Maller, J.B. (1931). Studies in the intelligence of young Jews. *Jewish Education*, 3, 29–39.

Ma'oz, M. (2000). Changing relations between Jews, Muslims and Christians. In A. Levy (Ed.) *Jews, Turks, Ottomans*. Syracuse, New York: Syracuse University Press.

Marsh, M. (1874). Jews and Christians. *The Medical Surgical Reporter*, 30, 343–344.

Martin M.O., Mullis I.V.S., Gonzales E.J., and Chrostowski, S.J. (2004). TIMSS 2003. *International Science Report*. IEA, Boston College.

McDermott, M. (2002). Trends in the race and ethnicity of eminent Americans. *Sociological Forum*, 17, 137–160.

McMullin, J. (2004). *Understanding Social Inequality*. Oxford: Oxford University Press.

Medved, M. (1999). Is Hollywood too Jewish? *Moment* (August), 37, 1–12.

Mendelsohn, E. (1983). *Jews of East Central Europe between the World Wars*. Bloomington: Illinois University Press.

Michaelis, M. (1978). *Mussolini and the Jews*. Oxford: Clarendon.

Mickelson, R.A., Nkomo, M., and Smith, S.S. (2001). Education, ethnicity, gender and social transformation in Israel and South Africa. *Comparative Education Review*, 45, 1–35.

Miner, J.B. (1957). *Intelligence in the United States*. New York: Simon and Schuster.

Minkowitch, A, Davis, D., and Bashi, J. (1982). *Success and failure in Israeli elementary education*. New Brunswick: New Jersey: Translation Books.

Miron, M. (1977). A validation study of a transferred group intelligence test. *International Journal of Psychology*, 12, 193–205.

Montgomery, M.I. (1904). Turkey. *Encyclopedia Judaica*. New York: Funk and Wagnalls.

Mosse, W.E. (1987). *Jews in the German Economic Elite, 1820–1935*. Oxford: Oxford University Press.

Mosse, W.E. (1989). *The German-Jewish Economic Elite, 1820–1935: A Socio-Cultural Profile*. Oxford: Oxford University Press.

Moyles, E.W. and Wolins, M. (1973). Group care and intellectual development. *Developmental Psychology*, 4, 370–380.

Moynihan, D. and Glazer, N. (1970). *Beyond the Melting Pot*. New York: Random House.

Ms, J.R. (1960). Jews: *Encyclopedia Britannica*. Chicago: Benton.

Mullis, I.V.S., Martin, M.O. Gonzales, E.J., and Chrostowski, S. J. (2004). TIMSS 2003. *International Mathematics Report*. IEA, Boston College.

Murdock, K. (1920). A study of race difference in New York. *School and Society*, 11, 147–150.

Murray, C. (2003). *Human Accomplishment*. New York: Harper Collins.

Murray, C. (2007). Jewish genius. *Commentary*

Murphey, R. (2000). Jewish contributions to Ottoman medicine. In A. Levy (Ed.) *Jews, Turks, Ottomans*. Syracuse, New York: Syracuse University Press.

Nakhaie, M.R. (1995). Ownership and management position of Canadian ethnic groups in 1973 and 1989. *Canadian Journal of Sociology*, 20, 167–192.

Napier, L.B. (1934). Introduction. In A. Ruppin (Ed.) *The Jews in the Modern World*. London: Macmillan.

Nardi, N. (1948). Studies in the Intelligence of Jewish children. *Jewish Education*, 19, 41–45.

Neisser, U., et al. (1996). *Intelligence: Knowns and Unknowns*. Washington, D. C.: American Psychological Association.

Nemeck, O. (1916). Zur psychologie christlicher u judischer schuler. *Beitrage zur Kinderforschung*, 128, 1–24.

Neubauer, A., Grabner, R. H., and Stern, W. (2006). How much g is needed to play chess successfully? *Proceedings of the 7th Annual Conference of the International Society for Intelligence Research.*

Neuman, S. (1998). Occupational segregation in the Israeli labor market. *International Journal of Manpower*, 19, 571–591.

O'Grada, C. (2006). *Jewish Ireland in the Age of Joyce*. Princeton, New Jersey: Princeton University Press.

O'Grada, C. (2006a). *Dublin Jewish demography a century ago*. Dublin: UCD School of economics.

Ones, D.Z., Viswesvaran, C., and Dilchert, S. (2005). Cognitive ability in selective decisions. In O. Wilhelm and R. Engle (Eds.) *Handbook of Understanding and Measuring Intelligence*. London: Thousand Oaks.

Ortar, Gina R. (1967). Educational achievements of primary school graduates in Israel as related to their socioeconomic status. *Comparative Education*, 4, 23–34.

Ortar, G., Hagari, A., and Kartoni-Manor, H. (1966). *Milta Intelligence Test*. Jerusalem: The Hebrew University (in Hebrew).

Patai, R. (1977). *Journey into the Jewish Mind*. New York: Schribner.

Patai, R. and Patai, J. (1989). *The Myth of the Jewish Race*. Wayne University Press, Detroit.

Pearson, K/ and Moul, M. (1927). The problem of alien immigration into Britain, illustrated by an examination of Russian and Polish Jewish children. *Annals of Eugenics*, 2, 111–244.

Pintner, R. (1931). *Intelligence Testing*. New York: Holt, Rinehart and Winston.

Pintner, R. and Artensian, S. (1937). The relation of bilingualism to verbal intelligence and school adjustment. *Journal of Educational Research*, 31, 255–263.

Pintner, R. and Keller, R. (1922). Intelligence tests of foreign children. *Journal of Educational Psychology*, 13, 214–222.

Pintner, R. and Maller, J. B. (1937). Month of birth and average intelligence among different ethnic groups. *Journal of Genetic Psychology*, 50, 91–107.

Plomin, R. (1994). *Genetics and experience: The interplay between nature and nurture*. Thousand Oaks, California: Sage.

Pollack, S. (1993). Epidemiological and immunological study of HIV-seropositive Ethiopian immigrants in Israel. *Israeli Journal of Medical Sciences*, 29, 19–23.

Porter, J. (1965). *The Vertical Mosaic*. Toronto: University of Toronto Press.

Post, Rchard H. (1962). Population differences in visual acuity. *Social Biology*, 9, 189–212.

Prais, S.J. and Schmool, M. (1975). The social class structure of Anglo-Jewry 1961. *Jewish Journal of Sociology*, 17, 5–15.

Preston, Samuel H., Ewbank, D, and Hereward, M. (1994). Child mortality differences by ethnicity and race in the United States. In S. C. Watkins (Ed.) *After Ellis Island: Newcomers and Natives in the 1910 Census*. New York: Russell Sage.

Raviv, A., Margalith, M., Raviv, A., and Sade, F. (1981). The cognitive patterns of Israeli learning disabled children as reflected in the Hebrew version of the WISC-R. *Journal of Learning Disabilities*, 14, 411–415.

Raviv, A. (1989). School psychology in Israel. In P. A. Saigh and T. Oakland (Eds.) *International perspectives on psychology in the schools* (pp. 11–124). Hillsdale, New Jersey: Lawrence Erlbaum Associates.

Riess, S. (1998). *Sports and the American Jew*. Syracuse, New York: Syracuse University Press.

Rim, Y. (1983). Eye-color, ethnic origin or family size? *Personality and Individual Differences*, 4, 101–102.

Roberts, J.M. (1996). *A History of Europe*. Oxford: Helicon.

Romanoff, J.S. (1976). *Birth order, family size, and sibling spacing as influences on intelligence and academic abilities of Jewish adolescents*. Ph. D. Thesis, Temple University.

Roof, W.C. (1979). Socioeconomic differentials among socioreligious groups in the United States. *Social Forces*, 58, 281–289.

Roth, C. (1946). *A History of the Jews of Italy*. Farnborough, United Kingdom: Gregg.

Rosen, B. C. (1959). Race, ethnicity and the achievement syndrome. *American Brain Sciences*, 12, 503–559.

Rowe, D.C. (1994). *The Limits of Family Influence*. New York: Guilford Press.

Rubinstein, W.D. (1987), *Jews in the Sixth Continent*. Sydney: Allen and Unwin.

Rubinstein, W.D. (1993). Genes and genius. *Generation*, 3, 12–24.

Rubinstein, W.D. (2000). Jews in the economic elites of western Nations and anti-Semitism. *Jewish Journal of Sociology*, 42, 5–32.

Rubinstein, W.D. (2004). Jews in grandmaster chess. *Jewish Journal of Sociology*, 46, 35–44.

Rushton, J.P. (1989). Genetic similarity, human altruism, and group selection. *Behavioral Brain Sciences*, 12, 503–559.

Rushton, J.P. (1997). Race, intelligence, and the brain: the errors and omissions of the "revised" edition of S. Gould's The Mismeasure of Man (1996). *Personality and Individual Differences*, 23, 169–180.

Russell, B. (1945). *A History of Western Philosophy*. New York: Simon and Schuster.

Russell, C. and Lewis, H.S. (1900). *The Jew in London*. London: Harper Collins.

Rutland, S.D. (1988). *Edge of the Diaspora: Two Centuries of Jewish Settlement in Australia*. Sydney: William Collins.

Rutland, S.D. (2005). *The Jews in Australia*. Cambridge: Cambridge University Press

Sachar, H.M. (1992). *A History of Jews in America*. New York: Alfred Knopf.

Safir, M. P. (1986). The effects of nature or of nurture on sex differences in intellectual functioning. *Sex Roles*, 14, 581–590.

Sachs, L. and Bat-Miriam, M. (1957). The genetics of Jewish populations: 1. Finger print patterns in Jewish populations in Israel. *American Journal of Human Genetics*, 9, 117–126.

Sacks, M.P. (1998). Privilege and prejudice: the occupations of Jews in Russia in 1989. *Slavic Review*, 57, 247–266.

Samuelson, F. (1982). H.H. Goddard and the IQ of immigrants. *American Psychologist*, 37, 1291–1292.

Sarason, S.B. (1973). Jewishness, blackishness, and the nature-nurture controversy. *American Psychologist*, 28, 962–971.

Sarton, G. (1948). *Introduction to the History of Science.* Washington, D. C.: Carnegie Institute.

Savage, S.W. (1946). Intelligence and infant mortality in problem families. *British Medical Journal*, 19, Jan., 86–87.

Sarfatti, M. (2006). *The Jews in Mussolini's Italy.* Madison, Wisconsin: University of Wisconsin Press.

Scarr, S. (1995). Inheritance, intelligence and achievement. *Planning for Higher Education*, 23, 1–9.

Schellekens, J. and van Poppel, F. (2006). Religious differentials in marital fertility in The Hague, 1860–1909. *Population Studies*, 60, 23–38.

Schmelz, U.O. (1971). *Infant and Early Childhood Mortality among the Jews of the Diaspora.* Jerusalem: Institute of Contemporary Jewry, Hebrew University.

Schmelz, U.O. and Della Pergola, Sergio (1985). The demography of Latin American Jewry. *American Jewish Yearbook,* 85, 51–104.

Schmelz, U.O., Della Pergola, Sergio, and Avner, Uri (1990). Ethnic differences among Israeli Jews. *American Jewish Yearbook*, 90, 3–206.

Schmool, M. and Cohen, F. (1998). *Profile of British Jewry.* London: Board of Deputies of British Jews.

Seago, D.W. and Koldin, T.S. (1925). A comparative study of the mental capacity of sixth grade Jewish and Italian children. *School and Society*, 22, 564–568.

Seligman, D. (1992). *A Question of Intelligence.* York: Carol.

Shavit, Y., Cohen, Y., Stier, H., and Bolotin, S. (1999). Ethnic inequality in university education in Israel. *Jewish Journal of Sociology*, 41, 5–21.

Sheldon, P.M. (1954). The families of highly gifted children. *Marriage and Family Living*, 16, 59–61.

Shuey, A.M. (1942). Differences in performance of Jewish and non-Jewish students on the American Council Psychological Examination. *Journal of Social Psychology*, 15, 221–243.

Silbiger, S. (2000). *The Jewish Phenomenon: Seven Keys to the Enduring Wealth of a People*. Atlanta, Georgia: Longstreet Press.

Silvera, A. (1995). North African Jewry. In D. Chirot and A. Reid (Eds.) *Essential Outsiders*. Seattle: University of Washington Press.

Slezkine, Y. (2004). *The Jewish Century*. Princeton, New Jersey: Princeton University Press.

Sm, K. (1960). *Lithuania*. Chicago: Encyclopedia Britannica.

Smilansky, S. (1957). Evaluation of early education. In M. Smilansky and L. Adar (Eds.) *Educational Achievements*. Israel: Henrietta Szold Institute.

Smilansky, S. and Shephatia, L. (1977). Connection between integration and other classroom variables and achievements in grade 1 and 2. *Megamot*, 23, 79–87 (in Hebrew).

Smilansky, S., Shephatia, L., and Frenkel, E. (1976). *Mental development of infants from two ethnic groups*. Jerusalem: National Institute for Research in the Behavioral Sciences.

Smilansky, M. and Yam, Y. (1969). The relationship between family size, ethnic origin, father's education and students' achievements. *Megamot* 16, 243–273 (in Hebrew).

Smith, M. (1958). *History of Mathematics*. London: McMillan.

Sombart, W. (1919). *Die Deutsche Volkswirtschaft im neunzehnten Jahrhundert*. Berlin: Springer.

Sorsby, A. (1951). *Genetics in Ophthalmology*. London: Butterworth.

Solomon, E.S. (1956). Social characteristics and fertility. *Eugenics Quarterly*, 3, 100–103.

Sourasky, A. (1928). Race, sex, and environment in the development of myopia. *British Journal of Opthalmology*, 12, 17–212.

Steinberg, S. (1974). *The Academic Melting Pot: Catholics and Jews in American Higher Education*. New York: McGrew-Hill.

Steinberg, S. (1981). *The Ethnic Myth: Race, Ethnicity, and Class in America*. Boston: Beacon Press.

Sternberg, R.J. (Ed.) (2000). *Handbook of Intelligence*. Cambridge, United Kingdom: Cambridge University Press.

Stille, A. (2005). The double bind of Italian Jews. In Zimmerman, J. D. (Ed.): *Jews in Italy under Fascist and Nazi Rule, 1922–1945*. Cambridge: Cambridge University Press.

Storfer, M.D. (1990). *Intelligence and Giftedness*. Jossey-Bass, San Francisco.

Sward, K.T. (1933). Jewish musicality in America. *Journal of Applied Psychology*, 17, 675–712.

Sweetman, A.G. and Dicks, G. (2000). Education and Ethnicity in Canada. *Journal of Human Resources*, 34, 668–696

Szeinberg, A. (1963). G6PD deficiency among Jews: genetic and anthropological considerations. In E. Goldschmidt (Ed.) *Genetics of Migrant and Isolated Populations*. New York: Williams and Wilkins.

Terman, L.M. (1925). *Genetic Studies of genius. Vol. 1. Mental and Physical Traits of a Thousand Gifted Children*. Stanford, California: Stanford University Press.

Tolts, M. (2003). *Mixed marriage and post-Soviet Aliya*. Unpublished.

Torczyner, J.L. and Brotman, S.C. (1995). The Jews of Canada. *American Jewish Yearbook*, 95, 227–260.

Tropp, A. (1991). *Jews in the Professions in Great Britain, 1981–1991*. London: Maccabeans.

Twain, M. (1985). *Concerning the Jews*. Philadelphia: Running Press.

Tzuriel, D. and Caspi, N. (1992). Cognitive modifiability and cognitive performance of deaf and hearing preschool children. *Journal of Special Education*, 26, 235–252.

Van Solinge, H. and van Imhoff, E. (2001). Social-demographic profile. In: H. van Solinge and M. de Vries (Eds.) *De joden in Nederland anno 2000*. Amsterdam: Aksant.

Veblen, T. (1919). The intellectual pre-eminence of the Jews in Modern Europe. *Political Science Quarterly*, 34, 33–42.

Vernon, P.E. (1951). Recent investigations of intelligence and its measurement. *Eugenics Review*, 43, 125–137.

Vincent, P. (1966). The measured intelligence of Glasgow Jewish schoolchildren. *Jewish Journal of Sociology*, 8, 92–108.

Vital, D. (1999). *A People Apart: The Jews in Europe, 1789–1939.* Oxford: Oxford University Press.

Von Hentig, H. (1948). *The Criminal and His Victim.* New Haven: Yale University Press.

Waterman, S. and Kosmin, B.A. (1986). *British Jewry in the Eighties.* London: Board of British Deputies.

Weinryb, B.D. (1972). *The Jews of Poland from 1100 to 1800.* Philadelphia: Jewish Publication Society of America.

Wendt, R.A. and Burwell, E.. (1964). Test performance of Jewish day school students. *Journal of Genetic Psychology,* 105, 99–103.

Werner, P. (2003). Knowledge and correlates of osteoporosis: a comparison of Israeli-Jewish and Israeli-Arab women. *Journal of Women and Aging,* 15, 33–49.

Wertheimer, J. (2005). Jews and the Jewish birthrate. *Commentary,* 120, 39–44.

Weyl, N.. (1966). *The Creative Elite in America.* Washington, D. C.: Public Affairs Press.

Weyl, N. (1969). Some comparative performance indexes of American ethnic minorities. *Mankind Quarterly,* 9, 106–128.

Weyl, N. (1989). *The Geography of American Achievement.* Washington, D. C.: Scott Townsend.

Weyl, N. and Possony, Stefan. (1963). *The Geography of Intellect.* Chicago: Henry Regnery.

Wilder, E. (2000). Contraceptive use at first intercourse among Jewish women in Israel. *Population Research and Policy Review,* 19, 113–141.

Wilson, J.Q. and Herrnstein, R. J. (1985). *Crime and Human Nature.* New York: Simon and Schuster.

Yaish, M. (2001). Class structure in a deeply divided society: class and ethnic inequality in contemporary Israel. *British Journal of Sociology,* 52, 409–440.

Yisraeli, E. (1998). *Ethnic representation in universities.* Jerusalem: Mashov.

Zavodny, M. (2003). Race, wages, and assimilation among Cuban immigrants. *Population Research and Immigrant Review,* 22, 201–219.

Zaridze, D.G., Boyle, P., and Smans, M. (1984). International trends in prostatic cancer. *International Journal of Cancer,* 33, 223–230.

Zeidner, M. (1987a). Gender and culture interaction effects on scholastic aptitude test performance: some Israeli findings. *International Journal of Psychology,* 22, 111–119.

Zeidner, M. (1987b). Test of the cultural bias hypothesis: some Israeli findings. *Journal of Applied Psychology,* 72, 38-48.

Zeidner, M. (1987c). Validity of college admission indices for Jews and Arabs in Israel. *Personality and Individual Differences,* 8, 587–588.

Zimmerman, J.D. (2005). *Jews in Italy under Fascist and Nazi Rule, 1922–1945.* Cambridge: Cambridge University Press.

Zoossmann-Diskin, A., Ticher, A., Hakim, I., Goldwitch, Z., Rubinstein, A., Davis, J.A., and Smith, T.W. (1996). *General Social Survey.* Storrs, Connecticut: Roper Public Opinion Research Center.

Zuckerman, H. (1977). *Scientific Elite: Nobel Laureates in the United States.* New York: Simon and Schuster.

Zuzovsky, R. (1987). *Science attainment in the Israeli elementary school.* Ph. D. dissertation. The Hebrew University, Jerusalem (in Hebrew).

Index

A

Abbasid dynasty 22
ABC (American Broadcasting Company) 307
Abrikosov, Alexei 230
academia. *See* education
Achievement Quotients, Jewish 6–10, 36, 37, 42, 45, 46, 48, 53, 67, 81, 83, 84, 85, 86, 89, 107, 114, 125, 127, 128, 144, 146, 157, 189, 200, 209, 230, 231, 242, 251, 265, 289, 293, 294–300, 321, 343
Adam, Adolphe 124
Agursky, Mikhail 227
Albu, Sir George 238
Alekhine, Alexander 66
Alexander II, Tsar 220
Alferov, Zhores 230
alleles 336–337
Allende, Salvador 197
Allen, Woody 305
American Jewish Yearbook 42, 63, 238, 260
American National Opinion Research Center 345
American Psychological Association 18, 351
Amsterdam, Jews in 65
A. M. Turing Awards 2
ancient Greeks 6, 8
ancient world, Jews in the 6, 22, 181, 253, 336
Anglo-American Corporation of South Africa 238
anti-Semitism 354, 355. *See also* discrimination, anti-Jewish; *See also* persecution, anti-Jewish
anti-Semitic violence 23, 206, 208–210, 213, 220, 245, 246–247, 254, 262, 329. *See also* pogroms
  in Britain and Ireland 92
  in Central and Eastern Europe 35, 49, 51, 206–208
  in France 121, 122
  in Germany 15, 62, 132, 330
  in Italy 183, 185
  in Latin America 193, 199
  in Romania 262
  in Russia 224, 226
  in Switzerland 249
  in the Ivy League 284
  in the Ottoman Empire 23
  in the United States 285
  in Yugoslavia 264
  National Socialist 62, 208, 249, 260
Antokolsky, Mark 218
Antonescu, Ion 263
Antwerp, Belgium 58, 59, 61
Applebaum, Anne 303
Arabs
  in Israel 152, 160–166, 357–358. *See also* socioeconomic status
  intelligence 152–153
  Jews under Arab rule 22
Arber, Werner 250
Argentina, Jews in 192–194
  population estimates 193
Aristotle 8, 24
Aron, Raymond 124
Aryans (Northern Europeans) 3, 121, 187
Ashkenazim. *See* Jews
Ashkenazi, Szymon 207
Ashley, Lord (Anthony Ashley Cooper) 3
Asser, Tobias 67
assimilation, into Gentile society 61, 112, 133, 135, 141, 184–186, 192, 224, 234
  Jewish resistance to assimilation 354
Atlantic Monthly, The 308

Attali, Jacques 124
attitude towards Jews (Gentile) 233
Australia, Jews in 33–40
Austria, Jews in 42–45

B

Babylon 22. *See also* ancient world, Jews in the
Backman, Margaret 281
Baghdad, Jews in 22
Bailey, Pearce 279
Baker, Benny 305
Bakst, Leon 217
Balfour, Arthur 150
Balfour Declaration, the 150
Balkans, the
   Jews in 253–270
Bamberger family (France) 120
banking, Jews in 13
   in Benelux 59
   in Central Europe 49
   in France 120
   in Germany 135, 136
   in Italy 185, 186
   in Latin America 196
   in Poland 205
   in Russia 220
   in Switzerland 250, 251
   in the Austro-Hungarian Empire 42, 43, 49
   in the Middle East 319
Barnes, Binnie 305
Barron, Clarence 308
basketball, Jews in 309
Basov, Nicolay G. 230
Basser, Sir Adolph 34
Bat-Miriam, M. 26
Becker, Ernest 303
Becker, Gary 14, 342, 351
Beers family (Germany) 135
Beit, Alfred 238
Bell Curve, The 278, 353. *See also* Murray, Charles; *See also* Herrnstein, Richard
Benelux, Jews in 57–70
   population estimates 62

Benny, Jack 305
Berezovsky, Boris 233
Bergson, Henri 125
Berhanu, Girma 172
Berlin, Irving 303
Bernal, Maestre 191
Bernhardt, Sarah 120
Bernstein, Leonard 304
Berry, Colin 8, 320
birthrates, Jewish. *See* fertility, Jewish
Birt, John 87
Bischoffsheim family (France) 120
Bishr, Sahl ibn 319
Bismarck, Otto von 132, 134
Bix, Herbert 303
Bizet, Georges 120
Black Death, the. *See* bubonic plague
Blacks, in America 13, 353
Bleustein, Marcel 124
Bloch, Felix 250
"blood libel" accusations 245, 246
Blum, Léon 120, 123
Boas family (The Netherlands) 60
Boas, Franz 218
Bohr, Aage Neils 113, 114
Bohr, Niels 113
Bolshevik Revolution 218, 221, 250
Bolshevik Party, the 221
Borge, Victor 112, 306
Bosnia-Hertzegovina 255, 259
Boston Globe 308
Botvinnik, Mikhail 2
Boublil, Alain 124
Bourgain, Jean 67
Bovet, Daniel 250
boxing, Jews in 309
Brazile, Jews in 195–197
   population estimates 195–196
Brenner, Sydney 242
bridge, Jews in 2
   in Britain 88
   in France 128
   in the United States 301–302
Brigham, Carl 273
Britain, Jews in 71–96
   population estimates 73–75
British Academy 85–86
British Chess Federation 88

Brodsky, Joseph 230
Bromberg, Edward 306
Brookdale Institute 169
Brook, Peter 87
Brook, Stephen 73
Brown, Herbert 89
Brown University. *See* Ivy League, Jews in the
bubonic plague, the 58, 119, 132, 245
Bulgaria
　Jews in 259–261
　population estimates 260
Bunin, Ivan 230
bureacracy, Jews in. *See* civil administration, Jews in
Burns, George 305
Burnstein, Paul 17
Byzantium. *See* Roman Empire

C

Canada, Jews in 97–110
　population estimates 98
Canetti, Elias 124, 265
Canetti, Jacques 124
Carasso, Isaac and Daniel 124
Caribbean, Jews in the 60, 61
Caro, Heinrich 135
Carol, Sue 305
Cassin, René 124
Castro, Isaac de 195
Catholic Church 182, 183, 329
CBS (Columbia Broadcasting System) 307
Ceausescu, Nicolae 263
celibacy, Catholic 327–328
Central Europe, Jews in 41–56
Central Intelligence Agency 358
Cervantes, Miguel de 319
Chagall, Marc 217, 321
Chamberlain, Houston Stewart 13, 14
Charlemagne 25, 117–118, 131
Charles V 58
Charpak, Georges 207, 209
Chávez, Hugo 199

Cheka, the (Soviet Union) 221
Chemistry, Jews in. *See* Nobel Prize winners, Royal Society
Cherenkov, Pavel 230
chess, Jews in 2, 16–17, 318
　in Benelux 66
　in Britain 87
　in Central Europe 45, 53, 208, 210
　in Germany 143
　in Russia 228–229
　in the Balkans 266
　in the United States 300
Chile, Jews in 196–197
Chiswick, Barry 290, 291, 310, 342, 351
Christopher Jencks 5
Citroën, André 124
civil administration, Jews in 122, 187
Classical music, Jews in 304
Cochran, Gregory 322, 331–333, 337–339, 351
Coetzee, J. M. 242
Cohen family (Australia) 33
Cohen family (London) 73
Cohen, Irma 279
Cohen-Tannoudji, Claude 125
Cohn-Bendit, Daniel 124
Coles, Robert 303
Columbia University 187. *See see* Ivy League
Columbus, Christopher 191
Commentary (journal) 6, 308
Conquering Jew, The 3
Constantine, Emperor 253
Constantinople, Byzantium 253, 254, 257
conversion, religious 335. *See also* Apostasy Hypothesis
　to Christianity 254
　in Italy 184
　in Latin America 191–192, 195
　in Spain 24, 191
　to Judaism 28, 167
Conversos. *See* conversion
Copland, Aaron 304
Cormack, Allan 242
Cortez, Hernando 197

Cossacks 329
"Court Jews" 132, 133
crime, Jews in 64, 138, 171, 311–312
Cromwell, Oliver 72
Crusades, the 72, 118, 132, 203, 354
crypto-Jews 191, 195, 254
Cullen, Paul 33
Curtis, Tony 306

D

da Costa family (Germany) 132
Dagobert, King of the Franks 25, 117
Darity, William et al. 287
Dark Ages 10
Dar, Y. 157
Dassault, Marcel 124
David, Hanna 163
Davis, David Brion 303
Davis, Martin S. 307
Debré, Michel 123
Deligne, Pierre 67
De Pass brothers (South Africa) 237
Derrida, Jacques 124
Deutsch family (France) 120
Diamond, Jared 303
diamond trade
    importation 60, 61
    mining in South Africa 238
diasporas, Jewish 22
Diller, Barry 307
Discount Bank & Trust Company 251
discrimination, anti-Jewish 354
    in Britain 72
    in Central Europe 51, 206–207
    in Denmark 111
    in France 118–119, 123
    in Germany 132, 133, 143
    in Italy 183, 185, 187
    in Latin America 193
    in Romania 263
    in Russia 214, 220
    in th Soviet Union 225
Disraeli, Benjamin 72, 319
Distel, Sacha 124
Douglas, Melvyn 305

Dreifuss, Ruth 251
Dresdner-Kleinworts 318
Dreyfus Affair, the 122
Dreyfus, Alfred. *See* Dreyfus Affair, the
Dreyfus Bank (Basel, Switzerland) 251
Drumont, Édouard 121
Dublin, Ireland 91, 93
Durant, Ariel 303
Duras, Oldrich 46
Durbin, Deanna 306
Durkheim, Emile 120
Dutch East India Company 59, 237
Dylan, Bob 303

E

Ecole Polytechnique 121
Edirne (Adrianople), Balkans 254, 255, 256, 264
education
  higher education, Jews in
    in Benelux 60, 65, 66
    in Britain 84–85
    in Canada 101–102
    in Central Europe 42, 46, 48
    in Denmark 112
    in France 119
    in Israel 163–164
    in Italy 185, 187
    in Russia 216, 223
  Jewish achievement in
    in Australia 36
    in Britain 78–79
    in Canada 99–102
    in Israel 157–158, 161–164, 169–170
    in Latin America 193
    in Russia 216, 218
    in South Africa 239
    in the United States 285
  Jewish valuing of 14, 66, 326, 342
Edward I, King 72
Eichmann, Adolf 193
Eilenberg, Samuel 209
Einstein, Albert 135, 250, 296
Eisner, Michael D. 307

Index 393

elites, Jewish. *See also* "significant figures"
  academic 294
  economic/business 36, 49–50, 80–81, 139–140, 141, 233, 287, 293
  in Australia 37
  in Britain 86–87
  in Central Europe 48, 207
  in Germany 135–137, 139–140, 141
  in Latin America 197, 198
  in South Africa 238
  in Spain 24
  in the Soviet Union 13, 221, 224–225, 226
  in the United States 287, 292–296
  media 308
  professional 223, 225, 228, 232
Ellis Island 273. *See also* immigration
emancipation, Jewish 10
  in Austria 42
  in Benelux 60, 61
  in Bulgaria 262
  in Denmark 111
  in France 119
  in Germany 133, 134
  in Italy 182–183
  in Latin America 193–192, 195
  in Poland 205
  in Switzerland 247, 248
emigration, Jewish
  from Central and Eastern Europe 25, 35, 36–37, 61, 63, 72, 73, 91, 97, 104, 108, 111, 112, 150, 151–152, 192, 193–194, 199, 203, 204, 209, 210, 261, 263, 265
  from Ethiopia 152
  from France 192
  from Germany 132, 150, 197, 199
  from Hungary 254, 305
  from Israel 63
  from Latin America 195, 196
  from National Socialist Germany 119–120, 199
  from North Africa 123
  from Portugal 58, 97, 119, 182
  from Russia 61, 91, 97, 108, 112, 119–120, 134, 150, 193–194, 216, 232, 272, 283, 288
  from South Africa 35, 238
  from Spain 24, 97, 182
  from the Middle East 35, 123, 151–152, 193
  from the Near East 35
  from the Soviet Union 151, 227
  from Western Europe 203
eminence, Jewish. *See* elites, Jewish
Emmanuel III, King Victor 184
Englander, Martin 141
Ephtussi family (France) 120
Erikson, Erik 303
Ernst, Richard 250
Ethiopian Jews. *See* Jews
Euclid 8
eugenics 325–328, 352–353
Euwe, Max 66
expulsion of Jews 25, 329
  from Benelux 58
  from Central Europe 41
  from England 25, 57, 72, 204
  from France 25, 119, 123, 204, 213, 254, 256
  from German states 25, 132, 204, 213
  from Hungary 41, 254, 255
  from Italy and Italian cities 181–182, 188
  from Palestine 149
  from Portugal 24, 58, 72, 151, 254, 266
  from Spain 24, 72, 151, 191, 195, 254, 266
  from Switzerland 245, 246–247
Eysenck, Hans 5
Ezra, Abraham ben 318

F

Fabius, Laurent 123
Fairbanks, Douglas 306
Falashas. *See* Ethiopian Jews
Falk, Gerhard 136
family, Jewish the 13
Farron, Steven 284
Fejgin, Naomi 349
Ferdinand II of Aragon 191

Fermi, Enrico 187
fertility, Jewish 356
  in Benelux 67
  in Canada 107
  in Germany 134
  in Israel 173–174, 357
  in Italy 183, 188
  in Latin America 194
  in South Africa 242
  in the Balkans 267
  in the United States 273, 310–311
Fields Medalist, Jewish
  in Britain 91
  in France 126–127
  in Germany 146
  in Russia 230
Fine, Reuben 301
fingerprint (whorl) analysis 26
Fisberg, M. 28
Fischer, Bobby 2, 301
Fischer, Edmond 250
Flohr, Solomon 46
"Flynn Effect". *See* intelligence
Flynn, James 348
Forbes 308
Ford, Henry 309
Foster, Norman 87
"Fortune 400" richest Americans 287
Fox Pictures 306
Fox, William 305
France, Jews in 117–127
  population estimates 119–120
Frankfurt, Jews in 132
Frank, Il´ja M. 230
Fraser, John 3
Fridman, Mikhail 233
Friedlander, Saul 303
Friedman, Steve 307
Frydman, Marcel 17

G

Galton, Francis 3
Gama, Gaspar da 195
Gamala, Joshua ben 335
Garfield, John 306
Garland, Judy 306
Gaucher disease 337
Gelfand, Izrail 226
General Electric Co. 306
General Mental Ability. *See* intelligence
General Social Survey 278, 286, 345–347
genetic affinity of Jewish peoples.
  See Jews
genetic drift 27
genetic mutations 27, 337–340
genetic profile of Jews. *See* Jews
Genetic Similarity Theory 257
genetic studies of Jews 26
  mitochondrial DNA analysis 29
  Y-chromosome analysis 29
German Jews. *See* Jews and Germany
Germany, Jews in 131–148
  population estimates 133–134
Gershwin, George 304
Gessen brothers (Russia) 214
ghettos and ghettoization, Jewish
  in Germany 132
  in Italy 181–183
  in Switzerland 246
Gintsburg family (Russia) 214
Ginzburg, Vitaly L. 230
Girodias, Maurice 124
Glazer, Nathan 16
Gnesin family (Russia) 217
Gobineau, Joseph Arthur Comte de 3, 121
Goddard, Henry Herbert 273
Godley, A. 17
Goldman-Sachs 318
Goldscheider, Calvin 311
Goldschmidt family (Germany) 135
Goldsmid family (London) 73
Gompertz family (The Netherlands) 60

Gorbachev, Mikhail 232
Gordimer, Nadine 242
Gorky, Maxim 215
Gould, Stephen Jay 273
Graham, David 79
Great Council of Helvetia 247
Great Terror, The. *See* purges in the Soviet Union
Greece, Jews in 261
Grey, Brad 306
Guggenheim, Meyer 248
Guide to the Perplexed 24
Guillaume, Charles 250
gulags, Soviet 224
Gusinsky, Vladimir 233

H

Haber, Fitz 135
Hammer, M.F. 27, 28–30
Hamon, Moses 256
Hardy, Jason 322, 331–333, 337–339, 351
Harpending, Henry 322, 331–333, 337–339, 351
Harris, Sir David 238
Harvard University. *See* Ivy League
Hassidic Jews 205, 358
Hayek, Friedrich von 44
Heifetz, Jascha 304
Heine family (France) 120
Heine, Heinrich 135
Heisenberg, Werner 113
Henry II, King (France) 119
Hentig, Hans von 311
heraldry 86–87, 135–136
Hereditary Genius 3
Herrnstein, Richard 5, 54, 278, 351, 352, 353
Herschel, Sir William 72
Herzog, Chaim 92
Herzog, Emile 120
Hess, Walter 250
Hevesy, Georg von 52
Himmler, Heinrich 188

Hirsch family (France) 120
Hirsch family (Germany) 135
Hitler, Adolf 143
Hobsbawm, Eric 87
Hobson, J. A. 238
Hoffman, Dustin 306
Hoffman, Roald 209
Hofstadter, Richard Pu
Hofstatder, Douglas 303
Holiday, Judy 306
Hollinger, David 15
Hollywood, Jews in 305–306
Holocaust, the 35, 42, 53, 62, 134, 143, 151, 188, 207, 208, 209, 210, 249, 260, 265, 272
  compensation for victims 249
Holy Roman Empire 246
Horowitz, Vladimir 304
Horthy, Miklós 49, 51
Hsu, Francis 348
Hungary, Jews in 46–51
Hunter College, Jews in 284
Hurwicz, Leonid 230
Hutchins, Stilson 308

I

Iger, Robert 306
immigration, Jewish
  into Australia 25, 33, 35
  into Benelux 24, 63, 204, 254
  into Britain 25, 73
  into Canada 25, 97, 104, 108
  into Denmark 112
  into Eastern Europe 25
  into England 61, 72
  into France 24, 119–120, 123, 126
  into Germany 58, 134
  into Ireland 91
  into Israel 24, 25, 150, 151–152, 196, 216, 227, 261, 263, 265. *See also* Zionism
  of Ethiopian Jews 26, 152
  into Italy 24, 182
  into Latin America 192, 193, 197, 199

into North Africa 24, 266
into Palestine 150, 207
into Poland 203, 210
into South Africa 25, 238, 239
   1930 Quota Act 238
into South America 25
into Switzerland 247
   flight from National Socialist Germany 249
into the Balkans 24
into the United States 25, 227–228, 232, 272, 283, 288, 305
into Turkey 264
infant mortality, among Jews
  in Austria-Hungary 54
  in Benelux 67
  in Britain 75
  in Canada 108–110
  in Germany 138
  in Ireland 93
  in Israel 174
  in Italy 189
  in Poland 205
  in Russia 220
  in the Balkans 259
  in the United States 310
Inquisition, the 58, 119, 183, 192, 195, 198, 254
Institute of Literature of the Academy of Sciences 224
intelligence
  Ashkenazi superior intelligence 29, 153–156, 157–164, 175–178, 316, 341
  definition of intelligence 18
  denial of Jewish intelligence in scholarship 351–353
  determinant of success 18
  evidence for heritability 159–160
  "Flynn Effect" 98, 274, 277
  general intelligence 18
  genetic basis 321–325, 336–338
  intelligence testing 141, 276–281
    Armed Forces Qualification Test 5, 278
    Army Alpha test 276
    Binet test 273
    British National Cohort Study 77
    College Entrance Examination Board 283
    Colored Progressive Matrices 168
    Dominos Test 156
    Key Stage 2 test 78
    Milta test 153
    Mory House Test 76
    National Intelligence Test 276
    Northumberland Test 75
    Otis Test 277
    Pintner-Cunningham Primary Mental Test 276
    Project Talent 281
    Standard Progressive Matrices 168
    Stanford-Binet Intelligence Scales 274, 277
    Third International Mathematics and Science Study 160
    Wechsler Adult Intelligence Scale (WAIS) 274, 280
    Wechsler Intelligence Scale for Children (WISC) 98, 152, 153, 160
    Wechsler Preschool and Primary Test (WPPSI) 153
IQ
  correlation between IQ and income 5
  "Greenwich standard" IQ 29, 168, 175, 274, 276, 280, 316
  of Ashkenazim 29
  of Ethiopian Jews 29, 167–168
  of Jews in Australia 39
  of Jews in Britain 75–77
  of Jews in Canada 98–99
  of Jews in Israel 152–157, 175–176, 267
  of Jews in the United States 273–280
  of Mizrahim 29
  of Northern European Whites 29
  of Sephardim 29, 266
  of Turks 255
Jewish intelligence in literature 3–4, 139, 283
mental retardation 279
  of Jews in the United States 273–280

of Mizrahim (Oriental) Jews 153–156
theories of Jewish intelligence
315–340
  Apostast Hypothesis 335–336
  environmentalism 322–325
  Eugenic Hypothesis 325–328
  genotype-environment co-variation
    324
  Miscegenation Hypothesis 334–336
  Persecution Hypothesis 329–332
  varying intelligences among Jewish peoples 157–164, 175–178, 316–317, 328
  verbal vs. spatial intelligence among Jews 83, 154–156, 281, 320
intermarriage and interbreeding
  between Sephardic and Ashkenazi Jews 59
  Jewish and Gentile 28, 29, 134, 334–336, 356
  in Australia 38
  in Benelux 63, 65, 68
  in Canada 107
  in Central Europe 46, 50, 211
  in Denmark 112
  in Germany 133, 141, 143
  in Italy 184
  in Latin America 192, 196, 199
  in Russia 224, 233–234
IQ *See* intelligence
IQ and Global Inequality 5
Ireland, Jews in 91–94
  population estimates 92
Isaacs, Sir Isaac 34
Isabella I of Castile 191
ISI Web of Science 30
Israel, Jews in 149–180, 225, 356–358
  population estimates 150–152
Istanbul, Jews in 255, 264
Italy, Jews in 181–190
  population estimates 184
Ivy League, Jews in the 271, 283

J

Jacob Berkman 287
Jacobsen, I.C. 112
Jacobs, Simeon 238
Jaenisch, Carl von 229
Jencks, Christopher 352
Jewish Anti-Fascist Committee 225
Jewish Colonization Association 193
Jewish Journal of Sociology 6
Jews
  Ashkenazim 5, 24–25, 27, 28, 29, 131, 151
  Ethiopian Jews (Falashas) 25–26, 27, 29, 152, 167–171, 317, 331
    question of Jewish ethnicity 26–25, 317
  the Israeli underclass 168–171
  four Jewish peoples 21
  genetic affinity
    among Jewish peoples 26–27
    with Africans (Lemba) 28
    with Gentile populations 28
    with North Africans 28
    with Turks 257
  genetic differentiations between Jewish peoples 27–29
  German Jews in the United States 288
  Indian Jews 26
  Jewish women 106, 233, 290, 356
  Mizrahim (Oriental Jews) 21–22, 28, 151–156, 319, 331–332
  Romaniot 253, 254, 255
  Russian Jews
    in Latin America 196
    in the United States 217, 218, 225, 276
  Semitic ancestry 27–28, 317–318
  Sephardim 23–24, 151, 330
  Tibeto-Burmese Jews 26
Johnson, Paul 16, 189, 253, 272
Jones, D.C. 160
Jones, George 307
Joseph Jacobs 4
Joseph, Sa'adia ben 319
Josephson, Brian 89
Julius Bar (Zürich, Switzerland) 251

K

Kadushin, Charles 295
Kahn, Philippe 124
Kamenev, Lev 221
Kanazawa, Satoshi 345
Kantorovich, Leonid 226, 230
Kapitsa, Pyotr 230
Kármán, Theodor von 52
Karrer, Paul 250
Kashdan, Issac 301
Kaskell family (Germany) 135
Kasparov, Gari 229
Kaufman, Alan 281
Kaufman, Victor A. 307
Kaulla family (Germany) 135
Kaye, Danny 306
Kazemipur, Abdolmohammad 104
Kern, Jerome 304
Khazars, Caucasian
 theory of Jewish descent 25
Khodorkovsky, Mikhail 233
Khvol'son, Daniel 214
Kische family, the (South Africa) 238
Klug, Aaron 230
Kluger, Richard 303
Kocher, Theodor 250
Koestler, Arthur 25, 48, 123
Kokovtsev, V. 220
Koopmans, Tjalling 67
Kouchner, Bernard 124
Krause, E. 79, 81
Krivine, Alain 124
Kun, Béla 49
Kuznets, Simon 230

L

Lacan, Jacques 121
Laemmle, Carl 305
Lamarckian evolution 16, 122
Lamarr, Hedy 306
Lambert, Emmanuel 120
Landau, Lev 226, 230
Landowska, Wanda 207
Latin America, Jews in 191–202
 population estimates 192
Latvia, Jews in 210
Lazard, Elie 124
Lelyveld, Joseph 303
Leningrad, Jews in 223, 226
Lenin Prize 231
Lenin, Vladimir 215, 218, 224
Lenski, Gerhard 13, 348
Lenz, Fritz 141, 320
Leontief, Wassily 230
Lerner, Jaime 196
Leroy-Beaulieu, Anatole 122
Lesser, Gerald 280
Levinson, Boris 278
Lévi-Strauss, Claude 120, 124
Levitan, Isaak 218
Lévy, Maurice 124
Lieberson, Stanley 351
life expectancy, Jewish
 in Israel 174
 in Italy 188
Lilienfeld family (South Africa) 238
Lippman family (France) 120
Lippmann, Gabriel 125
Lithuania, Jews in 209–212
 population estimates 209
Livingston, Mary 306
Lombroso, Cesare 183
London, England 61, 71, 72, 73, 75, 76, 81, 91
Luckey, Bertha 280
Lukas, J. Anthony 303
Lustiger, Jean-Marie 124
Luzzati, Luigi 183
Lwoff, André 125
Lynn, Richard 5, 17, 316

M

MacDonald, Kevin 258–259, 322, 325–328, 351
Mahler, Gustav 205
Mailer, Norman 303
Maimonides, Moses 24, 319
Majoribanks, Kevin 98

malaria
  genetic protection against 27
Maller, Julius 280
Manchester, England 73
Mandelbrot, Benoît 209
Manhattan Project, the 52, 113, 187
Marciano, Paul 124
Margulis, Gregori 231
Marranos. *See* crypto-Jews
Marx Brothers 306
Marxism 224
Marx, Karl 135
mathematics, Jews in
  in Benelux 67
  in Britain 91
  in Canada 106
  in Central Europe 52, 209
  in France 126–127
  in Germany 146
  in Israel 167
  in Latin America 200
  in Russia 230
  in Spain 318
  in the United States 300
Maxim Gorky 215
Mayerbeer, Giacomo 135
Mayer, René 123
McLean, John R. 308
Mechnikov, Ilya 230
media, Jews in the 306–309
Mendelsohn, Ezra 45, 207
Mendelssohn family (South Africa) 238
Mendelssohn, Felix 135
Mendes family 258
Mendes-France, Pierre 123, 258
Menuhin, Yehudi 304
Metro-Goldwyn-Mayer (MGM) 306
Mexico, Jews in 197–198
  population estimates 198
Meyer, Barry 306
Meyer, Eugene Isaac 307
Michaelis family (Australia) 34
Middle Ages, Jews in 6, 57, 213, 245–246
  restrictions, regulations, and legal status 58, 117–118, 131–132, 246, 246–247

Middle East, Jews in the 22, 29–30, 149–180. *See also* Israel
Mikhoels, Solomon 225
military, Jews in the 121, 122, 172, 184, 187, 279, 294
Milstein, Nathan 304
mining, Jews in 34, 214
Minkowitch, Avram 158
Mocatta family (London) 73
Modigliani, Amedeo 183, 321
Mohammed the Conqueror, Sultan (Ottoman Empire) 256
Moissan, Henri 125
Molotov, Vyacheslav 225
Monash, General Sir John 34
Monash University (Australia) 34
money-lending 25, 57, 94, 118, 246. *See also* usury
Montaigne, Michel de 119, 319
Montefiore family (London) 73
Montefiore, Sir Moses 72
Moonves, Leslie 306
Moravia, Alberto 184
Moscow Institute of Jurisprudence 224
Moscow, Jews in 222, 226
Mosely family (South Africa) 238
Mosenthal family (South Africa) 237
Mosse, Werner E. 133, 139, 141
Mottelson, Benjamin 113
Moynihan, Daniel Patrick 16
Müller, Karl 250
Muller, Paul 250
Mumbai (Bombay), India 26
Muni, Paul 306
Murad II, Sultan 330
Murphy, Thomas 307
Murray, Charles 5, 8, 9–11, 42, 54, 86, 127, 146, 231, 278, 293, 335, 351–352
musicals, Jewish composers of 304
music, Jews in
  in Benelux 66
  in the United States 304–305
Mussolini, Benito 185, 187
Myers family (Australia) 34
myopia (correlation with intelligence) 324–325

N

Napier, Lewis Bernstein 15
Napoleon 1, 61, 182–183
National Academy of Sciences 114
National Broadcasting Company (NBC) 307
National Socialist Germany 24, 143–144
 accords with Switzerland 249
 occupation of Denmark 112–113
 occupation of France 123
 policies in Italy 188
Near East, Jews in the 22, 255–259. See also Ottoman Empire
Neisser, Ulrich 18
Nemeck, Ottokar 141
Neumann family, the (South Africa) 238
Neumann, John von 52
Newman, Paul 306
Newman, Randy 304
New Republic, The 308
News Corporation 306
newspapers, Jews in 307–308
Newsweek 307
New York City College, Jews in 285
New York City, Jews, in 274, 280, 285
New York Review of Books 308
New York Times 307
Nietzsche, Friedrich 139
Nimzovitch, Aron 210
NKVD, the (Soviet Union) 222
Nobel Prize, the 8–9, 343–344
 in economics 19
Nobel Prize winners, Jewish 2, 343–344
 in Benelux 67
 in Britain 89
 in Canada 106
 in Central Europe 43, 44, 52, 209
 in Denmark 113–114
 in France 125
 in Germany 144–145
 in Israel 4, 167
 in Italy 189
 in Latin America 200
 in Russia 230
 in South Africa 241
 in Switzerland 250
 in the Balkans 265, 267
 in the United States 295–299
Norman Conquest (of England) 25, 71
North Africa, Jews in 22
Nuremberg Laws 143

O

occupations (professions), Jewish 342–343. *See also* socioeconomic status
 in Australia 37
 in Benelux 65
 in Britain 81–85, 267
 in Canada 104–106
 in Central Europe 43, 47–48, 49, 205, 207, 210
 in France 118, 121, 125
 in Germany 132, 135, 137, 140
 in Ireland 91
 in Israel 166, 170, 337
 in Italy 186–187
 in Latin America 194, 198, 199
 in Romania 263
 in Russia 214, 217, 219, 223, 232
 in South Africa 241
 in Switzerland 250, 251
 in the Middle East 22–23
 in the Ottoman Empire 257–258
 in the United States 288–290, 294–295
 in Turkey 264
Odessa, Russian Empire 218
Offenbach, Jacques 135
O'Grada, Cormac 18, 94
"oligarchs," Russian 233
Oppenheimer, Sir Ernest 238
Oppenheim family (Germany) 133, 135
Oriental Jews. *See* Mizrahim
Ortar, Gina 157
Ottoman Empire 22, 149, 254
 Jews in 22–23, 255–258, 330
  Jewish physicians 258
  population estimates 255

P

painting, Jews in 320
Pale of Settlement (Russian Empire) 213
Palestinian Arabs 357–358
  genetic affinity to Jews 27
Papaport family (South Africa) 238
Paramount Pictures 306
Paris Peace Conference (1919) 264
Partisan Review, The 308
Pasternak, Boris 218, 226, 230
Pasternak, Leonid 218
Patai, Raphael 7
Pavlov, Ivan 230
Pereire family (France) 61
Perelman, Grigori 231
Periere family (France) 120
persecution, anti-Jewish 329–332
  in Benelux 62
  in Central Europe 41, 51
  in France 118–119, 123
  in Germany 132, 143
  in Latin America 195, 199
  in Poland and Lithuania 204
  in Romania 263
  in Russia 73
  in Switzerland 246–247
  in the Byzantine Empire 253
Peru, Jews in 198
Pétain, Marshal Philippe 123
Peter Chernin 306
Pfeiffer family (Germany) 135
Phillips, Sir Lionel 238
physics, Jews in. *See* Nobel Prize winners, Royal Society
Pinter, Harold 87, 89
Pissarro, Camille 120, 321
Plekhanov, Georgi Valentinovich 250
pogroms
  as selectively eliminating the less intelligent 269
  in Central Europe 49, 208–210
  in Eastern Europe 269, 272
  in France 203
  in Germany 143, 203

  in Latin America 193
  in Russia 2, 25, 34, 93, 112, 193, 197, 214, 220, 329
Poland, Jews in 204–209
  population estimates 204–205
Polanyi, Michael 52
Polgár, Judit 53
Pope Paul IV 182
Pope Pius VII 183
Popper, Karl 42
Possony, Stefan 351
Preston, Samuel 310
Prigogine, Ilya 230
professions, Jewish involvement in. *See* occupations, Jewish
Prokhorov, Alexander 230
prostitution, Jews in 193
Protestant work ethic 12–13, 349
Proust, Marcel 120
Prussia, Jews in 132
PsychINFO 30
PsychNet 30
Ptolemy 8
Public Interest, The 308
public services, Jews in. *See* civil administration, Jews in
Pulitzer Prizes 302–303
purges in the Soviet Union
  anti-Semitic nature 225
  The Great Terror 224
Pythagoras 8

R

Rabinowitze family (South Africa) 238
Race Differences in Intelligence 322
Raymond, Henry J. 307
Redstone, Sumner 307
Rees-Mogg, William 87
Reichstein, Tadeus 250
Reinach family (France) 120
Reinach, Rabrice 123
Remnick, David 303
Renan, Ernst 121
Republic National Bank of New York 251

Revolution of 1848 182
Ricardo, David 319
Robinson, Edward 306
Rodgers, Richard 304
Rohrer, Heinrich 250
Roman Empire, Jews in the 23, 181, 246, 335
  Byzantine Empire, Jews in 253
Rome University 187
Rosenberg, Tina 303
Rosen, Bernard 348
Ross, Steven J. 307
Rothschild family 42, 61, 73, 120, 133, 135, 214, 318
  Mayer Amschel Rothschild 72
  Nathan Mayer Rothschild (fils) 72
  Nathan Mayer Rothschild (père) 72, 87
  Rothschild, Lionel de 72
  Rothschild, Maurice de 123
Rotterdam, The Netherlands 59
Royal Danish Academy 114
Royal Society, the 84–85, 114
Rubinstein, Artur 304
Rubinstein family (Russia) 217
Rubinstein, Helena 35
Rubinstein, William 16, 45, 80
Rushton, J. Phillipe 273
Russell, Bertrand 6, 90
Russia, Jews in 213–233
  in the Russian Federation 216, 232
  in the Soviet Union 221–228
  population estimates 215, 228
Rutland, Suzanne 14, 39

S

Saatchi, Charles and Maurice 87, 319
Sachs, L. 26
Sagan, Carl 303
Sakharov, Andrei 226
Salonica, Greece 255, 256, 259
Samuel family (London) 73
Saracens 118
Sarfatti, Michele 186
Sarnoff, David 307

Sarnof, Robert 307
Sassoon, Siegfried 319
Savasorda 318
Schnabel, Artur 304
Schönberg, Claude-Michel 124
Schorske, Carl 303
science, Jews in. *See* Nobel Prize winners, Royal Society
Scofield, Paul 87
Scots-Irish 287–288
Segrè, Emilio 187
Seligman family (Germany) 135
Seligman family (United States) 272
settlers, Jewish
  in South Africa 237
Sheehan, Susan Margulies 303
Sheldon, Paul 280
sickle-cell anemia 337
Sidney, Sylvia 306
"significant figures" (Charles Murray) 42, 86, 127, 146, 231, 293. *See also* elites, Jewish
Simon, Paul 304
Simpson, Jon 311
Singer, Isaac Bashevis 209
Six-Day War (1967) 199, 227
Slezkine, Yuri 14, 43, 131–148, 213–236
Sloan, Harry 306
Slonimski, Antoni 207
Smale, Stephen 299
Smith, David E. 318
Smolensky, Alexander 233
Smyslov, Vasily 2, 229
socioeconomic status. *See also* occupations
  Duncan Socioeconomic Index 287
  in Russia 214
  Jewish status hierarchy in Israel 267
  of Arabs in Israel 165–166
  of Jews in Australia 34, 36
  of Jews in Benelux 63
  of Jews in Britain 80–82
  of Jews in Canada 104
  of Jews in Central Europe 205, 210
  of Jews in Denmark 111
  of Jews in France 125–126
  of Jews in Germany 134

of Jews in Ireland 92
of Jews in Israel 154–155, 165–167
of Jews in Italy 186–187
of Jews in Latin America 193–194, 198
of Jews in South Africa 240
of Jews in the United States 274, 286–290
Wealth Quotients 80–81
Solomon family (South Africa) 238
Solzhenitsyn, Alexandr 230
Sombart, Werner 13
Sonnino, Sidney 183
Sony Pictures 306
Sophia, Bulgaria 260
South Africa, Jews in 237–244
   population estimates 238
Soutine, Chaim 210, 321
Soviet Union, Jews in. *See* Russia
Spain
   Arab invasion of 24
   Jews in 23
Spasovich, V.D. 220
Spassky, Boris 2, 229
Speyer family (United States) 272
Spielberg, Steven 306
Spinoza, Baruch 60, 319
Spitteler, Carl 250
sport, Jews in 309–310
Stalin, Joseph 224, 225
Starr, Paul 303
Steinberg, Stephen 16
Stein, Elias 67
Steiner, George 124
Steinitz, Wilhelm 2, 46
Stein, Joel 306
Stern family (France) 120
Stern, Isaac 304
stockbroking, Jews in 60, 219. *See also* banking,
Stoppard, Tom 87
Storfer, Miles 159, 323
St. Petersburg, Russia 219–220
Strauss-Kahn, Dominique 124
Streisand, Barbra 306
success, Jewish 342–349. *See also* work ethic, Jewish
   Theories of Jewish Success 12, 39, 94

Luck 17
Marginal Man Theory 15
Special Aptitudes 15–16
Strong Family and Ethnic Networks 14, 323
Strong Work Motivation Theory 12–13, 323
sugar industry, Jews in 195, 197
Sulaiman the Magnificent 257
Sulzberger, Arthur Ochs Jr. 307
Sutherland, Joan 87
Sverdlov, Yakov 221
Sveriges Riksbank (Swedish Central Bank) 19
Switzerland, Jews in 245–250
   population estimates 247–248
Szilard, Leo 52

T

Taiyib, Abu'l 319
Tal, Mikhail 2, 210
Tamm, Igor Y. 226, 230
Tay-Sachs disease 28, 337
Teller, Edward 52
Terkel, Studs 303
Theiler, Max 242
Thernstrom, Stephan 14, 345, 351
Thirty Years War 132
Thomson, J.J. 113
Time (magazine) 308
Time Warner Communications 307, 308
Timman, Jan 66
Tin Pan Alley 304
Tisch, Laurence 307
titles. *See* heraldry
toleration of Jews. *See also* anti-Semitism
   in the Ottoman Empire 255–257
Torres, Luis De 192
Treitschke, Heinrich von 139
Trianav, Rodrigo De 191
Trigano, Gilbert 124
Tropp, Asher 82, 351
Trotsky, Leon 218, 221, 250

Tuchman, Barbara 302
Turkey, Jews in 264
  population estimates 264
Turks 27, 254, 255, 257, 259, 266
Tuwim, Julian 207
Twain, Mark 3

U

United States, Jews in the 271–314
  population estimates 272–273
Universal Studio 306
University of Berlin 52
University of Copenhagen 112, 113
University of Kharkov 216
University of Melbourne 34
University of Pennsylvania. *See* Ivy League, Jews in the
University of Sydney 34
University of Vienna 43, 45
U.S. News & World Report 308
usury 57, 118. *See also* money-lending

V

Vanity Fair (magazine) 309
Veblen, Thorstein 4, 15
Venezuela, Jews in 199
Viacom 307
Vienna, Austria 43, 45, 54, 255
Villiger, Kastar 249
Visigoths, Jews under the 23

W

Waksman, Selman 230
Wald, George 209
Wall Street Journal 308
Walt Disney Co. 306, 307
Warburg family (Germany and Britain) 135
Warner Bros. 306
Washington Post 308

WASPs, the American Elite 284
Wasserman, Lew 307
Waterman, Stanley 73, 79
wealth, Jewish. *See* socioeconomic status
Web of Knowledge 30
Weidenfeld, George 87
Weil, Simone 124
Weimar Republic (Germany) 141–143
Weiner, Jonathan 303
Weinryb, Bernard 329
Weinstein brothers (Harvey and Bob) 306
Weizmann, Chaim 250
Wendt, R. A. 98
Werner, Alfred 250
Wertheimer, Pierre 124
Weyl, Nathaniel 5, 9, 292, 351
White, Theodore H. 302
Who's Who in America 292, 293, 351
Wigner, Eugene 52
William Lowell Putnam Competition 300
William Paley 307
Winawer, Szymon 229
Wittgenstein, Ludwig 42, 44
Wolf Prize winners, Jewish
  in Britain 91
  in Canada 106
  in Central Europe 52, 209
  in France 126
  in Germany 146
  in Latin America 200
  in Russia 230
  in the United States 300
women, Jewish. *See* Jews
work ethic, Jewish 342–349. *See also* success, Jewish
World War I 41, 204, 215, 220
World War II 24, 35, 46, 51, 63, 68, 113, 119, 121, 123, 184, 188, 196, 204, 208, 216, 224, 228, 249, 261, 272, 285, 309, 330
Wright, Robert C. 307
Wüthrich, Kurt 250

Y

Yale University. *See* Ivy League
Yergin, Daniel 303
Yiddish 1, 24, 61, 92, 192, 214, 274, 277, 278, 282, 286, 355
Yugoslavia, Jews in 264–265

Z

Zinkernagel, Rolf 250
Zionism 150–151. *See also* Israel
Zucker, Jeff 306
Zuckerman, Harriet 294
Zukor, Adoph 305

Richard Lynn

Richard Lynn graduated in Psychology and took his Ph.D. at the University of Cambridge. He has been Lecturer in Psychology at the University of Exeter, Professor of Psychology at the Economic and Social Research Institute, Dublin, and Professor and head of the Department of Psychology at the University of Ulster. Currently, he is Emeritus Professor of Psychology at the University of Ulster, Coleraine, Northern Ireland. His main work has been on intelligence and personality.

His books include *Personality and National Character* (1972), *Dimensions of Personality* (1980), *Educational Achievement in Japan* (1988), *Dysgenics: Genetic Deterioration in Modern Populations* (1996), *Eugenics: A Reassessment* (2001), (co-author) *IQ and the Wealth of Nations* (2002), *Race Differences in Intelligence* (2006), (co-author) *IQ and Global Inequality* (2006), and *The Global Bell Curve* (2008).

He has received awards including the Passingham Prize at Cambridge University for the best Psychology student of the year and the U.S. Mensa Awards for Excellence in 1985, 1993, and 2007 for work on intelligence.

Cover images, clockwise from top left:

Sigmund Freud, Felix Mendelssohn, Maimonides, Karl Marx, Mayer Amschel Rothschild, Albert Einstein, Ludwig Wittgenstein, and Baruch Spinoza.